"*The Secrets to Stepfamily Success* will certainly lead to positive change in step and blended family members' lives. Not only is it rich with valuable tools, learnable skills, and resources to enable a successful remarriage, but it is also inspirational as it calls everyone on the remarriage journey— whether you are considering remarriage or already experiencing step or blended family living—to action; i.e., to explore his or her own self-growth development. For those who want a lasting and happy remarried life, this book is a must-read.

Congratulations and thank you for helping to improve the lives of millions of remarried people who are raising step and blended families!"

— Paula Bisacre, CEO, Remarriage LLC, Publisher, *reMarriageMagazine.com;* Creator, "On Remarriage" column, *The Washington Times*

"This is the most thorough work on stepfamilies I have seen—the depth and breadth of *The Secrets to Stepfamily Success* make it a handbook of great value for both professionals and stepfamily members in navigating the complex territory of stepfamily life."

— Joan Sarin, M.S., Founder, Stepfamily Solutions (www.StepmomSOS.com)

"I've been working through your book. I tend to look at it as more of a stepfamily life workbook rather than a book to read through quickly.

As I have read through, stopped to make notes, made charts, lists and had insightful conversations with my children and the man I've begun dating, I've learned so much and have been able to define more of what I want and need in a relationship, what reasons I have for wanting to be in a relationship and a possible re-marriage, what I think a healthy co-parenting stepfamily will look like and what it will/may be like to merge two family units one day.

This book is a valuable resource that I will recommend to everyone I meet who is either divorced and starting a new relationship or who is already part of a stepfamily. Wouldn't it be great if this were required reading for every newly divorced person? Think of how healthy all of their new relationships/re-marriages would be!"

— Natalie Franklin, Administrator, Life in a Blender

"One of the hardest things about being a parent is becoming a stepparent. When I met my husband in 1990, I didn't think much about the difficulties of raising someone else's children. I thought that since I was a parent myself, we would get along so well. That's not what happened. Reality set in pretty fast.

What I wasn't prepared for, was all the complexities of having other people involved in our families, all the decision making that needed to be done by more people than just my husband and I.

Twenty years ago, stepfamily information wasn't as readily available as it is today. Internet was in it's infancy for those that knew about it and searching for information was a lot more complicated than today.

Stepfamilies are now becoming more aware that they are not all the same and in order to succeed they need to understand what makes them different. And yet, many refuse to look and face the issues that can make or break relationships. This is apparent with the high rate of divorce in remarriages.

Gloria's book *The Secrets to Stepfamily Success: Revolutionary Tools to Create a Blended Family of Support and Respect* provides the tools and skills to make stepfamilies more successful. She approaches the issues with a lot of open and positive insights that make changes possible, even in challenging relationships.

Many stepfamilies have a hard time finding good resources all in one place. They often go here and there to look for what they need for their particular situation. Gloria brought all this information together. This book is more than just a collection of data on stepfamilies. It's about becoming empowered and hopeful that your family will succeed.

This book starts with the importance of grieving the dissolution of the nuclear or traditional family, for if these issues are not resolved, they will affect any future relationships you will have and those of the children. Gloria also addresses the importance of defining your roles and rules within the home, dealing with money, sexual attractions between stepsiblings, setting boundaries and the issue of discipline. Each topic has great examples of what it looks like in a successful stepfamily and ideas of what to do. It also addresses the more than 60 ways stepfamilies are different from nuclear or traditional families, addressing why communication is often a big problem in relationships and how to address this.

Gloria mentions that flexibility is key to a healthy marriage; 'how can you be flexible if you do not know where you, your spouse and the children stand and what everyone needs right now.' (p. viii)

This book really helps change the perspective many have that stepfamilies are second best or inferior to a perspective of hope and possibility. It's not just about stepmoms or stepdads or their children, it's about the entire system, including grandparents as well as other extended families members. Gloria addresses in detail many of the issues stepfamilies refuse to look at such as grieving, money and sex. She demonstrates over and over again just how successful stepfamilies get there, in a way that encourages positive changes.

The information here is a great resource for all, from clinical and social workers that help individuals and families, to teachers, pastors, and coaches as well as anyone contemplating entering in a relationship as a stepperson. As a stepparent and a coach, this book will be highly recommended as a starting point for our work together.

The book also provides a list of great resources to those seeking help at different stages of steprelationships

I hope you enjoy this book and get as much out of it as I did."

— Claudette Chenevert, Stepfamily Life Coach, AKA The Stepmom Coach, www.coachingsteps. com

Gloria Lintermans has written a golden book which honors the unique qualities of StepFamily life. Her wisdom applies to all families in many ways, but the complexities and complications of being in a stepfamily are special. She deals honestly, compassionately and with great insight into how to turn those sometimes challenging issues into strengths which make stepfamilies such a solid part of our culture, producing successful and loving and loved human beings. Her book is optimistic and provides solid information on how to be one of those highly successful stepfamilies we all wish to be. My experience is that many times parenting classes and books do not address the unique issues of stepfamily life and can leave stepfamilies feeling discouraged as so many exercises and suggestions cannot be implemented in a stepfamily. This book adds the missing pieces for all of us who work with stepfamilies, and are in one.

— Eleanor Spackman Alden, LCSW, BCD

Recently I had the great pleasure to interview Gloria Lintermans and discuss her fabulous book entitled *The Secrets to Stepfamily Success: Revolutionary Tools to Create a Blended Family of Support and Respect* on my radio show 'Living on Purpose'.

Thoroughly researched and engagingly presented, fascinating and detailed information fills the pages of Lintermans' book. An invaluable and essential resource for all people involved with, and about to become involved in a stepfamily, Lintermans addresses a full range of issues, including finances, communication, addiction, identity, trauma, grief, roles, rules, and problem solving. These issues, which are all important aspects in any relationship, have an exponential impact when applied to the stepfamily environment, which differs in sixty different ways from an intact biological family, as evidenced by the author's research. Once readers have reviewed the implications of the stepfamily model as illustrated by this instructive book by Lintermans, at the very least they will be guided by much more information than the majority of people who create stepfamilies with little forethought about the effect on the children involved.

Our interview, featured on WomensRadio in October 2010, is heard through this link: http://www.womensradio.com/users/Lynn-Thompson/85/episodes.html. Gloria spoke informatively and with clear passion about her findings, including what she considers to be the main ingredient for success for members of step and blended families: respect.

I have warm appreciation for Gloria Lintermans for her visionary concern for children and their families, through which this inspiring (and sobering) book *The Secrets to Stepfamily Success* was created.

— Lynn Thompson, Vancouver Island, B.C. Canada, LivingOnPurposeLynn.com

THE SECRETS
TO STEPFAMILY SUCCESS:

REVOLUTIONARY TOOLS TO CREATE A BLENDED FAMILY OF SUPPORT AND RESPECT

By

Gloria Lintermans

Llumina Press

ISBN: 978-1-60594-418-0 PB
        978-1-60594-506-4 HC
        978-1-60594-422-7 EB

Printed in the United States of America by Llumina Press

Library of Congress Control Number: 2010902574

In Recognition of
Peter K. Gerlach, M.S.W.

This book is a tribute to the pioneering and ongoing work of Peter K. Gerlach, M.S.W. and his 30+ years of specializing in stepfamily dynamics and solutions. He is the co-founder of the non-profit Stepfamily Association of Illinois, a former board member of the Stepfamily Association of America, and is currently a member of the National Stepfamily Resource Center (NSRC). He is the author of *Who's Really Running Your Life: Free Your Self from Custody and Guard Your Kids*; *Satisfactions—Seven Skills Your Parents Never Taught You*; *Build a High-Nurturance Stepfamily: A Guide for Co-Parents, Stepfamily Courtship; The Re/marriage Book;* and, *Build a Co-Parenting Team After Divorce or Re-marriage*. Gerlach has been a step-grandson, stepson, stepbrother, and stepfather.

Oddly enough, Peter and I have never met, in person that is. Peter was one of those wonderful surprise Internet appearances when I needed expert information while writing my book, *The Newly Divorced Book of Protocol*. Over the years, by e-mail and phone, we've shared our thoughts and philosophy, and I offer tremendous gratitude to Peter for his major contribution to this book, which has made THE SECRETS TO STEPFAMILY SUCCESS a reality.

Complementary worksheets are available for further self-discovery on the subjects covered within this book at http://sfhelp.org, the "Break The Cycle!" non-profit Web site by Peter K. Gerlach, M.S.W. Listed at the end of each chapter, I urge you to use them as your key to understanding feelings and thoughts of which you may have previously been unaware.

The World of Stepfamilies

In 2001, there were 72.5 million children under 18 living in the United States. Fifteen percent of children (10.6 million) lived in blended families. About half of these children, 5.1 million, lived with at least one stepparent. *Source: U.S. Department of Commerce / U.S. Census Bureau.* These statistics underestimate the number of U.S. stepfamilies. According to *The National Stepfamily Resource Center*, if a child lives with a divorced, single parent and the nonresident parent has remarried, the child is not included in the calculations as being a member of a stepfamily. Also, about 25% of current stepfamilies are actually cohabiting couples. Two-thirds of all women, and 30% of all children, are likely to spend some time in a stepfamily, using the more liberal definition that includes cohabiting adult couples.

1,300 new stepfamilies form every day!
Source: Stepfamily Foundation

More than half of Americans today have been, are now or will eventually be in one or more *blended* or *step* situations during their lives.

TABLE OF CONTENTS

PART FOUR:
SUPPORT YOURSELVES

CHAPTER THIRTEEN: Evolve and Use a Stepfamily Support Network Together **247**

DEDICATION

The late morning sun shines through stained-glass windows, the deep colors saturated with light. A gentle kaleidoscope of dust softly streams over the congregation. My precious step-niece is being inducted as a religious leader today. Sitting in a pew, in a row directly behind me, is my step-cousin, my step-grandfather's nephew. I sit between my husband and his half-brother. My mother-in-law and my sister-in-law and her ex-husband are seated a few rows away, but within sight. I feel a tremendous bond, at peace with this sense of belonging. It is perhaps at this moment that fully and finally I have come to realize that family is truly where your heart is, regardless of the titles we know these people by.

A number of years have passed since that treasured event, as has my husband. I have grieved, healed, tucked his precious memory into my heart and moved on, adding even more members to a family of my heart. To Marsha, my first best friend and loving sister, for that fuzzy, warm spot you keep for me alone. To my supportive, loving, patient partner, Hal, for your valuable input and belief that there is no mountain I can't climb. To my dear brother, Bill, for our renewed friendship for which I am comforted and grateful. To my very special biological and step-children, grandchildren and "grandfriend," all whom I love and treasure: Evan, Richard & Amy, Bernie, Kim & Mark, Allyson, Rachel, Samantha, Eliezer, Grace, and Jonathan, Art, Amanda, Tessa, Sean, and Hannah, Lauren & Bruce, Eva and Lilly, Stacy, Joe and Nick, Dennis & Courtney, Sophia, Doug & Jeff, Hylee & Ethan, Noah, Zack & Abby, Cara & Michael, Alexander, Gabriel, Tamarra, and West. To dear friends and family who offer support, comfort, and laugh at my jokes: Marjie & John, Erin & Tony, Mitzi & Ross, Gail & Steve, Linda & Gerry, Sheila & our "guru" Nate, and Claire.

To Alice and her meticulous attention to detail and quiet patience, thank you for putting my best face forward.

Gloria Lintermans

INTRODUCTION

*"Many people are married to people who have been married to other people who
are now married to still others to who the first parties may not have been married,
but to who somebody has likely been married."*

Lionel Tiger, "Omnigamy: The New Kinship System."
Psychology Today

Almost 55 percent of first marriages in the United States end in divorce. Most divorced parents remarry (often more than once), and form (or join) blended or stepfamilies of which roughly 74 percent fail.

Studies show that only 18 percent of re-married parents who have all of their children after the remarriage are happy; the rest see family life as mildly stressful to miserable. One reason is that within our society, there are no cultural scripts, no set of socially prescribed and understood guidelines for relating to each other or for defining responsibilities and obligations in these families. Although our society tends to broadly apply to second marriages the rules and assumptions of first marriages, these rules often ignore the complexities of stepfamilies.

Be aware that the term "blended family," currently popular and often used interchangeably with stepfamily, can also be confusing; you do not blend in the sense of losing the character and identity of your original family. Nor are families reconstituted or put back together. However, there is a difference between step- and blended-families in that in stepfamilies the child(ren) is of one co-parent; in a blended family, there are children from both co-parents. For the purpose of this book, both groups will be referred to as step.

In stepfamilies, although one biological parent lives elsewhere; virtually all family members have recently experienced a primary relationship loss; the children are members of more than one household; and one adult—the stepparent—is not legally related to the stepchild unless legally adopted. For children, the transition from one family structure to another, and another, creates a long period of upheaval and stress. Generally, children are forced to adjust first to a new single-parent household before adjusting again to the new two-parent stepfamily—two difficult transitions. And, more likely than not, a very tight, emotional bond developed in that single-parent household.

Children can also find it difficult to bond with their new stepfamily because there is a biological parent outside the new family unit. Remember, most of these children hold membership in two households, with two sets of rules. Additionally, role models for stepparents are poorly defined and blended/stepfamilies come together from diverse backgrounds, which means everybody needs to have (or develop) the ability to tolerate differences.

Relationships in blended/stepfamilies are new, untested, and not *a given* as they are in traditional families. Even when everyone is in tune, what is missing is the comfort of knowing that there is a bond taken for granted, a biological bond of caring and love. Now, outward signals and signs are continuously needed to show that caring and loving, or respect, really exist. Children in blended/stepfamilies also have at least one extra set of grandparents and extended family which can leave everyone on both sides confused about what to do.

Blended/stepfamilies come in all shapes and sizes. The simplest is one in which a divorced or widowed spouse with one child remarries a never-married childless spouse. In a more complicated case, both partners bring children in from previous marriages and also have a child together. If this marriage is followed by another divorce and remarriage, the new family gets even more complicated. Ex-spouses remarry, too, to people who have ex-spouses from previous marriages, and who then have children of their own. The result is an extraordinarily complicated network of family relationships in which your role can include that of parent, stepparent, spouse, ex-spouse, custodial parent, non-custodial parent, or absent parent.

Your children become siblings, residential stepsiblings, nonresidential stepsiblings, residential half-siblings, and nonresidential half-siblings. There are even two subtypes of half-sibling roles: those of children related by blood to only one of the adults, and the half-sibling role of the mutual child. Children also have step-grandparents and ex-step-grandparents.

Even though blended/stepfamilies are a large segment of the American families today, our language has not yet caught up with the proliferation of new family roles. As family members separate and join new families, the new kin do not so much replace as add to kin from the first marriage. What are the new relatives to be called? There may be stepparents, step-grandparents, and stepsiblings, but what, for instance does a child call the new wife that her or his non-custodial father has married? Or, if a child alternates between the two households in a joint-custody arrangement, where does he or she call "home," and where is his or her "family"? It takes the entire family working together to make the adjustment easier for everyone.

There is also a lack of legal definitions for the roles and relationship in blended/stepfamilies. Because family law assumes that all marriages are first marriages, there are no legal provisions for remarried-family problems, such as: balancing the husband's financial obligations to his spouses and children from current and previous marriages; defining a wife's obligations to husbands and children from new and old marriages; or, reconciling the competing claims of current and former spouses for shares of the estate of a deceased spouse. Not surprisingly, research suggests that remarried people may be reluctant to commit all of their economic resources to a second marriage, taking care to protect their individual interests and those of their biological children.

Legal regulations concerning incest are also inadequate. In all states, marriage and sexual relations are prohibited between people closely related by blood. Many states have found that these restrictions do not cover sexual relations or marriage between family members not related by blood—as between stepsiblings or between a child and a stepparent, for example—and have moved to modify their laws to protect children in remarried families from abuse. Incest taboos serve the important function of allowing children to develop affection for and identification with other family members without risking sexual exploitation.

In some states, a stepparent does not have the authority to see a stepchild's school records or to make medical decisions for them. The preservation of stepparent-stepchild relations when death or divorce severs the marital tie is also an issue. Visitation rights (and corresponding support obligation) of stepparents is only just beginning to be legally clarified. When a biological parent dies, the absence of custodial preference for stepparents over extended kin or even foster placement may result in children being removed from the home where they had close psychological ties to a stepparent—ties which may have taken a long time to develop.

In remarriages, stepchildren and finances present the greatest challenges to a successful remarriage. Many studies have found that children in blended/stepfamilies *can* be just as happy and well adjusted as children in traditional families, or nearly so. But, even though stepchildren may turn out to be happy and well adjusted, being a stepparent (or married to one) can bring its share of problems to any marriage.

About half of the women who remarry have a child, usually within two years after the wedding. This is most often the case when women have no children, or only one, from a previous marriage. Adding another child to your stepfamily is bound to be a complex adjustment. Even though these children bring none of the complications that come with expanding families across households, or the complex structure of family roles and relationships, the complication is from the viewpoint of the children from the previous marriage.

Stepsiblings may not get along because they resent sharing their room, their possessions, and their parent. Ties between your stepchild and their non-custodial parent may create a triangle effect that makes your spouse's previous marriage seem "more real" than this marriage. Children, upset after visits with their non-custodial parent, are forced to make major adjustments that make life difficult for everyone, and you might often feel caught between loyalties to your biological child and wanting to please your new spouse.

Three potential problem areas are financial burdens, role ambiguity, and the children's negative feelings when they don't want the new family to "work." Problems frequently begin with the previous divorce, particularly with regard to finances. Money problems tend to come up because of obligations left over from a first marriage. Remarried husbands may end up financially responsible for children from their first marriage *and* for their stepchildren. In many states an ex-wife's alimony (although not child support) automatically ends when she remarries. One study found that remarriage by a custodial mother can prompt sizable reductions in child support from her ex-husband. Blended/stepfamilies as a whole tend to have lower incomes than do other married couples.

Even though disproportionately more second wives are employed outside their homes than are first wives, husbands sometimes feel caught between the often impossible demands of their former family and their present one. Some second wives also feel resentful about the amount of income that goes to the husband's first wife to help support his children from that marriage. Or, a second wife may feel guilty about the burden of support her own children place on their stepfather.

The emotional impact of the previous divorce can also cause money problems. Some women stash money away in case of a second divorce, and some men refuse to revise their wills and insurance policies for the same reason. For many couples, money is a sensitive issue that's not talked about. You are less likely to think and act in terms of "our" money.

Another basic problem is that legal roles of stepchild and stepparent are neither defined nor clearly understood. The role of stepparent can be precarious because the relationship between a stepparent and stepchild only exists in law as long as the biological parent and stepparent are married. If the biological parent dies, the stepparent instantly loses any legal claim to custody over his or her stepchild, and custody reverts back to the surviving biological parent. The only way to cement your legal ties to stepchildren is by adopting them, but this obviously requires the cooperation of the non-custodial parent, which may not be realistic.

Legally, the stepparent is a non-parent with no prescribed rights or duties. Tension, compromise, and confusion can rule when the role of parent is shared between a stepparent and the non-custodial natural parent. Some people still feel that stepparents aren't "real" parents, but our culture has no norms to suggest how they are different. Some studies point out that stepparents are less involved as parents and that spouses of stepparents expect this. Meanwhile, other studies find that biological mothers are dissatisfied when stepfathers are not very involved. Regardless, the less our roles are defined, the more unhappy we are as both parents and stepparents.

Another role ambiguity is that society seems to expect acquired parents and children to instantly love each other in much the same way as biological parents and their children do. In reality, however, this is often just not so. A stepparent might feel a tremendous amount of guilt about his or her lack of positive feelings (or even the presence of negative feelings) toward the spouse's children. Discipline might be a constant source of family conflict: You might, for example, think your ex-spouse isn't being strict enough, when in fact, most stepfathers and stepmothers think the real parent is not being strict enough.

As a stepparent, you might feel like an unbiased observer with a grudge because you're an outsider and the very thing that's making you "unbiased" is something you resent, biology. Stepchildren, as well, often don't react to their parent's new spouse as though he or she were the "real" parent. The irony of expecting instant "real" parent-child love is further complicated by the fact that stepparents are not generally expected to be "equal" in discipline or otherwise controlling their stepchildren.

Adding to the problem, adolescent stepchildren may have considerable family power. Children are a force to be reckoned with in any family, but in most stepfamilies, mothers have more power over both major and everyday decisions than either stepfathers or adolescents. In other stepfamilies, adolescents have more power than either parent, particularly in everyday decision-making. Active contact with the non-custodial parent also gives the adolescent an option—an alternative home, and so, more power to be wielded.

It helps when stepfathers have children of their own from a previous marriage. Perhaps experience with parenting makes a stepfather more effective and more authoritative. Adolescents also have less power in stepfamilies of greater longevity, reflecting either the breakup of the most troubled families or a gradual coming together of the new stepfamily over time. Nevertheless, children's attitudes as well as their power can have an impact on the new marriage.

The third reason for a difficult stepparent-child relationship might be that your child does not want this marriage to work, and so, acts out with hostility. Commonly children harbor fantasies that their biological parents will reunite. If children had reservations about or strongly disapproved of your divorce, they may sabotage your new relationships in the hope that you will get back together. Children who want their natural parents to remarry may feel that sabotaging the new relationship will get them back together. In the case of remarriage after the death of a parent, children may have idealized, almost sacred memories of that parent and may not want another to take his or her place. Stepchildren can prove hostile adversaries, and this is especially true for adolescents.

For a young teenager, your new marriage may be more difficult to accept than was the divorce. At puberty, when children are discovering their own sexuality, it is remarkable how conservative they can expect their parents to be with regard to their sexuality. Adolescence can be a trying time for all, regardless of what's going on in the family. Teens tend to be impatient, self-centered, and argumentative. They can be especially distrustful, suspicious, and resentful toward a new stepparent, verbally critical of the stepparent's goals, values, or personal characteristics. Anger displacement may also play a part. Many adolescents blame their parents or themselves, or both, for the breakup of the first marriage, and the stepparent becomes a convenient scapegoat for their anger and hurt.

Although all stepchildren and stepparents are to some degree uncomfortable with some aspect of their new family role, certain difficulties are more likely to affect stepmothers, and others are more common to stepfathers. Conflicting expectations of a stepmother's role make it especially hard. As a stepparent, your best shot at happiness is to ignore the myths and negative images and to work to stay optimistic.

Stepmother Anxiety

As a stepmother, your work is cut out for you. In fact, the role of stepmother is thought by some clinicians to be more difficult than that of stepfather. One important reason is that stepmother families, more than stepfather families, may be born of difficult custody battles and/or have a history of particularly troubled family relations. A remarried wife, seemingly out of left field, more often than a remarried husband, may suddenly be surprised to find herself a full-time stepmother.

Society also seems, on the one hand, to expect romantic, almost mythical loving relationships between stepmothers and children while, at the same time, portraying stepmothers as cruel, vain, selfish, competitive, and even abusive (*Snow White, Cinderella,* and *Hansel and Gretel* are just a few bedtime stories we are all familiar with). Stepmothers are also often accused of giving preferential treatment to their own children. As a result, a stepmother must be much better than just okay before she is considered acceptable. No matter how skillful and patient you are, all your actions are suspect. Is it any wonder that stepmothers tend to be more stressed, anxious, and depressed than other mothers and also more stressed than stepfathers?

Some researchers have found that stepmothers behave more negatively toward stepchildren than do stepfathers, and children in stepmother families seem to do less well in terms of their behavior. In fact, the relationship between stepmother and stepdaughter is often the most difficult. Yet, other studies indicate that stepmothers can have a positive impact on stepchildren. Because stepmothers are much more likely to play an active part in the lives of children than stepfathers, perhaps there is simply more to go wrong.

Still, some step-mothering situations can make this role especially complicated. You may, for example, be a part-time or weekend stepmother if you are married to a non-custodial father who sees his children regularly. You may try with all your heart to establish a loving relationship with your husband's children, only to be openly rejected, or you may feel left out of part of his life because of his relationship with his children. In addition, a part-time stepmother can feel left out by her husband's relationship with his ex-wife; for example, non-custodial fathers need to spend time communicating with their ex-wives about their children's school problems, orthodontia, illnesses, and even household maintenance and repairs.

Stepfather Anxiety

Men who marry women with children come to their new responsibilities with a mixed bag of emotions. Your motivations may be far different from those that make a man assume responsibility for his biological children. As a new husband you might react to your "instant" family with feelings which range from admiration to fright to contempt. You might even see yourself as less effective than a biological father.

A new stepfather typically enters a household headed by a mother. When a mother and her children make up a single-parent family, she tends to learn autonomy and self-confidence, and her children do more work around the house and take more responsibility in family decisions than do children in two-parent households. These are good things, but to enter such a family, you must work your way into a closed group. For one thing, mom and kids share a common history, one that does not yet include you.

Moving into your wife's house can make you feel like the "odd man out." It might be months before you feel comfortable and at home. In truth, initially, stepfathers do have less power relative to stepchildren, particular adolescents, when they move into the mother-child home.

You might feel out of place because of a different background or because you have a different perspective on what family life is all about. After years of living as a single-parent family, for instance, both mom and kids are likely to have evolved a fair chore allocation system. As a newcomer, especially if you assume the traditional male role in a two-earner remarriage, you may draw complaints that you are not contributing enough. Or, while you think it helpful not to interfere, your behavior might be seen as an unwillingness to contribute.

The hidden agenda is one of the first difficulties a stepfather runs into: The mother or her children, or both, may have expectations about what you will do, but may not give you a clear picture of what those expectations are. You may also have a hidden agenda of your own. You may see your new stepchildren as spoiled and unruly and decide they need discipline. Or you may find that after years of privacy, a bustling house full of children disrupts your routine.

A part of the stepchildren's hidden agenda is the extent to which they will let you play the father. Children can be adamant in their distaste for, or jealousy of, their stepfather, or they may be ready and anxious to accept you as a "new daddy." This last is particularly true of young children.

Stepfathers tend to be more distant and detached than stepmothers, and this is not necessarily a bad thing. Some detachment might be just what's needed in order to have a workable relationship with your stepchildren, especially during the early years of your marriage. Teenagers may be mature enough to think of you primarily as their mother's husband rather than as a stepfather. Teens, and younger children, may be unwilling to go back to being "children"—that is, dependent on and subject to adult direction. To you, they may seem spoiled and undisciplined rather than mature. Try to keep in mind that as part of a single-parent family, their responsibilities and participation in decisions were probably encouraged. The hidden agendas of mom, children, and you may be over simple matters of everyday living, things like food preferences, personal space, and the division of labor.

Discipline is likely to be particularly tricky for everyone. Two parents rather than one now establish house rules and influence the children's behavior, but you and your spouse may not agree. A second problem can be the influence of the biological father. To you, there may sometimes seem to be three parents instead of two—especially if the non-custodial father sees the children regularly—with the biological father wielding more influence than you, the stepfather. The key is for everyone to work together.

You might react to all of this in one of four ways. First, you might be driven away. Second, you might take control, establishing yourself as undisputed head of the household, and force the former single-parent family to accommodate your preferences. Third, you might assimilate into a family headed by a mother and have relatively little influence on the way things are done. *And fourth, you, your new wife, your stepchildren, and their non-custodial biological father can all negotiate new ways of doing things by taking to heart and incorporating the information you are about to learn—the most positive alternative for everyone.*

One Day at a Time

Okay. So now you have a pretty good feel for what everyone is going through. How do you start to make it better? How can you give yourself breathing space—time to catch your breath while your new family begins to come together emotionally and learns how to work together, a process that can take years? First you must be very clear about what you want and expect from this marriage and the individuals involved, including yourself. What are you willing to do? What do you need from your spouse in order to feel supported physically and emotionally? In a loving and positive way, now is the time to articulate, negotiate, and come to an agreement on your expectations and about how you and your partner will behave.

The best marriages are flexible marriages, but how can you be flexible if you do not know where you, your spouse, and the children stand and what everyone needs right now. *And, this may change over time, so there must be room for that to happen as well because the truth is that people change and promises will not prevent change.* People who vow never to change often try to hide their personal growth from each other, and the result, of course, is lost intimacy. People that are not flexible, that cannot change, may be left with a permanent, but stale, relationship.

In flexible marriages partners are freer to reveal their changing selves and the parts of themselves that no longer fit into their old established patterns. You and your partner must continue to be in touch at a deep emotional level even when the outer framework of your lives changes. The more you know, the more you grow. You couldn't possibly have known at the beginning of your new family what you know now and will learn later. Flexibility in your relationships will enable growth rather than tearing them apart.

Begin today by working with this book. Get in touch with your expectations and encourage every family member to do the same so that you can compare and negotiate the differences. Your goal, and your partner's, are to actively begin to define and built a healthy, supportive relationship. Talk over specific problems. Just because you were unable to predict some of the problems, don't let that stand in the way of dealing with them now.

It is not uncommon for people who marry again to feel reluctant to fully commit themselves emotionally, even though they want the marriage to work. The struggles of your first marriage and divorce can leave scars. When not openly acknowledged and healed, past failure, rejection, loss, and guilt can undermine a new intimate relationship without either of you understanding what is happening. One way to release these feelings is to share them, and to make it safe for your partner to do the same. Each of you needs to feel secure, respected, positive about yourself, and as comfortable as possible in your new family unit.

You may feel the "conflict taboo" even more than in your first marriage. It is understandable that you want to make this marriage work. You might feel too "battle-scarred" to open "a can of worms." And so, you gloss over differences that need airing and resolution—differences over which you may not have hesitated to wage war in your first marriage. Avoiding airing your differences is a serious mistake. It is important for you to understand your own and your partner's needs because society hasn't a clue how stepfamilies should work. Unless you talk about your expectations, they are likely to be unrealistic.

Legal Anxiety

Legal issues have to be aired. One important topic often swept under the rug is inheritance. Do you want your money and property to go to your new spouse or your children? What does the law in your state have to say about this? As a custodial parent, you may want your new spouse to adopt the children. This generally involves a waiver of parental rights by the biological parent, for many an unrealistic expectation. Recent court cases have addressed this issue and such termination of parental rights is extremely rare. Further, children above a certain age, perhaps 14, may or must give their own consent to stepparent adoption in some states.

Rights of stepparents to visitation or even custody of a stepchild in the event of the biological parent's death or divorce from that biological parent is a crucial issue because so many people become closely attached to stepchildren. Case law and legislation in this area are rapidly changing. Although it seems unlikely—and with reason—that stepparents will legally replace biological parents, it is important to indicate in a will or other statement that the biological parent would like his or her children's relationship with a stepparent preserved through visitation, if that is the case.

Your chance for a stable, happy marriage is greatest when you have strong social support, good communication skills, a positive attitude about the marriage, and low role ambiguity, and when you are able to dismiss negative stereotypes and myths about remarriages or stepfamilies. Open communication and flexibility can help to establish support, understanding, and stability where few social norms exist.

Blended/stepfamilies are an ancient, normal kind of human family unit. They have been around as long as our human ancestors have lived in communal groups. Anthropologists define this ancient human institution as characterized by non-DNA related adults nurturing and protecting immature youngsters who have survived the death, divorce, or absence of a parent. Unlike foster parents, stepparents are emotionally (and perhaps financially and legally) bonded to a child's biological parent.

Until about 1950, about 90 percent of American blended/stepfamilies were founded after the death of a child's biological parent. Since the "sexual revolution," about 90 percent of U.S. stepfamilies now follow the divorce of a child's biological parents. One implication of this swift shift is that our culture has not had time to produce, distribute, and widely accept any norms for people in prior divorce-based stepfamilies to follow. Another implication is that both biological parents are now alive and often maintain contact, about child support, visitations, holidays, education, and myriad other stepfamily co-parenting topics. If both biological parents eventually remarry, their biological kid(s) may have four stepfamily adults in two homes telling them how to eat, brush their teeth, and do their homework.

On one level, stepfamilies are "just like" conventional biological families: adult couples, usually of different genders, and one or more minor kids living and growing together, and doing "family things" together. Step-people and biological people both pay bills, go to work and school, have holidays and cavities, pets, problems, and triumphs.

One another level, typical two- or three-home stepfamilies differ from one-home biological families in over 60 ways which are discussed later in the book. These combined differences cause most step-homes to feel and act as different from a "normal" biological family as a poodle differs from a rhino.

Because of these many unexpected dynamic and structural family differences, and the lack of social norms and support, typical newly remarried people soon become uneasy with what they bought into. Rosy romantic visions tarnish as stepfamily realities set in, and original shared expectations prove unrealistic. Resident and visiting step-kids are confronted with several dozen unique adjustment tasks, many of which their stepfamily adults aren't aware of, or cannot empathize with. Relatives—untrained in the dynamics and uniqueness of stepfamily life—are unrealistically critical or unfairly judgmental, automatically using biological family yardsticks.

The kaleidoscope of unexpected and alien stepfamily stress can often turn the hopes and romance-based confidence of remarried couples into mounting adult confusion, resentment, distrust, and anxieties. When troubled remarried couples look for professional help, they discover to their frustration that there is little or none.

Ultimately, the unexpected complexities, confusion, disillusionment, and lack of accessible, *informed* help combine to crack and ultimately destroy 50 percent or more of typical U.S. blended/stepfamilies. In stunned disbelief, previously-divorced biological parents and their minor (and grown) kids find themselves re-experiencing the horrors, agony, and financial and social convulsions of family breakup and divorce—*again*. The personal and social impact of this stepfamily re-divorce epidemic is tragic and incalculable.

This book is for women and men who are considering forming a new stepfamily; those who already have, and are finding it more challenging than they thought; well-meaning relatives; and professionals (clergy, counselors, educators, doctors, and family lawyers and judges) who want to support these couples. This book is as much for single, non-custodial divorced biological parents as it is for their remarrying mates and new stepfamily adult partners.

Indirectly, this book is really for our country's millions of struggling step-kids who depend on their three or four stepfamily adults to provide them with the stable, safe, comforting, nurturing home(s) that they did not have the first time around, despite their parents' best efforts. Their parents very much wanted to do just that, but, without awareness, determination, and education, truly did not know how.

It is my hope that this book will bring you a fresh—and useful—view of the complex, challenging, and often *alien* world of multi-home stepfamilies. More to the point, that you find here *validation* (of your impressions and, perhaps, confusion); *clarification* of what is probably going on with and among your (many) family members; and, the *inspiration* and *knowledge* needed to not only set your stepfamily course together, but to navigate safely through the coming storms and years.

You will find, throughout this book, the word "*enough*," which signifies that while perfection might be attempted, not quite reaching it must not be viewed as failure or as an excuse to just give up. You are asked only for an awareness, a strong heart, and repeated attempts in the right direction.

Well-run by knowledgeable, confidant stepfamily adult *teams* (not just couples), this modern version of an ancient family form *can* provide the warmth, comfort, inspiration, support, security—and *often* (not always) the love—that we adults and kids all long for.

Benign ignorance, unresolved childhood issues, and incomplete grief will derail your journey if you choose to keep them hidden. You know what your life has been like keeping them underground. Here are the tools you need for positive change. The choice is yours.

CHILDREN LEARN WHAT THEY LIVE

Dorothy Law Nolte

If children live with conditional love, they learn to distrust.
If children live with deceit, they learn to be false.
If children live with criticism, they learn to fight.
If children live with ridicule, they learn to be shy.

If children live with neglect, they learn to abandon themselves.
If children live with inconsistency, they learn to be furtive.
If children live with violence, they learn to be numb or scared.
If children live with shaming, they learn to feel incompetent.
If children live with perfectionism they learn to feel inadequate.

If children live with excess worry, they learn to feel anxious.
If children live with unconditional love, they learn to love back.
If children live with tolerance, they learn to be patient.
If children live with encouragement, they learn confidence.
If children live with praise, they learn to appreciate.

If children live with fairness, they learn justice.
If children live with security, they learn to have faith.
If children live with genuine approval, they learn to like themselves.
If children live with acceptance and friendship, they learn to give and receive closeness,
care, and love.

A True Story

I have listened to well over 2,000 stepfamily adults—and some of their minor and grown kids—since 1981. Their stories have been as unique as hand-woven tapestries, yet common themes usually emerged. Without fail, a common reason for their calling, or attending a stepfamily co-parenting class, or coming into my office for a consultation, was *anxiety*. Low-grade or distilled *fear*. Worry. A rainbow of other emotions, too—frustration, sadness, shock, disbelief, hope, humor, rage, and the feeling of being overwhelmed—the gamut.

This book tries to organize the common elements of their complex stories. Before looking at these elements, note one stepfamily, one of the almost 100 kinds of stepfamilies which, together, offer an infinite range of step-person personalities. This story is meant to capture the *spirit* of their satisfactions and anxieties, rather than provide a comprehensive rendering. This story is real; the names of the people are not.

--- *Patty, Sarah, and Jack* ---

Patty came into my office with her biological mom, Sarah, on a Saturday morning. At 13, the slender, pretty brunette had never worked with a counselor before, although she knew her mother had gone to several for something. Patty had asked to "talk to somebody" about "something" to do with her stepfather Jack.

Sarah, who had a high school education and worked as a beautician, had already been in to see me several times. She had originally came in because of a mix of tensions around her one-year-old remarriage to a wonderful divorced man with two kids of his own. She was struggling with a collage of personal, parental, and re-marital "problems." (Just before she had brought Patty in, she had disclosed matter-of-factly that she had been sexually molested at 13.)

As Sarah had previously sketched her story, it appeared that she had again chosen a strong-willed, take-charge partner—although Jack was not an alcoholic like her previous husband, Patty's biological father. At my urging, eventually Jack came in with Sarah and Patty. He was a dedicated dentist, with a successful suburban practice. He was a compact, talkative, opinionated, forceful man in his early forties, who felt he had given "his all" to his former wife and kids. He was still angry and "mystified" about his wife's divorcing him, claiming "irrationally" that he was "impossible to live with." At one point, Jack mentioned that his father had deserted him and his mom when Jack was six.

Sarah's new husband was quite clear that his new family was not a "*step*family." His firm opinion was that labels were not important, *love* was. He was there to provide love, support, and strong male guidance to Sarah and Patty, while devotedly being a "good" absent father to his own preteen kids—and a responsible professional in the community.

As I learned more about their stepfamily, it quickly became obvious that Jack had come to "save" Patty and her mom from chaos and worry. He seemed to see his wife and stepdaughter (and most things) in black-and-white terms. His view was that—while lovable—his wife was incompetent at just about everything—especially parenting Patty.

Soon after their marriage, Jack had enforced a rigid code of discipline with Patty in their house, because Sarah was "too soft" on her early-teen daughter, and that Patty "was headed for trouble." He was irate that Patty's father had "weaseled out" of his parental responsibilities, leaving Jack to "clean up their mess."

Sarah seemed to be overwhelmed with Jack's righteous, rigid forcefulness, and had taken to explaining lamely to Patty that Jack "really meant well" (which he *did*!). Her attempts to get Jack to compromise and "be softer" with her daughter harvested predictable condescending monologs on "correct parenting," "it's for her own good," and her inadequacies as a mother and wife.

It was clear to me that neither stepfamily adult knew how to *listen* or problem-solve, and that they were locked in a (common) corrosive, lose-lose *values* conflict over "good parenting." Because Jack was unflinching in his views, and Sarah felt uncertain and poorly about herself as a person and mother, she felt "powerless" and despairing. She was getting increasingly angry with her husband and was withdrawing emotionally and physically, which made him "irritable" (i.e., *enraged*).

Sarah had brought Patty in because the girl was having trouble in her new school and had begun hinting that she was thinking of running away. I spent half an hour with Patty and her mother to help the girl start to build some trust in me and our process. I asked their permission to meet with Patty alone, and both agreed.

As soon as her mother left the room, Patty's big brown eyes filled with tears, and her mouth quivered. In bursts and sobs she told me (some of) her story. We met several more times, and a predictable, heart-wrenching tapestry emerged. She felt despairing and overwhelmed by a set of tensions she could barely describe, let alone cope with. She knew her mother loved her, but felt intensely angry and scornful that Sarah wouldn't "stand up" to Jack and protect her from his endless lectures, rules, and groundings.

Part of her stepfamily pain was periodic. When her stepsiblings, Annie (12) and Dickie (14), came to visit every other weekend, she always felt that Jack favored them over her— although he fervently denied that. For example, when Annie would leave her clothes strewn around the house, her father never yelled at her the way he did at Patty. He was especially supportive of Dick's progress at school sports, while he seemed indifferent to, or critical of, Patty's gymnastics efforts.

When the time seemed right, I asked if either of her biological parents had explained to her why they got divorced. She dropped her eyes and said quietly, "well, sort of." On further questioning, it seemed that she really wasn't clear on why and felt much inner confusion and conflict about the stress her parents' divorce had brought into her life. Patty said sadly that her "real" father really didn't seem to care about her much. She described several instances where he had promised to attend school parent conferences and gymnastic meets, but didn't. "He always has excuses," she said flatly. When I asked about his drinking, she looked away. "It scares me sometimes. Mom won't let him drive me anywhere now, because she thinks he'll have an accident."

Much of the mosaic of Patty's story was about instances where she felt Jack was unfairly and harshly critical—"over *nothing*!" He often restricted her phone calls with friends as punishment for her "bad" school grades—cutting off her only current source of sympathy and support. "He *never* listens to me," she grimaced. "When Mom tries to argue, he just walks all over her. And she *lets* him! Our life wasn't all that great before he came around, but I *hate* it now!"

I asked if there was *any* adult in her life who understood how she was feeling these days. Patty's long straight hair swung as she shook her head. Her only nearby relative was her mother's sister, who lived about 50 miles away. I asked if there were things that got in the way of her talking honestly with her mother. She nodded and looked away. Eventually she was able to tell me she thought her mother was miserable and scared. "So I *can't* tell her how much I hate Jack in our life. She has enough problems. You know, she's already taking some medicine for depression." Then another part of Patty emerged: "Why did she ever marry that jerk, anyway? This is really *her* fault!" She began to cry again.

Patty described sadness and frustration about her social life. "Jack won't let me have friends in my room. I don't like to have them over anyway, because he's home all the time, and he's such a *dork*! And Mom's such a wimp." I asked how she got along with her stepsiblings. "Annie's all right, I guess. We can talk about some stuff, and we like the same music. She feels her father's too strict, too, but she never talks back to him. Dick is so stuck up. He thinks he's so great! He sucks up to Jack, and he (Jack) just eats that up. It makes me *sick*!"

Patty described at some length her anguish over really liking a boy at school, and Jack and her mother telling her he "wasn't her kind of boy." "What do *they* know about it? It's my life, isn't it?" She hinted that she was sneaking out to be with him, "no matter *what* they think!" I noted silently that Patty's big hoop earrings, tight clothes, and overdone makeup signaled both "growing up early in America" and her desperation to attract some approval and male closeness.

"Patty," "Sarah," and "Jack" are real people. This is part of a real story. It does not have a happy ending. Their tapestry is not an exaggeration of many stepfamilies' situations. It also is far different from the stories that step-kids in typical *successful* stepfamilies tell. Sure, they have gripes and anxieties, too—but unlike Patty, they have two or more stepfamily adults who are healing their own inner wounds, learning stepfamily norms, and are there consistently with encouragement, comfort, warmth, and *respect*.

When I last saw Sarah several years ago, she was going to night school, getting tutoring, and slowly becoming more self-respecting and assertive with Jack. She didn't want to be married to him, but economically couldn't make it on her own. Patty did try to run away—twice—which reportedly enraged Jack rather than *alerting* him. This strengthened the deepening emotional split between Sarah and Patty, and Jack and his kids. Despite my best efforts, neither stepfamily adult in this story (nor their ex-mates) was even close to recognizing their own deep childhood wounds, and how they were inexorably corroding their remarriage, as well as wounding Patty and her stepsiblings. If this stepfamily does break up *legally* (it already has, emotionally), I hope Sarah's and Jack's—and their kids'—pain will break through the adult's protective denials, and allow awareness and eventual personal healing.

Peter K. Gerlach, M.S.W.

"On Children"

From *"The Prophet"* by Khalil Gibran (1923)

Your children are not your children.
They are the sons and daughters of Life's longing for itself.
They come through you but not from you,
And though they are with you yet they belong not to you.
You may give them your love but not your thoughts,
For they have their own thoughts.
You may house their bodies but not their souls,
For their souls dwell in the house of tomorrow,
which you cannot visit, not even in your dreams.
You may strive to be like them,
but seek not to make them like you.
For life goes not backward nor tarries with yesterday.
You are the bows from which your children
as living arrows are sent forth.
The archer sees the mark upon the path of the infinite,
and He bends you with His might
that His arrows may go swift and far.
Let our bending in the archer's hand be for gladness;
For even as He loves the arrow that flies,
so He loves also the bow that is stable.

"Co-Parents" Defined

Stepfamily co-parents or "adults" are two or more adults in any stepfamily who intentionally nurture dependent kids together. Active grandparents, aunts, and uncles can act as stepfamily co-parents.

A stepfamily adult can be a biological parent, a childless stepparent or involved adult relative. Legally and physically, divorced-family and stepfamily adults are *custodial, non-custodial, or share joint custody.* "Adult" can be a family role (noun), a nurturing *process* (verb), or a person who conceives and/or nurtures a child (noun).

Some caregivers have stepparent and biological parent roles ("dual role stepfamily adults"). A nuclear stepfamily may have three or more stepfamily adults living in two or more related homes with their resident and visiting biological and step-kids.

The term stepfamily adult is emotionally neutral. That helps offset our old cultural bias that biological parents are "better" or more "normal" or "natural" than stepparents or foster parents.

PART ONE

STEPFAMILY PREPARATION

The following four chapters are for any prospective or committed stepfamily adult and supporter (i.e., clergy, mediators, and pre-marital coaches and counselors); however, these chapters are especially helpful to dating adults who may form or join a stepfamily.

CHAPTER ONE

THE REASONS FOR WIDESPREAD STEPFAMILY STRESS AND RE-DIVORCE

In any stepfamily at least three people are struggling to form new family relationships while still coping with reminders of the past. Each family member brings expectations and attitudes that are as diverse as the personalities involved. Creating a successful stepfamily, as with any family, is easier for all when each member tries to understand the feelings and motivations of the others as well as their own. Ideally, discuss the realities of living in a stepfamily *before* the marriage.

What can you do? Plan ahead. Look carefully at your motives, and those of your future spouse, for wanting to get married. Get to know him or her as well as possible under all sorts of circumstances. Consider the possible impact of contrasting lifestyles. If your lifestyles clash, the children are the ones caught in the middle. Discuss how your lives will change by bringing two families together. What do you agree and disagree on when it comes to your concept of child-rearing.

Talk honestly with your children about the changes this marriage will bring: new living arrangements, new family relationships, and how this will affect their relationship with their non-custodial parent. Give your children ample opportunity to get to know your future spouse well. Consider your children's feelings, but don't allow them to make your decision about remarriage.

Discuss the disposition of family finances with your future spouse. An open and honest review of financial assets and responsibilities may reduce unrealistic expectations and misunderstandings. Understand that there are bound to be periods of doubt, frustration, and resentment.

Any marriage is complex and challenging, but the problems of stepfamilies are more complicated because more people, relationships, feelings, attitudes, and beliefs are involved than in a first marriage. Because its members have not shared past experiences, the new family may have to redefine rights and responsibilities to fit your individual and combined needs. Time and understanding are key allies in negotiating the transition from single-parent to stepfamily status.

1

In a good stepfamily every member is treated with dignity, care, and respect (initially love may not be in the equation). A healthy step or biological family is one in which each person feels the support to grow to his or her full potential.

If you have already jumped into the role of stepmother or father, the following three points can ease the transition process for everyone and give you breathing space as you continue to explore and use the ideas presented in this book.

Help stepchildren to get over their loss (the divorce or death of a parent) if they have not yet (it takes about two years). Or, perhaps, regardless of the time lapsed, they have not been able to because there was no environment of emotional support and trust in which they could have their feelings and come to terms with the "I wish I had(s)" or feelings that they somehow caused the divorce (as children commonly feel). They need a climate of emotional safety to not only express, but acknowledge their feelings rather than just blindly acting out with rage. They need to heal their loss before they can move on emotionally to creating and being part of a new stepfamily. You see your new marriage as completing your life, but a child may see it as something which will take away from theirs. You see it as a plus; they see it as a minus.

It is more important to develop a relationship of caring, communication, and respect with a stepchild than to hope for or expect instant love. Love takes time; it must grow. Be real with your emotions. What you resist persists, what you accept lightens. Encourage your children and stepchildren to be real about their feelings. Set limits on behavior, not feelings; for example, you cannot allow them to act out their anger by burning down the house, but you can let them express their feelings that they wish this new "family" didn't exist.

Let your relationship with stepchildren develop gradually. Don't expect too much too soon—from the children or yourself. Children need time to adjust, accept, and belong. So do parents. Don't try to replace a lost parent; be an additional parent. Children need time to mourn the parent lost through divorce or death. Expect to deal with confusing feelings—your own, your spouse's, and the children's. Anxiety about new roles and relationships may heighten the competition among family members for love and attention as loyalties are questioned. Children may need to understand that their relationship with you is valued but different from your relationship with your new spouse and that one cannot replace the other. You love and need them both, but in different ways.

Help the child that goes back and forth between parents. Their lives are full of good-byes. Help children accept painful feelings so that these feelings can become smaller and more manageable. Let yourself and your children feel, so that everyone can heal. An idealized expectation becomes a prison while accepting the truth will set you free. If you are marrying into an existing family, TV and movies may have helped create unrealistic expectations of what a family is and how it functions. What it is not is a fairy tale of politeness and caring.

Why Most Stepfamilies Fail

One in three typical stepfamilies do succeed, long term. In order to find out how to accomplish this, you must be willing to first explore why most stepfamilies break apart. There seem to be five interlinked reasons why most average stepfamilies crash, often within 10 years.

1. The adults in many stepfamilies seem to come from families which were, to some degree, less than functional. Without awareness and personal growth, these adults unconsciously pass similar emotional traits on to their kids, repeating and spreading a cycle of unreasonable need and an inability to get these needs met.

2. Most stepparents resist fully accepting that they are forming a multi-home stepfamily, which will differ in over 60 ways from the one-home biological family they are used to. To make matters worse, many people overtly or unconsciously associate "step-" with failure, wicked, unnatural, second-best, and inferior. They do not want to learn about stepfamilies, let alone be one. This ignorance can be fatal, both as a partner and parent. Typical multi-home stepfamilies are amazingly complex and often take five to eight years, or more, to stabilize. Many unaware, love-dazed couples expect it will all come together in five to eight months.

3. One or more new-stepfamily kids or adults are often blocked in mourning their agonizing prior losses. Every remarriage follows traumatic endings from previous divorce or death. Remarriage and/or cohabiting cause more major losses (and gains). Parents who did not see their parents grieve well, regardless of why they were grieving, can't grieve themselves. How could they have taught you how to grieve. They repressed and avoided intense sadness and/or rage, and so were stressed and ruled by these emotions for years. Incomplete grief promotes crippling addictions and illnesses, nourishes post-divorce hostilities, splits biological kids emotionally between warring ex-mates, and prevents even adult step-kids from accepting the kindest of stepparents. Blocked mourning has clear symptoms. Once recognized, frozen grief can be thawed, over time.

4. For most, the decision to remarry is made in a shared, wonderfully distorted state-of-mind: romantic love. Combined with the illusion that stepfamilies are not all that different from biological families, these distortions often cloud an awareness of what the couple is really undertaking, and what practical preparations they should make. Sobering divorce statistics imply that almost three of four stepfamily adults marry the wrong people, for the wrong reasons, and at the wrong time. They commit to mutual illusions.

5. The final reason for such widespread re-divorce is that our media and most communities offer little or no informed, effective support for remarried people and their kids. There are few or no stepfamily co-parenting classes, support groups, newsletters, or aware

counselors. Few clergy, teachers, therapists, mediation lawyers and judges, or medical professionals know how different, complex, and risky multi-home stepfamilies are. Stepfamily re-divorce seems to be a social-science black hole, though so many remarriages involving prior kids are highly stressful and ultimately fail.

Why Do Some Stepfamilies Survive

However, since roughly one out of four stepfamilies do survive—even thrive—we know that stepfamilies *can grow* the safety, support, warm closeness, strength, and comfort that only healthy families provide. The following, explored in detail throughout this book, can insure your success:

- Each adult must learn the symptoms, if any, of their own troubled childhood. You must identify your major destructive emotional traits and evolve a self-motivated, high-priority personal plan for healing. You must commit to it, and begin. Next, evaluate the odds that your prospective partner may have troubling emotional traits. If so, unless they are aware of their problems and are in solid recovery, settle for friendship.
- You must assess, as a couple, how well you accept and resolve conflicts with each other and key others. Learn and steadily work to develop important verbal skills: talking about how you communicate, empathic listening, effective assertion, and problem solving. Learn to manage your inner and personal conflicts. The emotional highs of new love can disguise deep disagreement on parenting, money, family priorities, and home management, i.e., values that will surface after the wedding.
- Together, accept your prospective identity as a normal, unique, multi-home stepfamily versus "We're just a *family"* (with unreasonable expectations). Then, stepfamily adults and kids (minor and grown) can try to agree on who *belongs* in it. You need to admit and resolve strong disagreements, well *enough* for positive results.
- Learn how your stepfamily differs from typical biological families, and the related typical stepfamily myths. Then, discuss realistic expectations for each of your many marriage and family roles. Be realistic, because without steady work on these, you and your kids will in all probability divorce within seven to 10 years.
- You and your partner must learn the five stages of healthy grieving, and the specific symptoms of incomplete grief. Then run a check on yourself, your partner, and each child, for major prior losses. If anyone is seriously blocking mourning their unique losses, you and your partner (including ex-mates) must agree on a plan to deal with that. And you must act on your plan. *Consider specifically what each child and adult will lose with your marriage and living together.* Evolve a clear policy for good grief and use it to guide and support all of you through your inevitable life losses.

- You and your partner should (separately) explore the following questions honestly: Why should I remarry? Why now? Why this person and their kids, ex (if not their first marriage)? If I have to, can I often put this adult ahead of my own kids without major resentment or guilt? (Stepfamily parents are inevitably forced to choose and often.) Can my partner do that?
- After the wedding, merge and stabilize your two biological families' assets, beliefs, habits, values, rituals, priorities, and lifestyles. Everyone in your new multi-home stepfamily must give up some cherished things and accept new things. Support each other in mourning key personal losses.
- Consistently resolve the many values and loyalty conflicts that will result from your marriage. The most important and dramatic conflict of all needs to be mastered. Each parent must decide whose needs usually come first with them, their partner's or their children's. To protect your kids from another divorce trauma, you might need to put your marriage first. Also, clarify whose needs control each of your stepfamily's homes. Learn how to problem-solve effectively together.
- Evolve and use a stepfamily goal plan. Stabilize your stepfamily roles. Revise most of your old biological family roles. Evolve new intra- and inter-home rules for these roles that everyone can accept well *enough*. Help each other admit and grieve key personal losses along the way.
- You must consistently balance and co-manage all of these tasks, plus a myriad of other responsibilities well *enough* on a daily basis to: build a solid, high-priority marriage; enjoy your kids; and, to keep growing emotionally and spiritually as individual people. And, don't forget to laugh, play, and relax together along the way.

The Parents

Most dating adults are in their late 20's to mid 40's. They have had more life experience than first-married couples, and are further along in their careers. These women and men have a different mix of values about money, leisure, child conception, relationships, work, spirituality, and other things compared to when they first married in their late teens to late 20's. There is a higher chance that their religion, race, and/or "class" differ from their new partner than the first time around.

One or both of the new partners have been married at least once before—for about seven years, on average. About 90 percent of them have been divorced, often within the last two to five years. Few had amicable breakups. Many describe their former mate as abusive, materialistic, indifferent, workaholic or alcoholic, selfish, "really screwed up," and/or unfaithful. These judgments are often vehemently returned by their former partners. Their kids suffer silently in the crossfire.

One or both have been custodial or part-time parents to one to three preteen or early-teen kids for several years. A minority of these biological parents have joint (split) physical and legal custody. Usually the woman has been a single custodial mother, with a full-time job inside and outside her home. She is often tired, but "pressing on." Following divorce, her standard of living went down, usually a lot. She has learned to be more independent and usually likes that.

Either she, her ex-husband, or both may have tense, diminished, or no relations with the "other half" of their biological kids' relatives—their ex in-laws. They have all had several seasons of awkward holidays, and often haven't discussed this openly with their ex, or with their daughters and sons.

Most of these adults decided to form a stepfamily when in a seriously altered state-of-mind: infatuation or deep romantic love. Some fell into this delicious condition before separating from their spouse, i.e., during an affair. If they live together, they imagine their current shared experience to be a pretty reliable model of how remarried stepfamily life will be. This almost always proves to be false.

Most of these women and men do not see or talk of themselves and their kid(s) as a "stepfamily," claiming they just don't like the sound of *that*. Those who were never married before may long to be part of a *regular, ideal biological family,* especially if their early years were lonely. Feeling excited, hopeful, and mature, few have researched the realities of stepfamilies. Many have declared, out of love laced with divorce guilt, "My kids will always come first" to their love-struck partners—who nod supportively.

Some new mates are marrying from a deep wish to rescue an alluring, overburdened single parent and their appealing youngsters. However, some of their kids don't *want* to be rescued. Others are delighted. Some of their grandparents and other relatives are delighted, too. Some ex-mates are relieved, others threatened and jealous, and still others are detached and indifferent.

Other than by court order, divorced biological parents have rarely gone to post-divorce counseling to heal their wounds, mistrusts, and misunderstandings. They are wearily practiced in fighting or avoiding, but not in listening and cooperative problem-solving. These split biological parents may sporadically hang up on each other in phone struggles over the kids and/or ongoing, deathless, sacred marital grievances. They have never met with all the people in their two to three plus homes, which are about to be joined, to discuss and plan their common complex enterprise. The other stepfamily adults probably wouldn't come anyway, feeling disinterest, distrust, and/or dislike. Who would suggest and run such a meeting, anyway?

Although the partners claim to be able to talk about everything, they seldom have had blunt, practical discussions about blending their values and priorities about managing money and assets (including wills); child management; and, building an effective joint way of resolving values conflicts. They have never imagined or discussed drafting personal, marital, household, or multi-home stepfamily goals.

The couples do not know or particularly care what their joint policy on mourning is, although they and their kids have much to grieve. They are typically unaware that their coming nuptial ceremony will cause searing new losses for any number of the people in their three-generation stepfamily. They understandably focus on the coming gains and dreams.

Before saying "I do" again, the average new stepparent has seldom or never tried to discipline his or her partner's children, because "it's not my place." If they have, they've been very polite and pretty tolerant. Often, these stepparents-in-training have had little direct contact with their step-kids' other biological parent. They have heard a lot about them, usually from biased people.

If not numbed out, these other biological parents—especially those without custody or frequent visitation—feel many things as they imagine a stranger raising their children. They swirl in an emotional stew of resentment, anguish, relief, shame, hurt, fear, sadness, and anger, depending on the day and circumstance. Absent dads, especially, seldom talk about this emotional kaleidoscope—to themselves or others. They often seek distraction in overwork, sports, computers, or addictions.

The other biological parents' parents can feel anxious too, wondering how this new and unknown stepparent will influence their grandsons and granddaughters. Some speak out, wanting to learn or control. Others worry and repress. Some shrug. Many of these grandparents are carrying around unhealed childhood wounds themselves and are in major denial. Like the spouses to be, they and other DNA kin usually don't identify themselves as prospective stepfamily members, have little factual knowledge of stepfamily realities, and are not motivated to investigate. Stepfamilies based on divorce were rare in their younger days.

The romantic love that envelopes typical thirty-something partners is an effective balm and universal solvent for their present or glimpsed problems. Their joint excitement, thrill, and hope have not yet mellowed into a clearer, deeper bond of mature love. These good people, understandably, cannot know what they don't know about the astonishingly complex enterprise they are starting together. Neither do most of their kids or supporters. At this stage, another divorce just is not a meaningful possibility.

Few dating or remarried biological and stepparent couples read material like this book. If they do, they often feel a bemused detachment or put it down uneasily before finishing. Their relatives, friends, clergy, therapists, doctors, and lawyers, if any, seldom know about the almost 60 differences between typical step and biological families. Most of them have never read about or attended a class on multi-home stepfamily dynamics. If a supporter advises the couple to learn about remarriage and stepfamily co-parenting challenges, they usually hear something like, "we know what we're getting into—we'll be fine!" Benign ignorance.

Beyond the Obvious

Roughly four out of five of these typical adults considering remarriage also were *accidentally* deprived of an emotionally and spiritually healthy childhood—and don't know it. Most had abusive, emotionally absent, or over-anxious enmeshed caregivers, who were themselves in the same emotional boat. Their personal characteristics typically include a palette of excessive shame, guilt, rage (or numbness), anxieties, trust problems, reality distortions, horror of abandonment, and deep longings for peace, love, and hope.

These traits may be deeply buried, well disguised, and protectively denied. Symptoms of these traits include recurrent illness, addictions, isolation, failed relationships, emptiness, and depression. The dating adults might be starting to worry about these traits, or they are, at least, becoming apparent. Whether their emotional wounds are moderate or major, these people know little about recovering from them. Those that do, feel it certainly has nothing to do with them and their new love (relationship).

This new romantic partner is probably an appealing, wounded, wonderful trouper in denial, just like themselves and their ex. They may have kids of their own, or never been married and have idealistic (biological-based) images of what kids need and how they *should* behave. A minority of these dating adults were co-raised by a step-dad and/or step-mom. Some have active, yet denied, addictions, or are in 12-step recovery programs.

Now that you have met a stereotype of the typical adults who initiate average stepfamilies, what are the minor kids like?

The Dependent Kids

Depending on their age, step-kids-to-be have often had extra freedom in their custodial parents' post-divorce homes. Some have become junior parents for younger siblings. Others are becoming little adults, by parenting or being surrogate emotional partners for their depressed or overwhelmed custodial mom or dad. Most pre-step-kids are used to regular or chaotic inter-home visitation routines, and often two very different sets of household values, priorities, roles, and rules.

Some have been helplessly enmeshed in recurring bitter battles between their biological parents over money, child custody, holidays, visitations, and exposed to differing discipline, moral, and health standards in their two homes.

Perhaps half of these children have seen the presence of their non-custodial parent (usually dad) dwindle or vanish through decreasing calls, cards, and birthday, vacation, graduation, or other contacts. The inescapable, shaming message seems to be: "You're not very important to me." These kids don't understand—or care—that visitations with them often bring their non-custodial biological parent piercing waves of guilt, longing, frustration, and pain. Sometimes contact decreases or ceases altogether because the child was a "surprise," one whose conception was not planned or really wanted by one or both biological parents. Either way, the child feels acutely unloved and unwanted.

Other girls and boys are getting more consistent attention from one or both parents than before their divorce. Some youngsters have been turned into spies, messengers, or mediators between warring biological parents. Still others have seen a small parade of parental boyfriends or girlfriends come and go. Such kids are distrustful of and cautious about befriending parental suitors; they may have risked it once and the new adult eventually disappeared or was "mean."

Many children of ruptured biological families have had several strangers as caregivers—usually female—in day care and/or at home. Whether they bond or not, these females always eventually leave. Some kids have been co-raised by relatives, often grandma or an aunt and uncle. With their own agendas, these kinfolk may be painfully critical of one (or both) of the children's biological parents. Where this is so, kids often translate that attitude magically (and silently) into self-blame.

Commonly, neither biological parent has told their dependent children clearly and honestly why the marriage and family split up. Many preteen kids silently blame themselves. Others have been rewarded with power, strokes, and freedom if they revile their absent biological parent to please their bitter custodial mom or dad. Most hate doing this, but give in to the powerful need to please their resident caregiver. Thankfully, a few boys and girls have attended *Rainbows*, a grief-support group held at school or their house of worship, and vented, questioned, and cried with other kids like themselves.

All these youngsters are trying to adapt to major life changes and losses they only partially understand. Some, lacking consistent love, support, and empathy from one or both biological parents, have become apathetic, numb, or started to "cause trouble." Some feel like they "don't belong anywhere," while others who get consistent adult nurturing are regaining some trust that they are safe, worthy, and loved. None know that their parents' divorce and eventual remarriage will bring them up to two dozen new personal tasks (discussed in a later chapter) on top of their normal developmental tasks—that their intact-family peers don't face. Few of their parents, teachers, and friends have any real clue about these complex extra tasks.

Even into adulthood, these girls and boys may ignore realities, and dream fiercely and idealistically of parental and biological family reunion. Such dreams greet even the nicest of potential stepparents, seen as dream-busters, with cloaked or up-front hostility, distrust, and rejection. Other step-kids-to-be welcome friendly new adults, relieved that someone can help their sad, lonely, and/or overloaded parent. Just as their dating biological parent dreams of forming a happy new family, older teens are dreaming of breaking away and gaining new freedoms—and are experimenting toward this.

Many children of divorce have lived with open or covert family anxiety, anger, pain, and confusion much or all of their lives. To them, these are normal and unremarkable. In every family kids have unique ways of adapting: some (often the eldest) become super responsible. A sibling may have turned invisible. Another may act out constantly. Any one of them may have turned into a resident social worker and peacemaker, sacrificing his or her own needs and dreams.

If their parents' divorce is a sign that these adults cannot function well for the good and emotional well being of all, most of these dependent kids have already begun to experience the social and physical consequences of their own unfulfilled emotions. They may befriend other "troubled" kids, act out or appear "hyper" at school, or withdraw into their own secret worlds. They may exhibit symptoms of Attention Deficit Disorder (ADD) or hyperlexia (a learning disorder that involves children who exhibit an above normal ability to read at a very young age while their communication and comprehension skills are below normal. Due to his fascination with the written word, a hyperlexic child often does not interact well with others. He may exhibit abnormal and awkward social skills and have problems relating to his peers.). Even if caring adults ask them what's going on, these youngsters typically lack the world experience, knowledge, vocabulary, and courage to answer clearly.

CHAPTER TWO

ASSESS FOR PSYCHOLOGICAL WOUNDS
AND BEGIN PERSONAL HEALING

They come to tell their stories. Stories about unexpectedly confusing relationship struggles with ex-mates, troubled kids, and each other. They speak in pain, bewilderment, blame, and anger. Sometimes they laugh, but seldom from the belly. "*I never knew it'd be like this*," they cry.

These women and men all deeply want a happy remarriage and a loving, normal family, yet find these elusive. Many are reluctant or embarrassed to say "we're a stepfamily," or "I'm a stepparent." Spouses and caregivers often seem uncomfortable describing their family conflicts and frustrations. Men in particular find it hard to look in their partner's eyes.

Nina and Tom

Having a second marriage start to wobble forces even self-reliant people to seek help, especially if they live with one or more beloved kids who are in obvious pain. Nina and Tom are one such couple. She, a vivacious 40-something redhead and mother of Bill and Anita, had recently quit work because of depression. Several years before, she had divorced her first husband. She had endured nine years of his drinking-and-remorse cycles, punctuated by many episodes of physical and verbal abuse. "*I kept hoping he'd change, and we'd be all right*," Nina says. "*Finally, I had to accept that he wouldn't.*"

Tom is a solid, smiling man who sits close to his new wife on the couch. They hold hands and lean into each other as they talk. They had remarried eight months ago, sure that their shared love would iron out the complexities of their three-home stepfamily. Tom had not seen much of his two preteen kids recently, who lived with their mother. "*She and I don't talk much*," he says. "*She won't listen to me. She's pretty bitter about our divorce, though she asked for it. Never have figured that out.*"

Nina had called for the appointment. "*It's about Tom's rages*," she explained. "*They really scare me and the kids. He gets totally out of control. We have to do something, but I don't know what.*" Their story is unique in detail, old in theme: Tom is hurt and frustrated by his teen stepdaughter who "*ignores*" him although he is now the sole breadwinner for her, her brother, mom, and grandmother. When he blows up at Anita, Nina feels caught in the middle: a normal stepfamily loyalty conflict. He becomes enraged when she seems to side with her daughter. "*We just don't know how to talk together about this,*" she adds. "*I feel so torn.*" Tom smiles, in his pain. "*Yeah, my anger scares me too. I know I have to knock it off, but it's hard.*"

Asked about their childhoods, Nina says almost offhandedly, "My mom was tough, at times." *She broke a lot of plates over my brother's head. He was pretty wild though. She used to hit us and she was an alcoholic.*" "*Yeah,*" says Tom, "*That's another thing we have in common: my dad was a heavy drinker, too.*" Asked whether he thought he was addicted, Tom looks at the ceiling. "*Hard to say. I suppose so, never really thought much about it.*"

Many step-adults were unintentionally neglected emotionally and/or abused spiritually, emotionally, physically, and/or sexually. Few are conscious of it. Fewer want to be, fearing disloyalty to their caregivers and confronting long-hidden agonies. Their parents were not monsters. Almost always, they too were accidentally deprived and deeply wounded as children, and do not know it. They loved, and literally did the best parenting they could.

These are wounded adults who usually deny or minimize their early abuse and neglect; the resulting intense shame, sorrow, fear, and rage; and, their own denial. Without awareness of and recovery from these wounds, these adults seem to repeatedly pick each other as partners. Add normal stepfamily complexities and conflict, and these deep emotional and spiritual wounds often block healthy marital intimacy and interdependence. This starts a spiral of stepfamily stress, conflict with the spouse, and eventually another divorce—and, a new set of wounds.

Already sustaining major parental death or divorce losses, most minor children of re-divorce are traumatized again, and as such are likely to be at high risk of major developmental and relationship problems of their own. Many will need professional help to heal the emotional deprivations unwittingly passed on to them by their wounded caregivers. Without help and true emotional and spiritual recovery, they are likely to create dysfunctional families of their own, continuing the cycle.

Are you an emotionally wounded adult who comes from a traumatic childhood? The hard truth is that a large majority of stepfamily adults are from this type of background and are, to some extent, in complete denial of the situation. Also, you repeatedly pick each other as partners and associates like magic, i.e., unconsciously. Until you recognize this problem and take the steps needed to heal, your combined core emotional and spiritual wounds are guaranteed to interact and preclude the joys of family relationships and safety you long for.

Equally important, you cannot help but to pass them on, even though it may be totally against your wish or awareness, to your dependent kids—just as you inherited them from your well-meaning, wounded parents and caregivers. Until surfaced and healed, these core emotional wounds silently pass down the generations in a widening fan of family and personal tragedy and pain.

Any human group—like a family—can fall somewhere on an imaginary line between totally healthy and totally unhealthy. Like sports teams, or small companies, some families function to achieve their objectives better than others, because of this, it is important to come to terms with what an emotionally and spiritually healthy family is. The underlying premise is that for true individual and group holistic health, the leaders of any group need to consistently provide and promote many of the traits of a holistically healthy family or relationship for all of its members.

The more of the factors listed below any group of people has consistently, the better or more functional it will be because the group will then be able to work harmoniously and productively. A healthy family steadily fosters competencies, self-sufficiencies, and balanced personal growth in all of its members. The unfortunate truth is that most families rarely have most or all of these factors consistently. Have you ever known, or been a part of, a really holistically healthy group?

Traits of a Healthy Family or Relationship

The Keys to Success

Keeping in mind that holistic health means balanced *physical, emotional,* and *spiritual* well-being, which of these traits describes your family or relationships:

- The adults are clearly and consistently in charge of the family. The minor kids are not called on to do significant care-giving for younger children or disabled adults, or to make major household decisions.
- The family leader(s) (each) have specific, realistic, harmonious goals for what they are trying to do as people, partners, and stepfamily adults. They have viable plans to reach their main goals.
- Each member consistently feels unconditionally loved, wanted, and prized for who they are, rather than for what they can do or contribute.
- Each member consistently feels physically, emotionally, and spiritually safe enough, short- and long-range.
- Each member is basically honest with himself or herself, and with all others; there are few or no taboo subjects or family secrets.
- Members often exchange respectful assertion, genuine listening, and cooperative, effective interpersonal problem-solving.
- Each member gets enough appropriate nurturing (such as hugs) as opposed to painful, intrusive, or shaming physical contact.
- Members exchange steady encouragement to fully develop their unique natural talents, and to be their real self, rather than an ideal, false self or someone's clone.

- Members exchange prompt, honest, constructive feedback instead of manipulative or shaming feedback.
- Members are encouraged and rewarded for taking non-shaming personal responsibility for their choices, rather than blaming others, deflecting, manipulating, or hiding.
- All members feel open to freely experience and evaluate others' ideas, customs, and beliefs, as opposed to being bound by a rigid, bigoted *"our way is the only true way"* of thinking.
- Minor children are steadily encouraged to be themselves, i.e., kids, without guilt or shame, instead of little adults, clones, or super-achievers.
- Each member is genuinely supported in developing his or her own spiritual curiosity, reverence, and a deep, nurturing faith in a benign, reliable, personal Higher Power based on unconditional love and hope, not on fear, guilt, shame, and/or duty.
- Family and household rules are consistent, clear, appropriate *enough*, and flexible. Consequences are clear to all, respectful, prompt, and appropriate *enough*, and aim at teaching and guiding, not at punishing and forcing compliance based on fear or shaming.
- Personal adult-child and family-outer world boundaries are clear, appropriate, and consistent *enough.*
- Leaders confidently, rather than fearfully, delegate increasing responsibility and autonomy as individual abilities grow.
- Members openly enjoy *reasonable* pride, pleasure, and satisfaction in personal and group achievements.
- Leaders provide children enough effective training in living, social, and learning skills—especially in effective verbal and written communications and problem-solving.
- Members are encouraged to feel and safely express all their current emotions, especially anger, sadness and despair, and fear. Members support each other in grieving their major life losses promptly and well *enough*, over time.
- Each member values and strives for healthy interdependence, rather than excessive dependence or premature independence.
- All members have a healthy balance between work, play, and rest; and between group, couple, and personal times.
- Members value chances to make safe mistakes and to learn from them without excess anxiety, shame, or guilt.
- Members all respect, prize, and care for their bodies and are comfortable *enough* with (not excessively guilty about or ashamed of) their physical endowments or lack thereof, and with their gender and gender-preferences.
- Members share an appreciative interest in, and respectful concern for, the Earth and all things on it.

- All members feel an appreciation and serene acceptance of the natural differences and sameness among each other and among all other people, cultures, and nations.
- All members are appropriately encouraged in the responsible, shame-free enjoyment of personal sensuality and safe sexuality, within the moral norms of the group and society.
- Members are steadily encouraged to adopt attitudes of realistic hope and optimism, versus unrealistic pessimism, doubt, and fear.
- All members often feel free to be spontaneous, play, and relax *enough*. Exchanged humor is spontaneous and affirming, not shaming, belittling, or hurtful.
- Each member steadily feels an unshakable, deep, balanced respect and love for himself or herself, and for all others.
- Each family leader can spontaneously quote many or most of these traits and values.

The more of these factors you, as the leader(s) of a relationship and family consistently and spontaneously provide, the more functional it is. How do you feel about the list you have just read? Do you agree with most or all of it? No? Then, what do you believe? Scan the list again. Reflect. Could you honestly omit one or several of these traits without reducing the probable harmony and emotional health and growth of your family, or of any human relationship or group?

What happens to children who are deprived of too many of these traits as they are growing up? The truth is sad. Kids who are deprived of too many of these factors, for too long, predictably develop specific emotional and spiritual wounds, i.e., inner pain or gnawing emptiness.

Take a moment to take in the full scope and depth of these many healthy-family factors and you will begin to appreciate just how very complex the challenge of really effective family management is! Make no mistake—these factors are equally important to biological, foster, adoptive, gay, absent-parent, and multi-home stepfamilies. If you, as the family leader(s) cannot clearly describe your specific ideas of what a healthy or functional family is, and what you are trying to achieve with your family, the odds of your family being unable to meet the needs of its members rise steeply.

Common Emotional Wounds & Their Symptoms

What happens to typical young kids who grow up, even accidentally deprived of too many of these factors, for too long? How does all this relate to marriage and stepfamilies? Take a look at the 15 common, unrecognized, unresolved, and unhealed inner wounds and their symptoms. Do any of these feel familiar?

1. Excess toxic shame, i.e., "I am a bad thing." Low or inconsistent self-love and self-esteem, *automatically* putting others' needs first. Constantly shaming yourself through

perfectionism, rigid and unrealistic standards, and harsh inner verbal abuse long after your childhood critic is gone. Hyper about real or imagined criticism, you are constantly defensive. (This blocks real listening and makes interpersonal problem-solving hard or impossible.)

2. Excess guilt, i.e., "I always do bad things." Toxic (rather than healthy) shame has been called "the gift that goes on giving" because caregivers with low self-esteem often repeatedly shame their kids without meaning to.

3. Inappropriate over-trust or distrust of yourself and/or others. A terror of, and certainty of, emotional or physical abandonment. Combined with excess shame, guilt and distrust, this unconscious horror of being left alone fosters adult jealousy, possessiveness, manipulation, relationship addictions, fear of real commitment, and come here/go away at the same time, dances.

4. Social and spiritual emptiness, a deep inability to really connect and bond with other people, and with a loving Higher Self or Power. Feeling like there is a hole in your soul. To excess, these early wounds block real adult intimacy, the giving and receiving of real love. You find it difficult to feel, accept, and believe in others' genuine love.

5. Self-protective inner and outer reality distortions, i.e., seeing things or conditions that are not there, and/or not seeing things that are obvious to unbiased, informed others. A fierce authoritarianism and/or excess independence. Compulsive self-reliance that blocks mutual problem solving and often frustrates and discourages mates and friends, which leads to loneliness, isolation, and sadness.

6. Unconsciously associating adult love with combinations of pity, anxiety, chaos, lust, caretaking, and/or rescuing another, rather than with healthy, interdependent, mutual empowerment.

7. Terror, not just fear of rejection and abandonment by key people, and expecting it without reason. The core primal terror here is of being ultimately alone in the world and being unable to care for oneself, i.e., of dying.

8. Habitual self-abuse and neglect. Relentless, harsh self-criticism, perfectionism, and harmful personal health habits. This often includes harmful diets, exercise, social habits, unrealistic physical expectations, and self-sabotage at school, work, or in key relationships.

9. Repeatedly and unconsciously picking "toxic" associates, partners, and settings which share and foster these negative traits, especially shame, frustration, fear, and rage.

10. Personality splitting or dissociation (an extreme case would be multiple-personality disorder). Common symptoms include: endless, chaotic "mind chatter"; chronic indecisiveness and anxiety; inability to sustain focus; and erratic cycles of impulsiveness, moodiness, and/or childishness and play acting at being an adult.

11. An unreasonable, compulsive dread of the unknown, or no fear at all. The former leads to compulsively over-controlling feelings, relationships, situations, the future,

and some perceptions. Combined with shame and distrust, it also promotes rigid, righteously judgmental black-white thinking patterns.

12. Confusion about personal boundaries, abilities, and limits. Vague, distorted, or no solid sense of self. Operating from a false self.

13. Repression of old or current feelings (numbness) and/or of related childhood memories (amnesia). This often leads to a reservoir of repressed rage and/or deep sadness—which "leak" or explode erratically until genuinely acknowledged and healed.

14. A reflex fear of other peoples' strong emotions, leading to habitual fear and avoidance of normal interpersonal conflict. An alternative wound is feeling persistently uncomfortable without enough excitement, chaos, and conflict, and acting impulsively to create those.

15. Unconsciously denying, minimizing, or rationalizing these wounds, or consciously projecting most or all of them onto other people, i.e., "it's *your* problem, not mine," while vehemently and rigidly denying doing any of these protective things.

In truth, we all have some of these deprivations and resulting wounds. Our parents were, after all, only people and products of their own childhood, with all the good and bad just waiting to be passed on to another generation. And so, deprivations and their resulting wounds are "normal." Each of our childhoods can be pegged somewhere on a line from a little dysfunctional, to moderate, to very dysfunctional. The trick is to understand just where you fall on that line. Are you an adult with many or most of these psychological wounds to excess? Sure, "excess" is a subjective judgment, but do you fiercely and protectively deny any of these early deprivations and resulting traits? Are you in pseudo, i.e., intellect-only, personal recovery? Or, real self-motivated versus dutiful recovery?

Pseudo-recovery is a protective delusion, much like a reality distortion, which inexorably stunts and stresses your relationship not only with others, but with yourself. It normally results in an inner impasse: one part of you really wants to recover; the other part is terrified to try. For example, an alcoholic in pseudo-recovery becomes addicted to recovery, turning it into a passionate, righteous religion while others soar and free their real selves from this life-long inner bondage, over time.

Though agonizing, these repeated knee-jerk choices appear to happen because these are powerfully shame-driven people with low self-esteem who seem to relentlessly seek their own level in others. Also, they seem to automatically associate love with control, anxiety, pain, pity, and guilt. Because that is all they have ever known, they do not know or really trust that better options exist.

Their dependent kids are usually developing their own versions of their parents' psychological wounds. These kids often have combinations of school, health, emotional, and social problems—which concern, stress, and frustrate their biological and stepparents, relatives, and teachers. Any couple which unconsciously co-mingles the partners' sets of excess, denied wounds will have a tough time relating—and stepfamily co-parenting—well.

When two unhealed partners experience the added complexity and stress of an average multi-home stepfamily, it is no wonder that most eventually divorce—again. What is scary is that most dependent step-kids are now shuttling between two homes co-managed by two to four moderate-to-major unhealed adults—most or all of whom are in fierce, protective ignorance of their deep emotional wounds. Most minor kids in U.S. single-parent homes are in the same boat, because the massive trauma of family divorce or parent death both adds to, and often further masks, adults' and kids' years of earlier deprivations, loneliness, and pain.

Societal and personal ignorance—and tolerance—of this dynamic is the biggest single reason for the currently sky-rocketing divorce rate. As a pleasure- and speed-focused society, we seem presently to have no clue about this, or to care little about it. Despite an appearance to the contrary, we are in mass, culture-wide denial.

The Challenge

As a prospective stepfamily adult, your challenge is to unflinchingly appraise your and your potential spouse's emotional and spiritual health by honestly answering the following questions:

- Am I an adult in moderate-to-major denial of excess accidental childhood deprivations? If so,
- What are my specific emotional and/or spiritual wounds?
- And how can I start healing them?
- Is my current partner probably or surely an adult in moderate-to-major denial? If so, why should I commit to her/him, forming a high-risk stepfamily?

You and your partner need to think about and answer these questions separately in order to cut down on distortions from the excess empathy, fear of conflict, and defocusing you may be feeling. If you need to, you can shrink the risk of coming to the wrong conclusions by using an informed, objective counselor to assess these important questions. Fortunately, public and professional awareness of the epidemic "Adult Child (of childhood dysfunction)" syndrome has exploded since the early 1980's and really effective education, assessment, resources, and recovery programs are now widely available. Sadly, this was not true for most of our ancestors and their kin.

Do not underestimate the importance of this work. You do not want to pass crippling psychological wounds to your children, as your caregivers did. Toxic shame, as opposed to healthy shame, continues right down the generations, until identified, owned, and courageously converted into self-respect and healthy self-love. Also, if you do not do this work, the odds are high you will automatically pick a partner with unhealed wounds. They may have their wounds marvelously camouflaged and be very appealing—just like you. Because of their wounds, however, once your romance fades, they are likely to emerge as seriously compulsive, emotionally unavailable or enmeshed, over- or under-needy, and/or over-controlling people. How often have you heard a friend complain, "*After we were married, he (or she) turned into someone else.*"

On the other hand, if all the stepfamily adults in your multi-home stepfamily are aware of any of these traits of unhealed wounds, and are actively working to heal them—terrific. The vital, initial target here is for you to identify and safely dissolve most personal unhealed wound denials *before* you get married.

Do you still not know if we are talking about you? If so, a normal reaction now will be to trivialize or blank out what you have just read. The bulk of this life-changing information is about identifying, owning, and healing your specific emotional wounds, over years of patient effort and reward. Once begun, thankfully, some benefits will emerge quickly. This is probably not what you expected to find in this book, but it is important. If you need to, take a break—stretch, move around, and then come back when you are ready to read on. Take your time!

CHAPTER THREE

LEARN HEALTHY GRIEVING BASICS AND CHECK FOR INCOMPLETE GRIEF

Sample Good Grief Policy

> *We all will experience major losses throughout our lives. We will consistently, gently, and lovingly help each other <u>admit</u> and <u>talk about</u> them as they happen; fully <u>feel</u> and <u>express</u> our normal shock, anger, and sadness; and respect all people's different ways of saying their final good-byes to precious tangible and invisible things that end.*

The next step, after assessing and beginning to heal old psychological wounds, is the newer life cycle of grief, the healthy, natural emotional-physical-mental process which allows us to successfully deal with divorce or the death of a mate (major tangible and invisible losses for everyone), heal the pain, and eventually move on. Mourning these cannot be hurried, but can be slowed or stopped by inner and outer forces. Such blockage promotes personal anxiety, major relationship tensions, and sometimes even physical illness. Additionally, when biological parents both remarry, they and their kids have two new sets of major changes to deal with on top of those from their biological family shattering. For example:

Philip and Sarah had lived well together for 17 years. They had three children and were a close, loving family. At 47, Sarah developed a malignant tumor. She died a year later at home, surrounded by her sorrowing family. Philip fell into a deep depression and gratefully accepted the compassionate support of friends and relatives. The youngest children mourned in their own ways. The eldest son, Jack, appeared remarkably steady and often helped the others while excelling in high school.

Three years later, Philip married a lovely divorced woman. Sheila and her two daughters moved into Philip's house, making a noisy and confusing stepfamily of seven. Sheila had known Sarah and the family from their church. She accepted that her step-kids found it hard to have her "replace" their mother, especially in their own home, and so she made sure they included her "spirit" in their stepfamily.

On the anniversary of Sarah's death, Sheila made a special dinner and Philip recalled things they had all loved about his children's mother. Sheila suggested they all go to the cemetery to honor and share remembrance of Sarah. All agreed but Jack. He had eaten very little during dinner and had been unusually quiet. He snapped at his younger stepsister rudely, in a way that no one had seen before.

Despite repeated invitations of friendship and support, Jack maintained a cool distance from his stepmother over the next several years. He began to drink and smoke heavily at college and his grades declined while he sharply maintained, "Nothing's wrong!" Jack always found reasons to be absent from the annual meal celebrating his mother. He never visited Sarah's grave and would change the subject or leave if conversation focused on her. He grew sullen and isolated, and scornfully refused suggestions of professional help.

The young man became rude and sarcastic with his stepmother and stepsisters. He pointedly ignored them when he came home, despite his father's demands for courtesy and respect. Sheila gradually lost patience with this and admitted her hurt and growing resentment. She became protective of her daughters around Jack, which began to split the stepfamily.

Philip felt torn and confused. He began to blame Sheila for being "immature" and "insensitive." Even when Jack was away at college, mention of him often provoked blame, defensiveness, anger, and fighting in their home.

Things came to a head on their fourth stepfamily Thanksgiving. Jack had had too much to drink by dinner and blew up at Sheila in front of the family. He screamed, *"You don't belong here! You never did! This is my mother's house, not yours!"* He raged at his father, face distorted, *"You betrayed us, Dad! Betrayed me! You're a coward and a traitor! How could you get married so soon? How dare you bring them to live here? How could you do that to Mom?"*

Everyone was stunned. Jack had never said a word to anyone about his cauldron of feelings about his mother's death and father's remarriage. His avoiding the agony of truly saying *good-bye* to his mother and birth family—and denying this—had brewed a massive remarriage and stepfamily crisis.

It had blocked him from accepting Sheila and her daughters for four years, through no fault of theirs. Jack's rejections had repeatedly forced his father to choose between him and his wife and her girls. Philip's pained decisions to usually side with Sheila and their marriage hurt and outraged Jack beyond words. His grief had "frozen." The family had not looked for or understood his many signals. The holiday explosion began Jack's mourning and the stepfamily's full bonding.

If Philip and Sarah had been *divorced*, this story would have been the same, though more complex. Jack would have avoided accepting the reality and finality of his parents' divorce and the irreversible shattering of his dream of birth family reunion.

Why This Chapter?

Every remarriage and multi-home stepfamily is based on at least two sets of *profound* losses. Family separation and divorce, or the death of a spouse, are agonizing partings to parents, kids, and close relatives and friends. Surprisingly, parental remarriage can *add* new losses for all three stepfamily generations.

Most step-people have neither the training nor the wish to fully assess their losses, or their grieving progress, especially amid the joys and dreams of a new love. Our normal drive to avoid pain, along with our American idealization of "the *good* life," can block remarrying people from healthy mourning. Frozen grief can slow or stop both personal growth and the healthy bonding of a new couple and stepfamily. Chronic sickness or depression, substance or activity addictions (like workaholism), obesity, "endless" rage or sadness, ongoing hostility between ex-spouses, promiscuity, repeated law-breaking or school troubles—and divorce—are all possible symptoms of blocked mourning. It is a serious *hidden* problem in many biological families and stepfamilies.

If anyone in the several homes comprising your stepfamily is "stuck" in mourning their key losses, it will hinder the healthy bonding among you. It can also stress and threaten the person's physical, emotional, and spiritual health. Practicing *good* grief and helping dependent kids learn to do it is a *key* stepfamily adult task.

Incomplete grief is one of the reasons so many typical U.S. stepfamily remarriages fail. Toward shrinking that sobering fact, this chapter aims to inform (rather than entertain) stepfamily adults and interested others how to avoid this pitfall, and build a thriving remarriage and multi-home stepfamily.

This chapter will provide perspectives on normal life losses and the five stages of *good* grief. You will learn what, specifically, you and other family members have lost from divorce or death, and from remarriage.

Overall, this chapter seeks to strengthen your remarriage and stepfamily by stimulating awareness and discussion of your and your kids' losses, and of your mourning beliefs, habits, and progress.

Let's start with some definitions. Here *"loss"* means a current or foreseen event where people are deprived temporarily or permanently of part or all of something they prize. It also may mean the thing that is reduced or gone. A *"griever"* is one who is deprived of something cherished. *"Grieving"* and *"mourning"* both mean the natural mental and emotional process that heals the pain of loss over time—unless blocked by the griever and/or their environment.

A surprising number of adults only associate *"grief"* with the death of a loved person. It helps to realize that our many losses inevitably follow the minor and major attachments we make throughout our lives. These losses can be tangible or invisible; may be either expected or unforeseen; may be very slow or sudden; may have a cumulative impact on us; and, always cause a *beginning*.

Losses Happen Naturally Over Time

Our lives are given structure by emotional bonds to special people, things, beliefs, dreams, and activities. Most, or perhaps all, major life changes cause losses of these bonds—and (usually) some gains. For example, childbirth causes the loss of sleep, energy, social freedoms, financial flexibility, "non-parent" identity, space, etc. Puberty ends sexual innocence and infertility, among other things. School graduations reduce youthful irresponsibility. Job firings, changes, or retirement force changes of identity, security, income, and perhaps self-respect. Major illness or disability ends wellness and choices such as mobility and independence. Thus the need to grieve recurs *often* over the lifespan of any person and family.

Our Losses are Physical and Invisible

Tangible losses from family breakup and remarriage abound: pets, dens, rocking chairs, neighborhoods, fireplaces, gardens, cars, tree houses, pictures, nooks, utensils, schools, window seats, holiday ornaments, and so on. Large and small, concrete losses can have enormous emotional impact on kids and adults. This may be felt in advance, or only after the *things are clearly gone.*

Invisible losses cause emotional holes in our lives which are just as painful as physical partings. They cannot be held, photographed, or recorded. The following are examples of invisible losses.

Relationships: Even if a griever still sees important relatives or friends after divorce or remarriage, the prior *quality* of some relationships may be lost because of anger, guilt, judgment, distrust, geographic distance, loyalty conflicts, etc.

Perhaps the most agonizing family-separation and divorce loss is LOVE: the priceless feeling of being special, appreciated, supported, desired, companioned, and preferred by a rare other—and feeling the same about them. That loss is usually sustained well before marital and biological family separation. Loss of self-love is just as agonizing.

A normal adult relationship loss is that of *romance*. This seems to happen naturally within several years after a love partnership begins. In a healthy situation, the gradually growing "hole" it leaves is well filled by a calmer, deeper, and richer love.

More common invisible divorce or death, and remarriage loses are:

Lost roles, status, and identity: For example, "I used to be the smartest/fastest/youngest/favorite/funniest/only (child/boy/girl) in our family, but now I'm not"; or, "I never thought I'd have a divorced child, much less be a grandparent to someone else's kids"; or, "I used to be their daughter-in-law. Now I'm not sure I'm even a friend ..."; or, "Yesterday, I was single and childless. Today, I'm married, a stepparent of three, and have an ex-spouse-in-law." Both divorce and remarriage cause *many* unseen *role* and *rank* losses (and gains).

Lost respect for self or others: For example, "We've *never* had a divorce in our family—I've *failed* as a (parent/Christian)"; or, "Mommy and Daddy are divorcing because I was *bad*"; or, "I'm *weird* because I'm starting to love my stepparent as much as my real (Mom/Dad)"; or, "Now *this* marriage is starting to feel rocky; something must be *really* wrong with me"; or, "My spouse lets his/her ex walk over her/him, s/he's a wimp!"

Lost faith and trust: When personal tragedy strikes, some people find their faith in themselves, their God, friends, or families strongly shaken or gone. Trust that their world is safe and nurturing can vanish for a season or a lifetime. Major childhood abuses and parental deprivations wreck a child's basic trust in men, women, caregivers, or authority figures.

A related loss is the ability to build and share true *intimacy*. Without this, marital love starves after romance fades. If denied and unhealed, *distrust* and the resulting intimacy blocks are the root causes of divorce, and re-divorce.

Lost hopes, dreams, and ideals: For example, "(Mom and Dad/my son and his wife and family) will (stay happily married/get back together again)"; or, "My ex-spouse won't ever (be happy/have a baby) with someone else"; or, "Divorce is for others, not for (me/us/my parents)"; or, "*My* kids will never (love/be raised by) another (parent/man/woman)."

Lost access and freedoms: For example, "Before I moved in with Jill, we got a *lot* of time together. With her kids always around now, we rarely get alone-time"; or, "Because there are six in our house now, I never get to use the (TV/bathroom/hair dryer/washer/den/PC/car, etc.)"; or, "Before my (Mom/Dad) remarried, I always stayed up past 10:30. *Now* my stepparent makes me go to bed too early! And I always used to snuggle with (Mom/Dad) in bed Sunday mornings, now I can't."

Lost privacy and solitude: For example, "When I was single, I had peace and quiet. With step-kids, the phone's always ringing, the radio or TV's blasting, and someone's always yelling"; or, "With a stepparent and two step (brothers/sisters) around now, (Mom/Dad) and I have to be a lot more careful about being dressed and closing doors. I'm embarrassed when my step-(siblings) see my underwear when they help with the laundry."

Lost rituals and traditions: For example, "We've *always* gone to Gram's for Thanksgiving. Now we have to go to my (step-relative's) house. The food's different and it's boring"; or, "I really miss going to worship with my children. I don't think their stepparent cares if they go or not"; or, "Sharon always made this fantastic angel-food cake for my birthday. Joan's not much into baking"; or, "I used to give each grandchild $20 for their birthdays. I can't afford to do that for them and my four step-grandkids too, so I buy them all candy. It's just *not the same.*"

Lost emotional security: For example, "Now that my kids are being co-raised by (a distant stepparent), I worry that they'll stop caring for me"; or, "My real family didn't stay together—I wonder if *this* one will"; or, "Before my ex remarried, the child support payment was like clock-work. Now it's irregular and sometimes I have to call. What if it stops?"

Each of these abstract losses could have many more examples. Though they cannot be recorded, they all leave life holes that *hurt* just as much as tangible partings. They need the same kind of mourning to eventually heal. Their impact on your life adds up. Individually and together, invisible losses are much easier to ignore or minimize than concrete losses, especially in kids.

Some people believe that legal divorce proceedings and documents "end" a marriage. Some think that the (recordable) death of a spouse "ends" a committed relationship. Socially, legally, and physically, this is *true* in both cases. Unless surviving adults grieve their relationship well, though, they remain *emotionally* married. Child support, visitation, education, health, church, holiday, and custody negotiations can prolong an "after-marriage" relationship for years.

Hanging on to a mate, even with bitterness and abuse, often masks a deeper personal terror of truly saying *good-bye* to a cherished marital *fantasy* or a childhood caregiver. This often follows having felt agonizingly abandoned by key people early in life.

Sadly, it is common in many stepfamilies to find an ex-spouse or in-law who seems dedicated to persecuting their former mate or relative, regardless of the pain it causes any biological kids involved. This is often rooted in incomplete grief, mixed with shame and repressed anger at the mate and early caregivers. Such vindictive people usually come from agonizing childhoods and do not know it (or minimize it). Once protective denials are shattered, personal *recovery* programs can heal this blockage, over time.

Where former marriages and families are not well grieved by all survivors, remarriage of any partner will eventually and stressfully bring out the mourning block. We can mask—but not *avoid*—our losses and the searing wounds they bring.

Losses Happen In Different Ways

Some losses can be seen well in advance, like endings from graduations, marriages, births, moving to a new place, or job retirement. Yet even clear warning may not fully prepare some grievers because mentally imaging a loss is not the same as *experiencing* it. When partings are expected, we may either do anticipatory grieving or avoid recognizing the loss. When it actually occurs, the loss may have less impact if we begin our mourning process earlier.

Other losses happen very slowly, such as declining eyesight, agility, stamina, memory, respect, belief in a dream, job satisfaction, romance, or the quality of a marriage. The voids these cause enlarge gradually, which can camouflage early (unconscious) grief reactions. Often, conscious mourning starts when the griever becomes clearly aware of the gradual loss via some event.

Perhaps our most traumatic losses are those which happen without warning—like major accidents, firings, sudden illness or disability, unsuspected romantic affairs, and unexpected divorces. These normally trigger massive shock and chaos, at first. Adults and kids learning of divorce, remarriage, a new baby, adoptions, and home moves without forewarning can feel stunned and disoriented as the losses they create first begin to surface.

Usually, divorces and remarriages *both* create complex sets of expected and unexpected tangible and invisible losses. For example, there are dozens of myths about stepfamily life that commonly must be let go of and grieved. A common one is the gradual and painful loss of the dream that "my stepfamily will feel, act, and be just like a 'regular' biological family." Do you know what your divorce and remarriage losses have been? Your kids'? Your ex's? Your parents'?

The Impact of Losses Can Accumulate

On top of normal endings like graduations, and retirements, step-people have one or two extra sets of major losses to grieve. Biological parents and kids have lost their first-marriage family. Remarriage ends their absent-parent family or a single person's independence.

Such endings each create big sets of concrete and invisible losses (and some *gains!*) for all bonded family members. If time, custom, or personal values have not let much grieving happen between one set of losses and the next, the stresses from them can merge. When they list their losses, most step-people are amazed at how many they have had in just a few years. The combined impacts of normal and extra tangible and invisible losses can feel overwhelming to kids and adults alike.

People Experience Losses Differently

The loss of solitude and privacy for a remarried single person may seem trivial to a parent not having much of either. The loss of a pet via divorce or remarriage can feel far more traumatic to a child than an adult. A busy parent may not think to help the child mourn. They may even criticize the child for "making a big thing out of nothing," because they are uncomfortable with (or cannot relate to) the child's intense feelings. This is especially true for adults who were discouraged from grieving well as a child. Men may often have low empathy for a woman's feelings about divorce and remarriage losses—or for their own!

Also, adults may choose to endure losses because they are offset by wonderful gains like a new love, relief from anxieties and loneliness, and more social acceptance. Kids of divorce and remarriage usually do not choose their losses and may get far fewer benefits. It is often painful for parents to fully acknowledge this because they feel selfish, guilty, torn, and embarrassed.

To manage overwhelming pain or fear, many of us learn early to repress our feelings. People who have suffered repeated emotional or physical abuse or neglect can numb themselves without effort. They often deny doing so because it is unconscious. They may mentally acknowledge losses and "compute" what they feel, but are "dead below the neck." Such emotionally paralyzed survivors can have trouble *truly* empathizing with other grievers. Other childhood-trauma survivors have no personal emotional boundaries and are overwhelmed with the intense emotions of other grievers.

Endings Always Create Beginnings

In the longing, ache, and sorrow of major loss, it is easy to overlook or undervalue the new options that always appear. Ending a marriage and household eventually frees or shifts time, energy, and commitments. Focusing on new beginnings too narrowly or too soon can really hinder *good* grief. Conversely, denying or ignoring our new choices can prolong the pain of losses. Balancing grief-work with recognizing and exploring new opportunities is a healthy personal and stepfamily adult goal

What Is "Grieving"?

Children and adults naturally form *bonds* or attachments to special living, inanimate, and invisible things throughout their lives. Eventually these bonds break by choice or chance, causing minor to major invisible and physical losses.

Nature provides an automatic reflex to allow us to accept our losses and their impacts, and return to "normal" (a focused, clam, stable, balanced, purposeful) life again. Healthy grievers move through predictable phases in two or three levels, as they re-stabilize their emotions, thinking, and perhaps spiritual faith. Behavioral symptoms of these phases allow gauging a mourner's progress - or lack of it.

It is a natural, predictable sequence of mental and emotional states that relieves the distress of loss *over* time. Noted British researcher John Bowlby feels that young children's' grieving has three emotional stages: protest, despair, and detachment. Dr. Elizabeth Kubler-Ross, who has studied and written widely on reactions to human death, names five adult states of mourning:

1. **Shock**, numbness, disorientation, and/or hysteria;
2. Irrational pleading, fantasizing, or bargaining (**"magic thinking"**);
3. **Anger** and rage;
4. **Sadness**, apathy, despair, and depression; and eventually ...
5. **Acceptance**, and resuming life goals and activities.

We grievers can move through these stages in order, skip one or several for a while, or may move back and forth between them over time. We each have our own style.

By the way - medical research tells us that tears of joy differ chemically from tears of pain, because the latter contain compounds that cause depression and stress. By shedding these chemicals, crying is one of our body's natural way of staying balanced during times of trauma. Blocking the urge to weep *stresses* us!

The other half of the grief process is a gradual shift from mental chaos to realistic, consistent clarity on some important questions: *"What* have I lost?" "Is it *really* gone for *good*?" "How and why did my loss(es) happen?" "Am I to blame? Could I or others have prevented it?" "Why did this happen to *me*? Why *now*? "What does this loss *mean*, how will it affect me? How will it impact others important to me?" "Can I replace my losses? How? At what cost or risk? Do I want to? When?"

Stepfamily adults can gently and patiently help young grievers - and each other - find their own answers to these questions over time. *"Suggestions"* help more than giving mourners "right" answers. Lack of clear, realistic answers to questions like these can block the final *emotional* grief step of acceptance. Acknowledging truths about key loss(es) can take a long time, because they can be so painful ("I'll *never* have my birthday again the way we used to do it!").

In her book Second Chances, psychologist Judith Wallerstein observes that it takes some kids 10 - 15 years to *fully* adjust to their complex set of losses from parental divorce and biological family restructuring.

In healthy (unblocked) mourning, the emotional and cognitive stages are eventually complete *enough*. Loss tensions *gradually* subside. Inner wounds heal, and holes start to refill. **Each person's unique needs, traits, and situations shape if and how this completion occurs, and how long it takes.** Because mourning involves mind, body, and spirit, the conscious mind **cannot** speed it up. Yet, it *can* be unconsciously slowed or stopped.

Requisites for Healthy Mourning

So if we want to promote *good* grief in our lives and homes, what do we need? Six factors are key ingredients for most people and families:

1. Conscious awareness of our loss(es), their personal impact(s), and of the natural five-step, two-phase grief process
2. Confidence in surviving our loss(es), based on experience and faith
3. Commitment to healthy grieving as a personal priority, *without excess guilt*
4. Inner and outer permissions (support)
5. Times of solitude (with low distraction) to meditate, sort, and *feel*
6. And, time and patience

The more that some or all of these six factors are absent, the more likely a child or adult will move slowly through, or be frozen in, healing from their inevitable life losses. Let's take a look at these factors more closely.

1. **Building Awareness:** Simply put, to facilitate *good* grief, we need to be able to name our tangible and invisible losses and our related feelings, clearly and specifically. We also need to be able to articulate the main impacts of these losses on our lives. These conscious awarenesses help us to reflect on, discuss, and vent about them. In the opening example, Jack was unable to do these for many years.

   We usually find it easier to name our concrete losses. The invisible ones are easier to blur, discount or ignore. By the way, kids are either hindered at naming and explaining their losses and feelings (lacking concepts and vocabulary), or helped because they are freer than grownups to feel and vent.

   Grievers normally need no awareness of the mourning process, any more than they need to understand their breathing or digestion. When grief gets blocked, however, the conscious knowledge of normal mourning dynamics helps to decide what is wrong and how to fix it. If parents get stuck in working through their divorce and remarriage losses, their kids are at risk of the same.

   Because invisible losses (e.g., love, security, self-esteem, status) are so personally and socially powerful, the chance for blocking is higher than with some other endings. Remarrying adults need to know at least the symptoms of blocked mourning, if not the five grief stages.

   Stepfamily adults can help kids mourn major partings by helping them name specific losses, their impact, and explaining the grief process in age-appropriate, positive terms. Doing so, and clearly modeling the five-step process, validates children's feelings and raises their self-confidence. Such affirmations sound like: "You seem pretty (furious/depressed/sad/confused). I'm so glad you're going such a *good* job of grieving!" (This makes a pretty good inner affirmation for ourselves, too!)

   Note that grief may be sabotaged by unconscious fears of feeling and expressing anger and sadness. If a well-meaning stepfamily adult says, "Sandy, it's *good* to grieve," but does not honestly show their own rage and tears, kids get a confusing double message. What have your kids seen you do with your major losses? What did your key caregivers do?

2. **Confidence in Surviving Grief:** This mourning resource is hard to assess well because it is partly unconscious. If such faith is not felt, the imagined, or real, emotions from major losses can feel literally paralyzing or fatal ("If I cry, I'll never stop—I'll drown!" or "If I let myself get angry, I'll *kill* someone!"). Chronic depression can grow if grief feelings are seen as "endless."

   Confidence that the sadness *will* end, as a predictable part of the natural human mourning cycle, can help endure or manage grief's rage and despair. Key people around a griever who lack such confidence in the healing process can be a powerful external block to *good* grief. For typical stepfamily adults, getting clear on the differences and similarities of chronic depression and the *temporary* sadness phase of normal mourning is really useful.

3. **Commitment to Doing Good Grieving:** Even clear awareness of their losses, and great faith in the grief process, will not help grievers who do not care much about their own welfare. Once the mourning cycle and healthy-grief factors are known, we each have a conscious choice to avoid or resolve inner and outer grief-blocks! If we have such blocks and choose to not pay attention to them, *good* grief's healing will come more slowly or not at all.

    Adults seriously abused and deprived of respect as children are prime candidates for this self-neglect. They are also likely to be un-empathic and discouraging to other mourners, unless they are codependent or professional helpers (e.g., counselors, educators, lawyers, clergy, and medical healers). Such wounded professionals risk being over-concerned and so, cannot be of value as they loose their objectivity.

    Often, *good* grief is partly instinctive and partly a conscious choice. Conscious mourning is *work,* e.g., going to retreats, cemeteries, grief workshops, or therapy; reading relevant books; meditating; journaling, confronting and cleaning out painful mementos; saying real or symbolic good-byes, and choosing to be fully *in* painful and scary feelings at the moment.

    Mourners decide consciously how to use their free times. They can allot time to reflect, feel, and realize, or can medicate themselves for the pain of loss with activities, substances, or stimulation. In the long run, healing losses is easier if you give your grief-work, and that of close others, high priority. Currently, our speed-and-stimulation based American society usually does not. Did your birth family prize *good* grief? Do *you* now?

    How you use your free times is a good indicator of your grief priorities. Like other addicts, hustle-aholics are often frantically trying to dodge recognizing and feeling their rage and deep sadness from major losses. So are people with "mind-churn," whose thoughts are rarely quiet.

4. **Inner and Outer Grieving Permissions.** One of the most potent pairs of things that can block normal mourning in adults and kids is a lack of inner and/or outer support for the healing process to proceed. What are these "permissions" like? How can you tell if they are there or not?

    Building inner "permission" to grieve. A key factor in healing from loss is having inner support to grieve well. Our attitudes about feeling and expressing strong emotions either help or stop us. We learn these attitudes early, mostly from family adults, teachers, heroes, and the local culture we grew up in. Often we are not aware of our own values (*should's* and *ought's*) about mourning, because we have seldom thoughtfully considered and discussed them as kids or adults. They silently shape our loss reactions via feelings and inner "voices" (thought streams). Basically, these inner permissions sum up as either of these beliefs:

"It is okay and *good* for me to: (1) fully feel and openly express shock, confusion, anger, depression, and sadness; and to (2) find clear, believable answers to my questions of loss, over time, *without guilt or anxiety*"; or ...

"It is not safe or acceptable for me to do one or both of these things."

Between these two extremes are many variations; e.g., "It is okay for me to get angry, but *not* okay to cry," or vice-versa; or "It's okay to cry, but only (alone/at night/ in the car/...)"; or "Grieving is women's work"; or "It's proper to feel these things, but I selfishly burden others if I *show* them."

Our ancestors' values about grieving probably get passed on to us more by observing our parents react to loss, rather than by listening to them talk about it. As a child, what did you see your key caregivers (parents, key relatives, teachers, clergy) do about mourning their losses? What scripts or "permissions" about feeling and sharing strong emotions did you inherit from your ancestors? Did those adults who parented and taught you as a child promote healthy grieving? How do you judge that?

An important awareness about our inner permissions is: even if we were taught grieving inhibitions as kids, we can identify and intentionally relearn them as adults and replace them with more healthy beliefs and thought streams. We can also intentionally teach the younger people in our lives to have their own clear (versus ambivalent) inner support for healthy mourning. Doing so is a major gift!

Outer permissions to mourn. If the key people around a griever encourage and support healthy grief, they give "outer permission" for it. There are many ways we can grant—or block—such permission. To encourage and support a dear one grieving is a real challenge, especially if we are in our own pain! Are you generally such a person? Would your child(ren) say so? Your partner? Have you ever been consistently comforted by such a supporter? Remember what it felt like, over time. *That* is experiencing full outer permission to mourn well.

People who lack support characteristics often unintentionally hinder a griever's healthy mourning. They may be secretly fearful, shamed, needy, and ignorant. They usually will deny this to themselves and others, to avoid the pain of awareness. Their inability to feel, endure, and express intense feelings, and to comfort others experiencing the same, must be well guarded, especially if they are burdened with perfectionism. They are *wounded*, not "bad, people. Most come from a childhood of great emotional deprivation, fear, confusion, loneliness, and pain.

Such "blockers" can be blunt or subtle about withholding permission to mourn. Some are very clear: "Oh, stop being such a wimp!" "What's the big deal?" "Aren't you over moping yet?" "Come on—get on with your life!" "Isn't Jean great? Nothing gets her down!" "C'mon, cheer up—it could be a lot worse. Look at George's situation ..."

At other times, their discouragement comes via a glance, a silence, a turn of the head, an overdue phone call, or a reproving or sarcastic tone of voice. Some dependent people will block another's grief because they may unconsciously fear the griever will "collapse," i.e., will not be there to lean on. Some people with only vague personal boundaries deeply feel others' intense emotions. They dread feeling overwhelmed themselves if they let close grievers mourn fully.

Kids of divorced parents can unconsciously interfere with a parent's mourning, to save their dream of parental reunion or to protect the parent from feared "collapse." Stressed and guilty-feeling single parents may covertly discourage a child's grieving, fearing it to be a "last straw." An elderly or infirm parent can fear loss of support because of "probable" emotional collapse of their newly-divorced or widowed adult child. They can hinder their child's grief by increasing their calls for attention. All such blockers lack solid confidence in their own, and/or their griever's, ability to survive grief's intensities.

Kids learn how to mourn from personal heroes or heroines among their family, friends, house of worship, school, community, nation, and race. TV, sports, music, and fantasy heroes can powerfully model or inhibit *good* grief for kids and teens. Do the Chicago Bears, Ninja Turtles, Barbie, GI Joe, Batman, Madonna, Santa Claus, Captain Kirk, Led Zeppelin, Jesus, or the Masters of the Universe *have* losses? Obsess and cry? Rage? Get deeply sad and depressed? Seek counseling? What grieving permissions have your heroes or heroines given you? Your partner(s)? Your kids? Your parents and siblings?

Inherited cultural values are important here, too. Some British, Scandinavian, Asian, Native American, African, and Central European cultures prize stoicism, at least among males. Other Mediterranean, Latin, Arabic, and Indian groups expect males to feel and vent passions intensely and spontaneously. Some "permit" showing anger, but not weeping. Some the reverse.

Can you think of cultures that discourage females from healthy mourning, or encourage them to amplify and hang on to it? What culture(s) do you identify with? Do you know what ethnic traditions are shaping your, and your kids', reactions to loss? Can you discuss this together?

Getting consistent *outer* grieving support can be especially complex for stepfamily grievers. There are more key people and three or more sets of ancestral and cultural customs about feeling and expressing rage and anguish. These sets can clash, sometimes starkly. One family's tradition may be "boys grieve alone and real men don't grieve," while the new partner's ancestors taught, "males who cry and mourn openly are strong and healthy." Simply living with new people can impede natural grieving because full trust in their acceptance and support hasn't formed yet.

Paradoxically, close friends may *not* be the most helpful companions along our mourning path. If they have a high stake in the griever's quick recovery, do not understand the grief process, and/or carry strong biases about divorce, death, and remarriage losses, they can unintentionally hinder the five emotional steps. Some clergy can accidentally discount grief feelings by urging exclusive focus on God's blessings. Grief support groups (like "Compassionate Friends," "Rainbows," and "Kaleidoscope"), (some) divorce recovery groups, and qualified therapists can provide more objective and effective support.

If you or a loved one have "okay to grieve" inner permission, and get "not okay" outer messages from key other people (or vice-versa), confusion and stress can be high, especially without a clear awareness of this conflict. Do you know anyone with this kind of stress?

5. *Solitude, and 6. Distraction-free Time. Good* grief happens when we experience our feelings fully and repeatedly, and gradually let them go. Being mentally and physically busy all the time really hinders such experiences. The painful, and healing, alternative is to give yourself or another mourner quiet times to meditate and be open to feeling and expressing the emotions that need to surface—especially rage, despair, and sadness.

At such times, mourners need to be free of mind- and emotion-distorting chemicals like alcohol, nicotine, excessive food (e.g., sugar), caffeine, and some prescription drugs like tranquilizers and sleep medications. It also helps to minimize distractions like TV, phones, physical discomforts, other people moving or talking, thinking about other problems, and the like.

For many of us, being in nature or in a personally sacred, peaceful place at such times greatly helps to get clear and quiet. Soothing music, and journaling, can help do this.

Focusing and meditating on what we have lost, what our loss(es) mean to us, and how we feel, is hard and healing. Mourning some major losses fully can take months or years. Patience, faith, and repeated calm, clear, focused times nurture the natural five-step emotional, and related mental, clarity processes. Having an attentive supporter nearby during such times often, but not always, helps.

Together, these factors promote natural healing of the invisible wounds from life's endings, over time. What if a grown or young griever does not have enough of these factors?

Symptoms of Blocked Grieving

Lacking some of these *good*-grief resources consistently, people can either not start their mourning process, or can get stuck in one of the five emotional phases. Use the following list to check for frozen grief in yourself or one you care about. Look for repeated patterns over time:

Seeming "forever" sad, angry, or depressed, or often feeling numb or "nothing," either in general, or about the loss. People who *always* seem very intellectual or "unemotional" may be frozen in grief.

Repressed anger. Signs include *repeated*: procrastination; lateness; sadistic or sarcastic humor; cynicism; sighing; inappropriate cheerfulness; over-controlled monotone voice; insomnia or excessive sleep, waking up tired, tiring easily, or inappropriate drowsiness; irritability; clenched jaws ("TMJ") or teeth grinding (particularly at night); back pain; muscle spasms, tics, or twitches; and, fist clenching, or other automatic actions. Some of these may have medical causes, though our mind-body connection is a relevant mystery here (i.e., which causes what?).

Minimizations or denials. Consistently down-playing either the loss itself (" ___ wasn't *that* important to me"), or feelings *about* the loss ("No, I'm not *sad*—just tired again, is all."). *The ultimate denial is one's own denial.*

Chronic weariness, depression, or apathy. It takes a lot of personal energy to steadily repress frightening emotions and awarenesses. In his book *Healing the Shame That Binds You*," John Bradshaw likens this to trying to live while holding a big beach ball under water. Therapist Virginia Satir suggested it is like constantly holding a door closed against a basement full of starving dogs.

Addictions to activities (e.g., work, hobbies or sports, worship, committees, socializing, TV, personal computers, fitness and health, sex, cleaning, shopping, gambling, reading, or *endless* education); *substances* (nicotine, caffeine, food or sugar, alcohol or other hard drugs, or medications); or *"toxic" relationships* (those consistently producing shame, fear, rage, pain, guilt, anxiety, stress, and/or unhealthy dependence).

Often, people using addictions or obsessions to put off grief pain have several of the above ("cross addiction"). All will deny, minimize, or rationalize their compulsive dependencies, until real (versus intellectual) personal recovery begins. Usually, their partners or relatives, who may be addicted to their addict's feelings and welfare ("codependence"), will join them in such denial ("enabling"). Others may acknowledge their partner's addiction while fiercely denying their own.

Repeated avoidances. These can be verbal, mental, and/or physical. If the loss (or something associated or similar) comes under discussion, a blocked mourner will often become silent or irritable, tune out, try to change the subject, or leave. They may reflexively shun certain places (like former dwellings, neighborhoods, houses of worship, cemeteries, etc.); people; activities or rituals (holidays, vacations, births, death, graduations, etc.); or painful mementos (photo albums, movies, music, old letters, holiday ornaments, special clothing, etc.) that remind them of that which is gone.

Blocked mourners will often protectively deny or minimize such avoidances. Single-parent and blended families abound with such painful reminders. Are there any in your life? Your kids' lives?

(Some) **chronic pain or illness**, especially without clear biological cause. A growing number of professional healers feel that recurrent asthma, migraine or other headaches, digestive or colon problems, back pain, shoulder pain and neck stiffness or soreness, breathing or swallowing troubles, panic attacks, nightmares, allergies, and the like are body signals that emotions are being unhealthily repressed. Fearful mourners will often scoff at this.

Obesity and eating disorders. It's been said of some obese people that "every fat cell is an unshed tear." Adults or kids can numb the pain of unresolved loss by compulsive overeating. Others are metabolically unbalanced. Grief-work can be far more helpful than endless dieting/ regaining cycles, which typically build guilt, shame, and eventual depression and hopelessness. Other eating problems, anorexia (self-starvation) or bulimia (compulsive binge-purge cycles), may signal blocked mourning and deep shame.

Obesity can be a symptom of childhood sexual abuse. This indescribably painful personal violation forces the *massive* losses of innocence, trust, security, and self-respect in children too young and dependent to understand and protect themselves.

Anniversary depressions. Major apathy, sadness, sluggishness, sickness, sleep disorders, irritability, or feeling gloomy "for no reason" may recur annually at the time or season a major loss happened. This can appear to be (or be increased by) Seasonal Affective Disorder (SAD).

Enshrining or purging mementos. People who obsessively display, revere, discuss, or protect special real or abstract reminders long after a big loss can be blocked mourners. Such mementos can include foods, music, clothes, pictures, furniture, letters, jewelry, perfume, gardens, and many more. Revering or reacting to such reminders to perpetual excess is the key here.

The opposite may also signal incomplete grief; people who compulsively throw away every reminder of the lost person or thing can be avoiding the intolerably painful hole in their life.

Often having extreme reactions to the losses or traumas of strangers, acquaintances, animals, or fictional characters seen on TV, etc.. Such reactions include uncontrollable sobbing, lasting depression, intense rages, insomnia, obsessions, and over-identifications ("becoming" the hurt one).

Stuck mourners may have one or more of these symptoms and hide or disguise them out of shame, guilt, and anxiety. This is especially true when the key people around them disapprove. Having one or several of the symptoms does not *prove* a person is blocking major grief; it *does* justify honestly exploring the possibility.

Adult and child mourners who are not stuck are grieving *well*. How do they do it?

Steps to GOOD Stepfamily Grief

1. Accept that you are a *step*family (versus "Just a 'regular' family"), and therefore that all your members have major prior and recent losses to mourn.

You all are a stepfamily and your remarriage follows, and causes, major losses for all your multi-home stepfamily members. Your losses are both tangible and invisible. Accept that all your divorced stepfamily adults and their kin are full members of your stepfamily, and will be for years. Your step-kid(s) believe this, whether you do or not. These other adults are deeply linked to you biologically, legally, financially, historically, and emotionally.

Accept that grieving is a legitimate and vital life task for all members of your stepfamily. Believe that incomplete grief in one or several of your stepfamily members can cause *severe* re-marital and parenting stresses and serious personal problems An adult's resistance to consider or accept these step realities is a clear sign of incomplete grief.

Talk together openly and often about your key or collective losses and your mourning process. Accept that all your active stepfamily adults, including living bio-parental ex-mates, are responsible for promoting healthy grieving in themselves and all dependent related kids. Grown kids can need family help, too.

Also, decide if each stepparent is responsible for promoting *good* grief in each stepchild. If not, who should? If so, how should the stepparent(s) do this *well*?

2. All three to four (or more) stepfamily adults clarify and compare their definitions of "*good* grief." Build a shared definition you all believe in and can use together.

This shared clarity among all active stepfamily adults promotes cooperative decisions on whether your stepfamily members are mourning well or not. Once stepfamily adults have their individual definitions clear, forge a shared definition all can use. Include the kids in this process, so they know what you are doing and why. They probably have a lot of natural wisdom to contribute! This definition is the core of your stepfamily's grief policy.

An alternative to this step is to have vague and/or conflicting stepfamily adult definitions of *good* grief. Because our culture devalues mourning, a common *unhealthy* definition sounds like this: "Good grief is not whining or blubbering over stuff that can't be changed. We should all get on with our lives and not wallow in the past!"

Sound familiar? Yes or no, know that you do now have a personal definition of *good* grief and that your actions following major life losses need to be based on it. Reading this chapter will probably make you more aware of your real (unconscious) mourning "rules."

3. Identify your current personal, household, and multi-home stepfamily "policies" about mourning. Update them if they do not promote *good* grief.

A *grief policy* is a set of personal or group beliefs about handling life losses, and related reactions and behaviors. Every person and family has grief policies (*should's* and *ought's*), although often they are not aware of them. The task here is to learn yours and update them if they do not promote good mourning in keeping with your shared definition.

An effective grieving policy will give clear guidelines on some key questions for your members:

- Specifically: "How does our family now define 'personal loss,' 'healthy grief,' and 'effective mourning support'?"
- "In this home, what are our specific beliefs ('should's and ought's') about identifying and talking about our major personal losses; feeling strong emotions like rage, deep sadness, and despair; expressing them; and hearing these well?"
- "In our home and stepfamily, how long can grief take? Can members mourn differently and still be accepted?"
- "Who's responsible for ensuring that each of our members is encouraged to know their losses and to grieve well in (1) this home, and (2) our multi-home stepfamily?"
- "Who among us is responsible for teaching and coaching us on how to support a mourner well? Is everyone on their own? Should (or do) we have a family 'grieving specialist' or coordinator? If so, who? What's their job? How did they get it? Are they doing it 'well enough'? Do they feel appreciated enough?"
- "What key projects are generally more important to our home and stepfamily members than healthy mourning, and which aren't? What priority do we normally give healthy mourning?"
- "Is it okay to ask for grieving help in our home? In our stepfamily? Generally, how should we support each other in recovering from personal losses? How do we pick 'safe' grief supporters and what should we ask for and expect from them? Do we 'owe' them anything? If so, what?"
- "When should we get aid in grieving, for whom, and from whom? Who should make this happen in our home? In our stepfamily? Who should monitor such help to see if it's effective? Who should pay for the help? How and when? Within what limits?"
- "Who's responsible for making this grieving policy? Giving feedback on it? Resolving conflicts about it? Amending it? Putting it into practice? Appreciating *good* grievers among us?

All members of your multi-home stepfamily probably have *unconscious* answers to these questions now. These answers form your current personal, home, and family grief policies. If you have not discussed them together, it is likely they are at least partly unconscious, conflicting among some of you, uncoordinated, and under-enforced in your home and family. If true, that is fertile ground for incomplete grief and high personal, couple, and family stress.

Once everyone is clear on an effective home and stepfamily mourning policy, then:

4. Take detailed inventories of the invisible and tangible losses that each member of your stepfamily (including multiple households) has had.

   Identify specifically what tangible and intangible things you have lost. Then do the same with or for your present partner, any important young people in your life, and all other stepfamily adults. Trusted companions or professionals may help in verifying loss-related "holes," in case anyone is in denial to avoid pain.

   Consider endings stemming from both divorce or death, *and* remarriage or cohabiting. If your list is long, try grouping losses as high, medium, and low-impact. Doing this in a positive way as a household or whole (multi-generation) family can create real stepfamily closeness. It can grow empathic awareness of each member's "holes" and pain, and promote healing outer permissions.

   Once your losses are named, reflect on and talk about their meaning to you with safe people. Discuss each of the questions in the previous project. Such talk can sound like "Because of my divorce, I feel like I've lost some of my main 'roots'—I feel less secure emotionally, financially, and socially. I feel confused, too, about who I am—my identity is less clear to me now." Invite kids to talk about the meanings of their losses often and affirm them—without moralizing, correcting, thinking for, or trying to "fix" them. Show rather than tell them how to talk about their losses.

   The language of healthy mourning is full of "I"s and feelings words. It is full or energy and passion, too. "I sure miss ..." "I keep thinking about ..." "I remember ..." "I'm really *sad* that ..." "*I* hurt (versus '*it* hurts') when ..." "I'm really *angry* that ...."

   People who are ashamed or feel guilty or scared to mourn honestly (i.e., lack inner permissions) often use "you" and "we," instead of "I." Do you know anyone who does this? What has the grieving language in your home sounded like recently? In many step-homes, it is the sound of *silence*.

   Now you have acknowledged you all have important losses from divorce or death, and remarriage (or co-habiting). You have evolved clear definitions of *good* grief and a viable family mourning policy. You have identified your main tangible and invisible losses, and have begun to talk openly about their real impacts. The *good*-grief co-leaders in your home and stepfamily are now ready to:

5. Check each family member for signs of significant incomplete grief. If you find any, stepfamily adults decide together on how to unblock—and *act*! If unsure or scared, get qualified professional help. (Some counselors specialize in grief work.)

   If you think someone is significantly blocked, look for missing healthy-grieving factors.

   *   Does the blocked griever understand the grief process? (I.e., can they describe the five emotional steps and the chaos-to-clarity mental steps?) Can they name their key losses? If not, explain why that helps and encourage them to learn these at their own pace.

- Does the stuck person *believe* the hurt will go down and their mourning process will end? How can our family help them to realize they are moving naturally through the stages of grief, or can do so? What would grow their trust that there is a better life for them after mourning? Recall that natural mourning cannot be rushed.

  If this person feels no confidence in (or resists) the grieving process, maybe they are just not ready to say good-bye. How can your family support them until they are ready, without being over-stressed while waiting? If their resistance is self-harmful, get professional help. Seek counselors who have specific training and experience in facilitating healthy grieving. Beware of becoming obsessed with helping your stuck one. Ultimately, it is their decision if and when to say good-bye. What you can do is provide the best outer permission (support) you can—then let go!

- Is your mourner committed to mourning well? *Good* grief is a conscious choice. It may be that a stuck mourner has awarenesses and confidence, but puts most other life priorities ahead of self-healing. This often stems from deep shame, self-neglect and self-abandonment. These are typical core issues for survivors of childhood trauma. They are often denied, even when obvious to others. Acknowledging and working to heal these issues are essential personal, step-couple, and stepfamily adult tasks! Choosing to avoid these issues risks passing them on to future generations.

- One indicator of a mourner's commitment to *good* grief is their freely choosing times to be alone and quiet—even if others discourage this. Removing inner and outer distractions helps reflect on grief questions and fully experiencing the feelings tied to the answers that eventually appear.

- Help your mourner to review their inner permissions about grieving. If their "should's and ought's" are vague, work to clarify them. An option: without judgment, describe in detail how the mourner typically behaves when they are (1) angry (or have reason to be), (2) deeply sad, and (3) deprived of something they prize. Their actions indicate their true inner rules about feeling and showing strong emotions following important endings.

  Another option: ask the person some specific questions: "(When/how) should (men/boys/women/girls) feel and express (1) anger or rage, and (2) sadness or despair?" "If you feel and show these emotions, will you or someone else get hurt?" "How" "Why" "How do you know." Write down exactly what their inner voices say, *without judgment*. Several conflicting inner opinions are okay—at first.

- Once the inner rules are identified, decide if they clearly fit your stepfamily's definition of *good* grief. If not, learn what, if anything, is in the way of adopting healthier personal values. If this is confusing, or if family members have high resistance to these steps or improving their inner grieving permissions, get qualified professional help.

- Check their outer grieving permissions and the quality and availability of their mourning support. See if anyone important to them is now openly or covertly discouraging them from naming their losses, or from feeling or expressing their anger and sadness in their own way and at their own pace.

If there is someone, expect them to deny that they are interfering or to rationalize that "it's really best because ..." Respect their resistance, but do not accept it. They truly mean no harm, yet discouraging grief in a loved one *is* harmful, just as chronic constipation is. It blocks a mourner's natural way of relieving their distress. If prolonged, it can make them emotionally, relationally, and/or physically sick.

If a grief-blocker cannot accept what they are doing and change, the mourner can choose to reduce—or end—contact with them, to be with people who give positive grief permission and support. Chronically unhappy and codependent people can help themselves by limiting, or ending, relationships that impede healthy grief. If the blocker is a parent, spouse, old friend, religion, or employer, such decisions are scary—and ultimately *healing*. Mourners with low self-respect, and/or high fear of abandonment, often lack inner permission to do this.

Also, grievers may often fear that their "endless" sadness, depression, or rage will burden or annoy supporters. To avoid this, invite supporters to say honestly—without guilt—if they cannot listen to or be with you at certain times. Ask them to be responsible for their own limits, so that the mourner does not have to be. Consider that letting genuinely concerned others share your anguish is a gift, for it gives them a real way to help. How do you feel—and act—when a dear one shares their rage or sadness with you? Can you tell them *without guilt* if and when you have had enough for the time being?

Help your mourner be clear on when they currently want empathic companionship and acceptance, or solitude, rather than wanting advice or to do "problem solving." Because well-meaning supporters may offer the latter at the wrong time, mourners need inner permission—and maybe outer encouragement—to say, "Thanks, but that's not helpful, now. Just *hear* me and *be with me*, please," or "I need time alone right now to sort things out.

Grief supporters need guidance at times on what their mourners need at the moment. A grief policy option is that "it's okay for our supporters to ask, and it's okay for our grievers to tell them, even if *not* asked!"

Consider co-designing a ceremony or ritual to help the stuck person say "good-bye." Examples are: a special farewell meal, service, or meeting; creating a poem, story, song, prayer, sculpture, collage, or other final tribute; planting, burying, or burning something; making imaginary or real calls, or writing in detail about those things that will never be again, and sharing them with a trusted friend; reverently letting go of a symbolic object; making a last or special visit to a place tied to the loss; etc. Designing and doing a grief ceremony as a couple or a whole stepfamily can grow bonding and closeness for all.

A SAMPLE STEPFAMILY *GRIEVING* POLICY

(With editing, this can also become a *personal* grieving policy.)

Everyone in our multi-home stepfamily has experienced *big* losses from divorce (or the death of a spouse) and *blending* our several biological families. Losses *hurt*. Grieving is Nature's way of healing our hurts and sadness over time, so we each can let new people, ideas, and activities into our lives, and move on. This policy says clearly how we want our family members to mourn their losses. It defines *good* (unblocked) grief and guides us on how to lovingly help each other do it in a healthy way.

The natural process of *good grief* involves shock, pleading (maybe), rage, sadness, and eventual acceptance (but not forgetting). It also involves getting unconfused and clear, over time, on some normal questions about our losses and their meaning. Mourning is a *normal*, healthy reaction when females and males of any age attach to, and later lose, precious things. Some big losses take people years to mourn fully. We know, too, that adults and kids can get stuck in the grieving process if they don't feel safe enough to grieve.

The stepfamily adults in each of our stepfamily homes are in charge of (1) grieving their own losses well, and (2) respectfully helping our younger people (and others) to do the same.

In our special stepfamily, we strongly believe it is GOOD to:

ACCEPT that emotional attachments and losses are a normal part of every life, and that the people and things we lose will *never* come again in the same special way.

GET CLEAR on specifically *what* we each lost, *why* we lost it, *why* we miss it, and *how we really feel* about losing it. Losing special people (relationships), dreams, things, pets, customs, health, freedoms, places, securities, roles, identity, privacy, and opportunities all can hurt—*a lot!*

TALK OPENLY about important things that are gone for good—over and over, if we need to—until the hurt stays down. The other half of talking is listening with our hearts—without judgment—to ourselves and each other. That *really* helps!

USE MOURNING LANGUAGE. It sounds like: "I *hurt!*" "I'm really *sad!*" "I'm so *mad* that ..." "I miss _____ so much!" "If only ..." "I remember ..." "I'm not ready." "I wish ..." "I feel ..." "I've lost ..." And sometimes, "Good-bye, _____."

CRY, alone and with each other, when we need to. This is true for each of our boys, girls, women, and men. People who feel their anger and pain, and cry it out, are strong and healthy. It can hurt our health to block crying!

FEEL *ANGRY* about our losses and show it—as long as we don't hurt ourselves, others, Life, the Earth, or important things.

FORGIVE any person who caused us to lose someone or something dear—*when we're ready*. This is not a "should." We're not doing this only for the other one(s): forgiving is a good way to set our*selves* and others free from old anger, resentment, guilt, and stress.

REMEMBER the people and things we've lost, in our own ways, with deep love and appreciation. As normal grief ends, sorrow may stay.

ASK FOR HELP from God and each other when we need a hug or an ear, to be held or comforted, or some information about our losses or other people's related feelings or beliefs.

PRAY for help or understanding or patience or strength or guidance—alone and together.

INVITE people in and outside our family to tell us *honestly* if they feel burdened by us, or if they can't listen to or support us at the moment. It's okay to *not* help a griever when someone feels really distracted or overloaded at the time!

SAY—and mean—"I did" and "I'm sorry" when any of us causes a painful loss to another.

ACT to help ourselves and other family members move through our mourning. Each of us can decide for ourselves what things and memories to keep, which to let go of, and when to do so. We can't decide these for someone else.

KNOW that we can't "fix" or heal another person's hurt or fill the holes in their life that losses make. We *can* love, support, and be with them, as they fill these holes themselves.

WRITE in a special diary or make a scrapbook about *what* we lost, *what* we miss, how we *feel*, and anything else we need to do. If anyone does this, they can keep their writing private *without guilt or shame*, or show it to people they trust.

BE ALONE with our thoughts and feelings—as long as we don't overdo it. It also really helps our grief progress when we talk to trusted others about our losses and our feelings.

BE *UNIQUE:* No one has to mourn like anybody else: we each find our own way of saying *good-bye* and letting go, when we're ready.

AFFIRM and encourage anyone who is grieving, if we *choose* to (we don't *have* to). Affirming can sound like: "*I **feel really** good that you're able to feel* _____/talk about ____ /cry about ____ / ____. **Good job!**"

EXPERIMENT AND CHANGE how we mourn, over time. There's no "perfect" way!

LEARN from our losses to really appreciate and enjoy the special people and things in our lives while we have them.

ENJOY LIFE as best we can and care well for ourselves, both while we mourn and after the hurt and anger soften.

GET PROFESSIONAL HELP, if anyone gets really stuck in moving through their grief. The adults in each of our houses are responsible for deciding if this should happen, and doing it.

SUPPORT EACH OTHER. When any one of us has an important loss, the others will try in their own way to:

- Understand and believe in our *good* grief process.
- Ask our griever what they need from us, if we're not sure.
- Be empathic, comforting, and available *enough*. [
- Really **listen** *from our hearts*, *often*—without trying to 'fix" the griever.
- Offer patient, warm acceptance and encouragement, without rushing their process.
- Honestly say when we've heard enough or need to attend to our own affairs.
- Be as steady, realistic, and optimistic as we can.
- Be at ease with strong feelings in us and our mourner.
- Avoid yanking our griever out of his or her feelings by asking too many questions.
- Hold and hug our griever when needed, and respect his or her wish to avoid these at other times.
- Work towards knowing how and when to smile, laugh, and share comfortable eye contact.
- Be comfortable with shared silences.
- Hold no secret bad feelings (like resentment) about giving of our time and selves.
- When it seems okay, gently remind our mourner of the new choices that always appear from their losses.
- Make our home a safe place for our family members and others to grieve well; and,
- Care for and love ourselves just as we do for our mourner.

These statements form our family's policy on how we mourn our life losses effectively and healthily. Using this policy is important to each of us, because *incomplete grief* can make our people and others stressed, unhappy, or even sick.

Suggestion

You are cautioned against using this sample policy as it stands for your home or family. A grieving policy works *best* when it comes from the hearts and minds of the people it applies to. Your own policy will best evolve through many talks together as family members, meditations, and several drafts. Allow your policy to grow and emerge as your stepfamily develops.

Also, brevity, simplicity, and clarity are important keys in evolving a family grieving policy that is really useful. If you can net your key grieving beliefs and goals down to one page and then display that page (maybe signed by all and/or framed) in a public part of your home, it will work for everyone!

CHAPTER FOUR

MAKE THREE WISE/UNHEALTHY DECISIONS

A stepfamily reality easily obscured by rosy romantic bliss and optimism is that adults do not just marry beloved partners. You are also committing to their partner's children, ex-mates, relatives, divorce and visitation decrees, child support obligations, and childhood and post-divorce (or death) family baggage, too.

Ask yourself: Why should I get married at all? What specific needs am I really trying to fill? Why get married now rather than months or years from now? If you are a biological parent: When no compromise appears, am I consistently able and willing to put my new marriage relationship ahead of my kids much of the time and without too much guilt, resentment, and shame? If you are a stepparent: Do I really trust that my prospective partner will put our relationship ahead of his or her biological children often enough for me when we cannot find a compromise? Will he or she feel too guilty or resentful about so choosing? If you will be part of a dual-role stepfamily adult household (one step and one biological parent), you need to look at both questions.

Why marry *this* person? Or, if the prospective partners is a biological parent, why marry this group (including kids, ex-mate(s), and relatives) and all its combined emotional, physical, financial, and legal problems?

What are all my other options for filling my current needs? Clearly, personal judgment on these questions is often *highly* distorted by romantic (versus mature) love, lust, weariness, loneliness, rescue fairy-tales, insecurity, and social pressures. Family and close friends are often biased in advising you here. It is helpful, if not essential, to get objective support on these important questions from professionals who are not unhealed wounded adults themselves, and who are stepfamily-aware.

The best time to ask yourself these questions, of course, is well before your vows, rings, champagne, and rice. Remember one of the common traits of un-recovered adults is excessive reality distortion. Another is unconsciously and repeatedly picking others in the same emotional boat. Lonely, empty, and longing, do you routinely protect yourself from scary marriage realities by avoiding these questions altogether, or giving them only a surface effort. Most of you will live to regret this, relentlessly haunted by the eyes in many mirrors and in your beloved, multiply-wounded children.

These questions are best thought through while alone. It is fine to discuss these questions with each other and other trusted people in depth, but only you can decide the answers that fit you and your kids.

Co-Creating a Healthy Remarriage

Meet Our Guides

To make our re-marital mission here more real and less academic, meet Ned and Laurie, Sally and Mike, and their ex-mates. They are imaginary composites of hundreds of average stepfamily couples. They will demonstrate stepfamily adults wrestling with the three pre-remarriage questions (picking the right people, for the right reasons, at the right time) as perhaps you are (or will be).

As you learn from them, note that they represent only two of the almost 100 structural types of multi-home stepfamilies. Nonetheless, the re-marital challenges they experience are common to all stepfamilies. For brevity and clarity, we will focus mainly on their relationships. There is much more to their stories!

As you meet these men and women, see if you identify with any one in particular.

~ Ned, Laurie, and Janice ~

Ned is now 34. He is the older of two brothers raised in Des Moines by a Methodist housewife and a police officer. Ned met Janice when he was 23, as he was being discharged from the Navy. They married seven months later, full of hope and love. Angela was born a year and a half afterward, followed in three years by baby Philip. Angie was planned, where her brother was "a surprise."

As three years passed, their relationship grew "flat" and distant. Soon after Janice discovered Ned had been having an affair with her best friend's sister, she angrily filed for divorce. Ned moved into a cheap apartment—the first time he had ever really lived on his own. After a costly, bitter, 17-month court battle, Janice was awarded physical and legal custody of Angie and Phil. A legal parenting agreement evolved painfully, including visitation and financial support guidelines and responsibilities.

During that time, the kids visited their dad every other weekend, and most Wednesday nights for dinner. Nine-year-old Angie became fiercely protective of (and worried about) Ned, who felt consumed with guilt and shame over the pain that "he'd caused." He sought no counseling for this. Angie also felt increasingly responsible for her little brother, as their mom was often distracted and weary from her full time office job and other responsibilities.

Laurie, 36, grew up in Wisconsin, the only daughter of a hard-working farm couple with Swiss Lutheran roots. Blond and athletic, she had dated several boys in high school and afterwards, but none "took." She attended Iowa State University and became interested in dentistry. She had several jobs as a dental technician in Des Moines and did well at them. She liked (most) people, and was personable, warm, and efficient. With a natural ability for organization and management, she became the indispensable office manager of a large, thriving dental practice.

The years passed, and although several men showed interest in her, Laurie felt no *electricity* happen. She shared an apartment with a schoolmate and established a small circle of common friends. After a nine-month dating spree Laurie became engaged to a charming and zesty young salesman, but broke it off as they began to talk about setting the date—something, Laurie thought, didn't feel *right*.

Over a year later, Ned walked into her dental office and "something *clicked*." She felt attraction and sympathy for him as a polite, quiet, clean-cut single dad. Laurie listened intently as he told her about his life. They began to date, both alone and doubling with Laurie's roommate and her partner. In the spring of the following year, heart beating and *sure*, Laurie accepted Ned's engagement ring.

During her increasing contact with Angie and Phil, Laurie became very fond of the little six-year-old boy. She grew mixed feelings for his sister, who seemed unpredictably to be several girls: friendly and perky, aloof and possessive of Ned, and at times, painfully indifferent and rude to Laurie. The adults smiled tolerantly and "knew" that Angie would mellow and eventually come around.

Neither Ned nor Laurie thought of themselves as a budding stepfamily. Laurie proclaimed—and believed—*"I'll never try to take your Mom's place. I'll be your friend."* Janice described Laurie as "Ned's girlfriend" to her relatives and friends.

Ned and Laurie have not yet set a wedding date, but are talking about her moving in with him. They enjoy sex together and had mutually agreed to limit Laurie "sleeping over" to times the kids were not visiting.

~ Sally and Mike, Frank and Debbie, and Susan ~

Sally is a vivacious, petite brunette. At 39, she is the leading producer for a large Atlanta real estate firm she has been with for nine years. She lives with her 15-year-old son, Jason, a husky, outspoken "jock" and lukewarm student at his public high school. His sister, Jill, 16, chose to live with her father, Frank, three years ago. Rather than forgive each other since their divorce seven years ago, Sally and Frank have nursed old marriage resentments and have grown to dislike and distrust each other even more. Their attempts to discuss issues around the kids usually result in raised voices, name calling, and hang-ups on either end. Each feels misunderstood and accused by the other of being a "bad parent."

Frank married Deborah three years ago. They had a baby within a year, Jill and Jason's half-brother Timothy. Deborah has two teen daughters, Anne and Sylvia, who live with her. All three females had mixed feelings about Jill arriving. Deborah and Frank both have full-time jobs, and their seven-person household often feels chaotic and stressful. The seventh person is Annette, a young nanny from Switzerland who looks after Timmy and the house.

While Frank and Debbie do call themselves a "stepfamily" and their three teenage girls "stepsisters," they both emotionally exclude Sally (and Debbie's ex, Edward) as family members. Neither has read anything about stepfamily norms. Sally intellectually acknowledged Debbie as Jill's step-mom and speaks to her as little as possible. She often smoothly changes the subject when Timmy's name comes up.

Sally has dated several men since her divorce. Last Christmas she met Mike at a business party. She was pleased and interested when he invited her out soon after the New Year arrived. They have dated for 11 months, and are each clear and open now that this is their primary adult relationship. Each says enthusiastically "I've never felt like this before!"

Mike is 41, a polished, charismatic, successful Atlanta attorney. His wealthy Irish Catholic parents still live together physically, but emotionally divorced long ago. His father, a Philadelphia circuit court judge, is politically well-connected and still fiercely ambitious. Mike and his sister Moira privately acknowledge their dad "has a temper" and "an old drinking problem"—but nobody really talks about these.

Mike had met Susan in law school 17 years ago and married her within a year. She was the good-looking, independent middle daughter of a divorced middle class couple. Susan and Mike had Sean, William, and Kathleen quickly, and lived an active, church-going busy life. Several years into their marriage, Susan began to complain of "dark moods" and "sleep problems," and started to gradually withdraw from everyone but her oldest son.

She began to drink mid-day Bloody Mary's "for her nerves," and pooh-poohed Mike's mild alarm. Over many months, Susan's behavior became increasingly moody and erratic. She finally went to a psychiatrist at Mike's urging. The doctor eventually prescribed medication and urged Susan to cut way back on the alcohol and smoking—or better, to quit both. She didn't—and became more moody and covert about her drinking.

Mike and Susan each responded to their growing anxiety and discontent by working even harder. Their sex life dwindled in the growing silences and banality between them. Outwardly, their family looked happy. It wasn't at all.

One evening, Mike was stunned to hear Susan say matter-of-factly "*I don't love you any more,*" and that she wanted to divorce and "*find herself.*" Over the next agonizing two years, Mike fought the divorce, alternating between rages, numbness, and pleading. Susan's psychiatrist recommended marital counseling, but Susan adamantly said, "*It won't matter.*" Despite friends' and relatives' advice, she moved out.

It was clear to most that she had a major alcohol abuse problem and was unable to acknowledge it. Susan said flatly that she wasn't a capable mother and that the kids should remain with their father. Everyone was torn, anxious, guilty, and confused. Their divorce was finally granted four years ago on "irreconcilable differences."

Do you see any elements to our guide's backgrounds and stories that feel familiar?

What Is "Marriage"?

This chapter is about making three complex *right* choices which lead to a stepfamily remarriage that "works" well, or succeeds. To gain a clear view of what "works well" really means here, we need to first get clear on "what is marriage"? For our purposes, we will acknowledge that it is many things:

- Shared personal attitudes and values.
- A unique, dynamic, six-phase relationship, powered by the mates' (often unconscious) drives to fill a set of core human needs.
- A model for dependent children, and a birth-family keystone.
- A voluntary spiritual commitment, or contract.
- A voluntary legal contract.
- The sole way to preserve ancestral values, names, DNA, and traditions down the generations.
- An ongoing economic enterprise; and...
- A key factor in community and societal stability or chaos.

Do you think Mike, Ned, Laurie, Sally, Frank, Deborah, Janice, and Susan would each define marriage like this? Is it useful for people like them to develop their own thoughtful definition? Have *you*?

* *When you can clearly define what "healthy marriage" is for you as a person and as a couple, your odds for each picking the right partners to succeed at it go way up.*

Do you buy that?

What is a "Successful" Marriage?

A simple answer is: "one that lasts." Yet we suspect that with a little thought, you can name some couples who are not divorced, but whose marriage you *would not* rate as "happy" or "healthy." Behind the reflexive response above are some other yardsticks. Shelves of books and research reports have been written on marital success. There are *many* points of view.

European, Asian, and African cultures currently weight marriage factors differently than our average American society. For our purposes, let us focus on only two of those factors: "marriage" is...

- A unique, dynamic six-phase *relationship*, powered by the mates' (often unconscious) drives to fill a set of core human needs; and...
- A relationship model for dependent children and a stepfamily adult's-family keystone.

The first of these provides a yardstick for assessing "does each partner feel the marriage is successful *now?*" The second factor is long-range, allowing assessment of a marriage's success across two or three generations.

So your question becomes: "how can I pick a re-marital partner who is highly likely to 'succeed' with me at (at least) these two objectives, over time? The divorces of Ned and Laurie, and Susan and Mike say that their original choices appear to have been wrong. For perspective, that is the case now for around half of American first marriages.

Why Marry?

Marriage is a unique relationship in that it is the only effective way most adults have to *consistently* fill a set of basic personal needs well enough. These natural core needs, or emotional tensions, are both conscious and unconscious.

Conscious needs: As typical adults, we each need (or want) these things, often *enough:*

- To feel special and important above most of their mate's other loves; i.e., to feel "primary" to their beloved and respected other.
- To feel emotionally and physically safe now.
- To feel heard, deeply understood; and accepted.
- To feel free to spontaneously be one's own unique self, without anxiety, guilt, or shame.
- To feel respected and validated by respected others.
- To feel sexually desirable and satisfied.
- To feel really known, appreciated, and enjoyed.
- To feel intellectually and emotionally stimulated.
- To feel deeply trusted and trusting.
- To share the adventures of daily life with someone who cares.
- To feel currently balanced and centered—emotionally, physically, spiritually, cognitively, and socially.

- To feel empathically comforted, accepted, and supported when worried, scared, or ashamed.
- To feel encouraged to grow freely as a unique person with special, valuable abilities.
- To feel companioned *and* separate (a balance).
- To feel needed by, useful to, and influential with a beloved partner—i.e., to feel "I *matter.*"
- To feel personally and socially normal (enough).
- To feel genuinely forgiven, when appropriate.
- And, to problem-solve effectively when any of these fluctuating personal needs are not met enough.

For many adults, one more deep personal need is:

- To co-conceive and/or nurture children.

Would you edit this list of primary human needs? Seen all together, it is a pretty tall order for one partner to fill consistently!

* As long as each partner feels his or her unique mosaic of these needs is filled enough, the marriage may succeed long-range.

Unlike poets and song-writers, some sociologists view marriage as an ongoing unspoken "economic exchange": you voluntarily agree to fill enough of these needs for me, and I'll agree to fill enough of yours for you.

If you are divorced, which of the needs above were not getting filled well enough for you? For your mate?

Since our inner and outer lives change constantly, the balance of how well these individual needs are satisfied is ever-shifting. When someone's needs are too unsatisfied for too long, some couples (like Mike and Susan) split. Others choose to work to repair their relationship. Still others, like Mike's parents, numb out or separate emotionally, and endure.

Adults can partially fill many of these needs outside of marriage. So why then do we marry? Research consistently shows that compared to partnered spouses, single adults are less healthy, less "happy," and die sooner. Apparently our overall human need to be consistently well loved by one beloved partner cannot be well filled alone, or with even the best of kids, friends, or gods.

Maybe "I *love* you" means "I deeply delight in filling as many of these needs in you as I can—and I really enjoy that you reciprocate. This feels good!"

Many divorced adults cannot name their version of this needs list clearly. They certainly know *"something* didn't feel good" in their primary relationship. Most people who struggle in their marriage can passionately rattle off a list of "faults" in their mate. These faults and criticisms are usually coded for "I'm not getting *my needs* for _____ filled well enough with them—and they're supposed to fill my needs!"

Unconscious adult needs: There are other powerful emotional and spiritual needs we each long to have met. The trouble is they are usually unconscious. How can couples effectively "problem-solve" unmet needs, if they are not even aware of them?

Remarried pastoral counselor and author Dr. Harville Hendrix has studied Western marriage relationships extensively. We share his opinion that most marriage-mate choices are impulsive (rather than reasoned) attempts by partners to satisfy the needs above—*and* some core unconscious needs. The latter stem from our experiences in mom's womb, and the first six or seven years of life with our caregiver(s).

Henrix believes that our mate-choices are often basically unconscious because we adults have not lived alone enough to really get to know ourselves and to learn consciously about our unique set of unfulfilled childhood needs. His useful paperback, *Keeping The Love You Find,* proposes a way to help do that. In it, he suggests that a universal human need is to feel wholly alive, which is fully possible *only* (he feels) in a primary committed adult relationship.

Adequately describing these core unconscious needs is beyond our scope here. Basically, they have to do with (1) repairing emotional and spiritual "wounds" we got accidentally as very young kids, and (2) recreating certain primitive feelings of environmental security and pleasure we enjoyed before and after our birth.

For example, if we felt partially or consistently rejected by a primary early caregiver, (usually mom), we will "forever" choose partners in unconscious hopes of quenching our desperate need for *unconditional* maternal (or paternal) bonding, nurturing, protection, and approval. It is literally like our (very real) inner children are searching endlessly for the ideal (or real) mother or father we lost or never had.

The intensity of these needs, coupled with unhealed childhood shame, often promotes destructive relationship addictions (*codependence*). Conversely, if we were devastated enough by our earliest caregiver relationships, the unconscious terror of agonizing rejection and abandonment we retain keeps us in either stressful, cyclic approach-avoid relationship dances or lonely, solitary exile.

Until we adults become conscious of such powerful, ceaseless longings and fears, we may try a string of partners over time—and be ultimately disappointed by each one. Once we become aware of our hidden needs, work to mourn our early deprivations, mute the terrors, and find spiritual and internal ways of filling these core needs enough, we are freed at last from picking the same kind of partner over and over, or protectively picking *no* partner.

So how do we become aware of these unconscious needs? A thorough answer is, again, beyond the scope of this chapter, but here are three key ideas, and several references for more understanding:

Understanding Your Unconscious Needs

1. Invest some early-adult years in living alone. This grows your probability of really leaving home, emotionally and financially. That in turn promotes growing the belief, from experience, that "I *can* live well enough on my own, if I choose to"—especially for women. Without this deep, secure belief, mate choices are often subliminally based on "I have to have you (or someone) or else (some catastrophe will surely happen)."

Not having ever lived alone in turn promotes anxiously dependent, rather than healthily inter-independent unions. Inter-independent relationships sound like: "We each want very much to live intimately with each other, but if we don't or can't it will be okay *enough*."

2. Whether living alone or not, invest time, energy, and money in meeting your "inner family." Those of us who were accidentally too traumatized as young kids often adaptively split (*dissociate*) psychologically. You are not crazy or weird in the least! The result is a set of inner "energies" which collectively determine how you live your daily lives as kids and adults. These energies, or "subselves" war, compete, ally, get paralyzed or hysterical, and cause minor to major physical and emotional symptoms.

This group of normal psychological "parts" can realistically be thought of as an inner family, or team, which is somewhere between harmonious/productive and chaotic/unproductive. The dynamics and unity of our inner family often closely mirrors the dynamics and health of our childhood families. If we came from early lives of trauma, anxiety, anger, and confusion—that is how our inner crew lives today. This often leads to our current *outer* lives having many of these traits.

The good news is that with meditation, self-awareness, patience, and temporary informed professional help, we can come to know and harmonize these energies. The bad news is: most people are not even aware of their inner team, much less know how to work meaningfully at quelling the chaos within and empowering the natural, inner leader sub-self we each have.

The desperate inner children in most of us who long endlessly for an ideal mom and/or dad are powerful members of our inner crew. Other inner subselves (like our Perfectionist, Procrastinator, Critic, Rebel, and Controller parts) are equally powerful. They are dedicated day and night to protecting our vulnerable and needy young subselves at *any* cost.

Until they are acknowledged and harmonized, such groups of personality "parts" can literally take us over. They strongly influence or make key adult decisions, i.e., whom we choose as our primary partner, how we act with them, and what we expect and need from them.

One vital implication of this is that average couples are not "two people," but really two complex, dynamic, interacting teams totaling 20 to 40 sub-selves! To try and maintain ongoing harmony in such a crowd, especially if each inner family is in disarray, is a pretty steep challenge. If one or both partners are not even aware of their inner teams, it seems to be impossible to stay healthily self-aware for about half of America's first marriages. Re-marriers seem to have an even harder time!

The real victims of this hidden chaos are America's growing legion of bewildered, anxious, shamed children of divorce. Without informed guidance and compassionate healing, they are becoming the next generation of divorcers and re-divorcers.

Getting to know, harmonizing, and empowering our inner sub-selves is a normal, doable process anyone can do over time—even kids.

3. Attending this last step, meeting and harmonizing your inner team, is a major subset of a larger task. A high majority of stepfamily couples come from very traumatic childhoods. Most of them do not know it--and do not want to. They unconsciously bear up to a dozen or more significant emotional and spiritual wounds, which stress their loves (and their kids and partners) until healed.

*	The larger task for any adult considering a committed primary relationship is to assess yourself for childhood trauma and resulting "splitting," and core emotional and spiritual wounds.*

Depending on the findings, moderate-to-major unhealed adults need to patiently evolve and work a high-priority personal healing or recovery plan. A natural part of recovery is meeting and harmonizing one's inner family. Another part is recognizing your true unique gifts and gradually becoming aware of your life calling and main purpose.

An inevitable result of real (versus pseudo) recovery is the growing conviction and calm acceptance, "*I* am the only one responsible for my life and what I do with it." That leads to far more realistic expectations of oneself and interdependent partner, less blaming and more cooperative "problem-solving," and hence to strengthening their unions and families.

To bring this concept down to earth, are you aware of how these conscious and unconscious needs are being filled now (*if* they are) in your life? Are you clearly aware of your expectations of if and how your partner "should" fill them, and vice versa? If your answers are either "no," or "I'm not sure," what does that mean to you now?

Is Stepfamily Remarriage Different?

Most non-stepfamily people will impulsively (or thoughtfully) answer: "Not much." Others will say truthfully, "I don't really know." Typical veteran stepfamily adults will reply emphatically, "It's a *lot* harder! *Far* more than I expected!" Together, these replies form a mystery: how can the primary adult relationship in a stepfamily home be both "not much different" than a biological family (first) marriage, and also "a *lot* harder"? We'll explore both sides of this very real paradox.

Because they often do not know what they do not know, most couples like Ned and Laurie and Sally and Mike never really researched what they are taking on together. If they, you, or your kin expect stepfamily remarriage to be pretty similar to biological family marriage, everyone is in for some stressful surprises. To understand why, let us first look at one answer to the question above:

No, it's not different! People who claim, "First or forth marriage—the basics don't change!" are right. Reflect on what emerged above on "what is marriage"? It's:

- Shared personal attitudes and values.
- A unique, dynamic six-phase relationship, powered by the mates' (often unconscious) drives to fill a set of core human needs.
- A model for dependent children, and a birth-family keystone.
- A voluntary spiritual commitment, or contract.
- A voluntary, binding legal contract.
- A way to preserve ancestral values, names, DNA, and traditions across generations.
- An ongoing economic enterprise; and,
- A primary factor in community and societal stability or chaos.

Is each of these factors also true for average pairs of adults considering re-marring? We think so. Our guide Ned says, *"I have really learned from my first-marriage experience; I won't make the same (marital) mistakes I did with Janice. I know Laurie's really the one for me!"* Sally feels similarly: *"I'm a lot more mature, and so is Mike. We have a lot more life under our belts, and we each know the ropes now, including parenting. Besides, I've never felt love like this before. It's absolutely wonderful! I know we're going to make this work!"*

Laurie, who has had two serious romantic relationships but has not been married before, answers a little differently. She might review the points above and say: *"Well, yes, they're the same for a remarriage, but it's not so neat or simple. We'll have to deal with Ned's ex, Janice. And, I'm not sure how it's going to work between his kids Angie and Phil and me, or their grandparents and me. Ned and I are great when his kids aren't around. When they visit, we usually have fun together. But, uh, we ... things change, sometimes, when the kids come over. Ned says we'll all be fine together. I really want that ..."*

Other important things that are the same in marriage and stepfamily remarriage are each stepfamily adult's:

- Childhood experiences and memories
- Core attitudes and personality traits, and
- Personal needs, feelings, dreams, abilities (and limits), and personal-maturation stages, and,
- Marriage and remarriage are both embedded in dynamic, interactive family and social environments.

Now, we'll look at the other answer:

Yes, stepfamily remarriage is different! If two thirds or more of current remarriages split within 10 years despite most mates having "more experience under our belts," *something* must be different about remarriage:

Different inner environments. Compared to when they first said "I do!" most remarrying partners like Mike, Sally, and Ned are *personally* different in some key ways: their age and health; personal identity; relationship experience and expectations; and key life priorities. A devil's advocate would say: "So what?" *Here's* what:

1. *Remarried stepfamily adults are older.* Ned first wed at 23. Sally was 22. Mike was 25. As they each relish remarriage visions now, they are 12, 17, and 16 years older, respectively. Ned's new partner Laurie is now 36. Many of their ideals and attitudes have mellowed from experience. Some of their interests and priorities have shifted in the years since early independence from home. For example:

     Mike and Sally are each clear they want no more children. Laurie sees "the clock running out" and wants to have kids with Ned—*soon*. He has not really thought deeply about what that would mean to him and his existing children, but has gone along with Laurie's enthusiasm in the swirl of romance.

     Compared to their early to mid 20's, each of these adults now is more established in their communities and careers. They earn more and have different priorities about balancing work, play, and rest in their lives. Their bodies are different. Their parents and relatives are older. Most of their siblings have kids now, and several siblings have divorced. Our three biological parent guides—and their stepfamily co-parenting ex-spouses—have forgotten what it feels like to have no children and no parental responsibilities.

     Another aspect of stepfamily adults being older the second time around is their physical health. Among many implications of being older, one is especially important: addictions. There are three kinds: substance (alcohol, food, nicotine, pot, etc.), relationships (e.g. codependence), and activities (e.g. workaholism). All addictions serve to medicate inner pain. They evolve in a slow, predictable way to cause increasing personal and family disruption. Unchecked, they each shorten addicts' lives and often deeply affect their dependent kids.

     Because a high percentage of people who remarry seem to come from traumatic (i.e., painful and frightening) childhoods, many are addicted to one or more of these three types of self-distraction and -destruction. The normal human defense against admitting life-controlling addictions is denial. Ten to 15 years after their first union, their addictions, if not admitted and managed, have often developed into the serious—and more obvious—"middle-phase."

     In this stage, typical addicts tend to show serious health, work, relationship, family, and self-esteem problems, which were minimized or well hidden in prior years. Often such addictions were among the key causes of their first divorce. Susan's increasing alcoholic medication and emotional decline with Mike and their kids is a case in point. One of his responses to this was an equally destructive *activity* addiction: workaholism.

2. *Different personal identities.* Approaching their wedding commitment decisions, most stepfamily adults see themselves much differently than 10 to 15 years before. Before their first unions, each of our four divorced guides thought of themselves as a "young, single, independent adult." Currently, Sally laughs and says, *"Well, today I'm a divorced career woman, single mom, and multiple aunt."*

Mike publicly describes himself as *"a successful, hard-charging lawyer; devoted son, brother, uncle, and single dad; major taxpayer, undiscovered tennis ace, and a committed church volunteer."* In full denial, Mike still does not identify himself as a "definite middle-aged workaholic," "a secretly confused, guilty, uneasy divorced man," or "the un-recovered, oldest child of an alcoholic, major-dysfunctional Irish Catholic family, who married a deeply emotionally troubled woman for the wrong reasons." All are true.

Laurie says thoughtfully, *"Today, I'm a mature, grown woman; a loyal friend and daughter; a productive health professional; a cake nut, and an excellent baker. I'm really ready now to be a loving wife, a dedicated mom, and some kind of aunt to Ned's kids. I'm a solid Lutheran; an average classical piano player; a staunch Republican, active Iowa alum; and 11 pounds overweight. At 22, I was a feisty green kid who thought she knew a lot more than she did!"*

Ned sees himself as "an average guy just trying to get along okay in the world." If pressed, he says, *"Well, I'm also a good* lineman (for the local electric company), a Packers fan, an ex (Navy) swabbie, and a pretty good bass fisherman." Asked about his kids and ex-wife Janice, Ned gets quiet. "Yeah, I'm the best dad I can be, when I see my kids, and, uh, I'm a divorced guy, too."

Like his almost-fiancée Laurie, Ned does not yet see himself as being in an emotional (versus legal) stepfamily—although factually, they are. Neither of them has heard the term "stepfamily adult," and neither would be comfortable about adding that to their self-descriptions. They also each would be reluctant to say, "Along with Janice, I'm one of three stepfamily adults in our two-home stepfamily."

Besides differences in their ages and personal identities, people who remarry are also typically different in:

3. *Marriage experience and expectations.* Two major differences are: average divorcees' (and widows' and widowers') ideals and illusions about married life and parenting have been strongly influenced by the realities of their actual years as a spouse and caregiver.

They are much more likely now to consciously use their own first-marriage experience as a yardstick in forming remarriage goals and visions, rather than using observations of their parents' and key kin's relationships (and media illusions) as they did before. In times of conflict or uncertainty, their unconscious perceptions of their parents' marriage are often still a powerful influence on their choices and expectations.

Sally speaks for all our divorced guides: *"When I first married, I was sure we'd stay together forever. Divorce was for others—not for Frank and me. As I think about Mike and me marrying now, I guess I have to accept that maybe we could fail at this, although I don't think we will. I know I won't put our kids through another divorce, so I feel more committed to this relationship, because I know now it won't just automatically work because we love each other."*

A second major relationship difference among people who remarry is in their typical views about (biological) parenthood. At 22 to 25, our guides each had various sure and vague expectations and standards about raising infants and preteens. These ideals and best guesses have now been replaced by years of being in the trenches with their kids. Collectively, they chuckle and look back: *"I had absolutely no clue as to what it would really be like to be a parent."* Laurie says, *"I've heard enough of my married girlfriends talk about their kids to believe parenting's a lot harder than it looks. And, it's wonderfully rewarding!"*

None of our four dating guides have direct experience at stepparenting, or partnering a stepparent. Although genuinely "older and wiser," they are now in the same position of idealism and "guesstimating" about stepfamily co-parenting relationships as they were originally about biological parenting. A high risk for most women and men like them (e.g., *you?*) is to assume that step parenting is "pretty much like" typical biological parenting. "C'mon, parenting's just parenting" is a common illusion. Paradoxically, it is both right—and *very* wrong.

The many ways that stepparenting differs environmentally from biological parenting have been identified in this book. Learning to competently drive a station wagon (biological parenting) does not really prepare you to safely manage an 18-wheel tractor-trailer in the mountains (stepfamily co-parenting).

4. *More losses to grieve.* Still another major inner-environmental difference for three of our four love-struck stepfamily adult guides—and their three ex-mates—is that because of their divorces, they (and each of their kids and key relatives) have each had a set of major losses to mourn.

The traumatic impact of divorce on adults *and kids* has been rated by some professionals as second only to the death of a loved one. Sociologists studying the long-range impact of divorce on children and adults conclude that it may take some up to 10 years, or more, for the emotional impacts too really subside. Many divorced biological parents, especially men, begin re-dating within one to three years, or less. This raises the odds that some members of their stepfamily-to-be are not well along in truly grieving their prior losses.

How important these major losses are to a given stepfamily adult depends on how effectively they can grieve. Grownups who were taught as kids that it was okay to feel and safely express current emotions like shock, confusion, rage, and sadness, can usually grieve divorce losses well. They can also teach their biological kids to grieve their family-breakup losses well, unless their marital partner or others inhibited such teaching. Unfortunately, men especially do not know how to grieve well. They were taught directly or by example to numb, minimize, or repress key mourning emotions and just stoically tough painful losses out.

A sobering corollary is that often these divorced biological parents have not been able to teach their kids to mourn life-losses well. That often inhibits their kids from accepting the nicest of stepparents and stepsiblings. That stresses remarriages after the initial glow of romance and idealism wears off.

Another corollary is that where divorced mates have not grieved well, they have often not found effective ways to forgive themselves and each other for the pain and deprivation their splitting up (and prior behaviors) caused, especially for the pain and losses their young kids experienced.

That leads to ongoing waves of guilt, remorse, and shame, and sometimes the "endless" need to blame the other biological parent. These reactions are usually magnified for unhealed moms and dads from dysfunctional (shaming) childhoods. When a biological parent has such excess guilt, they tend to: (1) deny it, and (2) compensate by over-pleasing and under-disciplining their minor biological kids.

Over time, this guarantees a divisive loyalty conflict with live-in or visited stepparents, who usually push for setting realistic discipline. Over time, if they are pushing disciplinary consequences, they wind up resentfully feeling like "the bad guy." This especially causes conflict where the stepparent has been a firmer disciplinarian with his or her own kids. Such kids will quickly and loudly complain when their stepsiblings are treated "better."

An important final difference here is that normal stepfamily remarriages inevitably cause a second set of major tangible and invisible losses to most of the adults and kids involved. More grieving needed! Our social training and natures tend to only focus on the new mates' joys and gains, not the very real endings that come painfully with the stepfamily re-marital package.

Incomplete grief in one or more new-stepfamily members is one of the five main reasons that most remarriages eventually fail. It underlies much chronic physical sickness and "mental illness," and most addictions. Our instant-gratification feel-good society tends to pooh-pooh healthy mourning of the string of traumatic partings that we all encounter in life. This discounting makes it all the more challenging for the Miles, Sallys, and Neds of the world to grieve *well*, and to help their kids do the same.

If you are divorced, or your mate has died, have you ever thought about specifically *what* you have lost? Do you know what each of your kids has lost? Are you and they each grieving well enough? How do you know? What if you are not? Can you name the five stages of normal grief, and six or more behavioral signs of incomplete grief?

5. *Different personal priorities.* One more key inner difference between people who marry for the first time and those who remarry when they are older is their profile of current life priorities. Before their first marriage, Janice, Ned, Mike, Susan, Frank, and Sally probably focused their average days on their jobs, friends and family, fun, personal health, money, and some things—like cars, clothes, and home furnishings.

Ten to 15 years later, they have added the major priority of parenting to their daily mix. They may have begun to plan for their kids' college education and their own retirement. They probably have a growing concern about caring for their own aging parents. They have often emotionally taxing relationships with their ex-mates and their former relatives-in-law to negotiate. Several of our stepfamily adults have to add a priority for maintaining and managing the houses they did not have in their 20s. Managing their growing estates calls for attention now that they did not need to expend before.

Besides these new priorities, our stepfamily adults' ranking of weekly life priorities is probably different than at their first wedding. Health is often a higher concern. Family relationships are more complex and may be somewhat more important now, compared to work and "getting ahead," and socializing. Spirituality may be a growing priority, as our guides head into middle age and their death becomes more real. Volunteering for religious or community projects may have become more important in allocating weekly time and energy.

So our guides' respective inner landscapes are very different, as they begin to plan a second committed relationship and family.

Different Outer Environments. The emotional landscape *around* typical remarrying adults is also usually much different from their first union. Key differences include:

- Many more family relationships for each stepfamily adult to balance.
- Many alien, complex stepfamily tasks and roles to negotiate and master.
- More "busy-ness," and less couple time.
- Little social empathy for them as stepfamily members and stepfamily adults; and,
- Far less effective community supports.

Here's a brief perspective on each of these:

Many more relationships to balance. When Sally married Frank 17 years ago at 22, she generally divided her social time and energy between him, her parents, two unmarried sisters, two grandparents, and five or six good friends—12 to 13 people. Now at 39, she must juggle her social time and energy between Mike and his three kids, her own kids Jason and Jill, her ex-husband Frank and his wife Debbie and her kids' half-brother Timmy, her aging parents, her remaining grandmother, her two sisters and their families (nine people, total), and seven or eight good friends and their families—28 or 29 people.

There are several important personal and re-marital implications, including:

- She is routinely pulled in more opposing directions now, trying to balance her relationship needs, obligations, and satisfactions.
- The number of primary relationships in her life has greatly increased, and so has the number of social (versus work) roles she tries to fulfill. So have periods of frustration and low to high anxiety ("stress").
- So, it is now much harder for Sally to "find" (i.e., *choose*) undistracted intimate time with Mike than it was with Frank.

At 22, Sally was not a biological mother of two teens with a half-brother, an aunt of five, a stepfamily adult ex-wife, a godmother, a step-mom-in-training, a sister-in-law, and an ex-daughter-in-law. Ned, Mike, Frank, and Debbie all have similar stories.

The bottom line here is that one key outer difference for most re-dating adults is that their interpersonal landscapes are much more complex, and probably more *stressful*, than when they first said, "I do!"

The paradox here is that if you asked most remarrying adults to list the tasks they need to do to plan a successful honeymoon trip, they could tell you clearly and quickly:

- Choose a destination we both want.
- Estimate the costs and our financial limits.
- Evaluate transport options, and reserve planes, cars, rooms, and other tickets.
- Arrange for safe care for our kids while we're gone.
- Arrange for child, work, home, and other (e.g. pet) coverage.
- Notify key others of how to reach us.
- Select or buy clothes and other supplies, pack, and…
- Enjoy!

Adults know these steps from prior travel experience. Our legions of Neds and Lauries *do not* know how to prepare for their new stepfamily because they have never made the stepfamily-remarriage trip before. Understandably, most previously-married adults wrongly assume that remarriage will be "close enough" to their first experience.

More "busy-ness," less couple time. Meet successful stepfamily veterans Carlos and Rosita who liken their remarriage (with six combined dependent kids) to a new baby: *"To thrive, our relationship has taken steady high-priority commitment, attention, time, and nurturing from both of us, for a long time!"*

Among other things, it implies that *happily* remarried stepfamily adults steadily choose to make (rather than "find") enough time for talking, problem-solving, relaxation, and intimacy with each other—in a complex U.S. life often jammed with many competing activities, responsibilities, and options. Successful re-wed mates do that because they want to, not because they have to.

One implication is that other primary relationships, like those with dependent biological kids, kin, ex-mates, and key friends, must accept that the attention and ranking they have been used to (or longed for) will shrink and stay shrunk. Many are not happy campers with this loss, especially dependent kids. When they "act out" in response, it often causes shared guilt, shame, hurt, anger, frustration, aggression, and stepfamily stress. Not good for the infant remarriage!

Less empathic social acceptance. Yet another outer environmental difference that Mike, Sally, and their stepfamily co-parenting peers encounter is this: as they have myriad normal re-marital and stepfamily conflicts, confusions, and problems, very few non-step-people can really empathize with them.

Sally's ex, Frank, has been a remarried biological dad and the stepfather of two teenaged girls for three years now. When he confides to his married sister, Nina, that at times he gets upset with Debbie for being "so wishy-washy" with "her girls" (versus *"my stepdaughters"*), Nina says *"Why does that bother you? They're not your kids. Jill and Timmy are enough for you to manage!"*

Nina has no experiential empathy to help understand that what Frank is really saying is, *"It hurts a lot when I complain about Anne and Sylvia not helping around our house, and Debbie repeatedly blows me off and sides with her daughters. I feel unheard, devalued, and second-place!"*

Multiply this example by many accumulating re-marital frustrations over months, and similar well-meant, but uninformed responses from non-stepfamily relatives, friends, work mates, and professionals. The common growing results in typical stepfamily adults are:

- Personal self-doubt ("I must be weird or too sensitive").
- A sense of personal isolation ("no one *really* understands what I feel!").
- And, without effective adult problem-solving, marital and stepfamily co-parenting polarization ("it's me against them"), antagonisms, resentments, and rising personal, re-marital, and household stress.

In stark contrast, when our stepfamily co-parenting guides vented the joys and tensions of early biological parenting to kin and friends years ago, they often felt understood enough, and usually felt empathically supported. "Everyone" could speak knowledgeably of frustrations with "my" or "our" (bio) kids. That feels much different than "his" or "her" or "their" kids.

Different language. This last point highlights still another outer environmental factor that makes remarriage feel different for typical stepfamily adults: the terminology they use to talk about their unions and families. Consider:

"My family" is usually decoded to mean "my spouse and (bio)kid(s)"—or maybe "my mate, kids, and blood relatives." For remarrying stepfamily adults like Mike and Sally, "my family" can mean either:

- "The nuclear or extended families I grew up with."
- "The adults and kids living in my stepfamily home now."
- "All my custodial and non-custodial bio and step-kids, and my new and former mate."
- Or, "All the 87 living and dead people related by blood and past and present marriages who are emotionally important to each of us five stepfamily adults and five step- and biochildren now."

Typical stepfamily kids, adults, and their supporters, must work to distinguish which family is being talked about: birth family, first-marriage family, single-parent (post-divorce) family, one-home nuclear stepfamily, or multi-home, multi-generation stepfamily. If they do not, they risk minor to major misunderstandings, resentments, and conflicts.

And how about the titles "parent/mother/father"? Do those terms mean the same to stepfamily adults and kids as they did to first-time biological parents and their relatives and friends? A child saying "my parent" in an average stepfamily can mean:

- My custodial biological mom (or biological dad).
- My non-custodial biological dad (or biological mom).
- My live-in stepmother (or father), or,
- The man my mom's married to (or living with), whom I see every other weekend.

Many earnest stepparents have recoiled in hurt and confusion, hearing a stepchild angrily test them by saying *"You're not my parent!"*

Previously single stepparents are often ambivalent on whether they are a "real" parent or not. Often, veteran biological parents can subtly or obviously discount their inexperienced new mates' stepfamily co-parenting decisions "because you've never raised kids before" (implication: "I'm much more experienced—and therefore, a *better*—stepfamily adult than you").

The same kind of confusion regularly exists around all the other family-role terms like "brother," "sister," "relative," etc.

Yet another subtle, powerful difference of stepfamily adults' interpersonal language is the emotional "flavor" of common family role titles and terms. For biological kin and our society, "our family" usually carries feelings of normalcy and rightness about it. The phrase "our stepfamily" often carries a varying emotional bouquet of shame, failure, weirdness, and second-best-ness.

The term "stepchild" is often used in current media to denote a cast-off or adopted (non-natural) person, group, or idea. One result is an instinctive avoidance of these "negative (feeling) step terms—e.g., *the* kids" versus "my *step-kids*." This means stepfamily members often do not label themselves (or their family roles) realistically. This in turn muddies what members expect from themselves and each other, which makes their stepfamily relationship conflicts—including remarriage—even more confusing and harder to resolve well.

The cure for this is for stepfamily adults to get clear themselves on their multi-home stepfamily identity and all their various roles; then facilitate equal clarity in other willing family members; and then get collectively clear on all their stepfamily roles, terms, and titles, and all learn and use the skill of verbal "problem-solving."

Fewer effective community supports. A final major external difference between people married for the first time and remarried stepfamilies is the amount of *informed* professional and community support available to them in troubled times. Most communities now have a network of trained, experienced marital and parenting counselors, and effective educational and support programs, for members of biological families. This is rarely true for remarried stepfamily adults and their stepfamily members.

The vast majority of clinicians, medical professionals (including psychiatrists), clergy, family-law professionals, and educators have never had any informed, in-depth instruction on the many stepfamily uniquenesses and realities. Almost no such professionals in your community, we would bet, can accurately summarize what you are reading here.

Most of these people—even if *they* are in a stepfamily—are generally unaware of the 15 to 25 emotional tasks that most minor kids of parental divorce and remarriage must negotiate. Nor are they likely to know of, or fully appreciate the complex challenges typical stepfamily adults face. Although such helpers' hearts are filled with compassion, they usually rely reflexively on biological family theory, experience, expectatons, and tools. This is like a master carpenter trying to make an effective, complex plumbing repair with fine woodworking tools.

Few U.S. communities appear to have informed education programs or effective support groups for stepfamily adults. This is especially tragic, since typically about 20 percent of their populations are stepfamilies, well over half of which are troubled and will eventually split up.

Few clergy, however theologically experienced, have adequate knowledge to effectively guide average remarrying adults in decision-making or help stepfamilies resolve conflicts.So far we have taken a look at what *marriage* is, what a *successful* marriage is, *why* adults marry, and what is *different* about a stepfamily remarriage. These topics lay the foundation for the real meat of this chapter: how you and your partner can both wind up...

Making Three *Wise* Pre-Remarriage Choices

Romantic Distortions

One of the reasons most people who remarry and form a stepfamily wind up re-divorcing is that they are in a distorted state of being just at the time they need to be crystal-clear about evaluating and answering these five to six vital questions. Their deliciously altered mind-state is romantic love.

How would you describe the differences between romantic love and mature marital love? Our experience is that in romantic love, the wonderful traits of our beloved are amplified and enhanced. Flaws disappear or seem trivial. Our patience and forgiveness are magically elastic, and our willingness to sacrifice our current needs to please our magnificent partner is (close to) boundless. Our trust that the future will "take care of itself," and "our love will overcome *any* problem" is invincible.

Our shared dreams for the future are exciting and sure. The grass is greener, the sun brighter, and (at least some of) our self-doubts and anxieties melt away. "We talk for hours—about *everything*!" "I've *never* felt this way! I *know* this (relationship) is right!" "We never fight!" (Or, if we do, "We *always* solve the problem later!")

This happy state in each partner, unfortunately, usually distorts what is relationally and situationally real. One of the major aspects of this distortion is the blithe expectation that our mate will change some irritating or less than thrilling trait "after we're married a while." Countless divorcees' testimonies document that that rarely happens. They married the enticing vision of someone they thought they would get, rather than a real here-and-now mate, warts, snoring, bad breath, and all.

1. Remarrying the Right *People*

In a first (non-stepfamily) marriage, this challenge reads, "picking the right *person*." In average pre-stepfamily dating, at least one partner is dating a single parent, their kid(s), and probably a living ex-mate. The challenge for Laurie is *not* "Is Ned the right *man* for me?" The reality of her question is, "do I have evidence and intuition that says *clearly* that I'm sure to get my set of personal core needs met consistently over many years by Ned, his daughter Angela, his son Philip, his ex-wife Janice, any future partner(s) of hers, and all their relatives?"

"Maybe I can get along with Ned really well, but what if Angela and I don't like each other? What if Janice is jealous of me step-mothering her kids, and causes us trouble? What if Ned and I have a child—or several? How will Angela, Phil, and Janice react? What if Phil and/or Angela came to live with us? Can I love Ned's kids the same as my own biological baby? Would Ned love *our* child(ren) as much as Angela and Phil? What if he didn't?"

Ned's question here is, "Can Laurie and I live harmoniously enough with each other, Phil, Angela, Janice, and Janice's possible (now unknown) new mate? Will this network of relationships and competing needs be likely to allow me to get my core needs filled—well and often enough?"

A 43-year-old childless step-mom writes with flaying anguish, after three years of remarriage: *"I love my husband so much—yet, I'm not sure I can go on living with him and his two custodial (preteen) boys. The kids (versus "my kids") treat me so badly all the time—and he does nothing. I now dread coming home from work, most days, and feel I've totally lost control over my own home. I was confident when we married and they moved in we'd all learn to get along just fine. I never thought I'd feel like this."* Shattered romantic delusions—and unmet core emotional needs—in action!

Before marrying for the first time, dating couples normally do not have any of the difficult, and essentially unanswerable, wonderments that Laurie has (above). The moral here is that lovers weighing a stepfamily remarriage really must try to pick the right *people*, not the right person.

Single biological parents find another level of complexity to this first pre-marriage question. It is, "will *each of my kids* get along well enough with my prospective partner—and *their* kids, ex mate, and kin, if any? Is my choice to remarry all these new people in my *kid's* best interest, too?"

A metaphoric version of this question is, "Would I take me and my minor kids on a life-long world cruise with this adult, their and/or my stepfamily co-parenting ex-mates, and all their kids, on a 30-foot sailboat?" First-marriage sailors have only a crew of one mate to evaluate.

In a romantic-love mind state, where mutual needs and emotions are running high and thinking is rarely objective, it is hard enough to pick the right *partner*—let alone to rationally answer the "extra" questions like those above.

The good news is, there *is* a finite list of key criteria that can help you assess these extra remarriage questions clearly and realistically, to decide confidently, "yes, these *seem* to be the right *people* for me (and my child(ren)) to commit to."

"Standard" Mate-Selection Reasons

In describing why they have chosen their current partner (singular), dating men and women usually say something like, "Oh, we have ...

- The same interests, values, and dreams!
- Great fun together, alone and with mutual friends!
- Mutual respect, trust, and love!
- Great talk! We can talk about everything, for hours! We rarely (or never) fight!
- Great sex!
- And, (sometimes), my family just loves (Ned, Laurie, or _____).

These criteria all work for picking a remarriage partner, too. For people who remarry to form a stepfamily, however, there are important...

Extra People-Selection Criteria

There are specific vital additional questions to answer in your picking the right *people* for you (and any biological kids) to re-wed. These queries can be grouped into (1) key prospective-mate traits, (2) other stepfamily adults' traits, and (3) prospective-step-kids' traits.

What are you thinking? Feeling? There are no rights and wrongs. Does the reality of having to choose the right *group*, rather than just the right partner, seem more believable and real to you now?

2. Remarrying at the Right *Time*

In a sense, there is *never* "the right time" to commit to remarriage. Some factors are alays uncertain or unknown. So the real project here is learning as objectively as you can (given your romantic-love distortions): (1) "What specific timing factors should I assess here, for a high-odds successful-remarriage choice?" and (2) "What balance of "right time" versus "wrong time" factors seems like an okay-enough risk to me (and my kid(s)) now?"

There are many more variables affecting the long-range success of a stepfamily remarriage commitment than in a childless first-marriage decision. There are many more relationships and people, each with more developmental tasks, and many more potential values conflicts to master, to weave over time into a thriving remarriage and stepfamily.

Consider this. Excluding parents and siblings, when Ned and Janice first wed, they had three major relationships to balance: each of them with themselves, and the marriage relationship with each other. As Laurie and Ned consider setting up stepfamily shop, they have at least 10 relationships to harmonize and balance, over time.

For each person in their five-member stepfamily relationship "web," each of the other four relationships can generally either bring personal stress, a source of nurturing and satisfaction, or both. Each relationship will require time, energy, and prioritizing, over time. And, Laurie, Ned, and their other three members each have an ongoing relationship with themselves and with the several-to-many voices *within*. So there really are at least 15 relationships in Ned and Laurie's prospective stepfamily—excluding their relatives.

So when is the "right" time for Ned, Laurie, Janice, Angela, and Philip (or for Mike and Sally and their many web-partners) to commit to stepfamily remarriage? Once again, pause, and allow your thoughts and feelings to unfold without censure. Are you beginning to appreciate the real complexity of your stepfamily-remarriage enterprise?

To summarize, it all comes down to this. Starting with me and my partner, do *all* our kids' stepfamily adults now realize clearly that:

- "Via remarriage, we're now considering forming a normal multi-home stepfamily, with three to four, or more, stepfamily adults as joint managers."

- "Our stepfamily will feel and act very differently than an average biological family. We stepfamily adults and our minor and grown kids have many new norms to learn, accept, and adapt to; and many old biological family beliefs and ideals to modify or give up and grieve."
- And, "each of our minor kids and young adults has some or all of over 20 unique developmental tasks to master on top of their normal growing-up tasks. As their stepfamily adults, we need to: (a) learn specifically what these tasks are, and (b) determine who among our kids needs what kind of help and support from us all as they work their way through these tasks."

The bottom line is that as dating persons and stepfamily adults, are you each and all clearly "well enough" along with all of these now? How do you know? How can you decide objectively, in view of normal romantic distortions and unconscious needs? If you are not sure yet, how will you judge when you are?

3. Remarrying for the Right *Reasons*

Would you agree that there are healthy and unhealthy (or wrong) reasons to commit to a remarriage? Have you really thought about what your *real* reasons are for considering this once- or twice-in-a-lifetime commitment? How comfortable are you now with the idea that your *conscious* reasons may not be (all) your *real* reasons?

The real key to the third vital pre-marriage question is to not let your heart and unconscious mind impulsively or seductively out-maneuver your head. You can try this on your own, or you can invest in using an objective, qualified professional consultant to help you guard against your own subjectivity.

Pre-Remarriage Danger Signs

Is there a way that dating stepfamily adults like our guides (and you) can quickly guesstimate whether they may be making some unhealthy remarriage choices? We think so.

Here are some time-tested symptoms that should alert you and your partner: "probable major re-marital danger ahead!"

Persistent inner voices. *"Don't remarry these people now!"* If you repeatedly have thoughts like these, and/or persistent relationship doubts or worries when you let your mind get quiet, something is wrong. If you brush such thoughts aside, or avoid mental quiet times, you are at high risk of future re-marital stress. Your option is to meditate and invite your inner voice to tell you specifically *why* it is warning you. Try journalizing about their warnings, without editing for logic or making sense. Pay attention to your inner voice(s)!

Feeling high urgency or desperation to remarry and/or cohabit. A related symptom is feeling intensely like "I can't live without you!" Such intense feelings in you or your partner are surely a brilliant red light.

Another related symptom is seriously discussing remarriage within less than 18 months since you met, or less than 18 months since any marital separation. Stop and explore, perhaps with qualified professional help, what the inner pressure is about (usually ancient longing and fear).

If either you or your partner are a biological parent of minor kid(s) now, and say (or think) "my kids always come first with me," STOP all remarriage discussions! This is a clear, unmistakable indicator of almost certain future re-divorce. The biggest single conscious reason for the re-divorce epidemic in our country are bitter, disillusioned stepparents saying, *"I got too tired of coming in second (or fifth) with my mate."* If you doubt that remarried biological parents must choose, often, and that these loyalty conflicts are real, very frequent, and very divisive in normal multi-home stepfamilies, reality check these ideas with veteran remarried stepfamily adults, i.e., couples with minor step-kids who have been remarried at least five or six years.

Reluctance to read, discuss, and use this book. If you find yourself, and/or your partner, repeatedly doing almost anything other than reading and discussing this book (or other stepfamily readings), consider what that symbolizes. Listen closely to your inner voice(s). Something is not right.

Ongoing ex-mate hostility, and/or "end-less" hassles with them over divorce settlements, parenting agreements, and/or child visitations, custody, and/or support. If your and/or your partner's ex-spouse is ceaselessly angry, combative, uncooperative, dishonest, or secretive, they are not really (emotionally) divorced. Such behavior almost surely signals that the hostile one is an adult in full denial of major, unhealed childhood wounds. Do not expect that person's hostility to stop in the near future. Verbal and legal threats, attempts to confront and reason, and/or financial or child-related punishments, almost always make such behavior worse.

Often, such unwarranted venom masks a deep, unfinished relationship struggle with one or both of their original caregivers. Where this is true, the implacable truth is that you can do nothing about motivating them to acknowledge and heal their wounds, and grieve their divorce losses. That must come from inside themselves, at their own time. What you *can* do is:

- Work patiently toward seeing them compassionately as enormously wounded, rather than "evil," "twisted," or "a son of a bitch."
- Proactively avoid one-up contests, power or control battles, and adding new wounds to their old ones via emotional, verbal, or physical abuse.
- Stop reacting to them as you have been (it is probably exactly what they want). Develop a genuine attitude of equality toward them, and use positive verbal skills to defuse most arguments and conflicts with them.

- And, consciously keep your own life balanced so as not to become preoccupied with their "awfulness" and your related frustrations and anger.

In other words, you cannot change them, and so must: (1) accept who they are, and (2) steadily make an environment that promotes them healing themselves—when they are ready to. Steadily blaming, shaming, punishing, and frustrating them are the polar opposites of this and only reap more of the same, over time.

Fantasizing that your partner (and/or their kids and/or ex-mate) will change seriously unpleasant traits "somehow" after you remarry. They probably will not, no matter how loving, patient, pious, and reasonable you are. If they are not going to change, do you still want yourself and any dependent kids to commit "'til death us do part"?

Many recent major life changes or traumas in a short time for you and/or your partner, and/or one or more of your minor biological kids. Some examples are: Firings and/or new jobs, new homes, schools, or churches; divorce(s); sudden great financial losses or gains; deaths or major health losses; pregnancies and births; graduations or flunk-outs; legal suits or judgments; natural disasters, home break-ins or muggings; rape or murder; sudden family or home membership shifts.

Such major life events all cause disorienting emotional losses which require time to grieve. When many such events come back-to-back, the combined emotions and adaptations can really unbalance adults' and kids' judgment and needs. *Not* a good time to make major long-range life decisions like stepfamily remarriage! Take many months to sort everything out, do some healthy grieving, and rebalance your lives!

Active addiction(s) to substances, activities, and/or relationships. If you or your partner believe *anyone* in your stepfamily-to-be, including you two, any ex-mate, key relatives, and/or any minor or grown child are now addicted, caution is needed. Addictions like Susan's are almost certainly clear signs of major unhealed childhood wounds, which foretell ongoing stepfamily stress and conflict. Sally would do well to squarely face the probability that Mike now has a serious *activity* addiction (workaholism). Sally and he are both at high risk of denying, minimizing, or rationalizing this, to avoid the great pain and fear that would result.

Chronically ill or acting-out biological kid(s). Do you or does your beloved partner have even one minor child that has *recurring* (e.g., repeating for six months or more)…

- Serious school academic or social problems (including few or no friends, or "toxic" friends)?
- Trouble with truancy, gangs, cults, or the law?
- Non-experimental drug use or clear dependence?
- Threatened or actual running away from home?
- Excessive stealing, defiance, lying, or secrecy?

- Repeated excessively emotional outbursts?
- Suspected or clinically diagnosed attention deficit/hyperactivity disorder?
- Chronic depression, or sleep, digestive, or eating problems (anorexia, bulimia, obesity)?

Individually and in groups, these are all high-alert symptoms of prior and/or current major family (versus personal) dysfunction. Any ongoing (or escalating) symptoms like these are re-marital RED lights. They should cause you serious pause about planning to form a stepfamily, until you find the real cause(s) for these symptoms and progress toward healing them. Remarriage or cohabiting is probably *not* the appropriate medicine.

Ongoing or sporadic legal action between divorced ex-mates. If either of you is (or has been) involved in a string of court-suits over finances or stepfamily co-parenting with an ex-spouse (or a relative), this is also a red light! To oversimplify, this probably means one or both partners: (1) have not *really* grieved and accepted their divorce, (2) have not forgiven themselves or their ex for "what happened" (or didn't happen) between them, and/or (3) may be acting out old birth-family rage that has nothing to do with the divorce.

It also means any minor or grown biological kids are traumatically caught "in the middle," and are probably emotionally split and highly stressed, and may be acting out.

Get qualified post-divorce professional help on this one! If you do not, your future remarriage days and nights will probably be at least partly based on the ongoing anxiety or terror that "The Ex" will call in the cops and/or lawyers again "sometime" (or cause *you* to). Everyone will be walking on well-worn egg-shells for months and years, rather than on clouds. To repeat a painful stepfamily truth: your living (and sometimes dead) stepfamily co-parenting ex-mates are co-equal partners in your multi-home stepfamily—and will remain so after your youngest "leaves home."

A series of prior adult break-ups (including divorce(s) or approach-avoid relationships) or no prior intimate adult relationships. If you and/or your prospective partner have a historic string of "failed" intimate relationship (marital or not), another red light! This is a strong symptom of some serious core wounding, *which stepfamily remarriage will definitely not cure.* Self-motivated recovery can heal this serious personal problem, over time.

Keeping major secrets. If you, your partner, or any of your prospective stepfamily co-parenting partners are clearly in the habit of distorting or intentionally withholding key truths ("lying by omission"), rethink any re-wedding plans! Such behavior is a sure symptom of an adult with emotional wounds, usually excess shame, fear(s) (often of abandonment), distrust(s), and reality distortion(s). Get qualified professional help toward childhood-trauma assessment and personal recovery, without guilt or shame.

Repeated avoidance. If either you or your partner *consistently* avoids serious, intimate discussion (including conflicts) of *any* of the issues in this book, this is a bright-red re-marital light! Someone like this, or someone who "always wants to have fun," fears or distrusts something.

They are unconsciously putting their distrust and fear (rather than self and mutual love) in charge of the growth of the relationship. Some classic avoidances, or denials, to watch for are:

- "We are *not*—or won't be—a *step*family."
- "Stepparenting is basically no different than biological parenting."
- "We can and should handle or *own* problems (rather than using qualified outside help)."
- "A family's just a family. Stepfamilies aren't all *that* different. I/we do *not* need to study what's normal and real in a stepfamily now."
- "We've all lived together for ____ months without big problems, so—eventual re-divorce? Not us! No sweat!

These are the sounds of deep, perhaps unconscious, fear. Such fear probably will not alter from donning each other's rings and uttering heart-felt pledges and vows. Real commitment involves courageously learning and *confronting* such fear(s) together, quelling them, and putting love back in charge, over time. Try re-reading Chapter Two on communication. Learn an effective structure for safe talking and listening together and then work toward discovering together "what would make it safer to talk and "problem-solve" together, now?"

Recommendations

Ideally, you are reading this before you become emotionally attached to a prospective stepfamily co-parenting partner. The odds are, though, that you would not have begun reading this book unless you were already attached, and may have begun having relationship "problems."

Shelves of books, tapes, and legions of retreats, workshops, courses, and counseling sessions have been designed to inform adults on how to co-create a healthy, lasting marriage. Despite this huge effort of providers and consumers, half of our marriages currently fail. Even more of our remarriages do. *This inexorably implies that most adults cannot proactively think, read, or listen their way into a healthy primary relationship.*

There is little illusion here. Nothing that anyone writes will give you *the* sure-fire way to re-marital success. The fundamental reason divorce is rampant in our culture is that most marrying adults are not emotionally and spiritually whole enough to sustain a long-range committed relationship.

This is largely because *their* parents were fragmented and wounded by *their* parents. No one has blown the cultural dysfunctional-family whistle loud enough, yet.

Working with hundreds of fragmented, struggling adults and couples, we have yet to see anyone become significantly more whole just by reading (or hearing) information. What usually motivates us to change seems to be pain—real, imagined, and/or foreseen.

Increasing personal wholeness hinges on a persistent, conscious valuing of one's self and steadily envisioning and seeking inner harmony.

In our fast-paced instant-gratification American world, most adults (like you?) are not about to make evolving personal wholeness their highest priority. This is especially true when they are really lonely, horny, grieving, and/or in love—as many divorced or widowed parents of minor kids are. Still, there are practical steps you can take together to significantly raise your odds of re-marital and stepfamily success.

Improving Your Odds BEFORE You Remarry

Relax. Breathe well and become curious about what is about to safely happen. Let your minds become still as we paint a picture for you.

Imagine you and your partner moments before your long-awaited commitment ceremony. See yourself walking together into a special place filled with well-wishers, and music, and light, and flowers, and your kids.

Imagine the words you say and hear, and the moment of pledging. Feel the joy, and hopes, and excitement, and the love. See the faces of all who wish for your health and happiness. Let this rich, warm image fill you and enjoy it fully now....

Now imagine the years that follow beginning to roll past your eyes like a film on fast forward. Experience a safe kaleidoscope of scenes of you as a couple, and with combinations of your kids ... waking up in the morning ... meals together ... evolving a home together ... birthdays ... vacations ... maybe pets ... times alone. Imagine many tasks between you two in the light and in the night, about the concerns of your evolving lives: balancing work and family, time with friends and relatives, leisure, intimate times, illnesses, money, special gifts and glances; adventuring together, dreaming and planning, some arguments, parenting the kids, walking together in different places, maybe holding hands the way you do....

Imagine a series of special occasions like each child graduating, coming back from camp, opening presents in holiday gatherings.... Allow a sense of your growing years together flowing by to develop.... And imagine many conversations with your ex-mates about stepfamily co-parenting things—dental appointments, school conferences, health insurance, wills, parties, ... times with your bio-relatives and step-relatives ... picnics and dinners.... Imagine romance gradually dimming, and being replaced by a *different* feeling....

Let yourself relax even more, to a comfortable level. Breathe in just the right way. If you're a stepparent, begin to imagine times when you feel angry or disappointed ... or disinterested ... in your step-kids. Imagine them ignoring and defying you, and preferring your mate, despite all you do for them.

As your life tape rolls by, imagine an increasing sense of frustration, and hurt and anger with certain people in your stepfamily. Picture reaching out to your partner for empathy and support, to discover that they don't seem to understand. They even seem to often support their kids rather than you. Experience the feelings of unfairness, and disbelief, and disillusionment. It wasn't supposed to be like this!

Imagine reaching out to others for help and understanding, only to find they don't feel the aloneness.... See a gradual chasm begin to form between you and your step-kids ... a creeping coldness, and the sharp guilt that goes with it. Imagine forcing yourself to split, and try to act interested and caring, when underneath is resentment, and hurt, and longing. Imagine your partner's reactions ... puzzlement, reasoning, irritation, growing resentment, pleading, arguing ... finally, the chasm begins to grow between you two and your home splits into "us versus them" camps.

Your stepfamily-life tape rolls on and reaches a certain scene. Slow the tape down, now. Experience this imaginary scene with startling, memorable clarity, with every sense you have. Years together have come and gone. Dreams have flowered, and mellowed, and changed into realities. You, your partner, your exes, and each child are older.

You're having an exchange with your mate. It may be quiet, or sad, or angry, or loud. The essence of it is that one of you finally reveals that living together as a stepfamily is more pain than pleasure—and has been, for too long. One or both of you feels deep despair. You see no reasonable hope of relations getting better. You've tried what you could; nothing seems to work.

If you have prior kids, you're weary unto death of feeling endlessly trapped between them and your partner—and no one understanding how awful that feels. If you have step-kids, you've felt "second best" to them—or their other biological parent—for the last time. One of you says, "I called a lawyer this morning...."

Remember the feelings that billow as you experience the growing reality that your union is ending, your home is splitting, and your dreams are vanishing. You're middle aged and confronting life alone again. You're confronting yourself.

Imagine finding a way to tell the kids. Clearly see and hear their reactions and yours. Imagine the other stepfamily adults, and certain relatives, and key friends, learning of this. See the looks on their faces. Hear their words. Know the feeling of having to decide, "who leaves our home—me or them?" Picture in great, clear detail the time that inevitably comes when one of you takes a last look around the home you've shared for years ... and walks out the door for the last time.

Image your partner gone, your love gone, your marriage and stepfamily over, your re-divorce starting. Meetings with lawyers. Arguments over dividing up your property. Times alone, thinking all this over. How could this have happened to you? Why did it?

Take a few minutes of quiet now to finish any reflections and clarify any key awareness. Remind yourself that you can retain your version of this experience for future reference, should you need to. Understand deeply that this has not happened to you at all—but it could.... Know with total certainty that you and your partner can prevent this stepfamily scenario from happening. About 30 percent of the couples just like you do just that.

Take a special breath and regain a full, comfortable sense of yourself in this present moment. What are you aware of, now? Although it was not fun, take your memory of this along as a magic lamp to rub, in case your resolve falters, or you lose your vision and mission together. This guided imagery was not a forecast of your futures. It was a factual description of what *might* happen, if you do not build a strong stepfamily foundation now and patiently plan the rest of your construction project.

Building a healthy remarriage and stepfamily is one of the most complex and challenging projects you will ever experience. If you co-commit to it, the rewards are enormous—for you and each of your kids. The project also inevitably depends on evolving some degree of teamwork and cooperation with your kids' other stepfamily adults, over time. You cannot control or coerce them, or their willingness to join you two. You can appeal to them, as partners, and try to appreciate their needs and priorities as a co-equal human.

Samuel Johnson said, "Remarriage is the triumph of hope over experience." This is curiously both true and untrue in average stepfamily unions. True because the human needs that a marital relationship seems uniquely designed to fill are the same with any primary partner. Untrue, in that in a stepfamily union, the emotional environment around the adult relationship is vastly more complex and alien, invalidating much of any prior spousal experience.

The aim of this chapter was to provide you with a structured way of lowering your odds of making harmful choices. *Any* marital commitment involves an unquantifiable element of chance and risk. The more time you take to absorb stepfamily education and to learn about who *really* lives inside your skins before remarriage, the more your odds of long-term re-marital and stepfamily success rise. Fortunately, there's a lot of effective help available on both projects.

As you continue to read this book along the way, and as your stepfamily experience and wisdom grows, you'll find new things in them each time you do.

If you do each decide that these are the right people to remarry, that this is the right time to commit to them, and that your reasons are clearly the right ones—may this Coahuilla Indian blessing richly apply: *"May the four winds of heaven blow gently upon you and upon those with whom you share your heart and home."*

PART TWO

STEPFAMILY REALITIES

The following four chapters are to help you and supporters heal toxic misconceptions (myths) and unrealistic expectations which stem from a normal unawareness of vital stepfamily realities. Patiently learning stepfamily structural, developmental, role, and relationship realities is essential for making stepfamily co-parenting and relationship decisions as you, new-stepfamily adults, merge your several biological families.

Chapter Five

Replace Stepfamily Myths With Realistic Expectations

Typical multi-home stepfamilies are similar to intact biological families in a number of ways. At the same time, they also differ structurally, developmentally, and dynamically in *over 60* ways! People unaware of these differences, and what they mean to typical adults, kids and supporters, risk unconsciously using inappropriate or harmful biological_family norms and expectations to guide their stepfamily perceptions, goals, and decisions. This is like trying to play baseball with soccer equipment and basketball rules—a guarantee of confusion, frustration, conflict, and stress that will inhibit healthy stepfamily merging and bonding, and promote growing dissatisfactions.

This chapter introduces potential stressors by comparing common unrealistic stepfamily expectations to associated realities, and urges stepfamily adults to study, discuss, and accept these many differences and realities as they improve their communication effectiveness together. Doing this is an important step to benefiting from the ideas in the next chapters.

Learning, Teaching, and Applying Stepfamily Realities

Learning to live well in a new stepfamily has been likened to the challenges faced by a clan of Swedes pledging loyalty to a tribe of Tibetans, who all settle down together in rural Brazil. There is much for everyone to learn—new laws, customs, roles, and vocabulary, i.e., learning to cope in a new, alien environment.

There are three distinct, new challenges facing you and your child-raising partners:

1. You will need to learn specifically how your multi-home stepfamily differs in composition, norms, and dynamics from your respective birth-families and first-marriage families.

2. You will need to use these step-realities and make time together to evolve clear and realistic personal, marital, co-parent, and multi-home stepfamily goals and expectations over time. And, along the way...

3. You will need to teach your main stepfamily differences, realities, and goals to your kids, important kin and friends, and key professionals. Keep them updated. Expect some people to misunderstand and to criticize your new values, goals, and plans—or you. Realize they probably have their own unsolved problems and/or are stuck in a biological family mode of thinking. Befriend informed others who will empathize with and support you.

Here is a sample of common stepfamily myths and realties that you'll discover, discuss, accept, and apply:

Myth: "I love you and I must love your kids."

Reality: "I love you and will patiently work at respecting your kids. They and I may never love each other. If we do, it will feel different than biological parent-child love, and that's okay.

Myth: "Your or my ex-mate is not part of our family!"

Reality: "As long as your previous marriage biological children live, their other biological parent, and their new mate(s), if any, will emotionally, financially, legally, and genetically influence all of your lives. Ignoring or discounting the needs and feelings of these other adults will stress everyone for years.

Myth: "We're just a regular biological-like family."

Reality: No, because you have two to three linked stepfamily co-parenting homes, three to six stepfamily adults, six to twelve co-grandparents, 40 to 90 relatives, new alien family roles (such as stepfather, stepmother, stepsibling, for example), many major losses to mourn, and many conflicting values and customs to resolve among all your people. You are, however, *normal*—a normal multi-home stepfamily.

Myth: "Your or my kids will never come between us."

Reality: Stepfamily adults' inability to resolve clashes over one or more step-kids, including related money issues, is the most quoted reason for a stepfamily divorce. Underneath this usually lie your own unhealed wounds.

Myth: "Stepparenting is pretty much like biological parenting, without the childbirth."

Reality: While key aims of stepparents are about the same as those of biological parents, the emotional, legal, and social environments of average stepparents differ in numerous ways from typical biological parents. That usually leads to role confusion, frustration, and high stress, until all the stepfamily adults in your stepfamily agree clearly on what each stepparent's key responsibilities are.

Myth: "Your and/or my biological kids(s) will always live with us."

Reality: In about 30 percent of U.S. stepfamilies, one or more minor biological kids move sometime to live in the home of their other biological parent. This sends complex emotional and financial shock waves into and between the sending and receiving homes, especially if the move was on short notice or not agreed to by all involved.

There are many additional stepfamily realities which you will find in this chapter. Use this information to build realistic expectations for your new stepfamily homes, roles, and relationships. If you do not, collective, distorted expectations can cause great ongoing frustrations and disappointments, and even corrode your marriage. But by learning together what's normal in average stepfamilies—early on—minimizes much of this. (Be aware that if you are also carrying around unhealed childhood wounds, you might unconsciously resist doing this because your safety may have long been built on maintaining denials and illusions.)

Ideally, all of your stepfamily co-parenting ex-mates and key kin will join you in this goal. Be aware that some or all of your stepparents and biological parents may agree *intellectually* that you are a stepfamily together, but may not learn, adapt, and apply important step-realities to your expectations and relationships. If so, they risk expecting, deep down, biological family behaviors and outcomes. This will surely lead to mounting frustration, disappointment, and stress in and between your homes. This is especially true in the first years after the wedding, as alien stepfamily crises, like loyalty conflicts, begin to bloom.

Try this quick exercise. Can you can name 15 or more structural and dynamic differences between the average step and biological families, and describe clearly how each of those differences affects your home and family relationship? Though both are four-legged animals with mouths, noses, hair, and tails, poodles aren't ponies—despite wishing, praying, mantras, thinking, or hallucinogens.

Comparing Stepfamilies and Biological Families

Differences and Implications for Stepfamily Adults

Stepfamilies and biological families do have major similarities. Simultaneously, they differ structurally and dynamically in over 60 ways. If unexpected, these differences individually and collectively can startle, confuse, frustrate, and greatly stress all new stepfamily members—and their supporters.

Biological families and stepfamilies have each been around for thousands of years. They are both *normal*. Because in our era and culture there are many more biological families, people often judge stepfamilies to be "abnormal." Neither family type is inherently better; they are, however, vastly different.

Terms

Among the many confusions around stepfamilies, one stems from the terms that we all use to describe them. For clarity, let us remind you once again of the "new" terms we are using. In this book, stepparent means any adult who provides part-time or full-time guidance, nurturing, and protection to the minor or grown biological child(ren) of their current adult romantic partner.

The stepparent may be married to his or her biological parent partner, or cohabiting with—and emotionally committed to—him or her. A stepparent is usually, but not always, the opposite gender from his or her current partner.

A stepfamily is any family where at least one regular member of a parenting home is a stepparent. Typical extended stepfamilies (i.e., kids, stepfamily adults, and all relatives) can live in many related homes and may include 100 or more members. A *blended stepfamily* is one where both stepfamily adults have one or more biological kids.

A stepfamily adult is any biological parent or stepparent living in a stepfamily home. A stepchild is any biological child who lives with—or visits—a biological parent's committed adult mate. Step-kids can be grown or minor, and legally adopted by their stepparent or not.

An interesting paradox is that, depending on the yardstick you use, typical stepfamilies can be accurately seen as "just like" biological families, and *simultaneously* "very different." How can this be?

Stepfamily - Biological Family Similarities

Typical stepfamilies and biological families *are* alike, in that:

- Both family types are composed of adults and kids living together part or all of the time.
- The adults are (usually) in charge of their homes, and do their best to guide, nurture, protect, teach, and prepare their dependent kids to eventually leave and live well enough on their own.
- All members of each kind of family have daily needs and developmental life tasks to fulfill, as well as a range of daily activities, such as work or school, worship, socializing and play, meals, shopping, chores, and so on.
- Both kinds of normal families evolve through a predictable, natural sequence of developmental stages. Although stepfamilies have some different stages. For example: a minor step-kid(s)' key task is to test to learn clearly, "Am I safe in this family, or will it break up too?"; and members will need to resolve personal and family-role name confusions such as, "What should we call each other"?

- Both family types periodically have conflicts between their members, and with other people and the "environment." They use *tangible* resources (money, phones, cars, appliances, etc.) and *personal* resources (like love, humor, time, intelligence, patience, etc.) to seek resolution to their conflicts.
- Step-people and people in biological families each have individual and shared hopes, fears, goals, achievements, dreams, "failures," joys, health concerns, celebrations, depressions, identities, bodies, losses, etc.
- Both family types naturally develop sets of personal group *values*, group *roles* (who does what) and *rules* (when, how, and why), a *history,* an *"identity,"* and some loyalty or *bonding*. And,
- They both evolve with human and natural environments and interact with each as contributors and consumers.

So, when a stepfamily adult (or other) says, "Hey, we are just a *regular* family!" they are absolutely *right*. At the same time, there are over 60 ...

Stepfamily - Biological Family Differences

Average stepfamilies could not be more different than biological families! Typical multi-home stepfamilies have very different structures and developmental tasks than biological families. By these measures, they vary more from average biological families than do typical foster, "single" parent, or adoptive families. In reviewing the following information, notice both the individual differences and the collective impact of all of them.

Adopt a "learner's mind." Award yourself patience, solid permission to mess up and learn, and strokes for the smallest triumphs. Keep your emotional knees flexed, hold hands, and enjoy the adventure and challenge together. It is worth it. Average multi-home stepfamilies are simultaneously both the same, and enormously different than, typical intact (two-parent) biological families. You're beginning to glimpse what that simple statement really means.

What's *Normal* in a Typical Stepfamily?

Once again, a stepfamily is one where one or more adults are doing part-time or full-time parenting for their romantic partner's biological child(ren). Thus, parental cohabitation with a new adult partner after divorce or a mate's death forms a psychological stepfamily. Post-divorce stepfamilies have legal documents that further define them: property settlement decrees, and child custody, support, visitation, and sometimes stepfamily co-parenting agreements.

Older remarrying couples whose kids are all grown still form a stepfamily. They do bypass many, but not all, of the stress of stepfamilies with dependent kids (e.g., child visitation, support, and custody conflicts). They still encounter some of the most serious common causes of stress, particularly stepfamily ignorance, unhealed childhood trauma, incomplete grief, and divisive loyalty conflicts around grandkids, wills and bequests, holidays, and key traditions.

An intact nuclear (parents and kids) biological family normally lives in one home. Typical nuclear stepfamilies live in two or three stepfamily co-parenting homes woven tightly together by child visitations, legal agreements and responsibilities, genes, history, finances, and deep emotions. The only stepfamily that lives in one home is one where all biological kids or non-custodial biological parents are dead. Even then, there are usually emotional and other ties with living former in-laws and with step-kin living in other homes.

Because stepfamilies are adults and children living and growing together, sharing concerns with work and school, pets, health, bills, chores, religion, friends, etc., they do share some average biological family traits. Yet, some "common sense" biological family operating rules and values cannot only be ineffective, but even harmful.

Some key differences:

Unlike biological families, *normal/typical* stepfamilies…

- Live in two or three homes linked for a decade or more by genes, child visitation, support, and custody agreements; divorce decrees and obligations, history and mementos, and strong emotions.
- Always include one or more living or dead ex-spouses and their relatives, who are usually all emotionally part of the family.
- Are always founded on two sets of major losses (divorce or death, and remarriage and cohabiting). All three generations on both "sides" need to grieve these abstract and physical losses well.
- Have up to 30 family roles (e.g., "stepdaughter"), compared to 15 roles in typical biological families. There are no schools or accepted social conventions for these extra 15 roles, so they typically cause confusion and frustration in and between linked homes until a stepfamily-wide consensus evolves on them.
- Include many more people. Typical multi-home, three-generation stepfamilies have 60+ members.
- May have much complex confusion over priorities, values, names, rules, holidays, inclusions, traditions, money, and loyalties.
- Have common social isolation, misunderstandings, and biases to deal with.
- Stepfamily adults usually have to master numerous major developmental tasks, many of which have no equivalent in biological families—with little preparation or social support.

Because stepfamilies are so different from biological families, all remarrying adults and emotionally important kin, including their prior parenting partners, should study stepfamily basics, regardless of prior biological family experience. Note that growing up as a stepchild is probably not adequate preparation for being an effective stepfamily adult.

Over time, all parenting households evolve hundreds of rules about child discipline, finances, holidays, names, privacy, money, pets, home chores, grooming, health, worship, etc. Some of these rules are unspoken while others are vocal and clear. Because stepfamilies are so different, some "normal" biological family rules about co-living—and especially about parenting—can cause conflict rather than order. Other "normal' biological family rules about who's in charge of the home, hygiene, privacy, interpersonal respect, clear communications, honesty, nutrition, and the like, are still relevant and applicable.

Sometimes step-people are stressed by trying to force "normal" biological family priorities on their new household. For example, pushing step-kids to accept, respect, and like (or love) their new step-relatives quickly because "kids should respect (i.e., obey) their elders" can cause major resentment, guilt, and frustration.

Brady Brunch notwithstanding, new love is usually not enough!

Relatives and friends of remarried people often mistakenly expect the new household and kin to feel and act like a biological family. They also may not approve of either the prior divorce(s) or the remarriage. Therefore, friends and relatives may be startlingly non-empathic and critical, or offer unrealistic or inappropriate (i.e., biological family) suggestions if your new stepfamily runs into unexpected problems.

Ex-Mate(s) Challenges

Divorce and/or spouse death do end the physical and legal ties of a marriage, but they usually don't end the emotional ties of a marriage. They also usually do not end the emotional ties between the partners, especially if they have raised kids together. Re-weddings, cohabiting, births of new children, stepchild adoptions, graduations, and other family events can trigger unexpected strong feeling, including sexual, in and between divorced biological parents, well after their parting.

"Endless" ex-mate hostility and personal and legal battles over child custody, support, and visitation, or constant demands for personal attention or assistance can signal a marriage that is still emotionally alive. Other symptoms are a biological parent that is:

- Ceaselessly rehashing the good (or bad) old biological family or marital times.
- Forbidding their minor kid(s) to mention their stepparent, to obey them, or to call them "stepmother" or "stepfather."
- Steadily avoiding appropriate social or dating contacts.
- Refusing to accept their identity as a stepfamily member.

- Refusing to talk about (or with) their ex-mate, or to join them in normal stepfamily co-parenting responsibilities.
- Staying "over-close" (a subjective judgment call) with their ex in-laws.
- And, vehemently denying they are doing these things, or pooh-poohing them.

Note also that grandparents and other in-laws can deny the reality of their child's or kin's divorce and show similar symptoms. So can biological kids. The two core issues here are: (1) whether an ex-mate needs recovery from old childhood wounds, and (2) whether all affected by a death or divorce—and remarriage—have grieved their losses well.

Childhood Wounds Resurface

As discussed in Part One of this book and worth a reminder here, personal research since 1985 suggests that well over half of average remarrying U.S. adults come from a moderately to highly traumatic childhood. This means that as kids, they were unintentionally deprived—at home, at school, and/or within their religious affiliation—of consistent unconditional love and respect; healthy individuality, self-confidence, and esteem; encouragement to feel and express normal emotions; trust that others would effectively care about and help with their problems; and other essential emotional and spiritual nurturing.

As adults, such people with unhealed childhood wounds often protectively deny to themselves and others the deep inner pain, shame, emptiness, confusion, sadness, rage, and fear that remains from such early deprivations. These compound, hidden wounds can seriously interfere with achieving any healthy, lasting, committed relationships—time after time.

There is growing evidence that if not in a self-motivated healing program (i.e., "recovery"), these unhealed adults unconsciously choose and re-choose each other as partners. They are also at risk of unintentionally passing on similar deprivations and emotional wounds to their children, just as their key caregivers did.

Major symptoms of such early deprivations are: repeated relationship troubles, including divorce, codependence (compulsive over-concern with the feelings and welfare of key others), and other addictions to activities (like work, spending, or helping others) or substances (including food and prescription drugs). When coupled with the complexities and new tasks of stepfamily life, these emotional wounds in two or more un-recovering stepfamily adults often strongly promote mounting stepfamily stress and eventual re-divorce.

All marrying adults should assess their own and their mate's childhood for such traumatic family and school deprivations, and seek informed help if indicated. Such help is now plentiful and is effective with time. In case you are now thinking "Not me! Not my partner!"—note that the normal front-line emotional defenses against recognizing these painful early personal deprivations are unconscious emotional repression and denial.

Dating commonly evokes extra politeness and thoughtfulness, a reluctance to confront, and a high tolerance for different values and irritating behavior, especially in the beloved-other's kid(s). Romantic adult-child relationships often change dramatically soon after the remarriage ceremony. That ceremony instantly alters key roles: mother's boyfriend turns into stepfather; "your daughter" becomes "my stepdaughter"; "your woman-friend" is now step-mothering my granddaughter and is my new daughter-in-law; when your ex-spouse delays sending child support, it now affects "our" finances (versus just yours); "their nerdy (or cool) son" becomes "my stepbrother," etc.

These many simultaneous role and title changes often cause stepfamily members to either alter their expectations of each other ("*now* you must obey me"), or to feel suddenly confused on what to expect. If all stepfamily adults and kids are not expecting these many overnight changes, and do not accept a long period of home and family confusion and readjustment as normal, they can feel stressed, self-doubtful, anxious, and disoriented.

The bottom line here is that dating relationships and behavior is often not a reliable guide to what will happen after the remarrying and cohabiting. Similarly, living together before remarrying probably will not accurately foretell post-remarrying harmony or strife.

Legally and socially, remarriage does create a new family. However, it often takes five to eight, or more, years for most step-households to stabilize and start to feel closeness, bonding, and loyalty similar to a typical biological family. This is true even if one or more "our" kids are born to the new couple. Because of the large number of people and prior customs normally involved, it can take at least five or more annual cycles of birthdays, holidays, visitations, vacations, etc. to forge and stabilize a new stepfamily "identity" and a shared positive sense of "us-ness." The greater the dissimilarity of customs and values in the merging family, and the more rigid the members, the longer this stabilizing takes.

This stepfamily identity-formation involves members gradually clarifying and melding ideas on who has what "jobs" in their multi-home family, including non-custodial biological parents, their new spouses, step-grandparents, ex in-laws, and half-siblings.

Compromises also need to be reached on traditions and values relating to special events, e.g., graduations or retirements; major sickness, births, marriages, or deaths; altering wills and paying taxes; house moves or renovations; school, job, or changes of religious affiliation and/or house of worship; acquiring pets; communions, baptisms, or bar/bat mitzvahs; special anniversaries; reunions; etc.

Loyalty Issues

Sometimes the variables are so complex—or merging families' values are so different—that a multi-home stepfamily never fully bonds or grows an identity or loyalty like a biological family.

This does not mean it cannot be a viable family; it is just one that feels different. Stepfamily adults who define clear home and stepfamily goals early on, and commit to working patiently toward them, often achieve the most bonding over time.

Normal stepfamily structure forces biological parents to choose repeatedly between filling the needs of their new mate, one or more biological kids, and sometimes their ex-mate. These repeated stepfamily priority conflicts are normal, may go on for years, and are often unexpectedly stressful.

All families periodically have loyalty conflicts, in which one member feels caught between the opposing needs of two or more others. Such conflicts feel and sound very different in stepfamilies: instead of "you want x and our child wants y," it is "your child wants x and my ex wants y," or, "you want x and my child wants y." Usually "x" and "y" are about child visitations, support money, or parenting values or priorities. Loyalty conflicts in and between linked stepfamily co-parenting homes occur often in an average week, for years. They may or may not decrease with time.

Some step-kids may repeatedly force their custodial biological parent to choose between their new spouse and old, to test the safety of the new family. Stepparents are startled to find that occasionally, or even often, following an amicable divorce, their spouse puts the needs or values of their former partner ahead of theirs. This is especially likely when the focus is on a stepchild's welfare.

Most often, the biological parent feels painfully caught between the new mate and one or more biological kids, usually over conflicts on rules, discipline, and "fairness." If he or she agrees with one person, the other feels betrayed and resentful—a lose-lose situation. No one is wrong when these dilemmas happen; they occur naturally due to the structure of remarried families. Stepparents' normal personal needs for respect, recognition, and inclusion guarantee they will need their mate to choose between them and their stepchild(ren) often, over time. Dating politeness and tolerance fades with time, and resentment over feeling "second" (or "fifth") grow sharp and divisive.

Seductive non-solutions are to deny that these loyalty conflicts exist, minimize their stressfulness, or defer confronting them in hopes "they'll just go away." They will not. Expect and accept these clashes without blame as normal stepfamily dynamics, and seek negotiated compromises. Where none appear, for the long-term health of your stepfamily, the re-marital relationship should be primary with each biological parent enough of the time. Paradoxically, this puts their minor kids first by minimizing the odds of eventual traumatic re-divorce.

Love vs. Respect

Longing to build an ideal new family, remarrying stepfamily adults and their relatives commonly expect the members of their merging families to eventually exchange the equivalent of biological family love. This can happen, over time, especially if the children are very young and prior divorces were amicable. It also may never happen. Even if a stepchild does feel warmly toward the stepparent, their other biological parent may resent or fear such affection, and may criticize, manipulate, or discourage the child from feeling or openly expressing it.

A painful reality is that some stepfamily adults (or step-siblings) cannot ever find a way to even like a particular stepchild or vice-versa—the "chemistry" just does not fit. Experts advise making mutual respect the first relationship goal for stepparents, step-kids, and step-siblings. Gradually, this may ripen into friendship and affection, and—with luck—real love. If this does not happen, then, as therapist Fritz Perls said, "It can't be helped."

Some step-kids steadily reject a stepparent's genuine affection and support for no apparent reason. Perversely, the nicer the stepparent is, the more hostile or indifferent the child may be. Or, a stepparent can offer caring friendship, discipline, and guidance to his or her stepchild(ren), only to find that his or her spouse disagrees with these or resents the "interference" with the stepchild. Both result in stressful loyalty conflicts, which may stem from: unfinished grieving; denied or overt sexual attraction; excess guilt; premature or inappropriate stepparent discipline; biological parent enmeshment (emotional over-involvement); and/or the child instinctively testing marital and stepfamily structure, stability, and safety.

A stepchild may feel "if I show appreciation to my stepparent, my 'real' (same-sex biological) parent will feel betrayed and hurt." The custodial biological mom or biological dad can feel "if I side with your discipline of my child, my child (or my ex or other kin) will resent, criticize, and reject me." Adults who have not recovered from childhood wounds are particularly reactive to this scary threat.

Biological parents and biological kin usually do not expect thanks from their kids for their parenting efforts and sacrifices. Average stepparents do expect and need at least periodic acknowledgment, if not gratitude, for their stepfamily co-parenting efforts from their mate and their step-kids. Since most minor step-kids usually did not ask their parents to divorce and remarry, they are understandably unmotivated to say "thanks" for even the kindest stepparenting. In the best of worlds, stepparents may hear that welcome word many years later.

This uncomfortable, alien issue of gratitude causes many typical stepfamily adults to dread Mother's Day or Father's Day as stepfamily members pretend emotions and sentiments they do not really feel. A few U.S. states have instituted a separate "Stepparent's Day," and a few companies and stores now offer appropriate stepparent and stepchild cards.

Discipline

Even if all stepfamily adults agree that a stepparent has "authority" to discipline their stepchildren, the resident or visiting kids may not agree. Unless very young, step-kids usually feel the new adult has to earn the right to tell them what to do. Also, the kid(s)' other biological parent or key relatives may not agree. This puts the kids, and remarried biological parent, in repeated loyalty conflicts. These often cause the kid(s) to resist, act out, or become depressed.

Ideally, the biological parent will do most major disciplining for months after the remarriage, until the stepparent and stepchild have had a chance to build some mutual trust and respect. A stepparent forcing new rules and consequences on a stepchild "too soon" usually causes resentment, anger, and resistance. Waiting too long may prevent or lose the stepchild's respect, giving them the feeling the new stepfamily adult is wimpy or powerless. This happens also if the biological parent often sabotages the stepparent's efforts at child discipline.

If it is not practical to go slowly, it helps if the biological parent "authorizes" the stepparent in front of the step-kids, as by saying, "If Jerry tells you to do something, it's as though I'm telling you...." Some experts recommend that stepparents act like aunts or uncles at first, until full stepfamily adult authority has been earned over time.

Many well-meaning stepfamily adults and relatives, especially some religiously devout people, believe "stepparents should (immediately) care as much for their stepchild(ren) as for their own." Even if they arrived when their stepchild was, say, under four or five, many stepparents guiltily report favoring their own kid(s) (or close nieces and nephews) at first. This can be particularly true with biological teens. It is also true of many non-custodial biological parents during precious visitations.

Besides the unique genetic and ancestral ties that unite them, biological dads and biological moms have shared life experiences with their own children for years. Usually, they have spent much less time with their stepchild(ren). One way of assessing core reality here is to consider bluntly: "If our house was burning now, which kid(s) would you or I save first?" Usually blood is thicker than water. A rose does not have to apologize for not being an orchid.

Stepparents and step in-laws may genuinely feel equal concern for biological and step kids, after a long remarriage (e.g., five or more years) and active pre-remarriage friendship or custodial stepfamily history. Otherwise, the reality to accept without guilt is: "I love my own kid(s) more (or differently) than yours, so far—and that is natural in a stepfamily and okay."

Kids naturally test their power, and their stepfamily adults' priorities, by angrily complaining to either biological parent or stepparent, "*You're not fair! You treat (my step sibling(s)) better than me!*" One stepfamily adult usually has a more relaxed disciplinary style than his or her new mate—particularly if he or she is still feeling guilty over prior divorce traumas and/or is a previously over-loaded single parent with several children.

Treating all minor kids in your stepfamily "the same" is a worthy goal, but expecting to do so right after the remarriage is often unrealistic, divisive, and stressful. A stepfamily adult option is to honestly tell the resident and visiting kid(s) something like: "*We're working hard to be fairer. Our rules have been pretty different than* (the other family's), *and it'll take time for us to work these differences out. I understand that I seem unfair to you at times, and that that makes you hurt and mad. I'm really glad when you tell me how you feel.*"

"Relatives on all three or four sides of a stepfamily face the same potential inner conflict about genuinely including new stepchildren as family "equals." These dilemmas are most often felt at initial holiday or special celebration times, and when stepfamily adults or their relatives make post-remarriage wills. "Fairness" struggles usually recede as a stepfamily becomes more familiar and their history builds, but that is not certain. Openly acknowledging "inclusion confusion" and honest inequalities—with humor and without excess shame or guilt—is healthy. Un-recovered adults often have real trouble with this because of deep abandonment and shame wounds.

Financial Issues

After child-related disputes, money matters are the second most conflicted area for typical stepfamily adults. Some common financial stress includes:

- The "fairness," promptness, and reliability of receiving child support, and how the receiving stepfamily adult(s) choose to allocate and use it. Indignant stepparents can urge their mates to use the courts if necessary to raise, lower, get, or stop child support, which inevitably causes resentment in the other biological parent's home, and traps step-kids in powerful loyalty conflicts.
- The ambiguity and vagueness in many divorce decrees about which biological parent should pay for what child expense. Absent or "deadbeat" biological parents who avoid or resist child support cause everyone heartburn. Even if such matters have been stable for years, a medical expense or a biological teen's looming college costs can trigger high financial tension in and between linked stepfamily co-parenting homes.
- Biological families usually have two parents who blend their individual financial values and priorities to make money decisions. Stepfamilies have three or four stepfamily adults doing this, so reaching a real financial consensus is often tougher.
- Step and/or biological relatives can take sides over any of these financial stepfamily co-parenting decisions, adding to the intra-family complexity and stress.
- Major lifestyle differences between stepfamily adults' homes can cause trouble. If one divorced biological parent can only provide a frugal environment for their visiting or resident kids, and their ex can spend lavishly, the chance for ongoing comparisons, guilt, and resentment is high.
- Spousal (or relatives') resentment over "unfair" divorce settlements can linger well beyond biological family breakup. In unusual cases, active arguments over property settlements can extend far past the remarriage of one stepfamily adult (e.g., if a house or other jointly-held asset sells years later).
- Stepfamily adults trying to agree on how much money a stepparent "should" contribute

to normal and special expenses of each minor stepchild. If they are supporting kids of their own, the "fairness" of their money allocations can become the subject of raging loyalty conflicts. Spouses who equate their mate's financial contribution with a clear measure of re-marital love and commitment can feel pain and resentment, or gratitude. If all three to four stepfamily adults clearly acknowledge they are a stepfamily, expectations may get more realistic.

- Stepfamily adults and/or kin making new wills after a remarriage or the birth of a new child often brings out unexpectedly intense stepfamily-wide loyalty conflicts. The same is true with adjusting life and medical insurance coverage, and legal titles to homes, vehicles, and securities.

It seems common for remarrying couples to discuss these complex financial topics only vaguely, if at all, before their nuptials. Even if they do talk and plan early, realistically, and well, odds of intra-home financial conflict remain high if communications with their other stepfamily adults are poor. The complexity and intensity of stepfamily asset conflicts is usually far greater than in average two-parent intact biological families.

Legal Issues

In most states, remarriage does not endow stepparents with any legal parental rights, or all the legal responsibilities, of biological parents. For example, unless authorized by a legal document called "In Loco Parentis" signed by both biological parents, typical stepparents cannot legally demand to see their stepchildren's school or medical records, and cannot act as legal guardian to hospitalize a minor stepchild.

If even the most loving stepparent dies without a will, his or her assets will not go to the stepchildren. Specific rights and laws vary by state, so ask a local family law professional to tell you what pertains in your county—ideally before your remarriage.

Studies suggest that in one of three typical U.S. stepfamilies, one or more minor kids will move from one biological parent's house to the other's at some time. These moves may be well-planned and harmonious, or unexpected and highly disruptive emotionally and financially. Many things may lead a stepchild to move in unexpectedly with their non-custodial parent and stepparent, even years after their parent's remarriage. For example:

- The custodial biological parent "not being able to handle" a biological teen's "acting out."
- The custodial parent remarrying and a war breaking out between the custodial child and the new stepparent and/or a live-in stepsibling or step-relative.
- The death, injury, breakdown, illness, job loss, or jailing of the custodial biological parent.

- The other biological parent getting custody because the custodial parent is acting "sexually irresponsible," or is clearly abusing or neglecting the child(ren).
- The custodial stepfamily adults want to move out of state, and the other biological parent petitions for physical custody rights.
- A minor child becomes legally old enough to choose his or her primary home (typically 14 or so), and demands equal time with the other biological parent.
- And, a grown child separates or divorces, and returns to a remarried biological parent's home (perhaps with young kids) "for a while."

Even if well planned, such moves and custody changes can send shock waves through the routines, finances, holidays, space allocation, and roles, of both the sending and receiving homes. So stepfamily adults in each home should expect the possibility of kids' moving in or out, however initially unlikely, and develop at least a rough contingency plan.

Incomplete Grief

For personal and family health, all members of a remarrying family must thoroughly mourn many tangible and intangible losses from the prior divorce or adult death, and many remarriage and cohabiting changes. Previously single stepparents usually lose quiet, privacy, simplicity, and control (of finances, time and routine, space, decorating, meals, etc.) by moving into a home with a new mate and his or her visiting or resident kids.

Although mourning is a natural "built-in" human process, it can be blocked. If individuals who have losses have been taught to fear or suppress their own emotions, they will have trouble feeling and expressing the shock, rage, and despair that big (or multiple) losses normally bring. Also, if a young or grown person who has experienced loss lives among people who discourage honest, full expression of these feelings ("You're such a wimp! Put on a happy face right now!"), the healing power of good grief can be hindered.

Incomplete grief from childhood losses is a primary cause of most adult addictions and chronic physical and emotional disease. Our culture trivializes non-death losses and healthy grieving, which adds to this common stepfamily challenge.

Stepfamily adults can help by:

- Learning the stages of healthy grief (shock, denial, anger, depression, integration/ adjustment/transition), and the specific behavioral signs of incomplete grief (see Chapter Three).
- Assessing each adult and child member of their stepfamily for incomplete grief, and getting qualified help for them if warranted.
- And, intentionally making their homes safe places to feel and express all current intense feelings, without fear of shame. Stepfamily adults' making and using a clear family

policy on healthy grieving really helps. Do you know what your current (probably unspoken) home and family policies on mourning are?

It is essential for divorced biological parents to offer each of their children a clear, honest explanation of why their family came apart—in age-appropriate terms and language. If the kids are to grieve well, and have a real chance to build a healthy relationship with new step-kin, helping them make clear sense out of the chaos of their family split-up is vital.

This does not mean each biological parent should blame and smear their former partner or themselves. It does mean each mom and dad should first work toward realistically understanding their divorce themselves, forgiving themselves and each other, and then sketching the main reasons for their divorce objectively and in age-appropriate terms to their kids.

Adults with unhealed childhood wounds, unless well along in personal recovery, often have a very hard time doing these steps. Not doing them risks "endless" bitterness and hostility between ex-mates; bewilderment, confused loyalties, and high shame and guilt in their biological kids; and, growing frustration in new mates.

Many step-kids come from at least moderately dysfunctional early years; the divorce of their parents is a key symptom. Whether biological parents remarry or not, if they need personal recovery from dysfunction and do not work at it, their kids are at high risk of unintentionally inheriting some of the dozen or more emotional problems of their parents' childhood deprivations. These can include: excess shame and guilt, and self-defeating or limiting attitudes; reflexive fear of primary emotions, personal conflict, and true intimacy; unhealthy distrust, spiritual emptiness, reality and identity distortions; and, living from a false self.

Divorce itself does not cause these traits. Neither does parental remarriage or stepfamily life. It's when stepfamily adults constantly deny their own early deprivations and tolerate the resulting traits that similar deprivations and wounds are usually passed on to the kids. Following their parents' divorce, typical step-kids have up to two dozen developmental tasks or challenges that same-age kids in healthy biological families do not have.

If such kids are in a healthy multi-home stepfamily environment, and have stepfamily adults who all know of these special stepchild tasks and consistently provide effective help with them, there is no inherent reason that stepchildren will not "turn out" just as well as kids in functional two-biological parent homes.

Idealism & Guilt

Frustration blooms in many new stepfamilies when an idealistic new stepparent, or a guilty remarrying biological parent, assumes the crushing responsibility for "everyone's" happiness. Symptoms of this are adults' *overreacting* to family conflict, *repressing* personal feelings and needs, *avoiding* setting or enforcing appropriate child-disciplinary limits, or *excessive* worrying about intra-family relations.

Many un-recovered adults, and women raised in patriarchal homes, are at high risk of this. They are often compulsively over-responsible and approach remarriage and stepfamily co-parenting as a self-sacrificing rescuer. They can see their partner as a brave, overburdened single parent, and their minor stepchildren as emotionally battered, hurt, and needing "a good home life." Un-recovered biological parents can see a lonely single new mate as "needing a good, loving family."

While these perceptions may be true, if new stepfamily adults sacrifice their own personal needs and expect everyone to thank them for their selflessness, then disappointment, resentment, and stress are not far off. New step-moms can be particularly vulnerable to this from both their own genuine wishes, and/or social (and new husband's) expectations that she nurture "everyone." New stepfamily adults need to evolve viable family job descriptions to set limits on whose happiness they are responsible for—and how much.

Most divorced biological parents feel guilty and remorseful about the pain their kids experience from family tension and disruption, including later remarriage conflicts. Unless divorced dads and moms consciously work toward forgiving themselves and their former mates, they can be caught in a fruitless quest to "make up" for their kids' pain by constantly catering to them and shielding them excessively from new stress. This risks their kids getting inflated egos, and pitting the biological parent and biological child against a new stepparent or step-siblings.

Both create loyalty conflicts which are seriously divisive to the marriage. The healthiest approach for part-time or full-time biological and stepparents is to teach their dependent kids how to acknowledge and cope effectively with life's wounds, rather than to avoid or deny them.

Unlike most biological parents, step-moms and dads also often encounter:

- The need to resolve complex challenges around stepchild visitations, education, holidays, loyalty conflicts, worship, health, and socializing, with two or three other stepfamily adults, who may be friendly, hostile, or indifferent.
- Step-kids' rejection, scorn, or indifference.
- Jealousy, criticism, or opposition from other stepfamily adults and/or step-relatives.
- Feeling they have the responsibility to discipline their spouse's kids, but little or no authority to do so.
- Often feeling confused on exactly what they are responsible for, to whom.
- Feeling sabotaged and discounted in their stepfamily co-parenting efforts by their mate ("you've never raised a (child/boy/girl/teen/baby) before—you just don't understand ...").
- Enduring subtle or overt social discounting at school, religious functions, and within the stepfamily ("Oh, your Emily's *step*father...").
- Feeling powerless to shape or change stressful or "unfair" stepchild support, custody, or visitation "rules" imposed by their mate's divorce decree or prior court judgments.

- Finding little informed community understanding and support to help navigate these and many other stressful environmental stepfamily co-parenting challenges.

Historically, stepparents have bad press. In reality, most are average, caring, well-meaning adults optimistically undertaking complex, high-stress roles for which they are often quite unprepared. The quality of the relationship with their step-kids and step-kin is usually very different (not "worse") than biological parents.

If stepparents are (1) wounded adults in real recovery, and (2) can master the many environmental challenges in their family roles over time, and (3) get consistent empathy, priority, and loving support from their mate and kin, they can be enormously helpful influences on the dependent kids in their lives—i.e., they *can* be "just as 'good'" as effective biological parents.

It is not true that step-people, especially kids, cannot get the same nourishment, support, and appreciation that biological family people can. More stress and tasks may limit these, but if all the stepfamily adults in charge are informed, insightful, and committed to building a healthy multi-home stepfamily, it can "work" just as well as a functional biological family.

Sexual intimacy issues may be more transparent in a stepfamily than in an intact biological family. When adults have lived with children since their infancy, it seems to inhibit later sexual interaction between them. The instinctive and social taboo that (usually) prevents sexual interaction between biological siblings, or biological parents and children, simply is not as strong or sure in a stepfamily. Attraction and action between a stepparent and an alluring step-teen, or between adolescent step-siblings, is not probable, but is more likely than in a typical healthy biological family.

Recent research suggests that minor girls are four or more times more likely to be sexually abused by a male step-relative than a male biological relative. So, thoughtful adult modeling, guidance and enforcement of personal modesty and privacy rules are especially important in stepfamily homes.

In addition, stepfamily adults should generally avoid being overtly sexual in front of their minor kids, especially after a recent biological family separation. Seeing their parent and a "strange" adult sexually kissing or touching can evoke intense feelings of disgust, outrage, and guilt in a biological child who has not had a chance to grieve. This is especially true if the child has protectively allied with the other biological parent.

It is important to note that pre-teen kids normally need time alone with their biological parents, especially right after major life changes (i.e., losses). Biological parents have similar needs, not necessarily connected to a major event. Ideally, a stepfamily adult will not view this as "being shut out," but as a natural part of the biological parent-biological child relationship that can prevent stepfamily stress.

Stepparents may agree intellectually that their mate "should" spend alone-time with their biological kids, but resent this on a feeling level. This is especially likely when:

- The stepparent is childless and/or is an insecure, un-recovered wounded adult.
- Dating activities often excluded the step kid(s).
- The remarriage is rocky.
- The stepparent is feeling unappreciated and "second best" in his or her marital and stepfamily adult roles.
- A stepchild (or the other biological parent) is rejecting the stepparent. And, or
- The spouses have too little quality couple time and/or shallow communications.

A stepfamily adult who feels "we are a family, so we should do *everything* together" risks eroding, rather than building, stepfamily bonding, over time. To prevent the building of resentment, it helps if the stepfamily adults talk about the situation, without judgment. This includes the biological parent periodically asking their partner, "How are you feeling about my time alone with my kid(s), recently?" A related option is the stepparent telling his or her mate clearly, and without blame, of any growing resentment, so they can problem-solve together. The realistic aim here is to shoot for a changing, dynamic balance of individual, couple, stepfamily adult-child, and family times that suits most members enough.

Demanding that minor kids call stepparents "Mom" or "Dad" (or take a stepfather's last name) risks major stepfamily stress. Unless this is a free choice, and the reactions of all affected members are equally considered, such demands can cause either open family friction or guerrilla resentment and sabotage. Hearing his or her children call a stepparent "Mom" or "Daddy" can sear a guilty, non-custodial biological parent's heart. A biological child can be constantly anxious, having to remember that "in this house, I call my step-dad 'Pop,' but when I visit my 'real' father, I should call my step-dad 'Philip' (or not talk about him at all)."

Some flexible options are: "Mommy Alice and Mommy Trudy," "Dad and Pop," "Mom and Step-mom," etc. Note that "my 'real' (or 'natural') mom" implies that the step-mom is unreal or unnatural. "Biological mom" and "step-mom" or "co-mom" can minimize implied value rankings. The reverse situation can be tricky too: a well-meaning stepparent calling a stepchild "my son" or "our daughter" without checking around for reactions may cause unexpected resentment in some adult or child stepfamily members.

Therapists, clergy, doctors, and teachers can often cause unintended confusion by using labels that do not emotionally fit for a given stepfamily. As authority figures, their choice of title can carry more weight (especially with kids) than a non-professional's. Most stepfamilies find it best not to force names or titles on members, but to experiment over time and consider the comfort levels of all key people involved, including both biological parents and all grandparents. Each family will evolve its own titles—there is no absolute right way to label here.

Guilt is the normal emotion that rises in most of us when we feel we have broken an important rule (a "should"). There are many reasons why each member of a typical stepfamily may feel very guilty, during early years together. For example:

- "I should love my stepfather, but I don't."
- "I'm closer to my own daughter Susan than to my husband's girl."
- "I like my son's first wife better than his new one, though she's very sweet."
- "It's too weird; I'm really turned on by my stepbrother!"
- "I don't see my son as often as I should—and it's bittersweet when I do."
- "I shouldn't compare my new husband to Jack, but I do."
- "I really love my wife, but must admit I think she's not such a great parent."
- "It's dishonest not to say this is my second marriage, but I'm embarrassed to."
- "I can't stand my step-grandson—I should at least *like* him."

If people do not know what is normal in a stepfamily, they are at high risk of using biological family rules (shoulds, musts, and oughts) to guide their behavior. Notice the implied or actual shoulds in the examples above. One result is that veteran biological parents and new spouses can feel guilty about feeling guilty in their stepfamily ("I *should* know what I'm doing by now, but I'm really confused.")

Other remarried people may understand and validate the guilt you may feel. Non-step people may understand intellectually, but will often find it hard to really empathize. So, intense stepfamily guilt is normal, yet, can subside when stepfamily adults and kids learn stepfamily norms, talk honestly, practice appropriate grieving and amends, and give it time.

If a family is defined as "people bonded by genetic, legal, and emotional ties," then stepfamily co-parenting prior mates are (at least functionally) a part of each stepfamily—including yours. Even if one biological parent is long absent, kids will surely include both biological parents in their emotional (versus logical) definition of "who's in my family." Often, custodial biological parents and stepparents are likely to *ex*clude these divorced partners.

Such ex-mates may not see themselves as part of the stepfamily either, particularly if they remarry. Grandparents, step-grandparents, and other relatives each hold their own views about family membership, depending on how the first marriage ended.

The reality is that whether divorced or dead, absent biological parents—and their new partners and step-kids, if any—continue to play a major emotional (and often financial) role in the new stepfamily for years, even beyond the graduations and marriages of their biological children.

Rejecting biological parent ex-spouses and their stepfamily co-parenting, financial, and family needs usually promotes an ongoing bitterness among the adults, confusion and divided loyalties among the kids, and major stress for all. There is no comparable inclusion task in typical biological families.

The general reality is, expect the unexpected—both positive and negative—from ex-mates who make major behavior or situation changes that highly impact their stepfamily co-parenting partners, kids, and kin.

Well after your remarriage, important family events like births, graduations, job changes, disabilities, adoptions, remarriages, and deaths can trigger unexpected reactions in all stepfamily members, including ex-mates and ex in-laws. The advent of a new stepparent via the ex remarrying will almost certainly upset the prior balance around child visitations, finances, holidays, and perhaps custody.

The chance of a startling change in an ex's behavior can be minimized by inviting them to be an equal stepfamily adult (not just a friend) in your stepfamily, and working to build trust and open communications with him or her. Easy to say, usually hard to do! If ex-mates remain hostile or indifferent despite your best genuine attempts to include them, appealing to them to try post-divorce counseling may pay high long-term dividends for you and the kids involved.

Adoption Options

Adoption is usually the only way a stepparent can gain legal parenting rights, and responsibilities, for stepchildren. Such adoption is a highly emotional and complex stepfamily-wide decision, and normally requires the informed consent of both biological parents, if living. Typically, far more people's lives and feelings are affected by it than in a biological family adoption.

Stepchild adoption is most common when a non-custodial biological parent has died or been long out of contact. It is often motivated by overt or covert wishes to be "more like a real (biological) family." The vast majority of stepparents do not adopt their step kid(s).

Unless done from anxiety (about a weak marriage) or duty, adoption is a clear and powerful statement of a stepfamily adult's stepfamily commitment. Because it often increases the stepparent's family status, authority, and power, adoption can evoke respect, relief, and/or intense resentment or fears (e.g., of abandonment) among kids, ex-spouses, and the kid(s)' biological kin alike.

The idea of the process of adoption may cause a series of major stepfamily-wide loyalty conflicts, unless all affected have talked together thoroughly about their feelings and needs. Last names, bequests and estate planning, family rank and status, and parenting agreements may all change because of a stepchild adoption.

Patience, clear communication, honest inclusion of all stepfamily members' feelings, and stepfamily adults carefully debating "is this best for our marriage(s) (not *just* for the child(ren)?" can help all stepfamily adults make a healthy long-range decision on if, and when, to adopt. Getting qualified professional help to facilitate this complex and impactful process can be an excellent investment for everyone.

As with adoption, having an "ours" baby sends emotional and financial tremors through every corner of a multi-home stepfamily—even to relatively inactive members. Veteran biological parents may feel ambivalent about going through childbirth and rearing again, love notwithstanding. Kids still insecure from divorce may greatly fear the loss of parental time, love, and priority.

A new "ours" baby wrecks most minor step-kids' normal fantasies of biological parent and biological family reunion. The grieving that causes may be mistaken for "acting out." Ex-spouses can feel unexpectedly intense jealousy and resentment: their former mate's conceiving a child with another partner can seem like the ultimate rejection. Grandparents can see a new child as altering their estate bequests, or as an exciting blessing and joy.

In the wonderful haze of dating, it is easy to assume harmony on future child conception, and to avoid talking about it (and perhaps discovering a major values difference). Even if dating partners do discuss whether or not to plan a child together later, they often under-appreciate how such a future conception will upset their multi-home stepfamily's stability.

A major mistake that troubled step-couples make is to assume that having a child together will somehow improve a strained remarriage or a weakly-bonded step home. Usually the reverse happens and the changes brought by a baby in the family's financial, emotional, loyalty, and time balance add major stress for all stepfamily adults, and hence for half-siblings and kin. However, a new child in a healthy remarriage and stepfamily can bring shared joy and bonding.

Most mental-health clinicians, as well as doctors, lawyers, and clergy, lack meaningful training in, and true appreciation of, the complex stepfamily realities you are reading about here. Such health professionals are left to assume stepfamily and stepparenting dynamics and tasks are basically similar to biological families. This benign ignorance raises the odds that their well-meant counsel can often either be toothless, or at worst, harmful to new or troubled step-people.

In Summary

Recently, about 50 percent of U.S. first marriages have eventually ended in divorce. About 60-70 percent of American remarriage fails within 10 years. This high re-divorce rate comes from five interrelated reasons:

1. Most (about 70 percent) of remarrying adults suffer from a denial of significant unhealed childhood emotional and spiritual wounds.
2. These un-recovered adults often pick the wrong adult partner, for the wrong reasons, at the wrong time (before grieving is well along and learning about step norms and realities).
3. Stepfamily adults denying their multi-home stepfamily identity, and being benignly ignorant of the complexity, major unique tasks, and stepfamily realities you have read about here.
4. Some stepfamily members being blocked in healthy grieving for their major prior losses from divorce or death, and from remarriage and cohabiting.
5. A lack of informed, effective community help for prospective and troubled step-people.

The sobering reality is that against all common sense, most divorcing adults (with or without children) pick unsuitable partners (and family situations) again, and eventually re-divorce. Personal recovery, mourning childhood and prior-marriage losses well, patience, commitment, and informed stepfamily education can greatly help minimize the odds of this for people just like you and your kids.

If you now feel startled, anxious, or overwhelmed, that's normal. That is how many members of stepfamilies increasingly feel as they discover these may (often unexpected) simultaneous tasks of real multi-home stepfamily life, over time.

Usually, reading about and discussing these differences in advance does not really prepare stepfamily adults or their kids for how confusing and alien these many common stepfamily and remarriage tasks feel. Yet, by not studying and discussing them, you risk growing frustration, disillusionment, and stress for all stepfamily members.

Stepfamily adults who study these specific differences and tasks, and accept a suitably tailored set of them to fit their unique situation, are empowered to form realistic expectations of themselves and each other. This builds a solid basis for doing effective inter- and intra-home stepfamily problem-solving.

The alternative for any or all of an average stepfamily's three to six stepfamily adults is to deny that they are a stepfamily, or pay lip service to that identity, and assume that "normal" (i.e., biological) family values, role models, and expectations are okay enough to co-manage their homes. The majority of stepfamily adults follow this latter alternative, mainly from fear, repressed shame and guilt, and benign ignorance.

Another key implication of these stepfamily structural and task differences relates to the probable effectiveness of human-service professionals offering help to typical step-people.

Very few counselors, clergy, teachers, lawyers, and medical pros have ever seen a comparison like the one you have just studied. Most of them are in benign ignorance, too, of how different stepfamilies are from "normal" biological families—while they are truly just the same.

When seeking such professional help, ask candidates about their specific training in stepfamily tasks, structure, and dynamics. See if they can spontaneously name at least 10 of the common stepfamily myths and realities.

AVERAGE STEPFAMILIES VERSUS INTACT BIOLOGICAL FAMILIES: DIFFERENCES CHART RECAP

STRUCTURAL FEATURE	AVERAGE STEPFAMILIES	INTACT BIOLOGICAL FAMILIES
1. Number of related stepfamily co-parenting homes in the family:	*Usually two or three homes: the remarried couple's home and one or two other biological parents' (ex-mates') homes.*	Normally one home.
2. Number of biological kids living at the time of the adults' commitment ceremony:	*One to six-plus (his and hers) kids, dependent or grown. The average is two to four kids. Most remarrying couples have no initial kids together and never have any.*	Normally none, with some exceptions. When kids do exist, the marrying couple usually co-conceived them.
3. Number of stepfamily co-parenting adults in the family:	*Three to six: up to four divorced biological parents, and one to two stepparents.*	Always two, alive or dead.
4. Number of kids' absent biological parents in the family:	*One or two (his and/or her ex-mates or dead biological parents).*	None or one (jail, military service, travel, death).
5. Number of stepfamily co-parenting ex-mate(s) and their DNA and legal relatives:	*One to two+ sets: can collectively total dozens of people related to each stepchild; all become "step-relatives" at remarriage.*	None.

Structural Feature	Average Stepfamilies	Intact Biological Families
6. Number of living or dead grandparents:	*Six to 12 (biological + step).*	Four biological grandparents.
7. Half brothers and sisters:	*Possible.*	None.
8. Custodial minor kids living at home or away at school.	*More: typically two to six+.*	Less: typically one to three.
9. Physical and legal custody of dependent children.	*More complex: full, joint, or split; usually subject to legal decrees and parenting agreements which new stepparent(s) had no part in, but are bound by.*	Simpler: shared, full-time custody; no legal decrees or parenting agreements to follow.
10. Three-generation family size and complexity:	*Greater: typically 30 to 100+ biological + step members, living in many homes.*	Smaller: typically under 50 members, living in fewer homes.
11. Family sub-types—can stepfamily adults find other families like theirs for comparison, "normalcy," and support:	*Almost 100, considering combinations of his and hers prior and current child conceptions, custodies, and prior divorces and/or mate deaths. Commonly, "no one's like us."*	One "standard" family type: mom, dad, and biological kid(s)—so "most other families are similar to us."
12. Adults' ages at (re)marriage: amount of life, marital, and parenting experience:	*Older: typically 28-50+. Long age span = more life experience. Stepfamily adults may be more mature.*	Younger: typically 18-30. Shorter life experience. Typical adults are less mature.
13. Mates' prior family rules, rituals, and traditions to merge and renegotiate:	*More complex: four to six sets (hers +/-, i.e. plus or minus x birth family + "one-parent" post-divorce or mate-death family.*	Simpler: two sets to merge (each adult's biological family's rules, rituals, and traditions.

Structural Feature	Average Stepfamilies	Intact Biological Families
14. Adults' and kids' mementos and memories of the prior marriage and their intact biological family—and inevitable comparisons:	*Many tangible and abstract mementos; these may painfully and steadily remind step-people "we're not the firs—and never will be."*	Normally, no memories, mementos, or painful associations and comparisons.
15. Major tangible and invisible losses to mourn for members—kids, parents, and close relatives:	*Many tangible and invisible losses from divorce (or death) and remarriage. Stepfamily adults choose their losses; kids' losses are involuntary.*	No equivalent losses. All biological families do encounter other normal life losses along the way.
16. Adults' parenting values, priorities, and styles:	*Pre-formed—parenting values and styles conflict more often. More compromising needed.*	Evolved together over years—fewer values conflict "crises."
17. Mates' verbal communication and conflict-resolution styles and effectiveness:	*Pre-formed styles— more family members, differing cultures, and more values conflicts, all greatly raise the need for stepfamily adults' verbal problem-solving effectiveness.*	Adults' styles of conflict management evolved together over years. However, not necessarily effective.
18. Possible household interference from "outsiders" and resulting conflicts:	*More likely—ex- spouses, their new mates (if any), ex and new in-laws, and possibly lawyers and courts, may interfere.*	Less likely—relatives may interfere with parents' decisions, over time.
19. Prior adult and child divorce and family split-up trauma experiences:	*One or both stepfamily adults and their biological kid(s) may have experienced these, unless the first mate(s) died.*	None. Adults' parents may have divorced, but that is very different.

Structural Feature	Average Stepfamilies	Intact Biological Families
20. Stepfamily adults' legal rights regarding minor kids' school, health, custody, etc.:	*Stepparents have few to no parental rights without legal stepchild adoption.*	Biological parents share clear rights (and legal responsibilities).
21. Pre-nuptial contracts legally defining asset ownership and disposition in case of (re)divorce:	*More common. Symbolizes the real possibility of re-divorce, and battles over marital property. Can cause distrust, resentments, and conflict.*	Uncommon.
22. Divorced biological parents feel shame and guilt for "failing" and inflicting pain and loss on their minor biological kid(s) and parents:	*Typically minor to major feelings in one or both stepfamily adults. Where present, such feelings can powerfully corrode re-marital primacy and cause major loyalty conflicts until healed. Kids may exploit this guilt and shame.*	No equivalent feelings to invite biological parent depression or defensiveness, and confuse marital primacy.
23. Language is "traditional":	*"Unreal," "unnatural," "wicked," "abnormal," "minority," "stepmother." The root word "stoep" means "deprived."*	Biological families are "real," "regular," "normal," "natural," "standard."
24. Mates' initial marital expectations and motivations to succeed:	*More realistic expectations from experience: "We really might divorce." Or, higher adult re-marital motivations may include the intense need to avoid another divorce.*	Typically more idealistic and vulnerable to denials, "We'll never divorce!" No divorce-pain experience to add motivation.

STRUCTURAL FEATURE	AVERAGE STEPFAMILIES	INTACT BIOLOGICAL FAMILIES
25. Incest taboo—odds of inappropriate sexual attraction, action, and abuse in family homes:	*Taboo weaker or missing, so higher odds of harmful stepparent-stepchild and step-siblings' sexual attractions and actions.*	Lower odds: the incest taboo is usually stronger from the parenting adults living with their biological kids since infancy.
26. Last names:	*Remarried biological mothers' last names may differ from their own minor kids'. Step-siblings and half-siblings have different last names, and stepparents' and step-kids' last names may differ, unless the adult legally adopts the stepchild(ren).*	Biological parents and minor biological kids usually all have the same last name. This normally promotes un-ambivalent personal identity and biological family loyalty and bonding.
27. First names:	*Remarried couples may each have a biological child with the same first name; or a stepparent's and stepchild's first names may match; or new and former spouses may have the same first name. All these can cause confusion and misunderstandings.*	Biological kids and biological parents normally all have different first names; no identity confusion or misunderstanding. Any matching biological child first names are intentional, and evolved nicknames offset confusion.
28. Effect of minor children's presence on the stepfamily adults' relationship:	*Typically neutral to highly stressful for years, even with "our" kid(s). Stepparents may come to feel "I love you—and dislike (or "hate") your kid(s)."*	Usually strengthens stepfamily adults' commitment and enriches relationship. There is much social guidance and many precedents exist on how to "do each family role "right."*

STRUCTURAL FEATURE	AVERAGE STEPFAMILIES	INTACT BIOLOGICAL FAMILIES
29. Adults' and kids' household and family roles and rules:	*Many family roles possible of which half are unfamiliar and are learned by trial and error on the job. New rules must be evolved for each of these roles. Few to no social norms now exist to guide step-people in this.*	Rules for each role are usually learned from childhood.
30. Stepfamily adults' permission and authority to discipline minor resident and visiting kids:	*Initially unequal; stepparents may earn such authority over time, or may not. Step-kids' biological parent(s) and/or biological kin may undermine stepparents' attempts at child discipline.*	Usually co-equal, usually socially expected and accepted.
31. Members' definitions of "who is my (emotional) family—who belongs?":	*Definitions usually differ widely among various members. Initially very confusing. Differences often cause resentments, hurts, and loyalty conflicts.*	Major differences in family membership definitions are unusual, even if some members "aren't speaking."
32. Family bonding, identity, and loyalty:	*Initially, pseudo or none. These may or may not develop over time in and among related stepfamily adults' homes.*	Normally develops over years; often transcends caregiver neglects and abuses if present.

STRUCTURAL FEATURE	AVERAGE STEPFAMILIES	INTACT BIOLOGICAL FAMILIES
33. Stepfamily adults' emotional health:	*Estimate: 75+% of stepfamily adults come from moderate-to-major childhood trauma and unintended emotional depri- vations. Resulting emotional wounds promote repeated relationship con- flicts and breakups, without self-motivated, proactive personal recovery.*	Estimate: 50% of mates come from moderate-to-major childhood trauma and emotional deprivations. Biological parents' divorce and/or addictions are key symptoms of a dysfunctional childhood.
34. Counselors'/clergy's/lawyers'/educators'/ doctors' accurate knowledge of family norms, developmental phases and dynamics:	*Usually much lower. A common basic error: "stepfamilies = biological families, or close." One implication: much less qualified education and help available to typical stepfamily adults in crisis.*	Much higher, because biological families have been the "norm," and U.S. divorce and remarriage has surged just since the 1950's.
35. Couples negotiate courtship with existing kids and ex-mate(s) in the picture:	*Required. Logistics and emotions are often far more complex than typical first-marriage dating.*	No equivalent task (usually).
36. All adults and child members clearly accept "together, we are forming a normal, multi-home stepfamily." Members each decide "who belongs (initially) in my family now?" and resolve major differences:	*Required. A primary, must-do task. All three to six stepfamily adults must learn and accept their version of the differences shown here, and help other members do the same. Members usually have different definitions.*	No equivalent task.

STRUCTURAL FEATURE	AVERAGE STEPFAMILIES	INTACT BIOLOGICAL FAMILIES
37. Stepfamily adults learn "what's normal in an average multi-home stepfamily," and teach realities to key others:	*Required. Avoiding this project greatly raises the odds of building conflicting biological family-based expectations of each other.*	No equivalent project.
38. All members identify and grieve prior tangible and invisible divorce and/or death, and (later) re-marriage losses:	*Required. Prior grieving styles and rules must be merged. Parents ignoring this vital project promote stepfamily conflict and eventual re-divorce.*	No equivalent task.
39. Need to resolve minor biological kid(s)' (normal) dreams of biological parent and birth family reunion (logic doesn't count):	*Very common. If unresolved, this dream can block kid(s) accepting a stepparent, and grow stress in the remarriage. Often, a biological parent's remarriage shatters the dream, but not always.*	No equivalent task.
40. Biological parents, biological kid(s), and often biological grandparent(s) really resolve prior divorce guilt and shame ("failure(s)"):	*Required, unless the former mate(s) died. Failure at this task can skew stepfamily co-parenting priorities, inevitably stressing the remarriage(s), over time.*	No equivalent task.

Structural Feature	Average Stepfamilies	Intact Biological Families
41. Stepfamily adults and other members blend their styles of verbal communication and develop effective verbal problem-solving skills together:	*Required. Without mastering this project early, all three to six stepfamily adults are greatly hampered in accomplishing all other tasks in and between their homes.*	Required. Simpler in that only two stepfamily adults need to do this. (Still, many biological couples never do this task well enough.)
42. Dating adults each decide, "Is this the right person to (re)marry? Is this the right time? Am I doing this for the right reasons?":	*Far more complex. The 60-70+% stepfamily re-divorce rate implies that most couples don't evaluate these key questions well enough.*	Simpler. Couples have no kid(s) or ex-mates to consider in answering these questions. (Also less experience.)
43. Stepfamily adults make pre-nuptial agreement decisions:	*More common. Wealthier remarrying couples often want to guard against possible re-divorce asset conflicts and losses. Such contracts can breed distrust, hurt, and resentment.*	Unusual. Most first-time marrying couples aren't wealthy enough to worry about this and don't believe divorce could happen to them. Fifty percent are wrong.
44. (Re)marrying couples plan and hold a commitment ceremony for "the family" and friends:	*More complex. Who should come? Who should "stand up"? No social norms to guide here. Often, major loyalty conflicts arise.*	Simpler. Social norms are much clearer. Usually fewer people— and no biological kids—are involved.
45. All family members adjust to kids', ex-mate(s)', and ex in-laws' reactions to remarriage and cohabiting:	*Required. In some cases, kids, ex-mates, and kin can become hostile, rejecting, or intrusive. In other cases, most or all are supportive.*	No equivalent task.

Structural Feature	Average Stepfamilies	Intact Biological Families
46. Make harmonious dwelling, furnishing, decorating, and space-allocation decisions. Merge physical and financial assets, traditions, rituals, and values.	*Required. "Your home, mine, or a new one?" More people are affected, so these choices are usually more complex, which can cause conflict for members.*	Required. The dwelling is usually new to both mates. Far fewer belongings and assets to choose among.
47. Members resolve personal and family-role name confusions: "What should we call each other"?:	*Required. Often confusing, stressful, and frustrating, in and between linked homes and with kin and friends.*	No equivalent task.
48. Cope with stepfamily co-parenting ex-mate (or key relative) who won't accept the divorce, remarriage, and/or the new stepparent (i.e., frozen grief):	*Frequent. When present, usually the ex felt abandoned and abused, and has major denied childhood deprivations and wounds.*	No equivalent task.
49. Minor step-kid(s)' key task: Test to learn clearly (1) "Am I safe in this family, or will it break up too?"; and (2) "Who's really in charge of this home?":	*Required if step-kid(s) experienced prior parental divorce(s). Appropriate testing is often (wrongly) seen as "acting out," and kids are shamed or punished.*	No equivalent task.
50. Non-custodial biological parent(s) accept that they are missing much of their kid(s)' growing-up events, and that another adult (with different values) is co-raising their kids:	*Required, unless this other biological parent is dead or uninvolved. This biological parent may fight such acceptance (denial), accept and cooperate, or be indifferent and apathetic.*	No equivalent task.

Structural Feature	Average Stepfamilies	Intact Biological Families
51. Non-custodial stepparents cope with frequent guilt, resentment, and sadness that they're stepfamily co-parenting others' child(ren) instead of their own:	*Possible, if adult-child visitations and communications are infrequent, dissatisfying, and/or blocked by others.*	No equivalent task.
52. New mates make conception decision(s):	*Probable, before and/or after re-wedding. Mates are older and the odds are higher that one adult says, "No, I have enough kids." The decision is far more complex. If "yes," new birth(s) may cause three-generation loyalty conflicts.*	Simpler decision. The stepfamily adults are younger, and have far fewer financial issues and other people (e.g., existing step-kids, ex-mates, ex in-laws) who are affected.
53. All three to six stepfamily adults learn and help all dependent kids master the 20 complex, unique developmental tasks in addition to their normal growing-up tasks:	*Required. Stepfamily-identity denials and benign ignorance (most stepfamily adults can't name all these tasks) often hinder caregivers, raising the kid(s)' distress.*	No equivalent task. Biological parents strive to guide minor kids on many normal developmental tasks.
54. All three to six stepfamily adults evolve effective, compatible stepfamily co-parenting role definitions, and agree on stepfamily co-parenting responsibilities and priorities for each dependent child:	*Required. Post-divorce hostilities and distrust, ineffective communication skills, and adults' "benign ignorance" of step norms and unique stepchild tasks, often interfere. This task normally takes years.*	Only two stepfamily adults, so lower odds of conflict. Biological parenting norms are common and far clearer. They're learned over years before the wedding from parents, kin, and society.

STRUCTURAL FEATURE	AVERAGE STEPFAMILIES	INTACT BIOLOGICAL FAMILIES
55. All members satisfactorily resolve a stream of values and priority (loyalty or biological kids and inclusion) conflicts in and between their many linked homes:	*Required. Biological parent(s) must choose their mate "first" enough of the time (vs. putting biological kids, kin, or work first), or the stepparent grows resentful and eventually may re-divorce.*	Uncommon, unless one or both adults have not matured. Often, parenting values are not the key marital conflict.
56. Mates' verbal communication and conflict resolution styles and effectiveness:	*Required. Common conflicts include money, parenting values and priorities, religion, power, time, possessions, sexuality, holidays, etc.*	No equivalent tasks.
57. Making enough quality couple-time to nourish the (re)marriage:	*Often (much) harder, due to more people in the home and more simultaneous tasks.*	Easier, unless one or both mates shun intimacy. Few people and tasks.
58. Financial decisions I: Shall I include your kid(s) in my will? In my health and/or life insurance? Shall I help pay for your kids' education and special needs?:	*Required. Stepparents' decisions here can cause warmth, gratitude, and bonding, or resentment, guilt, or anger in and between stepfamily adults' and linked homes.*	No equivalent task.
59. Financial decisions II: All three to six stepfamily adults agree enough on child support amounts, timing, and allocations. Resolve conflicts cooperatively without putting the minor kid(s) in the middle:	*Required. This is an ongoing complex project that may cause conflict. It requires stepfamily adults' clear priorities, roles, and goals, forgiveness of old prior-family wounds, and shared effective verbal negotiating skills.*	No equivalent task.

STRUCTURAL FEATURE	AVERAGE STEPFAMILIES	INTACT BIOLOGICAL FAMILIES
60. Financial decisions III: (Re)married mates evolve a harmonious way of managing operating funds, investments, and savings plans, and deciding on asset titles (car, homeownership):	*Required. Common options: separate his, her, and our accounts, or one "common-pot" account, his and her savings and investments, or ours. Requires mutual trust and effective verbal communication skills!*	Required, but far simpler. The common choice is "our" checking and savings accounts, investments, and asset ownership.
61. Decision(s) "shall you or I legally adopt (your or my) minor biological kid(s)?":	*Possible. Many emotional and financial complexities. Usually needs absent biological parent's legal okay.*	No equivalent task.
62. All three to six stepfamily adults manage regular and special child visitations with one or two stepfamily co-parenting homes:	*Ongoing, unless the other biological parent(s) is/are dead or "gone." Often until kid(s) is/are late teens, and this may cause much conflict.*	No equivalent task.
63. Stepfamily adults adjust physical and legal child custody and any legal parenting agreements to changing conditions, over time:	*Frequent, unless the other biological parent(s) is/are dead, or all step-kids are grown and on their own. Many causes for adjustment are possible. Often fairly to very conflict-causing, without clear roles, prior losses well grieved, and effective shared verbal skills.*	No equivalent task.

Structural Feature	Average Stepfamilies	Intact Biological Families
64. All members adjust to minor children changing homes, schools, and custodial stepfamily adults:	*Common in about 30% of U.S. stepfamilies. May be unexpected. Can cause major financial, space, privacy, priority, and other changes and conflicts.*	No equivalent task.
65. Settle legal battles between divorced biological parents. Heal related guilt, resentment, hurt, and distrust, over time:	*Common. Conflict sources: child visitations, custody, and financial support, and enforcing prior stepfamily co-parenting agreement(s). Stepparent(s) can add to the turmoil.*	No equivalent task.
66. Build stepparent/stepchild respect (vs. love):	*Required, even if step-kid(s) are grown. Long-term success depends on many things— there's no guarantee. Without mutual respect, stepparent–stepchild discipline is crippled, usually stressing the remarriage.*	No equivalent task. Biological kids may lose respect for and trust in biological caregivers in a dysfunctional home. If parents divorce, this can hinder building trust in stepparent(s).
67. Members cope with social biases, misunderstandings, and probable social isolation:	*Required. Common: "stepfamilies are 'second best,' 'flawed,' 'not as good,' 'weird.'" "We know no other families like ours— we're alone."*	No equivalent task, unless mates form a "non-traditional" (e.g., mixed race or religious/ ethnic/ same sex) family.

STRUCTURAL FEATURE	AVERAGE STEPFAMILIES	INTACT BIOLOGICAL FAMILIES
68. Stepfamily adults break their denials of significant childhood abuses and neglects (deprivations), and steadily pursue personal "recovery":	*Estimate: 75% of stepfamily adults need to do this. This is probably the key to long-term remarriage and stepfamily success for most stepfamily adults.*	Estimate: 50% of biological parents need to do this. Most don't know it and don't want to know it. Promotes first divorce.
69. Stepfamily adults sorting, prioritizing, balancing, and successfully co-managing all these tasks plus "normal living" projects, every day, and making enough time to play, relax, and enjoy their shared family process.	*Ongoing. Far more complex. More alien tasks and higher odds of repeated conflicts and feeling over- whelmed. Keys to success are adults' awareness, matched priorities, effective communication skills, and the time and will to problem-solve together*	Ongoing, but far fewer tasks and people to balance, so lower odds of mates feeling overwhelmed.
70. Re-divorce. All family members resolve guilt, shame, anger, hurt, loss, and fear of trying again over years.	*More likely: 50% of remarried stepfamily adults (and their minor kids) re-divorce within about 10 years of the re-wedding*	**Less likely. About 50% of U.S. first-marriage couples now divorce.**

CHAPTER SIX

ACCEPT YOUR STEPFAMILY IDENTITY
AND WHAT IT MEANS

Stepfamilies *look* pretty much like biological families. They have many common characteristics. And, as you have learned, they also differ in about 60 important ways. There are commonsense things that work in an average biological family that will not work, or will even backfire, in a normal multi-home stepfamily. For example, an earnest stepfamily adult (or co-grandparent) believing they must quickly love their young step-kin just like their own blood will usually stress everyone out, starting with themselves. The reality? Shoot for initial mutual respect.

It is vital that you and all your two to five stepfamily co-parenting partners (ex-spouses included) fully accept that you all will probably never act or feel like a Norman Rockwell, or lesser, biological family. Understandably, if you are a love-dazed, lonely, hopeful dating adult, you don't want to hear this, especially if you are carrying around needy, unhealed wounds. But, the truth is, stepfamilies have bad press. Though they pre-date Moses, they are often linked to wickedness (courtesy Cinderella), failed marriage, and being a weird, abnormal, minority, second-best kind of operation. "Stoep," the centuries-old English root of the prefix "step," means "deprived." Who wants to proudly acknowledge being in a deprived family?

Take heart. Over some years, your stepfamily can *grow* to be a reliable, healing refuge of warmth, contentment, safety, respect, fun, and support. However, to get and savor these rare plums, the earliest challenge for you and your partner—and then your kids, ex-mates, and key relatives—is to clearly accept that together you make up a different kind of normal family: a stepfamily. If you do not accept your true multi-home stepfamily identity in your hearts, you are at great ongoing risk of striving endlessly to be what you are not—a biological family. For most stepfamily adults and minor kids, this becomes increasingly stressful and frustrating. It's like trying desperately to make your poodle be a pony. Real acceptance of your step-identity requires each of you to believe some pretty scary realities, such as:

- Even if you and your partner conceive children, you will probably never all feel the same closeness and togetherness as a healthy three-generation biological family bonded by ancestry, genes, names, memories, looks, ethnic heritage, and traditions. With love, effort, guts, and patience, you can build a shared history, good memories, and a different kind of deep, loving closeness together, over time.

- You and your partner, and your living and unborn kids, really are at high risk for another divorce, unless all of the stepfamily adults involved commit to mastering the "tools" being laid out in this book. If you do them well together, you can make your stepfamily thrive.
- For years to come, all of your kids' living and dead biological parents, and some of their key relatives, will be active members of your multi-home stepfamily. For the good of your kids, you need to honestly consider the needs and opinions of these people in all key stepfamily co-parenting decisions—despite old and recent disputes and wounds.
- Many of your existing biological-family ideas and values about mothering, fathering, and family behavior either will not apply to your new stepfamily, or will actually hurt you and your kids. You must learn together which old ideas fit and which need to be replaced and with what.
- At best, it will probably take you five to eight years after marriage (not just moving in together), to achieve stability and harmony in and between your stepfamily homes. *You will need patience.*
- As normal step-people, you and your stepfamily adult, and your kids and theirs, many never learn to like—let alone love—each other in a biological family way. That can't be helped. No one is wrong or bad. A practical, doable goal is to grow *respect*, over time.
- Custodial or not, your dependent sons and daughters may each have to master the numerous developmental tasks explored in Chapter Five that minor kids in intact two-parent biological families do not have. As their stepfamily adults, you are each responsible for learning clearly what these tasks are, forgiving yourselves and your kin where needed, and lovingly supporting and guiding your girls and boys toward mastering these tasks over many years' time.

Accepting step-realities like these can be especially hard if you have not healed your own wounds. Most of you long deeply for the warm, close, safe family you never had and see idealized in the media every day. Against all logic, your inner child wants your stepfamily to become this dream. You can get part of the dream, but it usually won't feel the way your inner child wants it to. Tune in to your feelings. When you and your partner can each say that in your heart you accept these points, and have well grieved any dreams they replace, you are ready to begin helping all of the other members of your extended stepfamily to accept your common multi-home identity, starting with your minor and grown kids. As they master this, all your members will need to give up some cherished hopes and grieve them in their own time and way. You can help—or not.

Once you all accept that you form a *step*family, your next task is to decide, together, who belongs in your family. Who are "we"? Expect some strong disagreement. Each biological child will count both living biological parents as "my family," and often will not *really* accept their step-kin. Divorced spouses rarely enjoy counting their ex as a full, respected stepfamily co-parenting family member, but that is what they are.

You may feel very uncomfortable partnering with your and/or your mate's ex, or they may become respectful stepfamily co-parenting partners. Ex in-laws may feel half in and half out of the new marriage family, or may endorse and support it fully because of their grandkids. There is much room for disagreement, ambivalence, and outright conflict over who you are, i.e., who your stepfamily really is. Clear-headed, grounded stepfamily adults will expect this and work patiently to build mutual acceptance and family membership for all members. Without this, related stepfamily homes will remain fragmented and conflicted over the coming years.

If any of your adults or kids do accept your stepfamily identity, but intellectualize it, or feel undue shame, guilt, resentment, or anxiety about it, it won't count. A simple test here is to note how comfortable each member is with speaking and hearing titles like "my step-mom," "your stepbrother" and "our stepfamily." Notice how you introduce or talk about each other. Usually given names only and/or avoiding stepfamily titles (or feeling very awkward and uneasy with them) suggest you need more work on this.

Only when committed couples and ex-mates really accept their true multi-home stepfamily identity, can they turn stressful step-myths into well-grounded, realistic family expectations.

Two vital questions that all stepfamily adults need to answer clearly, for the well-being of their home and multi-home stepfamily, are:

1. "Who are we? Who do we include in our definition of 'our stepfamily?' Who *belongs* to us?"
2. "Starting with *our* home, are each of our several related stepfamily homes emotionally healthy enough? Who is *really* running each of our homes now? Whose needs and actions are currently shaping the primary decisions, priorities, and "climate" in each of our homes? Who is directing our whole, multi-home stepfamily show now?"

A visual tool will help stepfamily adults and kids negotiate clear, honest answers to these complex questions, a "genogram".

A genogram is a diagram that shows all the people who genetically and emotionally comprise a family. Some scientists call these maps *sociograms*. They include three or even four generations of family members and show where each person "fits" in the family. With extra information and symbols, a genogram can show alliances, conflicts, emotional splits, and other important data that help describe the family's character. genograms can be especially useful to help new stepfamily members see and clarify "who *are* we?"

Why Make a Genogram?

All stepfamilies are formed after one or more divorces and/or adult deaths, by the merger of two or more multi-generation biological families. This complex blending is usually formalized and catalyzed by remarriage(s). One common result is that 50 to 100+ people in many homes are "suddenly" related by complex combinations of genes, emotions, history, last names, finances, legal obligations and contracts, cultural and ethnic traditions, hopes, needs, and expectations.

For the new stepfamily to function well, many new relationship priorities, a family-wide identity, and many roles, and rules, must be revised or created, over time. Forming a clear, shared, non-conflicting stepfamily identity is an important task, over time, for all the newly joined members.

Both before and after a remarriage, it is common for these many people to be confused and often conflicted about who they each now accept as "my/our *family.*" Often, because of negative associations ("wicked stepmother"), various family members don't want to acknowledge they are in a *step*family. (*"Nah, we're just a regular family now,"* and *"Oh no, that's their family now—not ours!"*) Even if they do acknowledge they are in a stepfamily, divorced adults and/or their new mates often want to reject their kids' other biological parent(s) from belonging to *"our* family."

A grown or dependent new stepchild normally has no strong urge to include a stepparent's kin or kids in "my family" and vice versa. *Half*-siblings can feel especially troubled and confused about whether to include some or all of these *other* kids, and their relatives, in defining *"my* family." Currently, there are no clear social rules to follow.

Conflicts among members over stepfamily inclusion are common. They typically cause relationships rifts, walls, and painful feelings of rejection, abandonment, resentment, and frustration in kids and adults. If unattended, these feelings impede the emotional bonding of the merging stepfamily and stress everyone involved. Stepfamily inclusion and loyalty conflicts usually surface for years after remarriage(s) at child visitations, birthdays, graduations, holidays, vacation, and other special family occasions.

Membership in average biological families and stepfamilies usually includes some key people who are physically or emotionally absent due to death, emotional or physical problems (e.g. Alzheimer's, AIDS), or unresolved feuds (like post-divorce and stepfamily co-parenting impasses). Even if they are not in vocal or written contact, absent people who have significant emotional impact on remarried people's immediate kin should be included in a genogram of their stepfamily. Excluding them distorts the full picture of who the emotional (versus physical) family really is and dilutes the reality, accuracy, and potential value of the genogram.

Biological family memberships shift over time with births, deaths, marriages, divorces, and kids growing up and leaving home. Stepfamily membership definitions shift more often than biological families because of these same factors plus child-custody and residence changes, stepchild adoptions, and rejections. One moral here is: even if all your members are fairly clear and harmonious *now* about stepfamily membership, that may change.

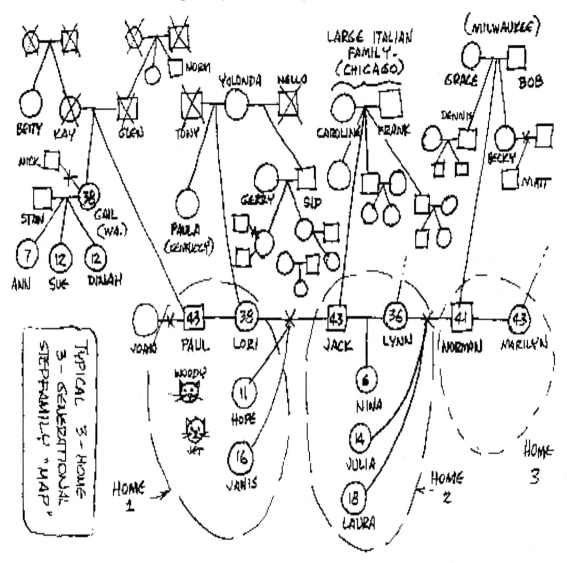

This is a partial genogram of a real six-co-parent, three stepfamily co-parenting-home stepfamily. It shows about half the members. Most information (names, dates, death causes, etc.) is omitted for simplicity. There are over 60 people here, and some are left out.

As you begin your genogram, here are some symbols to use. If these don't fit for you, have some fun inventing your own.

- Use circles for females and squares for males. Crosshatch or color these for people who are extra important to you. Use dashed circles and squares, or slashed or "X'd" symbols, to represent dead people.
- Horizontal solid lines show committed (e.g., remarried) relationships. Use dashed lines to show committed-and-unmarried adult relationships, and friendships and mentorships that are important to you.
- Vertical or slanted *solid* lines show biological (DNA) connections. *Dashed* slanted lines can show adoptions or other special adult-child relationships.
- Zigzag, double, or wavy lines can symbolize strong emotional, legal, financial, or other kinds of current relationship connections, including lust, anger, fear, and "hatred." If helpful, add relationship *polarity* symbols to these connector lines, like "+" and "-" for friendship and hostility.
- Use "X" to show divorce or death, and "---//---" for marital or other relationship separations.
- Include names, dates, pets, extra-important current friends, sponsors, or authorities, major illnesses and disabilities, arrows for child visitations, and any other symbolic or textual information that adds clarity, meaning, and "life" to your map.

Steps and Suggestions

Each stepfamily adult should draw his or her own map of at least three generations. You will discover more if you don't draw these together. Then explain the map-making purpose and steps to your kids (including grown ones) and invite them to draw their own genogram.

You can do this exercise any time and often (over time) in your stepfamily adventure. These maps can be especially useful around major events like weddings (including yours), births, divorces, home-leavings, geographic moves, and deaths.

First, check your initial attitude. Be open-minded and curious and give yourself permission to believe "there's no right or wrong" in anyone's map(s). Everyone has a right to their own opinion and definition. Avoid forcing anyone (including yourself) to include or exclude certain other members; that will only generate resentment and conflict. Other than DNA bonds, stepfamily memberships have to be offered or earned over time, through demonstrated caring, compassion, evolved trust, and shared experiences!

- Expect your members' genograms to disagree with each other. That's normal in typical stepfamilies. No one is wrong or bad. Discovering such differences, without judgment, is the first step toward resolving important identity conflicts among you all, and strengthening your multi-home stepfamily over time.

- Use a <u>BIG</u> piece of paper, flip-chart sized, or at least two 8.5"x11" sheets taped together. These diagrams get very complex.
- Draw your map in three stages: (1) stepfamily adults, (2) minor and grown kids, and then (3) biological and step kin, and other emotionally important people.
- Take your time. Expect that evolving your genogram will take up to an hour or more, perhaps over several sittings. The more undistracted focus and attention you invest in this exercise, the more you will learn.
- Consider journalizing about your map-making *process*. Often, the thoughts and emotions that bloom as you are making this map, and discuss it with others later, are worth the price of admission. *The map itself is not the object here.* The real payoff is what you all feel and learn as you draw and talk about your maps!

Start with all stepfamily co-parenting adults. Lay your paper long-side, horizontal. Start in the center, about one-third from the bottom edge. Use pencil to lightly sketch in a first, three-generation draft. Novice mappers often find that their first drawings are too cramped, and they have to start over to make more room for all the symbols, notes, and other information. Give yourself lots of space.

Draw a circle or square for you, and a short horizontal solid (if married) or dashed line to another symbol for your current partner. Put your current ages inside the symbols, and next to them note all the names you are each called by.

Next, add horizontal solid lines from your symbols to new squares and circles for each of your stepfamily co-parenting ex-mates (if any), whether alive or dead. If you have been married several times, or had children with several adults, show each of your partners. If you are divorced or widowed without biological kids, only include your ex if they, or any of their relatives, have significant emotional (or financial) meaning to you now.

If you are divorced, draw an "X" on the line connecting your symbol to your ex, unless there is still a strong love/hate (or just "hate") relationship. In that case you are still emotionally bonded, a frequent cause for major stress in many stepfamilies! If your former partner has died, draw a slash or "X" through his or her symbol, and note the approximate date and perhaps the cause of death.

If any stepfamily co-parenting ex-mate is seriously dating, cohabiting, or has remarried, add horizontal lines from that ex-mate's symbol to new symbols for his or her current partner. If the ex-mate has re-divorced or split up with an adult who still has emotional importance to any child of yours or your partner's, include that adult's symbol, and anyone related to them who is still emotionally important to your child (or to you.)

Look at what you have drawn so far. This is the "stepfamily adults' row" of your genogram. How many stepfamily adults are there in your stepfamily so far? How many homes do they live in? How do you honestly feel about including each one as an equal co-member of your stepfamily? Take a moment to journal your honest thoughts and feelings, without editing, for later reflection and discussion. Take your time here.

123

Now add all kids. Draw a symbol for each living custodial and non-custodial biological child, about two inches underneath his her custodial biological parent's symbol. If the child is living on his or her own, draw the symbol anywhere below the stepfamily adult row. Include symbols and connector lines for the children's spouses, kids, and/or any current key emotional partners. Put their current age inside their circle or square and note their first name or nickname(s). Add their last name because step-people, even in the same home, often have different last names.

Connect each biological child's symbol with solid, slanted lines to the horizontal line between his or her biological parents. If any custodial child currently visits the home of the other biological parent, add dashed arrows and dashed-line biological child symbols under the other biological parent to show this.

Now add a symbol under the appropriate biological parent(s) for each dead biological child (i.e., aborted, miscarried, stillborn, killed, suicide, and death through illness. Put a slash or "X" though the child's symbol and note the age at death. If the sex of an aborted child was not known use a diamond as a symbol. If you haven't included a symbol for the child's other biological parent, add one now on or near the horizontal stepfamily co-parenting row.

Note the date and cause of the child's death. Each such child is usually an emotionally powerful absent family member, long after his or her death. If such an absent child is well grieved by *all* living DNA relatives, draw his or her symbol with dashed liens, with a slash or "X." If he or she is not well grieved yet, in your opinion, make the symbol-lines solid.

Next, include symbols, full names and ages, for each emotionally important past or current adopted or foster child. Draw separate symbols for both of their birth (biological) parents, *even if they are not currently known or actively stepfamily co-parenting.* They are surely of major emotional importance to this child, even if the importance is repressed or denied.

Double check: look at each adult in your stepfamily co-parenting row (including each stepfamily co-parenting ex-mate's new or recent partner(s)) and ask, "Have we included each known living and dead child of theirs?" Pause for a moment and look at what you have drawn so far. You have just added the "children's row" to your genogram. Note your feelings and any thoughts and questions that come up. Write these down for later reflection. There is more to come. Remember, this is a *discovery* exercise.

Add significant kin and others. Starting with yourself, draw a square-and-circle pair three to four inches above your symbol for your birthparents. Connect these symbols with a solid horizontal line if they were married, or dashed if they weren't. If they divorced or separated, note that with an "X" or "//" on the connector line with the approximate date. If either is dead, put a slash or "X" through the symbol and note the date and cause of death. Add your parents' ages now, or at death, and any nicknames by which they are or were known to you and any grandkids.

If either of our biological parents remarried, or had a child with another partner, draw symbols and solid or dashed connectors for each of those adult partners and children. Add their names and ages, and any other information you feel is relevant to represent them.

Below the horizontal connector line linking your biological parents' symbols, draw down slanted solid lines to new circles and squares for each of your living and dead DNA brothers and sisters. Locate them about one-third of the way between the grandparents' row and your stepfamily adults row. If these siblings are or were married, add symbols and connectors for each of their partners, and each living and dead child of theirs. These are your kids' aunts, uncles, and cousins—and your step-kids' step-relatives. Add full names and nicknames, ages, and any other relevant information like major illnesses, disabilities, addictions, "in college," or "in the Army."

Now, repeat this multi-level "ancestor" step of your genogram for each of your stepfamily adults, one at a time. Stay focused on the goal here, for this can feel tedious and overwhelming: *your aim is to represent all the people who comprise the web of emotionally important relationships that currently form your whole multi-home, multi-generation stepfamily.*

Stand in the imaginary shoes of your stepfamily adult and ask yourself honestly, "Who do I count as my DNA and emotional family now—even living and dead relatives I 'hate' or have no relationship with?" Add names, ages, and any other relevant information. Include any forth-generation people, like great-grandmothers or great-uncles, of high current emotional significance to any stepfamily adult or child, whether living or dead.

Final check. One at a time, slip into the skin, mind, and heart of each biological and stepchild. Ask, "Is *everyone* I care strongly about, or have strong feelings about, on this map now?" If any people are missing, even if *you* don't feel they belong, add symbols and connector lines for them now.

If you are satisfied that everyone who is an emotionally significant member of your stepfamily, as judged by each stepfamily adult and each grown and dependent child (not just yourself), is included now, *darken the lines of all symbols and connectors with a pen or soft pencil.* The *structure* of your stepfamily map is now done. Once again, pause and note your emotions and "inner voices." Try for *objective*, thorough awareness, as though you were a reporter or scientist. This awareness is the real fruit of this endeavor.

Options. For a finishing touch, you may add some special notations for genogram "depth." For instance, use different colored pens or markers to circle or note: individual stepfamily members who are not currently accepted and included by you; individual members who are not currently accepted by other stepfamily members; strong antagonisms (use "lighting" lines to connect their symbols) or alliances (use double-parallel connector lines) between certain members; people who do not want to be included in your stepfamily now; members who need to deny, or do not fully realize yet, that you all *are* a normal multi-home, multi-generation *step*family; adult and child family members who may not, or surely have not, mourned the loss(es) of their prior families; and, the person(s) you feel wield(s) the most power in your stepfamily—who *"leads"* this multi-home family now, if anyone.

Keep in mind that a final, powerful use for your genogram will be for assessing how "functional" or emotionally healthy the birth-family of each of your stepfamily adults was.

Doing this thoroughly and honestly produces a strong indicator of how holistically healthy your present home and your whole stepfamily are now.

Using your genogram. These family maps are tools for *discovering, learning, planning,* and *teaching.* Discover and learn what?

- Who *are* we all?
- What does the term "family" mean to me/us now?
- How do we differ in composition from a typical biological family? ("What does a multi-home *step*family look like?")
- How likely is it that we *all* will ever feel like a unified, bonded, multi-home stepfamily?
- What would have to happen to promote that? Who should make that happen?
- Do full-time and part-time residents in our current home have very different definitions of "who comprises our stepfamily?" If so, how does that affect me/us? Do I feel something should be done about that? What, when, and by whom? What will probably happen if that "something" doesn't get done?
- What (specifically) do I need to learn from, or tell my partner about, what this map means?
- Is there any child or adult family member I feel uneasy about showing this map to, or asking to draw their own? Am I reluctant to compare and discuss our genograms with anyone? Is my partner? What's the discomfort about? "Discomfort" is probably a code for "anxiety" or "fear." If I or we don't resolve this "discomfort," what may happe, over time?
- How did I *feel* evolving this genogram? How did my partner? What does that mean?

To use your genogram as a *planning* tool, decide, after honest discussion with your other stepfamily adults, if there are now excluded (or rejected members. If so, decide if you all feel it would help your family as a whole (especially the kids) to offer them inclusion. In a practical sense, that amounts to inviting them to family gatherings (out of desire, not "duty"), informing them of key family events, and considering their needs and feelings in making key household and stepfamily decisions.

Keep your perspective: just as real friendships take years to grow and mature, feeling like a real family cannot be rushed or dictated. It is a sense that may or may not occur among some or all of your emotionally linked members after years of small and large shared events. If there are people who need to deny that you are all a *step*family, or need to reject membership in it, they are probably blocked in grieving some major divorce, death, and/or remarriage losses.

One big advantage of this diagram is that it can be used to teach certain members, friends, and even some professionals, that you are a multi-home *step*family. If stepfamily adults, kids, and/or key relatives do not fully accept this, they probably hold stressful biological family expectations of themselves and each other. They will also be unmotivated and will resist learning and accepting what is normal in a stepfamily. Understanding that stepfamilies differ from typical biological families in specific ways can greatly help stepfamily adults and kids avoid conflicts within and between themselves and each other.

What would happen if on some special occasion you mailed a copy of your genogram to every stepfamily member, with an appropriate note or letter? What if you invited *everyone* to assemble and meet each other? (Notice with interest what your inner voices have to say about that idea!)

How does family "loyalty" and "identity" build, over time? Did these exist in your biological family? Your first-marriage family? How has that affected you and your personal identity? How will the youngest kids in your stepfamily be affected if you all never develop a clear stepfamily identity ("We're the O'Rourke-Jacobsen-Miller clan, and proud of it!")?

When you feel "done" making and thoroughly discussing your genogram, put it where you can find it in the future. Comparing it to a future version can yield helpful insights about the progress of your identity formation, however *you* define that.

Another visual tool that can help you understand the nature of your stepfamily is a "structural" map. Peter Gerlach gratefully acknowledges Chicago therapist/teacher and Executive Director & co-founder of The Center for Contextual Change, Ltd., Mary Jo Barrett, MSW, for introducing him to this useful concept.

Stepfamily Structural Maps

One way of seeing the holistic health of any family is to diagram, or map, how it is structured *emotionally*. How this map is drawn is not important. The importance is the thinking that goes into it. Structure refers here to: who's included in the family—or might be; who's really in charge of any member's home, if anyone; relationship inclusions, exclusions, and emotional distance patterns; family-member alliances and oppositions; and, communication flows and blocks.

Stepfamily structural mapping is a relatively quick, win-win project. It identifies and validates what is strong about your stepfamily, and visually identifies structural things to improve.

Once completed, study and change them to fit your beliefs and situation better, if needed. Then try mapping your multi-home stepfamily at least twice: before and during child visitations, if any. Note any major structural changes that visitations cause. Discuss your observations and feelings with your stepfamily co-parenting partner(s). Invite the kids in your family to try mapping, too. Another option is to map your stepfamily homes before and after your (or someone's) remarriage. Stay focused! Like genograms, this is an *awareness* exercise, not a contest or a weapon!

Recall that all stepparents and custodial and non-custodial biological parents are stepfamily adults. In an average (post-divorce) stepfamily, there can be three to six stepfamily adults telling various minor kids what to do in two or three related homes ("ours, your ex mate's, and my ex's). In stepfamilies following a biological parent's death, there can be two or more stepfamily adults. In some homes, older siblings regularly share stepfamily co-parenting responsibilities for younger kids.

These structural maps are built on some basic ideas about the emotional health of stepfamilies. See if you agree with each of these beliefs (and add your own).

~ The Idea ~

1. A truly healthy or functional family's key purpose is to provide a reliable, safe haven, where every member feels consistently included, valued, respected, supported, and encouraged to develop and use his or her unique talents. Families that do not provide these consistently, or at all, to all their members can be called *dysfunctional.* The less the family provides, the greater the dysfunction.

2. Holistic (emotional, physical, and spiritual) family health is a continuum from low to high. Some families and households are more healthy, or functional, than others. Also, the same family or home can become more or less holistically healthy, over time.

3. The main factor determining a given home's or family's degree of holistic health is the combined personal holistic health of the home's or family's main leader(s). Because typical multi-home stepfamilies have three to six or more co-leaders, there are higher odds that the whole multi-home family is significantly dysfunctional than in an intact two-parent, one-home biological family. We believe that the stepfamily adult(s) living in each home are responsible for the emotional health of all *full-time* residents, over time. Do you?

4. A stepfamily adult may be a *biological* parent (who passes on genes), a *psychological* parent (who does child-nurturing things), or both.

5. A stepfamily includes **all** people regularly living in the one to three-plus homes of all step-kids' living biological parents, and **all** of their kids and current primary partners are members of the same multi-home stepfamily—*even if some are currently uninvolved or rejecting.* This means that a complete structural map of the whole *nuclear* stepfamily (excluding relatives) should include two or three stepfamily co-parenting homes.

6. Resident stepfamily adults should consistently make the major decisions and rules, and enforce consequences (co-manage) their home; this should not be done by a powerful child, relative, ex-mate, outsider, or no one.

7. The primary *adult* relationship in any healthy stepfamily adult home should consistently be that between the cohabiting stepfamily adults, not a stepfamily adult and a child, an ex mate, an activity (like work), or another adult. The less this is true over time, the less holistically healthy the home, the weaker the whole stepfamily, and the higher the odds that minor kids will eventually suffer another stepfamily adult re-divorce trauma.

8. For true holistic health, all individual home and multi-home stepfamily members, including stepfamily co-parenting ex-mates, should usually feel: (1) included *enough*

in key family decisions that affect them, (2) respected by other members *enough,* (3) safe *enough,* and (4) clearly heard ("open communications").

9. Stepfamily adults should generally share responsibility and authority for major individual and multi-home stepfamily decisions, with input from **all** relevant members where possible. *In new step-homes, biological parents (ideally) should do most of the disciplining of their kids until the stepparent earns appropriate respect and authority.*

10. Generally, the emotional and physical "boundaries" separating all persons, couples, and homes comprising the stepfamily should be clear and pretty consistent. Boundaries are conscious and unconscious inner decisions and reactions ("rules" or "limits") which define how close a child or adult will let someone else get to them, emotionally and physically. Boundaries also define what an individual will and won't tolerate from someone else. They are set by *words* (e.g., "No, I won't do that," and "Sure, glad to") and related actions.

    When two or more people are too emotionally entangled (i.e., having weak or no emotional boundaries), they are said to be "enmeshed" or "codependent." The opposite condition, excessive emotional detachment or distance between two or more family members, is called "disengagement." If excessive, neither of these conditions promotes personal, household, or family-wide holistic health. Adults unhealed from traumatic childhoods often tend to have one trait or the other, and unsuccessful relationships.

    In healthy stepfamilies, stepfamily adults (vs. kids, other, or no one) guide the setting of key boundaries within and between their related step-homes.

11. Available biological and step grandparents and relatives should support, rather than control or hinder, the stepfamily adults' marriages, homes, and multi-home stepfamily bonding and growth.

12. All stepfamily adults in a stepfamily should consistently strive for a multi-home united front in key decisions about, and the guidance of, minor step-kids. The less this exists, the more stressed all members feel (especially the kids), and the greater the stepfamily's dysfunction.

13. Unlike intact two-biological parent homes, most step-homes with resident minor kids have two or more different structural states: non-visitation and visitation. If both remarried mates have prior kids and living ex-mates (a blended three-home stepfamily), the home "in the middle" may have three or more visitation structures or states of which one may be functional and another very dysfunctional.

14. If all of the stepfamily's stepfamily adults are (a) clear on their respective beliefs about stepfamily health, (b) able to effectively resolve any major belief-differences between them, and (c) act consistently on their beliefs together as a team, they are more likely to build a holistically healthy multi-home stepfamily. Where all stepfamily adults *cannot* do these, members feel emotionally stressed, and the risk of eventual re-divorce rises.

Spend some undistracted time reviewing these core beliefs with your stepfamily co-parenting partners. Mull over your reality on the 14th premise. Have you ever thought about and identified your own "family-health" beliefs? Learned your partner's beliefs? Considered alternative beliefs? Be aware (and beware): if any of your stepfamily adults' key family-health beliefs are biological family-based, they may be toxic to your stepfamily.

Okay, now we have a foundation on which to build stepfamily homes, including yours.

Family structure maps use family members' names or initials, cartoon figures, face, or any other appropriate symbols. Be creative and inventive—doing these maps can be fun, as well as instructive. Consider using color markers or pens, too—whatever makes the diagrams clearer for everyone. We will start with maps of holistically healthy families (going with the ideas above). Then we will see some of the many kinds of dysfunction, for both biological families and typical multi-home stepfamilies. Again, the purpose of these maps is to visually show, in a simple, concise way, whether a given family or household is emotionally healthy or dysfunctional. *Don't use structural maps to expose, attack, or ridicule any member(s).* Do use them to provide an effective tool to help discuss and improve your family's structural and holistic health.

Baseline: A healthy two-parent biological family (emotional) structure

BioMom and BioDad are co-equally in charge of their home. Communication is open between all adults and minor kids. Family roles are clear. Kids are encouraged to be kids, rather than little adults. No interfering relatives or other people. No one is demoted, excluded, exalted, absent, enmeshed, or addicted. Household emotional boundaries are open, i.e., friends, kin, and ideas freely enter and leave.

Typical dysfunctional two-parent biological family structures

Dominant BioMom, blocked parental communications. Detached or absent biological father, blocked parental communications. Blocked parent-child communications, parents enmeshed. Child co-controlling the home, biological father ineffective. BioMom's dead mom controls the home, parents can't talk.

Or, two uninvolved biological parents, teen controls the home, no family boundaries. Overwhelmed mom, detached dad, BioAunt in charge. Rigid (closed) household boundaries. Enmeshed dad and controlling child, no parental teamwork or problem-solving. Enmeshed mom and (non-resident) BioUncle, dad dead but still key, kids unheard.

Or, regressed or overwhelmed biological parents. Nobody consistently in charge of the home. All family members isolated from outsiders.

Or, similar to the above, including a resident biological relative. Everyone enmeshed and chaotic, no personal boundaries, no clear family roles. Mates have no private time or space. Adults equal buddies, not parents.

How would you map the family that you grew up in? Over time, it probably had several key structures. Family structures change each time someone is born, dies (including abortions and stillbirths), leaves home, reaches puberty, becomes seriously ill or injured, gets married, and so on.

Typical dysfunctional two-home divorced biological family structure

BioMom has legal and physical custody, and controls her home. Regular child visitation with absent biological father, who is in charge of his home when the kids come to stay, but communications with his kids are blocked. Ongoing two-way hostility and poor communications between biological parents, with the kids caught in the middle.

Or, custodial BioDad enmeshed (emotionally *un*-divorced) with ex mate (via phone and visits), ineffective problem-solving, isolated, discounted step-mom.

Or, no effective stepfamily adult listening or problem-solving. Hostility and distrust, kids feel unheard by both adults.

Or, BioMom plus resident biological grandmother alliance. Step-dad undermined, ignored, and withdrawn.

Or, favored "ours" child. Resident half-siblings hurt and resentful, acting out.

Or, BioMom hasn't mourned her first mate's death, and can't help her kids do so. Her dead husband strongly affects the decisions in this home. Step-dad is increasingly resentful.

Or, two-home system where there is an emotionally unfinished divorce. Kids in the middle, polarized, rejecting step-mom. Step-mom resentful, feels unsupported, biological father denies they are a stepfamily or that there is a major loyalty conflict.

Or, all kids feel unsafe and confused, stepfamily adults often defensive, no three-home unity. Getting the idea?

There are many variations of their two-home split biological family, considering who is in charge in each home; the numbers, ages, and "parentification" of older kids; the availability and involvement of nurturing kin; and, how the "sending" home restructures if some of the kids leave, but some stay. The custodial biological parent is often overwhelmed and may "promote" an older child to co-control the home. Or else they may hire daycare or live-in help (who then should be included in any structural map).

If divorced, what did (or does) *your* two-home split biological family structure look like? Does it have several structures? Who is (was) in charge of each home when the kids were there? We have explored many ways multi-home stepfamily structures can be diagrammed. Time to try your wings!

A few preliminary suggestions:

- Stay focused. Biological, step, and other forms of family exist *primarily* to conceive and foster the healthy growth of dependent children. Of course they fill important adult needs for nurturing, procreation, shelter, comfort, and love, too. Focus your maps on understanding how the *emotional* structure of your stepfamily homes affect the ongoing welfare of (1) your remarriage(s), and (2) each of your dependent kids.
- Take your time. These maps are often complex, and can reveal insights and surprises only if you really concentrate thoughtfully on them. Build them slowly and deliberately, and they will pay off for you all.
- If you have not done your genogram first and formed a consensus on "who do we include in our multi-home stepfamily?" making *useful* structural maps will be hard or impossible. If you or any of your stepfamily co-parenting partners need to deny or minimize that you *are* a *multi*-home stepfamily, don't expect to get much from any of these maps.
- Draw these maps by yourself, not with your stepfamily co-parenting partner(s). You will discover more. Expect your map(s) to evolve through trial and discussion rather than expecting to "get it right the first time." Keep a large eraser handy, and sketch lightly until you have thought, mulled, and discussed together, *enough*. False starts are great here.
- Approach the process with the positive attitude of "doing this may lead to helping our remarriage, home, kids, and stepfamily," rather than adopting mind sets of anxiety, defensiveness, indifference, or attack. Catch the constructive spirit of these maps and invent your own rules. You are doing this to help and please yourselves, no one else.
- If you or a stepfamily co-parenting partner feels reluctant to do this exercise, what does that mean? That is a helpful learning by itself. We guess it means you or they have some anxiety, guilt, or shame about your present home and/or stepfamily that you do not want to confront right now.

As you have learned in Part One, *avoiding* is a common coping skill unhealed adults developed early in life to keep yourselves in less pain. Unfortunately, the risk here is that deferring painful stepfamily awareness often means it will get worse with time.

As with genograms, consider writing down any thoughts and feelings that surface both as you (1) evolve your structural maps, and (2) compare and discuss them with other members. Such journalizing can give you concrete information to draw comparisons if you map again in the future, a way of clearly affirming family growth and positive change (or lack of).

Starting With Your Home

Begin with a rough draft. Think of the people regularly living in (not just visiting) your home. You will do other maps on your child-visitation home and stepfamily structures later. Lightly draw a horizontal "stepfamily adult responsibility" line on a blank page. Now decide: "among all our stepfamily members, whose needs, opinions, and drives usually directly and indirectly affect the minor kid(s) in our home the most?" To put it bluntly: "who *really* runs the stepfamily co-parenting part of our home?"

Stay open to the possibility that the person(s) *really* running your house may be dead, or alive and living elsewhere. They may be one or more adults; a scared, depressed, or enraged child; a powerful relative; an absent biological parent; or some combination. They may also control everyone else by choosing to be over-helpless and a "victim." Remember, this exercise is not aimed at finding fault with anyone. It is about discovering what *is*.

Tentatively, put initials for the one or more "in charge" people above the line. Try to avoid preconceived expectations ("well, of course both of us resident adults are equally in charge here"). Of those above the line, is there one who is more in charge than another?

For example, it is common that in a new step-home, the resident (and maybe absent) biological parent has more authority over live-in and visiting biological kids than the resident stepparent. Or, a strong-willed, outspoken, or acting-out child, relative, or ex-mate may strongly influence the decisions in your home. If so, draw a shorter horizontal line above the responsibility line and put the name or initials of this "strongest" person above this line. If any home-leader is dead, put his or her name in parentheses or a circle.

Consider this "membership" spot check. Many homes are strongly influenced by certain members' spiritual beliefs. Such members' relationship decisions and boundaries are often affected by their deep belief in, and relationship with, a personal Higher Power. If this is true now in your home, find a way to symbolize the influence of such a *spiritual* home-structure member, e.g., {God}.

Also, many two-career homes hire part-time or even live-in childcare help. If you regularly use a nanny, babysitter, relative, neighbor, or other childcare provider to help parent any of your minor kids, decide how you want to add these individuals to your household's structural diagram. They *are* affecting your child(ren)'s welfare!

In the same vein, consider any professional counselors who are important to any regular member of your house. Psychological, financial, school, sports, or career counselors, clergy, lawyers, and medical professionals are affecting the emotional state of your members. How do you want to note their presence and "rank" in your current emotional structure?

Now consider each adult regularly living in your home (including grown biological kids) and pick a place on your diagram for them. Options include: (1) an active co-equal leader above the line; (2) a dominant leader above other members with some stepfamily co-parenting authority; (3) an emotionally regressed, overwhelmed, sick, or withdrawn role below the line (little or no authority or active influence on household activities); and (4) an emotionally detached—or passively ignored—stepfamily co-parenting role.

Now add each resident minor child by name or initials: where do they usually fit in your home's emotional structure (in non-visitation mode)? Common options: (1) co-equally below the line; (2) above the stepfamily co-parenting responsibility line, perhaps even running the whole home; (3) emotionally excluded, withdrawn, or detached; and (4) dominated by one or more other resident kid(s), a scapegoat or black sheep role.

You may notice that some kids may rise and fall above and below the stepfamily adult responsibility line (or a "scapegoat" line), depending on who is (or is not) at home or what is happening. Draw each child in their main place in your home or consider drawing several structures. Don't forget to include any unborn kids who are on the way—they probably have a BIG effect on your emotional structure! It may also be appropriate to include dead children who have not been well-grieved by all regular members of your home. They still influence some members.

Add communications factors. Once you have placed all residents in their main emotional position in your home's structure, focus on whether each regular resident can communicate "openly" or not in this (non-visitation) emotional structure. Think first about the adult couples (hopefully) above the stepfamily co-parenting line: does each adult *usually* feel: (1) Safe enough to say clearly and honestly what they currently *feel, need,* or *want*? (2) Respectfully *listened to* (not just agreed with)? And, (3) If these both are true, are these people able to discuss and *really resolve mutual conflicts* often enough (in your opinion)?

If they, or any two people on your diagram, can meet these three conditions, it is likely that they have generally effective ("open") communications. If they often don't meet these three conditions, draw a vertical line between them to symbolize a communications block. Use color for emphasis. If you feel a major trait of your home is that stepfamily adults and kids can't meet these three conditions regularly (now), make the main horizontal stepfamily co-parenting line solid. Who is responsible for removing any verbal communication block in your home?

Ponder whether you feel prayer or meditation is significant "communication" with important, absent real or spiritual members of your home. Also consider phone, e-mail, "chat" sessions (Internet), and written-letter patterns of communication, and their absences. They all count!

Add coalitions and antagonisms. Now you have members of your home located and family verbal communication factors symbolized. A final aspect of your home's emotional structure is any especially intense emotional polarization between certain members. These can be an unusually strong bond or closeness between adults and/or kids. Note such regular alliances by circling the partners, using "+" or other clear notation.

Sadly, dislike, distrust, rejection, indifference, and antagonism are common in and between average stepfamily homes. Be honest about acknowledging any such relationships regularly affecting your home's basic emotional climate (map what *is*, so that you can solve the problem).

Use "lightning lines, slashes, "x"s, or any other symbols to show conflicted members. Obviously, such relationships rarely feature *effective* verbal communication.

Add home boundaries. As a final option, ask yourself, "what's the unspoken rule that currently governs this home: are new people, customs, and ideas usually welcome here? Do the adults invite friends and relatives to visit fairly often? Are the kids' friends consistently welcome and do they feel comfortable visiting this home? Are the people in this home usually interested in the world, and in different customs, beliefs, and new ideas? Are our adults selectively open with some trusted people in sharing important aspects of our family and household life?

If you feel most of these are true, then the emotional and social boundaries of your home are open. Draw a dashed square or circle around everyone in the home to symbolize this. This implies that someone in the home sets these open boundaries (limits). Who?

If there were no boundaries, all kinds of other kids and adults would be free to enter the home, use the resources there, and leave when they wanted. Strangers, old lovers, remote kin would come and go without restraint. There would be no sense of privacy. If the adults in this house freely tell acquaintances or strangers intimate details of their relationships and home life, and encouraged their kids to do the same, the home would have no "container," no "us-ness." *Such homes are often seriously dysfunctional.*

At the opposite end of the spectrum, the adults silently or openly decree that new people, ideas, and beliefs are not to be trusted and are not welcome to cross the threshold. Kids are told rigidly who they can invite in or be with. It's clear that "people who act and believe differently (than we do) are wrong, untrustworthy, or bad. Such distrusting adults often rigidly enforce the rule "our family's affairs are nobody else's business, we don't talk_about ourselves with others!" Not freely describing yourselves as one of a set of linked stepfamily homes is a form of this. Such homes may be said to have *closed* emotional and social boundaries. If yours often seems to be like that, draw a solid circle or rectangle around it.

When adults feel an unusually high need for personal and household privacy, the prevailing emotional climate inside their home is often tension, anxiety, guilt, distrust, and repressed anger. Over time, this infuses the personalities and attitudes of any resident minor kids. Where post-divorce distrusts and wounds haven't really healed in and between ex-mates, the adults often unconsciously erect rigid emotional boundaries between their homes. Their kids are often caught in the middle. Insecure stepparents can promote similar distrusts and boundaries, or can feel increasingly conflicted and stressed because of them.

Final check. Look at the symbols and relationships you have created to show your home's (non-visitation) *emotional structure.* Stand in the imaginary shoes of each of your regular residents, one at a time. Would they agree that they and the other members seem to fit where you have mapped them? If you are unsure, sketch some other combinations and see how they feel. Come back in an hour or several days and scan again. Evolve your best fit. Avoid being perfect!

Add other stepfamily adults' homes. Now, on the same page repeat the same diagramming process you have just done, with all regular adult and child residents in the household of each of your stepfamily co-parenting partners. Include the home of each living stepfamily adult emotionally important to each of your minor biological and stepchildren, including biological parents you rarely hear from. These adults do help shape the emotional life and welfare of their biological kids, and so affect the emotional climate in your home and remarriage. Remember, you haven't begun mapping your homes during child visitations yet.

Do the same assessments and notations for special (spiritual, unborn, dead, absent, and professional) members; verbal communication blocks; key relationship alliances, and social and emotional boundaries. *Take your time mapping each home: the more time you take, the more awareness you will harvest.*

When you have finished this set of diagrams, be aware of your thoughts and how you feel. Write about these, without editing anything. See what happens.

Special variations. You have finished your baseline multi-home structural maps now. The next step is to evolve other structural maps for some special conditions. These include:

- Child visitation times.
- Child support "times of the month."
- Family celebrations.
- And, unresolved family conflicts.

Typical intact (one-home) biological families do not experience the first two of these. When average stepfamily homes experience any of these four, they usually undergo major structural (role and relationship) changes. Members typically feel extra stressed—or relieved if they gain privacy and quiet. If the stepfamily adults do not all cooperate, communicate, and try to problem-solve together, the emotional structures of their homes usually corrode remarriages and stunt stepfamily bonding over time.

Let's look briefly at each of these four special situations.

Child Visitation

When step-kids go to see or stay with their other biological parent, the emotional structure of both the sending and receiving homes changes. The network of emotional roles, priorities, activities, and relationships within each household shifts, either immediately or as time goes on. Who's "in charge" of each home may change a little or a lot. Resident kids may be "demoted" in importance or feel pleased with new co-equal playmates. Stepparents may feel ignored and resentful, as their biological parent mate focuses on visiting biological kid(s) (or dumps them on the stepparent). Conflict and chaos may erupt "endlessly" over child discipline styles, values, and preferences.

Stepparents and stepsiblings may feel "invaded" by visiting kids, while the visitors feel like strangers and invaders. Communication blocks, alliances, and rejections can bloom quickly or with time. Insecurities can activate, causing some members to demote themselves in the household structure. Child and/or adult scapegoats may appear. Certain adults or kids may withdraw emotionally or physically, or be rejected. These all may be triggered, amplified, or healed by phone calls with people remaining in the sending home.

Structural shifts in sending and receiving homes may differ between weekend visitations, week-long vacations together, and summer-long visitations. If any period of visitation time includes birthdays, anniversaries, or holidays, unique home restructurings may occur.

Depending on how many related homes you have, how many dependent minor kids, and how their various visitation schedules overlap and interact, you may have one or several different structural scenarios to map here. Experiment, using the same symbols and conventions you used for your non-visitation diagrams. Try for an attitude of *curiosity* and *wonder,* rather than blame or defensiveness. Once again, these maps are meant to be learning tools, not weapons.

Child Support Times

Another stepfamily factor that can cause a significant shift in both the sending and receiving homes' emotional structures is money. The basic issue is whether (some) stepfamily adults and kids are conflicted or not over the amount, timeliness, usage, attached conditions, and perceived fairness of child-support payments. If payments are late, or amounts disputed, stepfamily adults can fight in and between homes, and minor kids can be used as spies, weapons, threat-bearers, or victims.

Some stepfamilies have little or no conflict over these, while others (without effective stepfamily adult leadership and problem-solving skills) are increasingly driven and in turmoil. Biological and step relatives can get polarized and become involved. Such reactions may happen rhythmically every month or just occasionally (e.g., when special expenses arise or new wills are made).

Some stepfamily homes have both incoming and outgoing child support, at different times of the month or the same. Other homes have only a one-way flow. Some stepfamily adults have powerful, unfinished divorce-era stress attached to child-support payments due and received, so the stress cycles (and restructurings) that arise are about more than just current responsibilities and amounts.

One at a time, think of each child in your multi-home stepfamily for whom child support is due and/or paid. Considering the variables above, experiment with different structural maps of both sending and receiving homes, starting with yours, when funds are due and received. What do you discover? Pay special attention to whether communication blocks appear within and/ or between your homes, and whether certain family members withdraw, conflict, and/or shift positions above or below the stepfamily adult responsibility line.

Try journalizing about your thoughts and feelings as you focus on these particular stepfamily restructurings. If you have few or no emotional changes due to child-support stress, congratulations (or, you are in major denial)!

Celebrations and Conflicts

Other kinds of events that can cause major emotional step-home restructurings are regular and special celebrations, and unique or cyclic relationship conflicts. National and ethnic holidays, birthdays, weddings, funerals, graduations, retirements, births, christenings or Bar (or Bat) Mitzvahs, moving out of state, and the like, are usually emotionally charged family events. Their degree of emotional importance varies by family member, custom, and household. Typically, new stepfamilies normally have many unclear and conflicting values and priorities—and poor communication—over "who's to do what, when?" at these special times. Therefore, their household emotional structures commonly shift (perhaps chaotically) until "real life" resumes.

One of the most likely triggers of stepfamily stress at these times is if some members have not yet reached a stable consensus on "who *are* we as a family?" Depending on the nature and impact of the celebration, sometimes the structural shifts (e.g. relationship rejections and exclusions) become permanent. Once again, it often takes five to eight years of annual celebration (and vacation) cycles to begin to forge clear, stable expectations in and among all stepfamily co-parenting homes about "who's to do what, when?".

Another factor that can increase the structural impact of celebrations is whether the celebrating kids and grownups have grieved prior family and personal losses well enough. If they have not, stepfamily celebrations tend to be more painful, stressful, and confusing. The more people who are blocked in their grief, the greater the stepfamily's emotional polarizing.

The other major class of events that trigger big emotional restructuring of related step-homes is one-time or recurring conflicts between stepfamily adults, and/or stepparents and step-kids. Typical kinds of stepfamily conflicts that often cause big stepfamily relationship shifts are:

- Stepfamily adult court battles over child visitation, custody, or financial support. Legal battles can also erupt over enforcing or changing prior parenting agreements between divorced biological parents. These legal agreements are often forged in times of intense upset and conflict, and usually do not anticipate or fit multi-home stepfamily realities.
- Stepchild adoptions (by stepparents), stepfamily adults' wills and estate plans, and disagreements over the responsibilities and amounts of insurance coverage.
- Unresolved emotional cutoffs (unhealed hurts and angers, and communication stoppages) among former in-laws or biological kin.

- And, stepfamily adult loyalty conflicts. These are intense, ongoing values disagreements between biological and stepparents living together over the primacy of their relationship. When biological parents cannot find compromises, and can't spontaneously put their remarriage before their biological kids most times, stepparents grow increasingly disillusioned and resentful, withdraw or confrontational, and may ultimately find a way to cause re-divorce if their partner will not change.

The keys to "fixing" these predictable step-home and family restructurings depends on the stepfamily adults' motivation, knowledge and task awareness, and building *effective* problem-solving skills together.

Think about recurring specific holidays that emotionally affect your home and whole stepfamily. Using structural map symbols and conventions, sketch diagrams for all involved stepfamily adult homes that fit each of these times. Then review the list of reasons for typical step-stress above. List any "regular" stress in your and/or other stepfamily adults' homes, and map your homes' emotional structures when those conflicts are at their peak (in your opinion).

Using Your Structural Maps

Once you have invested time and energy to evolve these maps of your stepfamily, what can you do with them? Some options include:

1. Ask at least your stepfamily co-parenting partner to evolve his or her own sets of structural maps. Then compare and discuss them cooperatively, not combatively or defensively. You are all on new ground here, so give yourselves permission to not be perfect family leaders right off the bat. Go for progress, not perfection!

2. Consider explaining these mapping symbols and conventions to your older kids or provide simplified versions to younger ones. Have them draw certain structural maps (like the "baseline" and "visitation" homes) in the theme of exploration and creative learning, not "do it *right!*" If your kids trust that you and other members will not criticize or reject their renditions, their creativity and insight will teach you valuable information and give you all food for helpful discussions.

3. Show some of these maps to selected relatives—or any professionals (e.g., clinicians) you are using—to enhance their awareness of your stepfamily homes, relationships, and dynamics. Their constructive feedback can also add rich perspective (and some worthy reality checks) to your perception of your stepfamily's structures. Like genograms, these structural maps are powerful visual teaching tools for people who are not used to seeing stepfamilies as complex multi-home, multi-parent systems.

4. Consider adding some structural mapping terms to the way you all discuss (and problem-solve) events in your home(s). For example, after mapping and discussion,

some families start saying things like "s/he's above (or below) the line," and "there's a communication wall between Jack and Nita," as *non-blaming* ways of giving family feedback. If all members understand what "enmeshment," "alliances" and "exclusions" are (within a family-structure context), you will all have clearer language and more problem-solving tools together.

5. Redo these maps on your anniversaries, *without looking at the old diagrams.* Then compare old and new versions to see what has change, and what more you want to change.

6. If you are ever in a support group for stepfamily adults, consider having everyone make genograms and structural maps. Then use them, and the mapping process, as rich discussion topics together.

For productive discussions with yourself and with other people, here are some specific questions to explore:

- "How many stepfamily adults do we have in our stepfamily? How many homes do they live in now? Do they all accept they belong to the same multi-home stepfamily? If not, how is that affecting our minor kid(s)? What specific difference might it make if all our stepfamily adults acknowledged that we are all in this together, for years to come?"

- "In this house, and in our whole stepfamily, what are our specific structural strengths?" For example: Our stepfamily adults are solidly in charge of (a certain, or all) home(s). No one regularly feels excessively excluded or ignored. Verbal communications between various people in and between our homes are normally open and effective. There are no serious enmeshments, alliances, or oppositions now in and between our several homes. Our stepfamily emotional structure is pretty functional and stable, both before and during child visitations (and/or other especially stressful times.) We now have all the human resources we need to effectively make needed structural changes in this home or in our whole multi-home stepfamily. And, my partner and I can usually talk clearly and honestly enough together about our home's and stepfamily's structure. Etc.

- What other *structural* strengths do you see in your home? In your whole stepfamily?

- "In this house, who is *really* in charge most of the time?" If anyone other than the resident stepfamily adults is in charge, or if no one is, you have just defined a vital re-marital and stepfamily adult problem to resolve. It will not go away by itself.

- "If the resident stepfamily adults aren't in charge of (a certain home), how does that affect each of our resident and visiting minor children over time?"

- "If a minor child in this home is consistently above the (stepfamily co-parenting) line, or if a resident stepfamily adult is usually below the line, what would it take to get them to move across the line and stay there?" "Who is responsible for helping them do that?" "What will happen if they can't or won't?"

- "If there are significantly blocked communications between two or more members of this home—or between two of our stepfamily homes—what would it take to fix that?" "Who is responsible?" "If we don't get this fixed, how will that affect me/us?" "How will it affect our resident and visiting minor children over time?"

- "If someone in this home feels rejected or excluded, are they doing that to themselves or is someone else pushing them out? "What do I/we need to do about this, if anything?" "What may happen if I/we don't?

- "If the emotional and social boundaries of any one of our homes are too rigid—or too vague and flimsy—how does that affect me/us?" "How does it affect our minor kids living there over time?"

- "Who in our stepfamily generally determines the emotional structure of this home? Of our whole multi-home stepfamily?" "Is that okay?"

- "What would happen if I asked the other stepfamily adults in our stepfamily to draw their own structural maps and discuss these questions cooperatively?" "What benefits might that bring to *them*?" "To us all?" "What's in the way of doing this together now?"

Pause again and give yourself a chance to become aware of where your thoughts want to go and what you are feeling (or not feeling). Write about these now, for later review and sharing. They will never be as fresh as at this instant.

Summing Up

The majority of American multi-home stepfamilies fail within 10 years or so of their founding. One of several key reasons is their great structural complexity and the related challenge to stepfamily adults for managing them effectively.

The emotional structure of any family's home is composed of invisible things like roles, rules, leadership and power, communication barriers, inclusions and exclusions, and emotional boundaries. To avoid re-divorce trauma for you and your dependent kids, it can really help to see and understand the emotional structure of each of your stepfamily co-parenting homes and all your related homes together.

To help co-manage stepfamily complexity, genograms and structural maps serve to spark your curiosity, thinking, creativity, and sense of discovery, as well as constructive stepfamily discussions.

These maps are meant to help you get to know and more effectively manage your multi-home stepfamily—not to attack yourself or other members!

Try not to get hung up on "having to do these maps *right*," i.e., exactly according to these guidelines. Catch the spirit here and evolve your stepfamily's own "right" by choosing symbols and mapping conventions that really fit you and your unique people. The basic aim here is to help you visually symbolize concisely: (1) what are your household and stepfamily structural strengths, and (2) what are aspects of your emotional structures that you want to improve over time.

As stepfamily co-parenting teammates, work toward clarifying your common beliefs about "holistic family health." Then get clearer on what you are trying to do together as household co-residents and as a whole multi-home stepfamily. genograms and structural maps let you clearly symbolize your family goals, and measure your status and progress.

Evolving these maps together, and *using* them, is a key part of building and nourishing a successful remarriage and stepfamily. Learn the territory, set your sets, hold hands, keep your knees loose, take your time—and *enjoy the adventure together!*

CHAPTER SEVEN

LEARN HOW TO DO WIN-WIN
PROBLEM-SOLVING AND TEACH YOUR KIDS

All living things experience ceaseless discomforts or needs. All behavior is an attempt to reduce discomforts and increase pleasure—to fill current surface and underlying primary needs. Filling your and others' current physical, emotional, and spiritual needs is also called *nurturing* in this book.

Human families have existed in every age and culture because they consistently nurture their members better than other types of groups. As you have discovered in Chapter Two, multi- generational families vary on a continuum from "very low nurturance" and "very high nurturance." Where would you place your current (or prior) family on that continuum? Would your partner and knowledgeable others agree?

All creatures instinctively evolve ways of communicating (behaving) to fill their current needs. The more that communication fills everyone's current needs, the more effective it is. A major opportunity that forming or joining a stepfamily offers is the chance to patiently heal ineffective old ways of thinking, communicating, and problem-solving. Most troubled ("dysfunctional") and divorcing families don't know how to do this because their parents and society didn't teach them to.

All relationships and families have problems—unfilled needs. A priceless skill that anyone can learn in order to increase their daily serenity, effectiveness, and satisfaction is problem-solving. Currently, our society and most parents don't teach kids how to do this effectively.

Tragically, few adults know how to really talk and listen well together. Learning this skill can be a rewarding task, well worth investing your energy and time. There are five interrelated, learnable verbal communications skills. They are: process awareness; megatalk (talking together about how we communicate); empathic (heart) listening; assertion (versus aggression); and, conflict resolution or problem-solving. Stepfamily adults who work together to develop these abilities find the rewards great. Why is real communication so important? Typical multi-home stepfamilies have more people than biological families, which means more chances for complex interpersonal conflicts.

Unlike biological families, many step-people struggle with post-divorce hostilities, distrust, and ongoing disputes over child custody, visitation, discipline, and financial support. Typical step and biological parents discover major clashes over parenting values, rituals, customs, and priorities, which cause normal loyalty conflicts in and between their several related homes—for years.

There are also typically more minor children in related step-homes than individual biological homes, which means more sibling battles and more frequent needs for adult mediation and problem-solving. And finally, without significant, real recovery from unhealed childhood wounds in the adults, most people are ineffective verbal communicators, especially in conflicts. This is so because of a combination of excess distrust, shame, defensiveness, fear (or explosions) of strong emotions, a compulsive need to control, low self-awareness, and ineffective caregiver modeling.

Simply put, you just don't know how to problem-solve together. Until you have learned about and tried better options, you automatically use manipulative mind-reading, aggression, repression, double messages, withdrawing, threats, assumptions, and many other ineffective ways of trying to get your needs met via communication. They usually backfire and generate even more conflict.

Make no mistake about it, *normal* multi-home stepfamilies are complex, high-conflict groups co-managed by adults who are likely, to some degree, to be emotionally and relationship-handicapped, plus untrained in effective talking, listening, asserting, and problem-solving. You and your partner can build your ability to communicate effectively, if you decide to.

You may think this doesn't apply to you and say, "We agree on just about everything. We never fight." Like it or not, this is probably a red light. You have a major disadvantage in that you haven't had a fair chance to try out your conflict-resolving skills. Make no mistake about it, these abilities will be called upon, often, once the politeness and tolerance of dating fades and mundane, stepfamily living situations surface.

Never arguing or apologizing, often withdrawing, and quickly or never giving in are common symptoms of old, unhealed emotional wounds. From old habit and long practice, you will do anything to keep the peace. Never fighting also blocks your minor kids from learning how to handle interpersonal conflicts effectively. Whether you realize it or not, they are watching you.

"I know you believe you understand what you think I said. But I'm not sure
you realize that what you heard was not what I meant."

Sound familiar? To fill our daily needs we often depend on the ability to verbally communicate with others, yet few of us have studied how to do this well. On a verbal effectiveness scale of one to 10, most of us average three to five with the people who matter the most to us.

You are about to meet a cluster of related ideas that form a concept about effective verbal communication. While each idea adds to the whole, some are extra important. The * symbol flags these special points.

For our purposes, the word "communication" means "the dynamic interplay of mutual reactions between two or more people in emotional, spiritual, or sensory contact." In other words, anything you do—or do not do—that causes a physical, emotional, spiritual, and/or mental change in another is what we call "interpersonal communication." In these exchanges, each partner *simultaneously* sends, receives, and decodes meanings from up to four kinds of messages at once. For most of us, this complex process is largely unconscious until we focus on it.

Think about this: we can't *not* communicate. Why? Well, silence, and the lack of a look, touch, or note, cause meanings just as speech, touch, and eye contact do. If someone says, "s/he didn't say anything" or "I got no response," you know that there probably were meanings assumed—like, "You don't care much about me right now." That may or may not be what the silence was intended to mean, but that is often how the absence of verbal, visual, and/or physical communication is decoded.

Most of us do not know what we don't know about our communications skills, values, and habits. We learned to listen and talk from our families, teachers, heroes, and friends. Few of them knew what you are about to learn here. So we are often unaware of our communication process or of the many choices we have. Just as our hands reach to automatically tie bows, typewrite, or play an instrument, we talk and listen from habit—even if the results do not please us. Taking a "speech" class may grow diction, public speaking skill, or debating abilities, but probably will not cover the effective communication skills we are going to cover here. Sadly, few schools seem to.

These skills work between people and within you. We each experience *self-talk* much of the time: a group of inner voices (i.e., thoughts, hunches, intuitions, images, feelings, and visions.) These are inner-personal communications. They are so familiar to us that they often go unnoticed. The next time you feel conflicted about something, without judgment observe the dialog (or shouting match) between two or more voices inside you.

For example:

Voice 1: *"I wonder how Bob is recovering; I'll call him today."*
Voice 2: *"But you know he'll talk your ear off and then never asks about you.*

Talking to Bob gets boring and it hurts every time. Don't call Bob."

Voice 3: *"But friends should call! I'll feel guilty if I don't."*
Voice 4: *"Listen, this is too hard and confusing. C'mon, let's get a donut."*
Voice 5: *"Wait! You're 20 pounds overweight as it is. Don't eat that junk! Have an apple!"*

Sound familiar? The communication skills of process awareness, metatalk, empathic listening, assertion, and problem-solving will work between your inner voices just as well as with other people. Just think. What would your life be like with more inner harmony?

In a little while, we are going to target five communications skills. Be aware that just reading about them will not build your ability to communicate effectively. Trying the five skills is the only way you will experience their power and usefulness. It has taken years to develop your present talking and listening patterns. It will take time for these new skills to become comfortable habits, as well. Let yourself feel alien, awkward, and even phony for a time—without guilt! You couldn't play the piano the first time with concert ability. As with any skill, these take practice, feedback, and patience before they become familiar and fully effective.

If possible, practice with a partner. Having someone to share these experiences and offer feedback will speed learning and make it more fun. If you are not ready to explore this with your stepfamily adult quite yet, you can always ask trusted others for clear feedback on your communication behaviors. And you always have your inner partners.

Two of the most helpful learning attitudes are: *"Progress, not perfection" and "The road to success is always under construction."* Take them to heart.

As the skills start to work for you, avoid preaching about or selling them to insecure or uninterested partners. Doing so can seem to send a message that you are "one-up," which usually breeds resentment, defensiveness, and resistance. However, modeling these skills often catches the interest of others, over time.

Your first reaction to these new skills can be that they seem "phony" or "gimmicky," and that people trying them are "pulling something" over on their partners. Sure, these skills can be used to manipulate rather than communicate. But doing so eventually erodes trust and respect. If your steady goals are *"I want to hear you clearly and I want both of us to get more of what we need here,"* these skills will enhance all of your relationships, starting with yourself.

A tape or video recorder can not only help you to learn these new skills, but also to become aware of your present communication habits. They can also help you avoid the endless *"you said ... no I didn't"* cycles that erupt when insecure people don't get clear feedback. But be aware that recorders can also scare and distract uneasy partners from communicating freely. Be also warned, if these devices are used to trap, beat, or shame, then your relationships and self-esteem will suffer.

* When your (sincere) attitude about your partner is *"Your needs now are just as valid and important as mine,"* then these five skills you are about to learn will work. You cannot fake it. Any other attitude will automatically be sent by your voice tone, body, and face, and will dilute or reverse the usefulness and impact of these skills.

These skills are also interdependent. "Assertiveness" requires that you master "awareness," "metatalk," and "empathic listening." "Problem-solving" works only if the other four abilities are well developed. Highly effective communicators know all five skills thoroughly and switch among them fluidly as circumstances change.

You do not need these skills all the time. The goal is to grow automatic competence with them when important situations come up, and you or your partner(s) decide at any moment what qualifies as important.

Teaching these five skills to any young people in your life by modeling and instruction is one of the most potent and priceless gifts you can bestow. The skills will benefit and serve a lifetime, and will empower generations to come.

Overview

The Five Effective Communication Skills

Like pieces of a garment pattern, each communication ability makes more sense when seen as part of the whole concept. So we will begin with an overview and then explore each skill in some detail.

1. "Process awareness" is the foundation skill of effective verbal communication. It is being aware, without judgment, moment by moment, of your and your partner's key attitudes, physical and emotional feelings (including hunches and intuitions), thoughts (inner voices), real communication skills, and other needs and objective awarenesses, and, finally, how you are talking together. Use "process awareness" in all key situations, including when you are alone. With practice, it becomes a habit.
2. "Metatalk" is honest, clear, and cooperative discussion with a partner about how you are communicating together. It is based on mutual respect and process awareness, and uses a special vocabulary. You build this language over time, by fitting the concepts and terms in this book to your own personal values and style of communicating.
3. "Empathic listening" is a conscious decision to: suspend your opinions and other needs for the moment; briefly feedback your sense of your partner's main thoughts, feelings, and needs and vigilantly and objectively note their reactions. This is used when your partner's emotions are intense and he or she cannot listen to you. Listening empathically does not, however, mean you agree with your partner. Mastering these first three skills is essential for effective "assertion" and "problem-solving."
4. "Assertion" (the skill or art of) is: clearly knowing what you really need, right now; asking for it plainly and without guilt; calmly expecting a defensive response; respectfully listening to it; and then, firmly repeating these steps until you either get (1) agreement, (2) an acceptable compromise, or (3) switch to the last skill, "problem-solving."

   There are three effective-assertion essentials: (1) Valuing yourself and your partner's need to communicate equally; (2) firmly believing that your present needs are legitimate; and (3) knowing that if you are making a request, compromise and "no" are okay; or, if you are making a demand, they are not okay.
5. "Problem-solving" is used to meet enough of everyone's real needs when people disagree. This skill involves cooperatively uncovering what each person really needs

now, and creatively brainstorming all options to evolve a win-win solution. Effective "problem-solving" uses all of the other four skills and requires self-respect and mutual respect, optimism, imagination, patience, and good will. Well used, the power of this skill is enormous.

Before moving on to the details of each of these skills, let us agree on what is effective verbal communication. Basically, we communicate to meet our current conscious and unconscious personal needs. Agree? Needs are fluid combinations of mental, emotional, spiritual, and physical tensions. Moment by moment, you and each partner have major and minor needs that can conflict within and between you. (E.g., *"I want to both take the time to change my clothes and to please you - which means leaving immediately in order to be on time."*). Waking and asleep, we strive to reduce the discomfort of these combined tensions.

* So, verbal communication succeeds when each person involved gets enough of their present real needs met and feels good enough afterwards about themselves, their partner(s), and the communication process between them.

This definition implies that all people know their true present needs and their feelings during and after the process. The word *true* is key here. We are often not clear on, or honest with ourselves or our partners about, our real motivations. What do you think?

It is okay if our definition does not fit for you. To communicate *well,* however, you will need a clear idea of what "well" means. So, evolve a clear definition of effective communication that works for you. Then learn what your key partners' definitions are. If you postpone this or choose not to do it, the ideas in this chapter will probably be much less helpful to you.

Effective Communication Skills

One: "Process Awareness"

This foundation ability helps in all communication situations, including conversing among your inner selves. It is paying objective attention, from moment to moment, to at least six factors in and between you and another. These six are:

1. Relationship attitude. How do we each feel about the other's human worth, right now? Whose needs are more important? It is the single most powerful communication factor.
2. Communication needs. What does each of us really need from the other right now? Why are we each communicating? Do our respective needs match?
3. Focus. Is anyone so physically or emotionally uncomfortable that they cannot concentrate on our joint communication process? If so, what are the distractions and what would reduce them? Do we stay on target together until we both feel done?

4. How do our emotional levels compare, and which skills fit our mix best?
5. What is the outcome of our key exchanges of communication, now and over time?
6. And, what are our action/reaction communication sequences and patterns?

* Communication works well only when all partners get believable relationship messages that consistently say, *"I see you as my equal here and now."* Relationship messages are probably the most powerful factors in both inner- and inter-personal communication exchanges. Without "process awareness," they often go unnoticed, so they can silently wreck well-meant communication.

Really effective communication skills spring from this attitude about our partners and ourselves, a form of the Golden Rule: *"I now respect and value your dignity, needs, and opinions just as I would have you value mine."*

There are six key needs we try to fill by communicating: To feel respected by ourselves and each partner; to give or get information; to cause or block an action; to change (or solidify) our relationship with another person or ourselves; to vent; and, to end uncomfortable silences with other people.

* When your and your partner's inner and mutual communication needs match, you may (rather than will) get most of all you seek. The odds of this happening in key situations rise when you each know clearly what you both need. For example: If you need to vent now, and I need to cause change, our mutual communication needs clash. If you want to vent and I want to get information and strengthen our relationship, our mutual needs match.

Two: "Metatalk"

"Metatalk" is cooperative verbal communication between partners about their process of communication. It describes your mutual "process awareness." Rather than talking about "our fight last night," "metatalk" focuses on "how we are talking now about our fight last night." Shared "metatalk" is the raw material needed to resolve communication problems effectively.

Each of us develops our own style and vocabulary, but the theme remains constant: clear, objective descriptions of our "process awareness." Imagine you are talking with someone who repeatedly interrupts you. You become aware of this through "process awareness." You further realize you are feeling put down, unheard, and increasingly irritated. You then consciously decide to make a "meta-comment." You say: *"Sylvia, I notice that pretty often you start to talk before I'm finished. I'm not feeling heard by you and I'm starting to get frustrated."* You could stop there or you might add: *"Were you aware of doing that?"* or *"I'd like you to let me finish my thoughts."*

Another scenario: your partner laughs and says, *"I just had the most unbelievable fight with my sister. It was awful!"* You feel confused and say: *"I just got a double message from you, Burt, and I'm not sure what you're really feeling. Your words were 'the fight was awful,' but you chuckled and smiled."* Notice how this message would change if it were said blamefully or apologetically.

Three: Empathic Listening

The American College dictionary describes empathy as "mental(ly) entering into the feeling of a person ..., appreciative perception or understanding."

This skill is powerful because it allows you to: briefly tell the speaker, without judgment, your sense of what they are thinking, feeling, and needing at the moment; that you are prepared to listen with your heart to sense as well as you can what it is like to be the speaker; and then, to summarize your impressions of this from time to time as they talk, without extra comment. Stay clear that you are not "giving in" by doing this.

* Listening empathically does not necessarily mean that you agree with your partner. Sincere, versus manipulative, empathic listening is a win-win skill. It has many benefits for everyone because: it signals your respect for, and interest in, the speaker; he or she feels valued by you; and so, he or she is more apt to keep talking which builds trust, intimacy, and relationships. The speaker is also more likely to listen well to you later. Unlike saying *"I hear you,"* empathic listening demonstrates whether you truly comprehend what the speaker means and feels. This minimizes misunderstandings. At the same time, it may help the speaker clarify his or her ideas, emotions, and needs as they hear your non-judgmental summaries.

Choose to use this technique when you are aware of four conditions: (1) you now feel of equal worth with your partner; (2) you are genuinely interested in him or her; (3) you are able to focus on him or her now (you are not too distracted by the environment or your own current needs); and (4) your partner is so excited or upset about something that he or she cannot really hear you at the moment.

Confused? How do you listen with your heart? Internally reaffirm: *"Genuine listening is a gift, and it is not necessarily agreeing."* Temporarily set your own opinions and priorities aside. Focus mentally, without judgment, on your partner by watching his or her face, eyes, body, and hands. Note the partner's posture, motions, expressions, and gestures—or lack of these—and listen to the words and speech dynamics to estimate main thoughts, feelings, and needs.

Then, from time to time, tell the speaker the essence of what you believe he or she is thinking, feeling (emotionally and/or physically), and needing. Speak briefly (use a few words or a phrase at most), in your own words (do not parrot the other person's), and * without questions, comments, or solutions. Use attentive posture; comfortable eye contact; and gestures, expressions, and intensity that match the speaker's. When you are truly focused and empathic, these will happen automatically.

This skill is also called *active listening* because it involves concentration, awareness, and periodic, non-distracting talking by the listener—not just "sitting there nodding and grunting." You also may have heard it referred to as *reflective listening* and *mirroring*, because the listener returns only the gist of he or she is are getting—adding or subtracting nothing.

In his useful book, *The 7 Habits of Highly Effective People*, Steven Covey calls this skill *empathic listening*. This emphasizes the value of sensing your partner's current emotional experience as well as his or her thoughts. What does this skill sound like in action? *"So you think that ..." "It seemed to you that ..." "You're really feeling ..." "What you need now is ..." "... pretty tough, huh?" "So you were up against ..." "You're anxious about ..." "... really mystifying (to you)" "Now you look really ..." "Seems you're unsure of ..." "You were furious with me!" "... totally missed your point!" "Wow! Really confusing!"*

Notice the absence of "I." *"You're* wondering about ..." is a better choice than *"I think you're wondering about ..."* because it's briefer and it focuses on your partner, not you.

Four: Assertion

"Assertion is the art of saying something unpleasant ...
in a way than can be clearly heard and accepted."

This communication skill empowers you to respectfully confront a partner to get understanding—and agreement when needed. Using it may create a conflict that calls for all five communication skills.

By definition, "assertiveness" implies equal concern for your and your partner's present needs and feelings. Unless you are in a crisis, focusing on your needs without equally considering your partner's is aggressive. On the other hand, allowing others to put their needs first may be either compassion (if they are in a crisis) or submission, which erodes self-respect.

Mutually respectful "assertion" is the language of healthy frustration and anger. It builds self-esteem and honest, solid relationships. This skill is easiest to use with partners who are usually pretty comfortable with themselves. When your emotional level is high, and your partner's is not, use assertiveness to: prevent future conflicts; confront someone who has broken an agreement or is causing you stress now; or, give praise that cannot be discounted.

"Assertions" range from spontaneous and small (*"Please turn the radio down, okay?"*) to pre-planned life-pivoting ones (*"I need you to stop drinking for good or to get qualified addiction counseling, by May 1. If you choose not to, I need you to move out."*).

Successful major "assertions" include eight steps. Minor assertions need less. Compare the following steps to how you usually get what you want: Consciously ...

1. *Choose* to assert until it becomes a habit.
2. *Get clear* on what you feel, why, and specifically what you really need from your partner right now. If you are not sure of these, pause. Time will allow you to clarify them before asserting.
3. Make four quick *attitude checks* on how you honestly feel about the following:
   ➤ Your partner's needs. If they are as important as yours, go ahead. If not, lower your expectations about the outcome, or explore what is blocking you.

> Asking for what you need. If you solidly feel *"I have a right to say or ask for this,"* go ahead. The alternative is: *"I'm being selfish/pushy/greedy."*

> Your ability to handle your partner's reactions (e.g., anger, rejection, conflict) calmly. If you feel confident enough, go ahead. If not, work toward exploring and healing your fear and self-doubt.

> Finally, get clear on your expectations about the outcome. If you feel *"We both can get our needs met and will probably feel okay about it,"* go ahead. If you believe this assertion will not work, it probably won't.

4. State your need simply and directly, with steady eye contact.
5. * Without judgment, expect resistance. It is a normal human response, not a weakness or wrong. When it happens,
6. Use empathic listening until your partner's emotional level calms down and his or her ears open up.
7. Recycle steps four through six as needed. Keep restating your need(s) clearly and directly, and use "empathic listening" with each new resistance until you get clear agreement, an acceptable compromise or refusal, or new information that changes your needs or priorities. Or, until you run out of time. In key planned "assertions," arrange lots of time.
8. Note the outcome of your "assertion." If you and your partner(s) each got your main needs met, thank them and appreciate yourself. If someone did not get all they needed, without blame use "process awareness" and "metatalk" to discover what would work better the next time.

Notice what you are thinking now: what is your self-talk? Do you feel these steps really would work for you? Could you assert in important situations and leave any of these steps out? What would happen if you did not feel equal, clear, and confident?

For a fine meal to succeed, all ingredients have to be available and prepared well, and the setting and serving have to be right. Successful "assertions" are the same. They fail if one or several of the key ingredients we have just covered are missing, i.e., the preparation is rushed, the setting is wrong, or the presentation is off.

In major situations, attending to each of these elements is essential; successful "problem-solving" usually depends on effective "assertions" and the other three skills. As with the other communication skills, if you feel really one-up or one-down to your partner(s), "assertion" will not work. You must feel equal. The fundamental ingredients here are self- and mutual respect. Often, timid asserters do not believe their needs are legitimate. Hesitant or little eye contact is a major symptom of this. Repeated *"um's"* and *"uh's"* is another. Choice of vague, indirect, negative, or mild terms is a third. Using *"we need"* rather than *"I need"* is still another sign of a one-down mind set. The implied message here is, *"You probably won't agree or give me what I'm asking for...oh well ..."*

* There are three effective ways to promote yourself to an equal position, over time:

1. Develop a Bill of Personal Rights that you really believe in, and use it. (A Sample Bill of Personal Rights is available at http://sfhelp.org/basics/rights.htm) If you truly see your communication partners as equals, your Bill of Rights will apply to them, as well.

2. Read and apply *The New Peoplemaking*, a book by Virginia Satir (Science and Behavior Books, 1988), and *Healing the Shame That Binds You*, by John Bradshaw (Health Communications, Inc., 1988). Invest time in the healing exercises in Bradshaw's book.

3. Learn what your self-protecting inner voices say, i.e., negative self-talk. Develop and use affirmations that convert these messages to positive statements you really believe. Compassionately, notice your thoughts now. Are they anything like: *"Oh, I can't do that." "That won't work." "Too hard; too much work." "But I don't know how." "I have other things to do." "They'd laugh if I did." "That's really stupid." "I don't do stuff like that." "I'm not interested." "I will—soon ..." "Books are boring."*

These are examples of normal negative self-talk, a way out for our inner voices to protect us from trying scary new behaviors. It often stunts our growth. The main message is "Don't risk change!" Until we listen for them, such comments are often unconscious. They are whispers behind our thoughts that control us like iron shackles. If you elect to let such inner "laws" rule you, take a challenge and choose one or more of these: *"My Bill of Rights will help me!" "Affirmations work for me." "I can do each of these now!" "I'm finding the way ...!" "I'm learning how to do these!" "This makes sense to me!" "I'll respect me if I do these!" "I will start—now!" "I am the only person in charge of meeting my needs."*

These are positive affirmations or self-assertions. In building affirmations that really work, motivation experts suggest you keep them simple, clear, and specific. Focus on what you can do, e.g., *"I'm growing calm in the face of anger" rather than "I'll stop being so scared of angry people."* If you are visual, picture yourself doing each affirmation successfully—often. Imagine vividly how this feels. Say each one aloud, often, perhaps looking in a mirror, with steady eye contact. And then, write them out and post them where you will see them regularly, like your car dashboard, desktop, phone, bathroom mirror, PC screen, refrigerator, night stand, etc.

As you promote yourself to being equal, expect insecure others to resist and sabotage your changing. Respect their fear and need to control, but do not comply! They are responsible for managing their fear, not you.

What if you feel your present needs are greater than your partner's. Needs can be more important, i.e., more intense. For instance, easing the pain of your toothache now is more pressing than my need to mount photos in our album. If your needs seem to come first most of the time, however, look for a hidden compulsion to control situations. Verbal communication skills will not work consistently well for you until you heal this fear and shame-based attitude.

Regardless of the intensity of your needs, the worth and dignity of yourself and others are always equal. If you often feel entitled to more than those around you, you will broadcast that. Partners who regularly tolerate such a one-up attitude are usually shamed, guilty, and fear abandonment; they are *codependent*. A one-up/one-down partnership may be stable, but is usually unfulfilling and stressful for at least one partner. Important communication seldom happens effectively.

Like feeling equal, getting clear is an ingredient which can be amazingly elusive. There are four clarities to seek: What are my true needs right now? Realistically, can I fill them now? If I think so, how can I express my needs respectfully and unmistakably? And, what response do I need from you, specifically?

Needs are impulses to reduce inner spiritual, emotional, and physical tensions. Moment by moment, the needs of each communicating partner can: come in groups (though one or two may dominate for the moment); be conscious or unconscious and are often both; vary in intensity that can change instantly as our inner and outer environments shift (the normal differences between male and female need-priorities can hinder clear communication); and, conflict with us and/or between us at the same time, usually causing confusion, anxiety, and distrust.

As kids, we were often forcefully taught that some of our natural human needs and feelings are bad. Getting angry, lusting, lying, hitting, stealing, being selfish or lazy, and cheating are common ones. In our anxious, young need to be accepted, and lacking adult knowledge, we learn to deny, repress, project, or disguise such needs. We unconsciously numb, shame or guilt-trip ourselves when such needs appear.

Feeling a need means we are human, not good or evil. The keys are whether we act on these needs, how, why, and with what effect. My momentary need to *"kill you right now"* can be acknowledged without shame, guilt, or harm. It surely stands for a deeper normal need like *"I hurt, so a part of me wants to protect against repeat pain by hurting you back!"*

Try out believing that *"All my and your needs are legitimate and okay."* How does that feel? Do you buy it? What were you taught? We usually have overlapping physical, emotional, and spiritual needs at any moment. Some of these are conscious and others unconscious. How, then, can we learn our true current needs, to make a clear assertion?

For instance, *"I want you to be on time"* is code for *"I need to feel respected,"* i.e., *"I need to feel that you see my time as valuable."* Likewise, *"I wish you'd stop smoking in the house"* may really mean *"I'm scared you'll get cancer, die, and I'll be left alone. I need you to respect me and my fear!"*

* Often, our surface needs mask something deeper. *"So, how was your day?"* may cover two unspoken needs: (1) learning without seeming nosy, jealous, and insecure, if (2) you had lunch with your attractive coworker. These in turn mask the real need: to reduce insecurity and the fear of abandonment, and avoid guilt and shame. This illustrates a normal three-level, two-

part need. A spoken (conscious) need to get information, i.e., *"How was your day?"* Unsaid (conscious) needs: *"Did you spend time with Chris?"* (Don't think I don't trust you.) And, real, unconscious needs: (1) *"I need reassurance you won't leave me,"* and (2) *"I need to be nice and respect myself because nice people trust partners and don't pry."*

Like emotional needs, concrete ("thing") needs come in levels and clusters, too. *"I need the car this afternoon"* really means *"I need a convenient, reliable way to get to the bank by three p.m. and back here by 4:30."*

* Each partner usually has several needs at once. Learning them all clearly, and comparing and ranking them cooperatively, can take time. Success requires shared commitment, patience, time without distraction, and effective communication. The rewards are high. Fortunately, we usually do not have to scratch below our top layers of needs in order to get "good enough" assertions. For major conflicts or decisions, delving deeper before asserting raises the chance of getting your real needs met.

Once your real needs are uncovered, the second "assertion" clarity to seek is whether your partner is able (versus willing) to fill them. Other people may or may not have the resources or abilities to reduce our tensions. *"Could you scratch my back?"* or *"May I borrow your lawn mower?"* are easy enough. However, some basic needs that your partner cannot permanently fill for you are: to value yourself, feel lovable, trust yourself, reduce your guilt, learn who you are, set your life's goals, feel happy, find your serenity, find your power, feel real hope, accept help, accept love, heal your shame, risk new things, grow your skills, set your limits, lower your pain, ask for help, find your God, find your meaning, grow your courage, feel your emotions, choose your values, forgive yourself, grieve and accept your limits and your losses, and experience the beauty and wonders in and around your.

Other people can support and encourage us as we seek to fill these deep needs. Expecting, requesting, or demanding partners to reduce such tensions will surely create anxiety, frustration, anger, and resentment, and cause our relationships with others and ourselves to erode. Getting clear on our true needs, without guilt or shame, and taking responsibility for satisfying them, builds self and mutual respect.

Even if your partner can and is willing to fill a particular need, the timing of your "assertion" needs to be right. Are they distraction-free (enough) now? If all other ingredients are present and well prepared but this one, the "meal will fail." If the partner's emotional level is up, listen respectfully with your heart and invite his or her ears to clear. Then serve your "assertion."

It is important that you express your needs clearly. You know what they are, now you need to decide if your partner(s) have the capability to fill them now. Express your needs respectfully and without ambiguity. *Respectfully* occurs by itself when you see your partner as an equal. *Ambiguity* depends on your simplicity, directness, and choice of words.

The value of being simple and direct, versus hinting, is obvious. How do you know if you are being as "simple" and direct as possible? Ask yourself if you can phrase your need in less than three sentences. One is even better. The more words you use to express your needs, the greater the chance for confusion, misunderstanding, and resistance.

Since words and phrases mean different things to each of us, good assertions may fail by being misunderstood. "Be on time" may mean "no more than five minutes early or late" to you, and "within half an hour" to your partner. Asserting with simple, concrete, specific words and phrases, and perhaps respectfully asking your partner to rephrase what they heard, can really help here.

If your partner's actions bother you, can you describe their irritating behavior factually and objectively? Imagine capturing their disruptive actions on audio or video tape: you can record a specific tone of voice, expression, gesture, etc. You cannot record feelings or opinions like "idiotic," "abusive," "thoughtless," "wimpy," "insensitive," "inconsiderate," "nerd," and the like.

Limit describing your partner's behavior, and changes that you need, to things you could record. Asking, *"Please lower your voice"* is doable. *"Stop being so angry!"* demands a major attitude shift, and if sent with a demanding tone, dooms any success of communication.

"I" messages are powerful "assertion" tools. They are two or three parts: "When you ---," "I ---," and "---and I need you to ----." For example: *"Al, when you bring the car back 45 minutes late I get frustrated and angry because then I'm late for my bowling league!"* In other words, his *specific* behavior has a *concrete* negative effect. An optional ending is: *"If you'll be more than 10 minutes late, I need you to call me so I can arrange a ride. Will you do that?"* Omitting the ending gives your partner the dignity of offering his or her own solution. If the partner chooses not to, add your assertion and calmly expect resistance, without blame. This is clearer and certainly more respectful than, *"It really buts me when you're so incredibly selfish with the car, you jerk! From now on, be on time!"*

If your partner's behavior is not bothering you, but you still need something from him or her, describe clearly what, how, and when. For instance, compare: *"Jean, I need you to vacuum the living room by 5:30 tonight, including under the end tables and behind the aquarium. Okay?"* with, *"Hey! Clean up the front room later, Jean."* For important needs, get clear acknowledgment from your partner that he or she understands you and is willing to comply.

It is equally important to know the kind of response you need. This increases in value as the complexity or priority of your needs rises. Your options include: *"I'm venting"* (I need you to hear and accept me now. I don't need action or agreement); *"I'm requesting"* (I need action. I can live with a compromise or even a refusal right now); or, *"I'm DEMANDING"* (You must commit to taking specific action(s) by a certain time and/or in a particular way. Compromises, exceptions, or refusal are not acceptable to me here).

After feeling equal and getting clear, the last key ingredient for "assertion" is a trust in this skill and in your ability with it. This means believing that "assertion" and "empathic listening" will (usually) work for you and your partners, despite resistance, confusion, and conflicts.

Commitment to these communication skills, and practicing them patiently over time, will yield solid "assertion" confidence. An attitude that promotes this is: *"My 'failures' are priceless chances to learn."* How does this compare with your attitude about "assertion?" What are you saying to yourself right now?!

Does "assertion" seem complex? You usually need not be overly concerned with all of these ingredients. As the importance of our needs rises, so does the value of your feeling equal, clear, and confident in preparing and delivering an effective "assertion." To recap: Choose to be assertive rather than aggressive or submissive. Know and consciously get as clear as you can on what you really need; whether your partner can probably fill your need; how to describe your need simply and directly; whether your partner can hear you now because of his or her own emotional level; and what response you need (acceptance without action, agreement, compromise, refusal, or compliance and clear commitment).

Check your key attitudes: Are you feeling equal? Are your needs legitimate? Are you confident enough this "assertion" process will work now? With steady eye contact, calmly state your "assertion" and expect resistance without blaming your partner(s). Listen empathically to any resistance. When you can offer a positive response, i.e. when the partner's emotional level is steady again, restate your "assertion" firmly and clearly. Expect more resistance and repeat the last three steps again until you get enough of what you need or new information that changes your needs. Often, learning new information justifies shifting from "assertion" to mutual "problem-solving."

If it feels right, thank your partner for his or her cooperation. Appreciate yourself and note anything about your "assertion" experience you want to remember. "Assertion" is a dynamic process which offers choices all along the way. When it works, everyone gets his or her main needs met and feels good about how that happened. Any time you are unsure of your options or needs, allow yourself to tell (rather than ask) your partner that you need to pause while you get clearer. When you do, everyone wins.

Five: Problem-solving
Popular Alternatives to Problem-solving Are:

fighting	*arguing*	*demanding*	*Blaming*
analyzing	*rationalizing*	*explaining*	*lecturing*
preaching	*whining*	*complaining*	*worrying*
nagging	*manipulating*	*hinting*	*denying*
catastrophizing	*obsessing*	*joking*	*procrastinating*
threatening	*repressing*	*withdrawing*	*Submitting*

The final communication skill is "problem-solving," i.e., a cooperative process between or within people whose current needs clash. Effective "problem-solving" is based on the shared beliefs that (1) meeting all partners' real needs is the common goal, and that (2) the process will succeed for everyone involved. Based on mutual respect, the focus of this skill is on meeting needs, not power, control, punishment, fixing blame, or remaking personalities. "Problem-solving" could also be called "conflict resolution" or "joint needs satisfaction."

Consistent success at "problem-solving" requires fluency in the other four communication skills. When each partner knows and uses all five skills, most inner and mutual conflicts will be resolved with everyone feeling respected and satisfied enough. The basic "problem-solving" process is simple:

First, acknowledge that you have a conflict, without guilt, anxiety, or shame. Check for emotional levels and attitude. If no one's hearing is blocked by intense feelings and all people seem to feel equal now, and all expect "problem-solving" to probably work, then go ahead. Otherwise, your first shared "problem-solving" goal should be to listen to bring emotional levels down and/or achieve more of an attitude of equality.

Agree (out loud) to "problem-solve." Note and eliminate any major distractions. Cooperatively, use "process awareness," "metatalk" and "assertion" to explore below the surface needs to find the real tensions driving each of you. If discovering them evokes strong reactions (like shame, fear, resentment, or guilt), acknowledge the feelings honestly. Watch for and avoid slipping into "one-up" or "one-down" attitudes. Using "effective listening," confirm that each partner clearly understands the other's real needs, and values them equally (if true).

Decide together if your conflict is abstract or concrete, and set your goals accordingly. If your clash is abstract (differing opinions or values, like "*I like fish; you prefer red meat*"), aim to either compromise or accept disagreement. Trying to convert your partner implies your way is better and that he or she is "one-down." If you disagree over something concrete (like both needing the car at the same time), creatively brainstorm and pool all possible solutions, no matter how weird. Nutty ideas can lead unexpectedly to win-win outcomes. This is not a contest! It can be fun, even hilarious if your emotional levels are down and nobody feels overly "one-down" or anxious.

Pick the best-fit options and see if each partner is really satisfied enough. If not, avoid blaming yourself or another, and recheck your attitudes and expectations. Consider recycling the process, if time and energy allow. If your "problem-solving" works for everyone, appreciate each other and yourself. How do these steps compare with your normal response to personal conflict? Most people have never been taught any of these skills. Do you feel that learning and using these steps eventually will get more of your and your partner's needs met? What are you saying to yourself now? Is there anything blocking your trying these skills out?

How do the conflict resolution styles of you and your partner differ? Adopt an attitude of curiosity, neutrality, and expectation of improved communication, rather than defensiveness or fault-finding. This is not an exercise to find out "who's wrong or bad."

Here's an example of "problem-solving" at work between a couple who know what it is and have used it before with mixed success. Tony decided to use "empathic listening" when Beth first complained: *"I am really fed up, Tony! I need something to change, now!"* Her emotional level eventually came down as she felt heard and accepted.

T: *"Are you in a place to try some problem-solving?"*

B: *"Yeah. I'd like to try it."*

T: *"Okay. So, what do you need."*

B: *"It's about our nights. I need more cooperation with dinners during the week."*

T: *"If you don't get more help, what'll happen?"*

B: *"Well, I'm just so tired most nights after work. I get irritated and short-tempered if I can't get a breather when I get home. You know, I snap at you and the kids, and then I feel really guilty. It's getting to the point that part of me dreads coming home. I hate that!"*

T: *"So you need to recharge when you get home so you don't say things you regret to me and the kids."* (Using "empathic listening," Tony was able to discern Beth's real needs.)

B: *"Yeah, Tony, that's it exactly."*

T: *"Um. You need changes like starting right away, huh?"*

B: *"I really do! I feel at the end of my rope. I hate bickering at the dinner table. It's the only time we're all together and I want it to be nice. I need you to help!"*

T: *"Whoa. That's a solution, not a need. Hang on to that."*

B: *"Okay, you're right."* (Silence) *"Well, what do you need?"*

T: *"I don't want to jump right into dinner when I get home either. I work my tail off too, you know, here and at work!"*

B: *"You work just as hard as I do, and you need some quiet time after you get home, too."* ("Empathic listening.")

T: *"Yeah. And I need to not feel guilty that you're overloaded—and not to get into hassles with the kids over eating, too."*

B: *"So you don't want to feel responsible for me."*

T: *"Uh huh ..."*

B: *"... and, uh ... you don't want the kids complaining a lot."* (More "empathetic listening.")

T: *"That's it."* (Pause) *"Well, let's play with this. What are our choices?"*

In the next 10 minutes, Tony and Beth brainstorm cooperatively. They harvest these ideas *before* judging them: Start dinner half an hour later. Pre-cook more meals. Eat out more, within budget limits. Hire a part-time cook, maybe a foreign exchange student. Pay the older kids to cook. Trade responsibilities for dinner (one week "on," one week "off"). Simplify the menus. See if they could start and finish work earlier. Get Tony's bachelor uncle to cook some nights. Eat bigger lunches. Trade with the neighbors in cooking for both families together two nights a week. Order out some nights. Everyone cook for themselves. Ask the kids for ideas. One of them changing to part-time work. And, move closer to Tony and Beth's jobs to shorten their commutes.

Sure, many of these ideas were just too far out. But, after some experimenting, the solution turned out to be a combination of several less extreme options. This process of defining their respective needs and brainstorming ideas left both people feeling heard, respected, and closer to each other. They are not only motivated to use this technique again, but have successfully modeled it for their children. They invested about 35 minutes in the process and strengthened their marriage and their self- and mutual respect.

Can you imagine you and your partner handling problems something like this? What would have to change? Notice your self-talk now: is an inner voice really skeptical or negative? If so, do you want to change anything?

Example: Stepfamily Loyalty Conflict

Here's how this process sounds in a typical stepfamily loyalty conflict where all the members feel that they're okay and co-equals in worth. Here's the scene: Bill, 14, finishes dinner before his mom, Sarah, and new step dad, Sam, do. As the boy starts to leave the table, Sam asks him to stay until the adults finish. Bill looks at his mother and says ...

Bill: *"Do I have to, Mom"* (stay per Sam's request).

Sarah takes charge and calmly names the problem: *"Bill, sit down a minute and help us, please. We've got another loyalty conflict here. You want to leave right now."* (Affirms him: an =/= attitude). *How come?"*

Bill defines his needs: *"I want to call Carl about the game tomorrow, and I have a ton of homework. Besides—excuse me, but listening to you guys is not always the most exciting thing, you know? And you eat so slow!"*

    Here many adults—especially shame-based survivors of low nurturing childhoods—would semi-consciously feel attacked and disrespected, rather than decoding Bill's message as information about legitimate needs.

    With self-control and awareness, feeling attacked by someone (and/or by your inner critic) causes hurt, irritation, defensiveness, blaming, blocked listening, and escalating power struggles ("fights") about (a) who's *right* and (b) who's going to get their way (win/lose).

Sarah (grinning): *"So you want to check in with Carl, get at your work, and not get bored, eh? Okay, fair enough."* (Affirms his needs with "empathic listening" without agreeing, judging, arguing, or commenting). *"Hang in here a few minutes and help us, please. Sam, why do you want Bill to stay?"*

Sam: *"Well, dinner's one of the few times we're all together. It just feels good to me that no one leaves until we're all done. That includes me! I always had to stay at the table when I was a kid—I guess it just doesn't feel right that people scatter. I feel it's, uh, disrespectful."*

Bill: *"But Mom, I've never had to stay before* (Sam came) *…"*

Sarah: *"I know, hon. This is new for all of us!"* (She listens without taking sides and stays focused on the process.) *"So Sam, you need us to feel like a family, and sticking together at dinner is an important way of doing that, for you."* (Uses "empathic-listening" skill to affirm his needs, without agreeing, judging, or commenting).

Sam (feeling heard and respected): *"Yeah. I feel like we're all always racing around and this is one of the few times we can all be together and catch up."* He isn't aware of his underlying primary need to feel like an ideal "normal" (biological) family.

Sarah (smiling, without sarcasm or blame): *"Guess what, guys. I'm feeling caught in the middle again. I guess we need to find some kind of new rule for mealtimes, huh?"* She pauses to reflect and then says, *"I need each of us to feel clearly heard now, and to find some way to make this work for each of us so I can get out of the middle. What choices do you see here?"* (Mutually respectful assertion.)

As Sam and Sarah finish eating, all three come up with several options for lower-stress dinner times. The adults share an attitude of "our respective dignities and needs are of equal importance now." They settle on Bill agreeing to usually stay for about 10 minutes, maximum, if he finishes dinner first.

The adults agree to intentionally include the boy more (i.e., to listen to him with real interest) in their table talk and save most "boring" adult topics for their own time. This is a double compromise acceptable to each of them.

Note: If Sam and Sarah have made too little couple-time, this resolution probably wouldn't work. They also agree that there will be exceptions when Bill can leave quickly, and when the adults need to talk "boring stuff" with him present. This avoids stress from rigid black/white rule enforcement.

Six Problem-Solving Steps Recap

- Acknowledge that you have a problem (unmet needs).
- Use awareness and dig-down skills to identify your respective current primary needs.
- Decide if you have an internal conflict or interpersonal conflict, or both. Resolve internal conflicts first.
- Use awareness skill to check your attitude and focus.
- Ask your partner to "problem-solve" and reduce any distractions.
- Confirm that (a) each person understands his or her own needs and each other person's needs, and that (b) each of you has a mutual respect attitude (our needs are equally important, except in an emergency).

Putting It All Together

We rarely study the skills we rely on the most to get many of our daily needs met. Effective verbal communication happens when each person gets his or her major needs met *enough* and feels good *enough* about the way he or she did and each person involved.

Five learnable, interrelated communication skills which build healthy relationships and personal productivity over time are: "Process awareness" (what's happening in and between us now?), "metatalk" (discussing cooperatively how you communicate together), "empathic listening" (hearing with your hearts and knowing that listening well does not necessarily mean agreeing), "assertion" (knowing, stating, and restating clearly and firmly what we need, as opposed to aggression or submission, and handling expected resistance with equality and "empathic listening," and "problem-solving" (finding and meeting all partners' real needs in a win-win way, for both tangible and abstract conflicts).

A powerful key to success of which most people are unaware is the non-verbal relationship messages that we get from each other all the time. Only when we each decode these face, body, and voice-dynamic signals as "you see me as a respected equal here," can effective communication work. If any partner reads "you seem to feel 'one-up' or 'one-down' to me," communication withers. A deadly variation, "I see me as 'one-down' also steadily wrecks the outcome of any communication.

* The three most basic verbal communication tools to build are: a healthily love and respect for yourself and your own needs; an equal respect for every partner's worth, dignity, and needs; and, a knowledge and proactive use of all five of these skills.

Reading about these skills will change little. Trying them patiently and with cautious optimism will cause positive communication and relationship changes, over time. The skills work with adults, kids, and among the different voices within you.

The more you use communication basics and skills to do win-win problem-solving, the more automatic and effective it becomes. Highly nurturing stepfamily adults learn, model, and teach these basics and skills to their kids—a priceless life-long gift.

CHAPTER EIGHT

NEGOTIATE A STEPFAMILY MISSION STATEMENT & CREATE A STEPFAMILY ADULT'S JOB (ROLE) DESCRIPTION

"The mission of our family is ...
to create a nurturing place of order, truth, love, happiness, and relaxation; and...
to provide opportunities for each person
to become responsibly independent, and effectively interdependent, ...
in order to achieve worthwhile purposes."

"Personal Leadership Application Workbook"
The Seven Habits of Highly Effective People, by Steven Covey

A mission statement is a brief, well-researched document describing basic principles and long-term priorities and goals. It declares clearly, "This is what I or we stand for and what we're dedicated to doing long-term." A well-deliberated consensual mission statement can provide a solid basis for effective stepfamily decision-making, role definitions and conflict resolution.

Creating a mission statement requires stepfamily adults to *want to* reduce their psychological wounds and progress on any needed grief work, understand and accept stepfamily realities, fully accept their stepfamily identity and what it means, and be able to respectfully negotiate their long-term mission as stepfamily adults and teammates. Progress at these requires stepparents, biological parents and involved relatives to reduce major wounds and post-divorce barriers.

Typical stepfamily adults are confused and conflicted on who is "supposed to" do what with and for whose kids—especially if all adults haven't genuinely accepted their stepfamily identity. They're also often conflicted over how to nurture kids effectively. This chapter illustrates written stepfamily adult "job" (responsibility") descriptions, based on a consensual family mission statement. Investing time in these two vital tasks, combined with growing the effective communication skills covered in Chapter Seven, are major ways to avoid stressful values and loyalty conflicts and relationship triangles in and between related stepfamily co-parenting homes.

Family Roles and Rules

What are family *roles* and *rules*? A *role* defines "who among us does what?" Roles are sets of responsibilities and behaviors governing our social conduct. For example, we expect parents to procreate, love, nurture, provide, guide, and limit. Kids are "supposed to" depend, explore, test, make mistakes, test, retest, eat, learn, and follow (for a while).

Average three-generation biological families have a number of roles. So we can talk clearly about these, we assign them titles, such as: *mom, dad, sister, son, daughter, uncle, cousin, grandmother, "the baby,"* and so on. While most multi-home stepfamilies also share these roles, they also deal on a daily basis with a slew of additional roles, such as: *half-brother, step-nephew, stepdaughter, absent biological father, stepsister,* and *stepparent.* There are no schools and few social norms for these roles yet, so most step-people have to invent them as they go. What is a "good" step-dad, anyway? An "excellent" half-sister? Who decides how a non-custodial mother is supposed to act? What if others disagree—who is the authority?

Stepfamily *rules* define how, when, and where your old *and* new roles are performed. In biological and stepfamilies alike, there are hundreds of rules. They sound like: "Hang up your wet towel neatly (not wadded up), after drying yourself (rather than next week), on the towel bar (not the sink, the floor, or behind the door)."

Until they conflict, most family rules are invisible. Still, they are the yardstick against which your members and outsiders measure whether each person is "good" or "bad' at their several family roles. Two biological families merging via a wedding will have rules that mesh well enough and others that resoundingly conflict.

These rules govern your members' ways of handling a dizzying array of everyday things, like home maintenance and chores; shopping; parenting; privacy and sex; finances; pets; social and leisure planning; medical, legal, and religious decisions; spirituality and worship; holidays, birthdays, and special events; communication and problem-solving; ethics and morals; power and authority; emotional expression, touching; and humor and play.

Because they are made up of two or more households, and have tasks and roles that biological families do not, most stepfamilies have to invent new rules to govern child visitations, names, custody, financial support and inheritance, and perhaps adoption. Functional, intact biological families do not need such rules.

An important family rule governs rules themselves: who sets, judges, interprets, enforces, and changes each home's and stepfamily's rules? If all your members agree, well and good. What is your rule about family rules right now? Keep in mind that "no rule" *is* a rule.

Your emerging stepfamily roles and rules must usually be negotiated between three to six, often hostile, stepfamily co-parenting adults, many relatives, and typically three or more children. Normally, many of your people will hold conflicting values about "proper" family, parenting, and child conduct and priorities which evolved before your wedding. Probably most of their values and "should's" pertain to biological families, and so will need major revision over time. This guarantees you all an ongoing stream of loyalty conflicts, and therefore makes it very important that stepfamily adults grow shared assertion, listening, and problem-solving skills that work.

Since up to half of your stepfamily's roles are new, the rules for each role are initially vague and confusing, and are often in conflict in and among your two to three stepfamily co-parenting homes. It's normal, then, to be continually redefining and rebalancing the responsibilities of your three to six stepfamily adults, step-kids, and relatives, for five to eight or more years.

A vital role-rule question every family (eventually) decides is "who's really in charge here?" If you and your partner(s) do not feel like defining this clearly, your kids will demand that you do! One of their principal early stepfamily jobs is to test relentlessly for security, freedoms, limits, and leadership in their home(s). Often this is mistaken for "acting out."

Your fundamental stepfamily task here is for all your members to (eventually) agree enough on: "here's how we each and all shall act towards each other, across many, many kinds of situations." Your challenge as a stepfamily adult is to provide consistent effective leadership in reaching this complex, often confusing agreement. This implies doing a lot of patient negotiation and conflict resolution with just about everybody. That means making lots of time to talk and really listening to each other—without resentment.

Stepfamily adults who have not recovered from their own unhealed childhood wounds often have the most trouble mastering this role-rule task, because behind their social and the inner self they keep hidden, they are often combinations of people-pleasing co-dependents—in other words, anxious, withdrawn non-feelers; forceful or whiny control-addicts; noisy or covert teen rebels; or dreamy philosophers. But, self-propelled personal recoveries, where needed, can over time change such combinations into sets of cooperative, effective family leaders.

The mission statement, a tool that can greatly help you master your unique stepfamily, is borrowed from the business world. The leaders of the most successful businesses evolve early a clear guiding statement of the key principles and goals for their enterprise. From this mission statement emerge policies (rules), responsibilities and structure (roles), and detailed plans to reach key goals. All major decisions on running our enormously complex, dynamic country are founded on such a mission statement: the U.S. Constitution.

Does your employer have such a mission statement? If so, does it affect you? Is it used in day-to-day operations, or is it just words on filed pages and unseen plaques? Paradoxically, many of you come home from a job guided by some form of charter, yet never think of forging and using a similar statement of principles and aims for your homes and primary relationships. Marriage vows are such statements, yet rarely do you find them on family walls or refrigerator doors for daily reference and guidance.

Try this exercise. Ask several grownups and kids: "What's the purpose of your family?" Most people will at first be startled, reflect (perhaps), and then say something like, *"Uh, well, I'm not sure. Never really thought about it."* Some will joke to cover their discomfort. Dry cleaners, sports teams, Brownie troops, General Motors, interior decorators, and McDonald's restaurants all have clear written purposes. Probably your house of worship, bank, and grocer do, too. Does your family?

How would each of your parents have answered the question? Did they refer to specific mutual long-term objectives several times a month in making key family decisions across the years? Most parents do have goals. They would like "to build a good life together," "to be happy, healthy, and safe," "to give our kids better than we got," and "to share the good times and the bad together." While heartfelt, such aims can be toothless. They are often too general and vague to really guide major family choices or create specific long-range results.

Here's our point: to avoid another divorce and to *thrive*, stepfamily adults need a clear, workable joint plan toward specific marriage and child-raising goals. The goals you are working with in this book provide the raw materials for a stepfamily mission statement. What they do not provide is an underlying set of basic principles or values—like our U.S. Bill of Rights does. Your set of basic principles must come from deep within you.

Most adults with unhealed childhood wounds in denial have absolutely no concept of clearly defining their own personal rights and goals, and acting assertively on them. Most are used to focusing on others' rights, and feeling (resentfully and/or resignedly) obliged to fill them first. Others know only how to focus on their own needs. Recovery helps rebalance this over time.

From defining your basic relationship and step-family goals, family "job descriptions" can evolve under your *intentional* guidance for the new roles and their related rules that determine how you all live together. The alternative to tackling this challenge head-on is living defensively and semi-chaotically in an often stressful multi-home stepfamily environment, wearily putting out a relentless stream of small and large emotional fires, for years.

Pay attention to how you are feeling. How likely is it that average remarrying stepfamily adults and key supporters fully understand the gist and implications of what you have just read?

Family Mission Statements

A mission statement is a brief, well-researched document describing the basic principles and goals of a person or group. It declares clearly "what I or we stand for and what we're dedicated to doing." It may or may not include key guidelines on how to achieve the goals.

A mission statement is the foundation of all common policies, roles, and decisions. It is a blueprint that guides a person's or group's activities toward consistency, order, and desire outcomes. Such charters describe clearly "this is why I, or we, exist and where we intend to go."

For perspective, four kinds of common mission statements are: personal, relationship, organizational, and national. The first is a concise declaration of what a person is trying to do with his or her life. It implies the author has taken responsibility for the direction and outcome of his or her days and achievements. Most of us do not think seriously of drafting such a statement. We never saw our parents or key teachers do it, nor any heroes or heroines. Do you know anyone who has?

One way of answering the universal puzzle of "why am I alive?" is to believe "I have unique gifts, and my life's mission is to find, develop, and use them creatively to benefit the world as best I can." A personal mission statement might succinctly expand on that theme by naming the author's key talents and describing generally what he or she wishes to do with them over the years.

Have you ever thought about your life that way? Against what vision will you measure the "success" of your life when you are old? For most of us, it is far easier to live reactively several days or events at a time, without creating and striving intentionally, or proactively, for a clear long-term life goal. Our lives gradually evolve, then, as a mosaic of small plans and achievements, often well below what we are really capable of.

Wedding vows are the traditional example of a relationship (marital) mission statement. Ministers provide a generic statement for couples who have not devised their own ("Do you, John, take this woman, Teresa, to have and to hold ...") People who remarry seem more likely to create their own vows, which may include pledges of loyalty and support for each other's children.

Whether wedding vows are generic or personal, most couples lose track of them over time, as the romance of dating matures into humdrum daily living patterns. Can you think of a couple who framed and posted their nuptial pledges on a prominent wall in their home as a personal and public reminder? Most mates each have a general idea of what they are trying to "do" with their relationship, but rarely refer to their goals except perhaps on anniversaries, retreats, or in or counselor's offices.

What do you suppose would happen to the epidemic U.S. divorce rate if most couples made and used a meaningful relationship mission statement? What would be different in your life if your parents had devised and used a parenting mission statement, or did they? If you have children, do you know specifically what you are tying to do with and for them long range? Do your children know?

Organizational mission statements are the most common. Many religious orders, businesses, colleges, and financial institutions (trusts, funds, banks) publish brief declarations of their main values and objectives. If they are effective declarations, their personnel, financial, and operating policies and decisions are consistently based on them. Here is the current mission statement of a Midwestern hospital:

> *"West Suburban Hospital Medical Center is a community-based, not-for-profit, non-sectarian provider of high quality health care which is sensitive to the needs of people in our immediate and surrounding communities.*
>
> *West Suburban Hospital Medical Center prepares and educates health professionals to take their place in the health care system.*
>
> *The Medical Center has an ongoing commitment to the well-being of the community we serve, our charitable trust, and individuals we employ."*

We normally associate organizational charters with businesses, not families. Yet the leaders of every home and multi-home stepfamily, including yours, have basic principles, and at least short-term objectives, that shape their daily decisions. Though usually unwritten, these still govern how the family operates. In all families, personal, relationship, home, and family charters interact. When they harmonize enough with each other, local social values, and natural laws, the family works, over time.

The odds of a family being functional or effective go way up when its leaders are consistently clear and united on, and dedicated to, what they are tying to do together. Do you agree? Have you ever been in a family, team, or group like this? How did it feel to you? Did it work well?

Sadly, most U.S. stepfamilies ultimately do not work well, i.e., the remarriages on which the families are founded eventually decay and collapse. Troubled couples are either unclear on their shared marital and stepfamily co-parenting objectives, opposed on too many of them, and/or give them low priority.

For any family, person or relationship, the alternative to using (rather than just making) a mission statement is described by the title of a book on career planning, *If You Don't Know Where You Want To Go, You'll Probably Wind Up Somewhere Else.*

Jeanette Lofas, the founder of the Stepfamily Institute in New York, has said that forming a typical stepfamily is like merging two small companies. Salaried managers of merging enterprises would rarely try to blend their people, roles, assets, cultures, and objectives without a clear set of goals and a phased, consensual plan to reach these goals. Yet that is exactly what many, or most, step-couples set out to do. They assume "our love will see us though." More often than not, it does not.

Perhaps they began with a shared high-priority need, or dream, to intentionally fashion a "good life" for themselves and their children. Further, they felt responsible for making this dream happen, rather than assuming that it would "somehow" come true. Finally, they evidently spent a lot of time thinking and talking about specifically what comprises the "good life" they wanted to co-create over time. Do you agree?

Notice your feelings and "inner voices" now. Are you curious, interested, and energized?

Or are you feeling skeptical, resistant, or indifferent? If the latter, stop to examine your assumptions and visions about the stepfamily and remarriage you have formed.

Why Bother?

Picture a summer white-water rafting adventure down the Colorado River, through the Grand Canyon. You have never been on such a trip and trust the seasoned "rivermen" who pilot your two big pontoon rafts to keep you safe, from what you do not know. On the seventh day, you come to a boiling, 400-yard, boulder-strewn stretch of the river they had warned you about since you began. In the middle of this stretch is "The Devil's Hole," a foaming pit 12 or 15 feet deep formed by the water roaring around a cabin-sized boulder. Your pilots tell you, matter-of-factly, that some rafters and kayakers have died here, misjudging how to navigate the difficult and violent course. This sobriety is infectious.

With some anxiety, you watch as the "rivermen" beach the second of your two rafts and walk the shoreline of the roaring stretch ahead, assessing complex current flows and hidden rocks, and planning how to navigate this dangerous stretch of river. No one doubts that your lives are literally in their hands. Finally they return, and half of you intently watch the other craft gather speed upriver and shoot down the churning channel, bucking and twisting like a living thing. You cheer as they make it through, and then—hearts pounding—it's your turn.

This story parallels the re-marital journey you are about to take with your kids: it is smooth in places and dangerous in others. It is new and unknown territory, which can be lethal to your remarriage. Former (biological family) marriage and parenting experiences are not a reliable guide. You two, and your stepfamily co-parenting ex-mate(s), are the pilots, and your kids the dependent passengers. Your challenge is to either run your unique stepfamily river assuming it will be placid enough, or scout it out well in advance, forecast the rough stretch, and plan together where you want to come out and how you are going to get all of you there safely.

Over two thirds of American stepfamilies now capsize somewhere during their five- to 10-year trip, re-traumatizing all involved, especially their typical bewildered kids of parental divorce and remarriage who need help to:

- Convert vague or distorted self-perceptions, including gender identity, into a clear, healthy, and appropriate sense of their unique true self. This includes developing and accepting a realistic body image.
- Convert habitual self-doubt, ambivalence, and uncertainty into self-confidence, and grow merited trust in the dependability and good intentions of most caregivers and adult authorities.
- Develop the abilities to fully feel and express all emotions (especially anger, sadness, despair, and fear) within appropriate limits, without guilt, shame, or anxiety, and to

be comfortable enough with others doing the same. Failure to fill these needs will seriously inhibit a child's ability to grieve, communicate effectively, and manage interpersonal conflict well.

- Develop the abilities to tolerate change, uncertainty, inter-personal and conflict within themselves, imperfection, and healthy intimacies.
- Replace toxic ways of self-soothing (e.g., addictions, reality distortions, and avoidances) with holistically healthy habits and healthy sources of comfort and reassurance.
- Strengthen their ability to form real (versus faked) attachments to (bond with) healthy people, ideas and goals. And,
- Believe without ambivalence that their lives have intrinsic worth, promise, and real meaning rather than feeling old pessimism, worthlessness, and inner emptiness.

These are the re-divorced couples who underestimated the alien-ness, complexity, and risks of their adventure; and have no clear, informed goals or meaningful plan to reach them.

Many distressed remarried couples initially do not even identify themselves as a stepfamily. They also put careers, leisure, "things," and some other priorities ahead of co-managing their relationship and family. This is crudely equivalent to our "rivermen" focusing more on their personal investment programs, home repairs, and favorite sports teams, rather than responsibly getting everyone safely through the foaming rapids.

Creating a successful stepfamily is about the most challenging and risky event you have ever intentionally undertaken. Did you have clear goals and a well-researched plan, or did you just jump in, trusting that "somehow" you would be safe enough? What was the outcome?

What is your partner's style? Impulsive or prudent? If you are divorced, how did you each approach your first marriage—with a plan or by the seats of your pants? Can you imagine going through another divorce, with your and/or your partner's kids? How would you feel about yourself?

A final advantage of investing energy together in drafting re-marital and stepfamily mission statements is that with them in place, it becomes much easier to draft effective stepfamily co-parenting job descriptions. We will focus more on that a little later.

Making an Effective Mission Statement

Whether a mission statement describes an individual, a marital or parent-child relationship, or a group enterprise, there are some traits that distinguish statements that work from those that do not. There are three sets of keys to making a stepfamily mission statement effective: (1) The stepfamily adults' priorities, values, and knowledge; (2) the document itself; and, (3) if, how, and when the statement is used. Let's briefly explore all three. Assess yourselves thoughtfully on these factors as you proceed; build an honest report card together. Keep in mind this is about *learning*, not fault-finding.

1. Priorities, Values, and Knowledge

Stepfamily Adult Priorities

If you and your stepfamily adult partners do not now rank your long-range multi-home stepfamily emotional health highly, no document will help you succeed. Do you know what your current basic life priorities are? How you have used your recent waking hours points the way.

Values

Thorough exploration of this factor can fill whole books. Successful remarried adults have several key values in common. There are many others besides these:

- *Mutual and self love and respect.* Both mates rank their own personal needs, health, and worth as being consistently just as important as those of other prized people in their lives, including their kids.
  Women and men from seriously dysfunctional childhoods often put their own needs and worth last, from long habit, and inevitably grow dissatisfied and resentful. Many step-people are from significantly dysfunctional childhoods. People who feel genuine self-love with little guilt have no trouble in composing a Personal Bill of Rights, or in honoring the equal rights of others, including ex-mates!
- *Vision and planning.* All successful stepfamily co-parenting partners agree that they are electing a complex, long-distance project. They each feel that making and using clear, long-range personal and family goals (rather than just immediate goals or no goals at all) is vital to their eventual family and re-marital success.
  Effective stepfamily adults maintain a shared clear vision of specifically what kind of a multi-home stepfamily they want to build. From that, they form and use a plan to bring their vision to life.
- *Acceptance of interpersonal conflict.* Typical stepfamilies normally have major recurring clashes of needs and values in and between their several homes. Successful stepfamily adults each accept that reality, without undue blame, shame, or anxiety.
  They patiently develop tools to manage family conflict well enough. One vital tool is learning and using the five effective verbal communications skills you learned in an earlier chapter. A mission statement that works will probably clearly state the stepfamily adults' attitudes and aims on resolving family members' conflicting needs. What are your values and goals on this?
- *Commitment.* All three to four-plus stepfamily co-leaders are truly dedicated to making their own lives, their relationships, and their whole multi-home family, healthy and

functional enough. Adults who value themselves too little or too much, or have no clear, positive purpose to their life, will have trouble making effective mission statement.

Knowledge

Successful stepfamily adults can clearly describe what emotionally and spiritually healthy (versus dysfunctional or toxic) persons, relationships, and families are. This includes clear stepfamily adult awareness of what is normal in their multi-home stepfamily.
The next key to mission statement success is…

2. The Document Itself

Traits that promote the usefulness of any family mission statement include:

- *Brevity.* Notice that the example at the opening of this chapter is well under one page in length. Mission statements that are too long risk being too confusing, rigid, and complex.
- *Clarity and simplicity.* To keep the statement short and simple, every word counts. Though brief, the family mission statement in this chapter probably went through many drafts and adjustments before getting it "just right."
- *Flexibility and balance.* Effective mission statement guide rather than confine. They are general enough to avoid legalistic rigidity, and specific enough to provide clear direction.
- *Relevance.* Creating a meaningful family mission statement requires each of the co-authors to first get clear on these four fundamental questions: (1) "What is a family?" (2) "Who comprises our stepfamily?" (3) "What's an emotionally and spiritually healthy stepfamily?" (4) "What are the main purposes of our multi-home stepfamily?"
  For perspective on these questions, ask yourself: "What's the difference between our family and a baseball team? A travel agency? A school? What basic things can only be done in and by our family? Typical answers mention patiently preparing all dependent children to be safe, loving, independent, and productive; and empowering each family member's love, self-respect, holistic health, personal growth, security, support, and spirituality.
  Other family topics like home decorating, car maintenance, and pet care are minor compared to these, and so are "irrelevant" to your mission statement.
- *Reality.* Stepfamilies differ structurally and developmentally from typical biological families in over 60 ways, as explored in Chapter Five. Members of your stepfamily face well over a dozen personal tasks that people in biological families do not face. There are almost 60 myths that well-meaning, uninformed stepfamily adults stress

themselves and their kids with, because they expect their family to feel, act, and "be" a biological family.

A realistic stepfamily mission statement, then, may be a little longer than a typical biological family mission statement. It will describe goals on key focal points that biological-family mission statement do not include. For instance:

> - Adult and kids *grieving* major divorce and remarriage losses, and healing related emotional and spiritual wounds.
> - *Rebuilding* damaged interpersonal securities, trusts, and self-esteem.
> - *Child visitation, support, and custody* goals and values.
> - *Relations among step-siblings* and with other step-relatives, especially with absent biological parents.
> - And, *handling loyalty and other values conflicts*, which have to do with stepfamily adults choosing relationship priorities.

- *Focus.* An effective stepfamily or personal mission statement will highlight values and key long-term targets, rather than related plans and strategies. Family job descriptions may include the latter.
- *Integrity.* There are no self-contradicting goals in an effective mission statement. The stepfamily goals declared are in clear harmony with all stepfamily adults' personal life values and goals, and natural, civil, and social laws.
- *Format.* A final aspect of your mission statement document is its physical and visual form. A ball-point declaration on a grocery bag has a much different emotional impact than framed manuscript-quality calligraphy on fine linen-stock paper or parchment. Some appropriate graphics and artwork (e.g. a stepfamily crest you all create) can add dignity and importance to your statement.
- *Scope.* For best effect, your mission statement should apply to all residents in all the homes each of your kids live in part-time and full-time. Considering genetics, history, and emotional, financial, and legal links, your immediate stepfamily members live in two or three related homes. If you include all your kids' living and emotionally involved grandparents, aunts, and uncles, the scope of your mission statement can envelop 60 or more people living in a dozen or more homes.

Besides your (1) priorities, values, and stepfamily knowledge, and (2) the nature and appearance of your document, the final factor is…

3. Using Your Mission Statement

Personal, marriage, stepfamily co-parenting, household, and stepfamily mission statement either lifeless pieces of paper in a drawer or file, or truly helpful reference documents, like bibles, phone books, and dictionaries. What makes the difference is the motivation, thought, and cooperation that went into them, and how consistently motivated family leaders and members refer to them in making daily and special decisions. By definition, each mission statement is unique. The "right" way to make and use them depends on what works for you and your stepfamily members.

Several basic stepfamily adult's decisions here are: (1) When do you co-create your statement? (2) Where do you put your mission statement(s) in your home(s)? (3) How often do you refer to them, and why? (4) Who do you give copies to, and why? And, (5) do you *demand* compliance with the declaration from all family members, or *request and encourage* same?

Recommendations for Using Your Mission Statement

- Draft your own declaration together, rather than adopting someone else's. You are far more apt to respect your own heart-values and shared goals than those of other authors, no matter how venerated or articulate. Even changing, adding, or deleting several words can make someone else's inspiring words more yours.
- If it is not too late, draft and include your multi-home stepfamily mission statement in your wedding service. Doing so, especially if you have involved your kids (and their other parent(s)) in drafting it, can strengthen the emotional foundation of your union and extended family. Doing this can impart a special emotional power to your statement that can greatly add to its usefulness across your years together.
- Display your statement prominently in a place residents and visitors to your home will see it when they enter or socialize together. The alternative is probably "out of sight—out of mind."
- Review your declaration as a couple and family regularly, for example at anniversaries. Authorize yourselves to revise earlier drafts as your re-marital and stepfamily experience and wisdom grow.
- Consider giving a copy of your mission statement to your kid(s)' other stepfamily adult(s). In the best of all worlds, you will invite these other stepfamily adults to participate in drafting it. Because of post-divorce or new re-marital bitterness and hostilities, this often is not possible. If the language of your statement specifically includes co-honoring the needs, feelings, and rights of your other stepfamily adults, they may be more receptive. They may also draft their own statement. There may be value in giving a copy to your kids' grandparents or other key relatives, too.
- Read your mission statement together, perhaps out loud, when you encounter serious stepfamily or re-marital conflicts. Doing so can provide a steadying beacon in emotionally confusing times, when one or more of you have temporarily lost your bearings. It can also lead to important revisions.

- Avoid demanding that all stepfamily members follow your stated goals or adopt the values in your declaration. Evolve a statement that acts like a guiding keel for your stepfamily ship, rather than a confining, narrow channel.
- Use your mission statement as a foundation for evolving and applying job descriptions for some of your confusing and alien new stepfamily roles.

Stepfamily Job Descriptions

After drafting a mission statement, evolving specific job descriptions for the key new roles that you all are tying to fill can further help your stepfamily succeed. These descriptions might also (clumsily) be called "accountability declarations" or similar. In typical remarriage homes, the most important of these new roles are those of stepmother and stepfather.

Family job descriptions are like mission statements in that they clearly declare the author's basic values and goals. They differ in that they include more detail, and they may describe goals over a specific time period. The basic values and goals in a finished job description probably will not change too much. Specific short-term objectives will shift and need to be updated regularly.

Like your mission statement, effective job descriptions will be discussed openly and thoroughly with every person significantly affected by the role or job. A stepparent's job description, then, should include the thoughtful input and suggestions of at least all (older) kids and other stepfamily adults involved. These descriptions will ideally also be based on a clear understanding of the two dozen or so special developmental tasks most minor step-kids face.

Each spouse may make a separate goal statement for his or her relationship with the co-spouse and for co-managing the home. If this were true of the job description sample on the next page, it would be shorter, for the first two parts of it would be in these separate statements.

An optional third document is a specific strategy or plan to reach the key goals in the family job description. Plans may be blended into the latter, or may stand alone. Unless it is consulted and used, such a plan becomes just another piece of paper.

Sample Stepfather Job Description

The example that follows has four parts: "Basic Principles," "Common Parenting Goals," and "Specific Stepfathering Goals" for this man's stepdaughter, Ann (eight years old), and "Biological Fathering Objectives" for his biological son, Alex (15). Thus, this description defines two similar, and different, roles.

The author tries to reach a balance between being general enough to allow flexibility, and being specific enough to provide clear guidance. Here, Martha is the author's wife, Ann's custodial biological mother. Rick is Martha's ex-husband, Ann's biological father. Alex lives with his single biological mother, Nina (confusing, isn't it). Both kids visit their non-custodial biological parent periodically.

As you read this, note which parts you agree with and feel good about, and why, and which you would do differently. There is no right way!

My Key Responsibilities As Ann's Stepfather And Alex's Biological Dad

1. Basic Principles

- I will be true to my God and myself before all others. Keeping myself healthy and balanced is one of the greatest gifts I can give to Martha, Ann, and Alex. I'm responsible for doing so.
- I accept Rick and Nina as truly equal stepfamily co-parenting partners with Martha and me, except any time we feel their values or choices harm or threaten us, Alex, or Ann.
- Martha and I are equally responsible for providing a safe and healthy home for all under our roof. I will never consciously cause or allow verbal, emotional, physical, or spiritual abuse or neglect in our home, or to our members outside our home.
- My overall responsibility to Ann and Alex is to nurture, protect, and encourage them as unique children of God, in cooperation with Martha, Nina, and Rick.
- When people can't agree in and between our three homes, my marriage to Martha will usually come first. I ask and expect the same priority from Martha. I pledge my part in protecting us all from re-divorce. My loving bond with Alex will never break. My growing bonds with Martha and Ann are different and less sure.
- I will strive to stay clear on what an effective stepfamily adult is in our multi-home stepfamily, and will steadily work for excellence in this job, within my and our limits.
- As a stepfamily adult, I am a willing, temporary caregiver, guide, and protector for Alex and Ann—not an owner.
- Because I have known and nurtured Alex longer, I share more responsibility for his values and choices than I do for Ann's. I will become more responsible for Ann as we all build our stepfamily together.
- To me, parental love means consistently prizing and nurturing the spirit, talents, dreams, and uniqueness of any child. In this sense, I love Ann and Alex equally. Because Alex carries my genes, name, features, and lineage, I also love him deeply in a different way.
- Nina and I are jointly responsible for major stepfamily co-parenting decisions about Alex. Martha and Rick are primarily responsible for major stepfamily co-parenting decisions about Ann. Martha and I can advise each other on such decisions, where helpful. I share equal responsibility with Martha for daily living decisions in our home.

- I honor Alex's and Ann's grandparents and relatives as valued, special partners in our extended stepfamily. I respect their rights to know about and contribute to Alex's and Ann's welfare. But Ann and I don't have to follow their counsel. Martha may have a different view on this.

- I will never try to take Rick's place as Ann's biological father. I do fathering "things" with and for her every day. I will do what I can to respect and promote a healthy, loving relationship between Ann and Rick. If I feel Rick's actions seriously harm or threaten Ann, I will speak my opinion clearly and promptly, and seek peaceful change together with Martha.

- I will protect Alex and Ann from experiencing anyone, including Martha, me, and themselves, abusing, neglecting, or shaming them; or violating their personal boundaries.

- In guiding and protecting Ann, I acknowledge the real limits on me that exist in Martha and Rick's divorce decree. I claim the right to disagree with those limits, and to work cooperatively and within the law to change them, if Martha and I agree that would help Ann.

- In our home and stepfamily, I believe every member—regardless of age, gender, or ancestry—always has an equal right to:
  - Have their ideas, feelings, and dreams heard and respected.
  - Have their needs considered seriously and fairly.
  - Know clearly who's responsible for what, and what our rules and consequences are.
  - Make and learn from their own mistakes, without shame or excess guilt.
  - Be seen as a unique, special, and worthwhile person.
  - Learn and grow at their own pace and in their own directions.
  - Enough privacy, space, and freedom of choice.
  - Unconditional love, respect, and physical, emotional, and spiritual safety.
  - Their own friends, values, and activities—if not harmful, in Martha's and my opinions.

- I believe Alex and Ann each have the right to live at some time with their other biological parent if they want to, and if all adults affected by such a change agree on it.

- And, I'm open to constructive ideas from other people about my stepfamily co-parenting job. In the end, I am responsible for making, updating, and acting on this statement to be the best stepfamily adult I can be. I've never been in a stepfamily, so I'll make mistakes as I learn how to be an effective stepfather. That's okay, as long as I learn from them, and apologize when needed.

2. My General Stepfamily Co-Parenting Goals

- With Martha, provide a safe and loving home, with enough clothing, healthy food, spiritual and medical care, comfort, space, laughter, and peace for us all.
- Love Alex, Ann, my adult partners, and myself as human beings equally and unconditionally (where possible), and to be gentle with myself and them in those times that I fail.
- Enforce clear limits with other stepfamily members that allow Martha and me our own spaces, privacy, friends, and interests separate from theirs.
- Help both kids learn about our loving God and their own spirituality, and encouraging them to form their own healthy beliefs.
- Help Alex and Ann learn what their special personal gifts are, and how to grow and use them in a safe and balanced way.
- Set the best examples for the kids so that I can be consistently practicing what I preach. I'm specially dedicated to showing them with Martha what a healthy marriage looks and sounds like!
- Work patiently towards acceptable compromises when our former biological family customs clash with Martha's, Ann's, and Rick's former ways.
- Develop win/win ways of fixing stepfamily adult's problems between us all. This includes my really listening to what the others feel and need, and not forcing my solutions on them.
- I want to learn how to grieve well, and help our kids and my stepfamily adult partners identify and mourn our respective divorce and remarriage losses.
- Let Martha, Nina, and Rick know clearly and promptly if I have a stepfamily adult problem, and then either ask for their help or resolve it with them.
- Thank Martha, Rick, and Nina for their stepfamily adult's efforts and support, periodically; and thank the kids when they cooperate, try, or go above and beyond.
- Periodically ask Martha and Rick if they're feeling enough stepfamily adult's support from me, and if not, ask clearly what they need from me.
- Talk directly with Alex or Ann if I have a problem with them, rather than going through Martha, Nina, or Rick. Keep my stepfamily adult partners informed enough.
- Merit my own and others' respect by steadily acting on my stepfamily adult principles. This includes standing up firmly for my own rights as a person, and drawing clear, consistent limits on what behaviors I will tolerate.
- Periodically spend fun time with each and both kids, without distractions.
- Encourage each child to ask questions and take safe risks, without fear!
- Take a genuine interest in what and who Alex and Ann care about and hope for, where I can—and be honest when I can't. With my partners and their schools, teach Ann and Alex safe practices around drugs (including food) and sex when that's timely.

- Never use the kids to fill my needs, other than asking for reasonable help in our home.
- Get clearer on what "effective child discipline" means in our three-home stepfamily, and strive for it cooperatively with my partners. I want Ann and Alex to always know clearly what our main house rules are, and what will happen if they choose to not follow them.
- If any of us stepfamily adults disagree on house rules, my goal is to resolve this without catching the kids between us. Rick and Nina have the right to different house rules than we have, even though this is hard at times on Ann and Alex.
- Practice our family philharmonic orchestra regularly—we can be great!
- Learn with Martha by February if there's a stepfamily support group we could try out, and do so.
- Don't take my two jobs as biological and stepfather *too* seriously!
- Review this statement at least yearly with Martha, Rick, Nina, Alex, and Ann to keep it current, known, and *working*.

3. My Goals For All This Year

1. Remind myself regularly of the gifts, joys, and opportunities Ann brings into my life, to balance the hassles!
2. Look for chances to validate Ann's achievements, no matter how small. Let her know clearly I think she's special when I'm feeling that.
3. With Martha, help Ann learn to channel her anger instead of exploding. If no progress by summer, talk about counseling for her (all of us?) with Martha and Rick.
4. Learn "what's normal" from other parents of girls, especially from other step and biological fathers, including Dad and Martha's father.
5. Read at least two how-to step-fathering books by August.
6. Reduce our hassles about TV limits soon!
7. Stay clear when Martha and Rick disagree over Ann, unless they ask me for input or support.
8. Stop expecting Martha to discipline the way I do. Work patiently towards compromises and consistency together.
9. Remind myself when unsure that I'm co-leader of this home, and as such, I have equal right with Martha to provide limits and consequences for Ann.
10. Try to accept that, although I do more fathering things than Rick can, Ann's natural loyalty will be to him. This has little to do with my worth as a person or stepfather.
11. End the struggle among me, Martha, and her parents about Ann's church attendance. Keep what's best for our marriage clearly in mind.

12. Rethink my objections to a pet.

13. Don't get hooked when Ann accuses me of being unfair; try to see her side of this.

14. Split family taxi services with Martha without griping (too much).

15. When we have problems with Ann's visitations, consider Ann's and Rick's needs equally with Martha's and mine.

16. Stay informed on Ann's school grades, projects, and activities, and help where I can. Make an honest effort to go to all parent-teacher conferences with Martha.

17. Build a "Phantom Five" clubhouse in the back yard with Ann and her friends by May. See if Rick wants to help.

18. Help Ann and be with her in Indian Princess activities.

19. By 4/31, get clear with myself, then Martha on whether I'll contribute to Ann's college fund. If so, decide when and how much. Tell Rick and Nina. I want *both* kids to have an excellent education.

20. By October: think through how I want to provide for Ann, discuss with Martha, and revise my will. Tell Alex, Nina, and Rick.

21. Give myself permission to flex on any of these, or add new goals, as our year unfolds.

4. My Goals For Alex This Year

1. See or talk to him at least once a week, and don't try "too hard" when we're together.

2. Remember to tell him often how much I love him and how special he is, instead of assuming that he knows these.

3. Accept joint responsibility with Nina for working on healing our post-divorce issues, without involving Alex.

4. Work with Nina and Alex toward win/win solutions of our conflicts on Alex's dental work, weight, allowance, learning to drive, and smoking. Include Martha's suggestions on each of these.

5. With Nina, make sure Alex knows clearly within limits, and without blaming her or me, why we divorced, and why we'll never get back together. Ask for feelings about these. If he gives them, try to listen non-defensively. This is really *scary*!

6. Enforce healthy limits for Alex along with Martha and Nina, in spite of the guilt and sorrow I feel about his pain from our divorce and my remarriage.

7. With Nina, find out about the Rainbows program at school and encourage Alex to participate if he's ready.

8. Accept that Alex and Martha don't love each other the way I wish they could, and that it's enough to grow mutual respect for now. This is *hard*!

9. Remember that Martha's never been a step-mom before, that she's learning how, and will make okay mistakes just like I do. Get clear by June on what we each expect of her as

Alex's stepmother. Learn Alex's, Ann's, and Nina's feelings on this. I hope Martha writes her own stepfamily adult's job description by midyear.

10. Within limits, tell Alex my daily feelings, dreams, and problems—as information, not as a pal, whiner, or dependent. I want him to know what being an adult man, husband, and father is like, and help him grow healthy images of these roles.

11. See that Alex, I, and Dad get some "guy" times together this year, at least once a quarter. I take responsibility for initiating this.

12. Stay out of the middle between Alex and Martha, Alex and Nina, Martha and Nina, and Ann and Alex when I can. When I can't, and compromises don't work for everyone, our marriage will come first with me, often enough for Martha.

13. Pay regular and special financial support on time. Honor my half of the Parenting Agreement Nina and I worked out. Work with her peacefully for change if it becomes outdated.

14. Help Alex feel truly welcome and a full member of our home when he visits. That includes both privileges and chores.

15. When we have problems with Alex's visitation, balance his, Nina's, and Ann's needs equally with ours.

16. Stay informed on Alex's school grades, projects, and activities. Attend all parent-teacher conferences with Nina, and his games when I can.

17. Support Alex's Outward Bound trip in June and football camp in July. Coordinate our August vacation plans with Nina with enough lead time.

I freely choose to work hard toward these stepfamily co-parenting goals, balanced with the other responsibilities and goals in my life. I'm glad for the chance to do them!

Take time to notice your thoughts and feelings now. Reflect. Clearly, this husband and stepfamily adult did not just dash this job description off without a lot of reflection and soul searching! What does this document say to you about his priorities? How do you think his wife, ex-mate, and Ann and Alex would feel about his writing this? Do you think a job description like this would stress or strengthen their remarriage and three-home stepfamily?

PART THREE

MERGE AND EVOLVE AN EFFECTIVE TEAM OF STEPFAMILY ADULTS

These four chapters build on all prior ones. They propose specific steps that you can take together to patiently evolve a stable, highly nurturing stepfamily for yourselves, your dependents, and descendants.

CHAPTER NINE

FORGE A FLOURISHING REMARRIAGE AND KEEP IT *SECOND*

Primary factors that shape the ability to nurture in any family are the holistic health, integrity, priorities and knowledge of each family adult, and the quality of each primary adult's relationship to the other. By definition, in a successful or healthy committed union, each partner gets their primary relationship needs met well enough, often enough. That implies both mates need to be steadily aware of, respect and prize what they and their partner need. Divorce suggests partners were unable to do this well enough.

Typical minor step-kids have a mix of developmental and family adjustment needs that constantly compete for primacy with adult couples' needs. Stepfamily adults must often choose whose needs come first—their personal and marital needs, or the kids' needs.

This chapter urges you, when viable dispute compromises don't appear, to protect your kids, your mate and yourself from another multi-year divorce trauma by consistently *wanting* to put your partnership needs ahead of dependents' needs, except in emergencies. The rationale for this is a paradox: by putting your couple needs ahead of your kids' needs now, you really put your kids first *long term* by protecting them from family breakup and broken bonds (losses).

Taking this one vitally important step further, in order to maintain a highly nurturing home, union and family, each stepfamily adult must steadily want to put his or her integrity and holistic health ahead of everything else, including his or her primary relationship and kids' (non-emergency) needs!

This is a profound challenge for most stepfamily adults. Typically, adults with unhealed childhood wounds were taught as kids to devalue themselves and their dignity, worth and needs, and to do that automatically—before true wound-recovery and despite painful consequences.

A Personal Bill of Rights

Many of us were accidentally given self-abusive or neglectful "rules" about our rights as human beings by our childhood caregivers, often because they got the same from theirs. Until personal recovery has begun, many of these adults find the idea of declaring their basic human rights alien and confusing. They can feel extra guilty about defining personal tolerance limits to others' behaviors.

The following is a sample of a Personal Bill of Rights. Statements like it apply to any person, regardless of age, gender, color, or creed. Most of us are only vaguely aware of many of the principles by which we run our lives, yet they shape our every decision and behavior.

Read the sample bill below, note your reaction, and then try drafting a similar document over time for yourself. If it is honest, and you really believe in it, you will not hesitate to share it with others and encourage them to draft their own bill. If you are not interested in doing this now, what does that mean?

No matter what your stepfamily role may be, author your own bill. Give yourself permission to let these statements evolve rather than having to get them right the first time. You are all on unfamiliar ground here!

- A Person's Bill of Rights -

This statement will clarify and remind me of my rights as a dignified and honorable human being. I was not taught some of these beliefs as a child and can strengthen my belief in them today. Affirming my personal rights repeatedly will help free me of old inhibitions and distorted beliefs, and empower me to be firmly assertive (rather than. aggressive or submissive) with others in a clear, positive, respectful way.

It's healthy for me to honor and respect my own rights and needs as much as I do those of every other person. I can legitimately proclaim and act on these rights without shame, guilt, or fear, in any way that doesn't interfere with other adults' and kids' equal rights. I need no one's permission to adopt and live from these beliefs.

No matter what my age, experience, or situation, I am a rare, unique, worthwhile human being— as is every other person. I bring a blend of talents, knowledge, and motives to the world like no other living or dead person. I honor and respect my own uniqueness, and that of each other person in my life. I claim the right to be ME, without explanation, apology, or defense. I am responsible for being me at all times. I affirm others' equal right to be their own unique selves (plural).

I Declare My Human Right To:

1. *My own feelings. They are a natural part of being me. They include: fear, sadness, anger, shame, uncertainty, confusion, joy, lust, hope, pride, happiness, etc.—even "numbness."*

2. *Tell others of my feelings if and when I choose to, without feeling guilty. I am responsible for this choice, but not for their reactions.*

3. *Say no, without guilt or shame, and to be responsible for the consequences.*

4. *Choose if, when, and how to meet others' expectations of me. If I choose not to meet them, I need not feel guilty. I am responsible for such choices.*

5. *Choose my own friends and acquaintances, and how and when to spend time with them. I may, but don't have to, justify these choices to others.*

6. *Make my own mistakes, and profit by them if I can.*

7. *Choose if, when, and how to respectfully tell others clearly how their actions are affecting me, and to take responsibility for doing so.*

8. *Earn and maintain my own self-respect and pride, rather than depending on other people's opinions of me.*

9. *Seek, evaluate, and accept or decline help, without undue shame or guilt.*

10. *Give others the responsibility for their own beliefs, decisions, feelings, and thoughts, without feeling guilty or selfish.*

11. *Seek situations, environments, and relationships that I feel are healthy, promote growth, and are nurturing for me. I do not owe, but may choose to give, others explanations of my decisions on these.*

12. *Be spontaneous, play, and have fun!*

13. *Develop and grow at my own pace, and in the directions I feel are best for me. This does not mean I reject others' well-meant advice or counsel.*

14. *Appreciate my own efforts, and honestly enjoy my own achievements without guilt or shame.*

15. *Act to fill my own wants and needs, rather than expect others to do so for me.*

16. *Periods of rest, refreshment, reflection, and relaxation. These are as productive for me as times of work and actions.*

17. *Choose whom I will trust, when, and with what.*

18. *Take on only as much as I can handle at any given time, and to tell others if I feel overloaded, without shame or guilt.*

19. *Nurture, love, and value myself as much as I do others who are special to me. Pride, in moderation, is not a sin, and never was.*

20. *Choose the paths and goals I wish for my life, and to pursue them without guilt, shame, or the need to justify them to others.*

21. *Take all the time I need to evaluate and make important life decisions, even if this stresses others.*

22. *Care for my body and soul lovingly and respectfully, in my own ways.*

23. *Decide on my own priorities and limits at any given time, and act on them as I see fit.*

24. *Distinguish between who my family, work-mates, and friends say I am (or was) and who I really am.*

25. *Be heard and clearly understood. My thoughts, feelings, wants, and needs are as legitimate, worthy, and important as anyone else's.*

26. *Decide what "perfect" or "excellent" is in any situation, and choose whether to strive for these or not.*

27. *Choose how to spend my time, and take the short-term and long-term consequences.*

28. *Tell others respectfully what I expect of them, realizing they may or may not choose to fulfill these expectations.*

29. *Choose how and when to peacefully fill my spiritual needs, even if my choices conflict with others' values or wishes. I do not have the right to force my spiritual or religious views, values, or practices on other people, nor do others have the right to force theirs on me.*

30. *Heal past personal shaming and wounds over time, and replace unhealthy inner messages I've lived by with more nurturing and productive ones.*

31. *Listen to and heed my inner voices with interest and respect, and sort out my true voices from others I hear.*

32. *Ask (not demand of) others how they feel about me, what they think about me, and what they want of me. They may choose to comply or not.*

33. *Decide if, when, and how to forgive both my mistakes and any hurts received from others. I affirm that such forgiveness promotes healing.*

34. *Work respectfully and peacefully to change laws or rules I feel are unjust or harmful to me and/or others.*

35. _____

36. _____

Take a moment now and reflect. How do the "Human Rights" above compare with the beliefs you are using to run your life now? Which of these 34 statements bring up the strongest feelings in you? Why? Do any bring up anger, anxiety, guilt, or righteousness? Would you add any statements to your version of this personal "Bill of Rights?" As a stepparent, do you feel the adults and kids in your life are honoring your rights enough?

What might happen for you if you invested some quality quiet time to draft your own "Bill of Rights" and then began to use it? As with the sample mission statements and stepfamily co-parenting job descriptions in Chapter Eight, you are cautioned against copying this example and using it. These documents come alive when you create your own.

Our culture is built of millions of families. Well after their kids are grown, they and others outside the family judge: did this family *work*? The chances of answering "Yes!" rise dramatically if the adult leaders of the family know clearly what they are tying to do and why. They cannot decide this without first becoming aware and clear on what they are trying to do with their own lives, and then with their primary committed relationship.

Typical Ongoing Primary Marital Needs

It is not unusual for most couples to only be hazily aware of the mix of the primary needs they depend on, or expect, each other to fill, until personal discomfort sets in. "In our relationship, I feel genuinely and consistently loved by you, i.e., to feel …

Special to, and prized by you, among all your other relationship and priorities. This is a measure of your commitment to me and to our unique relationship." And I need to feel …

Needed emotionally and physically by you, but not over-needed (co-dependent); and …

Respected and appreciated by you as a unique adult person, a fe/male, a mate, a sexual partner, a home co-manager, a co-parent, a citizen; and I need to feel …

Liked and enjoyed by you often enough; and to feel …

Heard empathically (vs. agreed with), by you frequently; and …

And in our committed relationship, I need to feel genuinely and steadily …

Trusted by you with your deepest current dreams, fears, shames, doubts, and joys; and ..

Companioned by you, in a mutually-interesting, stimulating variety of social and other experiences; and to feel …

Accepted by you, with all my limitations, needs, wounds, fears, hopes, and dreams; and ..

Steadily encouraged by you to become my true Self and discover my life purpose; and .

Separate enough from you, so I can have my own friends, activities, and goals and keep my own identity as an individual; and …

To share the joys, sacrifices, and sorrows of conceiving and/or raising kids together.

The next step? How will you now interact respectfully and productively with your stepfamily mate?

What Are Relationship "Boundaries"?

If someone asked you to eat a live centipede, would you? Either "yes" or "no" demonstrates a personal boundary or limit. In our context, *boundaries* are invisible dividing lines between what people and groups will and won't accept, tolerate, believe, or do. Boundaries define what's currently acceptable physically, psychologically, and spiritually, and what isn't. "Acceptable" means "I can tolerate (something) without taking some action." For instance, *"I like red meat, but I refuse to eat horsemeat or raw hamburger."*

Your family members have many boundaries; even infants have them (*"Emma won't nurse now"*). We grow them automatically as we accumulate experience with pleasure and discomfort. Boundaries are universal, so we're often unconscious of how and when they regulate our lives until they're conflicted, violated, or absent too much. Some boundaries

189

change with age, experience, and our dynamic environments. Others remain constant across our years.

Adults and kids hint, imply, declare, or shout their boundaries verbally ("Okay," "No," "Not now,"...) and nonverbally, via eye, face, voice, and body dynamics. If you're being honest with yourself, your verbal and nonverbal boundary announcements match. If a false self group of personality parts controls your thoughts and behaviors, you may feel uncertain, mixed, guilty, or torn about your boundaries. You may then give or receive confusing double messages about them: *You say you're not bored, but I feel like you're disinterested...?!"*

Sometimes it's useful to differentiate between *limits* and *boundaries*. A *limit* is something you can't do, like levitate or chat with Buddha. A *boundary* is something you won't tolerate without taking some action. It may also help you problem-solve if you separate boundary conflicts from values disputes. The latter occur when people disagree over what is right vs. wrong, good vs. bad, safe vs. dangerous, and better vs. worse. Values and boundary conflicts are resolved differently.

Firmly boundaries are essential for persons, couples, and stable family systems. They help to define *identities* ("We don't eat meat on Fridays") and regulate the psychological distance between people and groups. When boundaries are compatible, stable, and enforced respectfully, they provide family kids and adults with enough identity, safety (comfort), privacy, and order.

Boundaries can be tangible (skin, doors, walls, fences, clothing, etc.) and invisible (thoughts, values, preferences, emotions). Both can promote order, harmony, and security, or frustration, anxiety, and stress. Remember the last time someone important violated (disrespected or ignored) your personal boundaries? Relationships fluctuate dynamically as each person asserts and enforces their boundaries to balance closeness and separateness.

A key boundary to manage is the invisible envelope around couples. Mates may conflict or agree on what their couple-boundaries are ("*Kids, when our bedroom door is closed, we need private time—unless someone needs an ambulance!*") Couples may also agree or conflict over how and when to declare and enforce their boundaries, and with whom ("*Jan, I need you to tell your sister to stop calling us at 6 AM!*"). Privacy is what happens inside your personal, couple, parental, and family boundaries.

One inevitable task while still dating is each partner learning to adjust their personal boundaries to mesh well enough with their partner's. Dating and cohabiting usually trigger two or more families merging. This forces the declaration and adjustment of many personal and group boundaries over many months. To succeed at this, typical adults need:

- To be steadily governed by their true selves.
- Have an awareness of boundary concepts and of their primary needs.
- Clear, stable, personal identities (a sense of self).
- Shared language to discuss boundary needs, conflicts, violations, and consequences.
- Effective communication skills—especially awareness, assertion, and empathic listening.

- A tolerance for (a) changing their family system and lifestyles, and (b) grieving any significant losses (broken bonds) these changes cause.

Do you know anyone who has had trouble merging biological families and forming stable new personal, marital, parental, and household boundaries?

Why Are Boundaries Important?

…Because they regulate your security, comfort, serenity, self-respect, and relationships. Specifically,

- Your boundaries determine what experiences you select or avoid, which limits your direct knowledge ("Yes" on fudge and waltzing, "no" on raising rattlesnakes and sky diving).
- They define your identity as a unique person ("Judi will talk about her spiritual beliefs, but not her brother's death or her sexual experiences).
- They regulate your emotional and physical security ("No, the roads look too icy. Let's stay home today.").
- They help control your health ("I smoke a pack a day, but I won't eat animal fat or use cocaine.").
- They specify the emotional distance or closeness between you and every other person ("Jerry, I need some alone-time right now. Do you mind?").

Boundary Conflicts and Violations

Because we're unique individuals, some personal and family boundaries will conflict internally (among personality sub-selves) and among people: e.g. *"You're okay with eating dinner after 8 PM, and I'm not."* A different stress occurs when one person accidentally or intentionally ignores ("violates") a significant boundary in another person, like *"I asked you not to buy so many lottery tickets, but you did anyway."*

Boundary conflicts are simpler to negotiate and resolve than violations because violations usually require rebuilding respect and trust, and healing hurts and guilt. Personal, marital, and/ or household boundary violations by kids and adults cause major home and family stress.

Boundary conflicts and violations can range from minor (no action required) to significant (some action or consequence *is* required). Each of these has two levels: surface boundary problems and the primary problems (unmet needs) that cause them.

Healthy and Toxic Boundaries

When boundaries and their consequences promote everyone's personal holistic health, safety, order, and self and mutual respect, they can be labeled healthy. Boundaries and consequences which diminish or block these and stress relationships and families can be called toxic. The latter usually means a false self controls one or more people. Thus, the personal and social *effects* of boundaries and their consequences, and the *way* they are set (e.g., respectfully and empathically or not) can be just as important as the boundaries themselves.

Enmeshment: Too Few Boundaries

Many American adults have survived a significantly low-nurturing childhood. A common legacy from that are psychological wounds, including excessive shame, guilt, and fears. Before hitting bottom and choosing to reduce their wounds, typical survivors tend to unconsciously choose each other as mates and associates repeatedly, despite painful results.

Sometimes the wounds manifest as rigid, aggressive boundaries and a high need to control relationships. Some shame-based survivors feel they don't deserve the right to have, assert, or enforce personal boundaries, and/or they don't know how to assert them effectively. When two such people choose each other, they may have few to no boundaries with each other ("Juan and Charlene are joined at the hip.") They (their ruling sub-selves) become fused or enmeshed, and they have wispy personal identities.

Symptoms of fusion include discouraging each other from having individual friends, hobbies, careers, thoughts, feelings, dreams, worship practices, and solitudes. Each partner feels high guilt and anxiety saying "no" or "not now" to his or her mate—or talking about this. Codependent relationships have unbalanced or too few healthy interpersonal boundaries.

An enmeshed relationship may satisfy some wounded couples who are unaware of themselves and their primary needs. A high cost they pay is stunted personal growth and muted or no personal life goals. As such couples age, factors can combine to cause one of them to need more personal boundaries. That inevitably raises the other partner's anxiety and causes boundary conflicts and violations.

A variation of this occurs when a parent is enmeshed with a child. Wounded, overwhelmed custodial parents with few resources can unconsciously require their child to become a "surrogate mate"—a confidant, partner, and companion. In the worst case, this includes toxic physical intimacy abuse. From unawareness, shame, and fear, the parent (i.e., his or her false self) discourages the child from developing an identity and other relationships, moving out, and choosing his or her own partner ("growing up," "maturing"). Some clinicians call such burdened kids "parentified."

Typical Boundary Conflicts

The basic interpersonal boundary conflict is: "*I will accept, tolerate, or allow (something) without reacting, and you won't.*" Like values conflicts, basic resolution options are: "You and I (a) acknowledge our mutual conflict and negotiate a compromise we each can live with," *or* (b) "we don't."

Many topics trigger surface boundary conflicts in typical families. For instance,

- Money ("*No, I won't agree to buy a $145 parrot.*")
- "Manners"
- Hygiene and health
- Food and eating
- Parenting
- Spirituality and worship
- Holidays and vacations
- Sensuality and sex
- Time balances (work, play, or rest)
- Privacy and solitude
- Socializing
- TV and leisure choices
- Home decorating
- Transportation
- Promptness
- Dress and appearance

Think about five or more things you feel intensely about. Have you experienced boundary (yes/no) conflicts with other family members on any of those vital areas?

Typical Boundary Violations

Boundary violations occur between personality sub-selves and between people. Let's look briefly at each of these.

Boundary violations among your personality sub-selves are so universal they go largely unnoticed. For instance your Health Director and Adult sub-selves say, "*We really need to call the dentist about these cavities today!*" This activates your Scared Child who remembers early dental pain and trauma, and distrusts this (new) dentist. That activates your Catastrophizer and Worrier sub-selves, who try to protect the Scared Child by causing you anxiety from images of the dentist discovering "*something really awful that will cost thousands of dollars.*"

Their persuasive ally, the Procrastinator, joins in by urging you to *"call later in the week,"* and your Magician sub-self provides convincing reality distortions like *"a few days isn't going to make any difference, and maybe the pain will subside by itself."* Result: you don't call the dentist and the boundaries of your Health Director and Adult sub-selves are violated (disrespected and overruled.)

Your Inner Critic may then chastise you for *"not taking good care of yourself (What would Mom say?)",* which may activate your Guilty Kid. Overall, your inner family of sub-selves is polarized and out of harmony, which causes you vague inner stress and maybe a headache or stomachache.

When the cavities get worse and cause serious pain and expense, all sub-selves feel anxious and insecure because no one among them was able to forestall that, i.e., they didn't trust the resident true self to guide them. If you were in true recovery from false-self wounds, your Nurturer sub-self would have effectively comforted the Scared Child, so the other Guardian sub-selves wouldn't have ganged up to take over your Self, Health Director, and Adult ("common sense"). That would free them to call the dentist and get appropriate self care.

Every time you feel "I know I shouldn't, but…," you violate some internal boundaries. That activates sub-selves who bring you guilt, shame, self-doubt, anxiety, and perhaps disgust. Those in turn promote false-self dominance and the temporary or chronic loss of your true self's wisdom and guidance. Personal wound-reduction via some form of inner-family therapy can reduce that over time, by harmonizing your inner crew and improving their problem-solving skills. If you've never communed with any of your sub-selves, this will probably sound like low-budget science fiction. If you're skeptical about personality sub-selves, we suggest that you try this safe, interesting exercise at: http://sfhelp.org/01/letter1.htm.

Violations Between People

The following are some examples of violations between people:

Miriam told her husband, Craig, that she doesn't approve of pornographic magazines or videos and wants none in their home. During a spring-cleaning session she discovers a box of such materials with recent publication dates hidden in their garage.

Robert let his wife, Anne, know several times that he's "uneasy" about her lunching alone with her former lover, Armando. Robert doesn't say, *"Don't do it,"* but implies that's what he needs. He hasn't said what he'll do if she chooses to continue. Anne enjoys friendship with Armando and has no interest in a sexual or romantic relationship with him. She feels Robert is being "immature" and "over-controlling" and resents his attitude (implied blame and distrust). A mutual friend tells Robert she saw his wife and Armando lunching yesterday, and Anne had said nothing to Robert about this.

Ned has taught his younger brother how to ride his motorcycle and asked him not to use it without asking. Ned comes home from work one day to find the cycle gone from the garage. His sister says, "Tommie took it."

Sam stoically implies hurt, resentment, and frustration that his wife ignores his request that she not read his email without asking. She blames him for distrusting her, keeping secrets, and being "a bad husband"; and says those faults justify her actions.

Other common examples of boundary violations include:

- Interrupting someone after they ask you not to.
- Willfully intruding on someone's privacy without permission.
- Telling others personal information that someone asked you to keep private.
- Spending significant money without consulting your partner.
- "Forgetting" your partner's request that you call if you'll be working late.
- Behaving seductively with a child and denying that, despite observer's warnings; and…
- Withholding or distorting information that would affect someone's perception of you and your relationship.

Physical violations come from disrespecting another person's bodily boundaries via unwanted or painful skin contact or penetrations. Others can come from ignoring someone's tolerances for noise, smell, taste, and temperature. Most aggressive (as opposed to assertive) behavior and all true abuse *always* cause significant emotional and spiritual boundary violations. The surface problem in conflicts like these is "*I need you to do (or don't do) 'x,' and you do it anyway—openly or covertly. Then you deny doing that, justify it, or blame me for it.*" All violations imply "I value my needs more than yours" and send a one-up respect message. The relationship impact of boundary violations ranges from trivial to major over time.

The roots of most (all?) boundary conflicts and violations inside and between you and other people are: (1) That one or more of you are ruled by a false self and you don't know that or what to do about it, and (2) you and/or the other person are unaware of the boundary concepts and terms above, and of the primary needs and values causing your boundaries, and (3) one or both of you lack effective communication basics and skills and don't know how to set and negotiate boundaries and consequences effectively.

How do these manifest with Miriam and Craig? Neither is aware of what you've just read. Her surface (conscious) boundary is: "*I want (you, Craig to bring) no pornographic materials in our home.*" Her implied (unstated) boundary is "*I will react (somehow) if you need to use pornography.*" A related (unspoken) boundary is "*I need to trust that you'll tell me the truth, and I'll react if you don't.*" Wanting to trust Craig, Miriam hasn't needed to define or state what she'll do if he violates her boundary.

Craig pledges that he understands and declares earnestly that he doesn't need pornography. One personality sub-self really believes this and wants to honor Miriam's request. Other sub-selves remember past arousal pleasures and want to re-experience them *despite* his wife's request (boundary). Periodically, these sub-selves generate thoughts and urges in Craig to fill two sets of needs: (a) get pornographic pleasures, and (b) hide this from Miriam and others to avoid major conflict, guilt, and family disruption. His Magician sub-self causes persuasive rationalizations why this is really okay, despite other sub-selves' counsel that it isn't.

Two of Craig's semi-conscious *inner* boundaries are: "*I will never betray or lie to Miriam*" and "*I will not be a man who needs pornography.*" He doesn't know about false-self wounds so he doesn't admit that his periodic guilty fantasies about viewing pornographic images are signs that he has significant unfilled marital needs. Implication: pornography is *not* the problem; *unawareness* and his relentless unfilled needs are.

Craig silently battles with an internal conflict: some sub-selves want to honor his and Miriam's boundaries. Others persuasively argue that violating the boundaries "isn't that bad," promising harmless pleasure (to fill undefined needs). At some moment in time, he buys pornographic magazines, experiences various excitements, and guiltily hides the magazines in the garage as he did as a youth. Like an addict in denial his false self now begins an elaborate inner and outer campaign to make this deception acceptable. The sub-selves that want sexual excitement and mental/emotional distraction from inner pain (the *real* problem) overcome other sub-selves (including his true self) that want to be honest and "porn-free."

From this perspective, Craig didn't lie to Miriam. The sub-selves that spoke the words "*I understand, and I'll never bring porn into our home*" were telling their truth. Unawareness, fear, guilt, and shame caused the sub-selves that *didn't* pledge that to remain silent. Because of unseen false-self control, Miriam was married to *two* Craigs in one body without his being crazy in the least. Neither mate knew this.

Time passes and Miriam discovers that her husband has broken two promises: to tell her the truth and to stop using pornography. Her respect for and trust in him drop sharply, she feels hurt and angry, and her anxiety blooms ("What *else* is he hiding from me?"). She confronts him, and—because they don't know inner-family, boundary, and communication concepts and skills—they *fight* (rather than problem-solve). This can have many outcomes, but none will illuminate the real problems without mutual awareness and Craig choosing a self-motivated program of personal healing.

When she discovers later that Craig is having an affair Miriam faces her own inner boundaries:

> "*I will not live with a man I don't respect and can't trust,*"
> "*I will never divorce,*" and...
> *I must honor and act on my own integrity to keep my self respect.*"

Other boundaries involve (a) who she may confide in about this situation (e.g., her sister but not her parents), and (b) her responsibilities to their kids and to God. The degree of harmony among her sub-selves will determine how she resolves her web of inner boundary conflicts and whether her vigilant Guardian sub-selves violate any of them.

An unseen prior problem promoted this situation. Because of their respective unawareness needs and inner wounds, Miriam and/or Craig also made several uninformed, unwise dating decisions. She committed to an appealing man with major hidden psychological wounds and unawareness. He committed to her without awareness of his wounds and what they meant. Both committed without knowing communication basics and skills.

If your family adults and kids have significant boundary conflicts and/or violations, the good news is once you acknowledge them, you can learn to avoid and reduce them together over time. The bad news is: until you all admit and reduce significant protective false-self denials and illusions, your ruling sub-selves will cleverly distract and deflect you from preventing violations and conflicts together—and will earnestly deny doing so.

Resolution Options

If you and your mate have significant boundary violations and conflicts, you may:

- Deny or minimize them ("Nah, they're not a big deal") and take no action.
- Agree that you *do* have a boundary problem, and avoid acknowledging that one or more of you will have to change something important to resolve it.
- Defer doing anything about it or make superficial changes. Your boundary problems will return and may escalate. Or,
- You may blame each other, avoid acknowledging your half of the problems, and endure rounds of lose-lose fighting, arguing, explaining (justifying), or withdrawal. Do the same with your other relationship problems, and become increasingly weary, distrustful, cynical, and dispirited. Or,
- Focus on "more important problems" and deny or minimize the effects of your avoidance.

Or you can reframe your problem from "boundary conflicts or violations" to "unawareness." Then, choose the attitude that *"We can reduce both of these as team-mates if we each accept personal responsibility for doing so."* If you can do this, then your options include: (1) Assess honestly for false-self wounds, and help each other harmonize your sub-selves under the wise leadership of your true selves, and (2) sharpen your thinking, focusing, and problem-solving effectiveness by working at it together. Doing so over time will help you:

- Identify the primary unmet needs causing your "boundary problems."
- Prioritize your needs and focus on filling a few at a time.
- Assert your needs and related consequences respectfully; and,
- Brainstorm as equal teammates to help each other fill your primary needs, while keeping your balance.

For boundary violations you identify, pay special attention to the skills of assertion, empathic listening, and metatalk. Also study your options for reducing disrespect and resolving self and mutual destruct. If Miriam and Craig were committed to these options and her self guided her personality, she might firmly say something like: *"Craig, when you pledge you won't use pornography or lie to me and then do both of those anyway, I feel betrayed, disrespected, disappointed, hurt, and resentful."*

This uses awareness, clear thinking, and assertion skills, and (hopefully) is delivered with respect. That is the first step in potential win-win problem-solving. If Miriam's false self were in charge, earnest sub-selves might cause her to say sarcastically or angrily, *"It's obvious I can't trust you with anything (generalizing) because you're weak and dishonest (labeling and blaming), and you don't care about my needs (accusing and punishing). You obviously have some kind of sick sex addiction (exaggerating, blaming, and avoiding her half of the problem), so don't expect to sleep in my bed until you get fixed, Craig (punishing and guilt-tripping)."*

Predictably, one-up communication behavior like this will probably evoke fight or flight among Craig's governing sub-selves unless (a) his Self (capital "S") was in charge, and (b) he knew communications skill. If so, he would assess non-judgmentally if her emotional level was "above her ears." If it was, he would realize she couldn't hear him until her emotional level dropped and could calmly choose the skill of empathic listening: *"So you feel betrayed and really hurt that I was dishonest, and you want me to acknowledge that."*

If that helped her regain her hearing, Craig might then say evenly, *"Miriam, I am really sorry that I betrayed you. I feel ashamed and I have no excuse. And (not 'but'!) I experience your false self is making your voice sarcastic, and I feel blamed, punished, hurt, and defensive. I don't want to fight or run away. I need you to get your self back in charge, and join me in some win-win problem solving, not attack or punish me. Can you do that now?"*

A third option you have to reduce your "boundary problems" is to seek qualified professional help. "Qualified" means trained and experienced at doing effective (a) personal trauma recovery and (b) communication skill-building work. If you're a stepfamily, any professional helper you hire (c) should have most of this special knowledge.

The paragraphs above are deceptively brief. Committing to their ideas will lead your family members to months of challenging, dedicated effort, and confront you with making some major changes in your lives.

A Recap

Self care and respect must first be within ourselves before we may truly care and be respectful of others. Personal boundaries divide what people will and won't tolerate without a reaction. The reactions range from minor (e.g., frowning or sighing) to major (e.g., divorce or murder). A challenge in growing any relationship is identifying and resolving boundary conflicts and violations. Typical adults and kids each have many ("yes"/"no") boundaries which define and separate them as individuals, and regulate their personal securities, comforts, and balances.

When boundaries clash (a) among your sub-selves and/or (b) between you and another person, you experience boundary *conflicts*. Boundary *violations* occur when some sub-self or person feels his or her stated boundary was ignored or betrayed—i.e., he or she feels disrespected. Resolving boundary violations usually requires rebuilding your trust, honesty, and respect, and healing any major guilt and resentments.

Help each other understand your ancestral wounds and commit to helping each other reduce any you find. Help each other grow proficient with effective-communication basics and skills and steadily use the skills together to resolve the inevitable stream of family role and relationship conflicts you'll encounter. Use the skills of awareness to monitor what you each need from your relationship.

As you do this, help each other learn to stay clear on, and firmly assert, your personal rights. Value your and your mate's respective integrities, needs, and opinions equally. Assert your needs respectfully, and set and enforce respectful boundaries with each other and others.

Help each other stay clear on – and honor – your personal and shared priorities, and co-commit to keeping your relationship second to your respective integrities and holistic health except in emergencies. If you have young kids or teens, usually keep their welfare third with minimal guilt to protect them from possible further divorce loss and trauma.

Chapter Ten

Merge And Stabilize Your Stepfamily Adults' Biological Families And Resolve *Many* Conflicts

Slowly evolving a highly nurturing multi-home, multi-generational stepfamily requires a willingness on the part of all adults and kids to merge the adults' three or more multi-generational biological families. That means they have to resolve significant differences concerning up to 16 important factors:

Family roles	Family rituals	Family rules	Boundaries
Names and titles	Parenting styles	Grieving styles	Goals
Dwellings	Assets and debts	Friends	Spiritual beliefs
Loyalties	Family memberships	Wounds ("baggage")	Family "scripts"

This stunningly complex, multi-year merger process *always* promotes major concurrent values and loyalty conflicts, as well as associated Persecutor-Victim-Rescuer relationship triangles, in and between stepfamily adults' homes. Typical stepfamily adults can't name or describe the 16 factors, and have no coherent long-range plan for how to merge and stabilize them together.

This chapter will help you deal with this inevitable, complex biological family merger process and its inescapable common stressors. It explains and illustrates each stressor and suggests ways you can effectively master them together. It also urges new stepfamily adults to negotiate and implement an effective biological family merger plan together. Doing this requires major progress on all the previous topics—especially psychological-wound healing and growing effective communication skills.

The Merger

How It Starts

Your complex merger actually began on your first serious date. You started noticing each other's values, preferences, customs, rituals, goals, and boundaries, and began deciding how compatible they were. The comparisons expanded as you met each other's relatives, minor kids, friends, and possibly ex mates. You probably didn't meet your partner's ex in-laws, but may have heard stories and comments about them.

As you continued to date, you began to discover more clearly where your personalities, lifestyles, and biological cultures meshed and clashed. Because you weren't committed spouses, you probably had much more tolerance for the differences, or kept quiet about any that disturbed you. Your mutual attraction and the excitement of dating probably overshadowed any major values clashes, or you had the comforting illusion "If we married, these will go away." Because no one was a stepparent yet, you experienced few or at least no major role or authority conflicts. You didn't yet wonder if you had the right and responsibility to discipline "their" child. If minor kids tested to see where their biological parent's loyalties lay, that may have felt amusing or irritating, but not disrespectful and divisive. You didn't know what you didn't know, and couldn't identify the stepfamily misconceptions and fantasies you each held... until now.

Sarah and Sam moved into Sam's home after their wedding. This accelerated the merger of an amazing array of things along with a series of complex, interactive changes rippling through their stepfamily homes.

What Do You Merge?

Physical belongings: Sarah and Sam had to blend their furniture, utensils, dishes, beds and linens, pictures, pets, vehicles, appliances, children's toys, tools, books, clothes, etc. Because these are tangible and many items are used often, they're usually the first things that merging adults and kids negotiate about. Combining the sets of *invisible* assets is just as real, and can generate far more conflict. For example ...

Customs and traditions: "Now that we're a family, you all will join us in saying grace before we eat, won't you?" "We never put uncovered food in the refrigerator, okay?" "I file every paid bill and cancelled check. I didn't know you throw all yours out ..." "We always open presents the night before. That's not a problem, is it?" "We've gone to the lake every summer for 12 years. You all will love it!" "We always had salmon at Easter, since I was a kid. Your mother and sister don't like salmon?"

Household and family priorities: "We're used to doing our work before playing, so I think you should do your homework before TV, okay?" "Well, I think all of us eating together is more important than your son making basketball practice." "My need to talk with our lawyer on the phone outranks your son's need to jabber with the buddies he spends most of the afternoon with!" "You're so afraid your ex will sue for sole custody that you let her blow off child support and walk all over you."

Communication styles: George D'Amato and his clan, for example, are used to all talking at once, and expressing anger, love, hurt, and frustration loud and clear. Family problem-solving routinely involves arguing, interrupting, demanding, threats, and sarcasm. Like their staid and stern German and English ancestors, Millie Friedrich's pre-teen daughters have been taught to be quiet, respectful, and (fairly) unemotional, in public. They're used to debating conflicts calmly and "never fighting." The D'Amatos and the Friedrichs are about to get remarried, and all six will live in the Friedrichs' home together …

Values/Standards: "You discipline to teach, but I discipline to punish. Kids won't obey or respect you unless they feel some loving pain!" "No, your phone calls should stop at 10 P.M., period!" "Well, I don't think it's too much to expect an apology from her …" "Ned should have the support check here by the third, at the latest!" "Tommy, in this home, we come to the dinner table with our cell phones turned off." "You guys put things off too often. We'll all do better if we never let the sun set on a problem. Don't you see?"

Household and extended-family roles and ranks: "But I always carve the turkey!" "I feel totally ignored, because your son talks only to you at dinner!" "I used to get the best grades. Now my stupid stepsister does!" "Since she remarried, my daughter doesn't call nearly as often." "Could my son like his new stepfather better than me?" "So what's more important, your daughter's braces or our marriage?"

Privacy and space: "I used to have my own room, but now I have to share it with my new stepsister Paula." "You mean I can't have my own bathroom in their (versus 'our') house?" "But where'll I park my car?" "It looks like we'll have to combine your home-office and mine in here." "I know you're used to coming into your mom's room any time, but we need our privacy. So please respect our closed door now, unless it's an emergency, okay?"

You get the idea.

Think about each of the following categories, each having scores of individual items that adults and kids must rank, sort out, and compromise on over time in order to achieve emotional stability and rhythm in and among your stepfamily homes and relationship. Imagine all of the adults and kids in your multi-home stepfamily working to concurrently blend and stabilize these groups of things peacefully:

Our physical possessions.
Our daily and weekly schedules.
Our communication and conflict-resolution styles.
Our personal and family goals and dreams.
Our kids' and adults' friends and socializing styles.
Our home and family beliefs, customs, rituals, and traditions, including worship.

Our personal inner wounds and "unfinished business."

Our individual and family experiences and expectations.

Our personal privacies and boundaries.

Our family roles, rules, and "ranks."

Our financial assets (including insurance) and debts.

Our ancestral and family "scripts."

Our personal and family preferences, priorities, values, morals, standards, and tolerances. This includes balancing work, rest, and play.

Our legal contracts, including court orders, mortgages, wills, insurance coverage, and any parenting agreements.

What to Expect as You Merge

What will this complex process (probably) feel like to you all? First expect that some kids and adults will need to grieve their tangible and invisible losses, to regain their emotional balance and accept your new stepfamily structure. If you and your kids are living in pro-grief homes and lives, you'll be helping each other mourn prior losses from childhood nurturing deprivations and biological family changes after the prior divorce or death.

If enough time has passed and you all have inner and outer permission to grieve well, then this group of losses from remarriage or cohabiting will feel manageable enough. If any adults or kids haven't mourned their prior losses, the expectation is that they will feel emotionally numb or overwhelmed by your merger. They may signal this by depression, apathy, rage outbursts, rudeness, indifference, super busy-ness, addictions, illness, and so on. Like pregnancy, grief can't be ignored, deferred, or rushed.

Secondly, expect the conflicts among many items in these categories to be concurrent. They won't line up like ducks in a row. This highlights the great value of the stepfamily adults' ability to cooperatively sort, rank, and focus, as you resolve your key merger conflicts one or two at a time. Some can lack the self-discipline, concentration, and empathy to focus and rank them effectively. Others may be obsessive and over-controlling in negotiating this complex, long-term merger process. Both are counterproductive.

As you merge, expect many inner and mutual values conflicts and power struggles. These will create an unsteady stream of divisive Persecutor-Victim-Rescuer relationship triangles among you all. Unless all stepfamily adults use the communication skills discussed earlier in this book effectively, you risk ongoing fighting or avoiding, and escalating hurts, resentment, guilt, and anxiety. (See more on "relationship triangles" further on in this chapter.)

Expect that some conflicts and losses that are major to a child may feel trivial to a stepfamily adult or relative, or vice versa, e.g., "We had to give away my cat because my horrible stepbrother is allergic to fur!" Personal awareness and empathy will help alert the adults to this.

Next, expect most other lay and professional people to not appreciate the scope of what you all face in your complex merger project. Ignorance, media distortions, biases, and lack of stepfamily experience and informed training all hinder their ability to empathize with you, despite wanting to.

Your long-term stepfamily merger is a great chance to put a glass-half-full philosophy to work. If stepfamily adults and kin really accept that you're all forming a new stepfamily and agree on who belongs, and if they understand that this complex merger of biological families will involve all your adults and kids for many years, then your merger can become a true team effort. The priceless rewards you'll earn over time are healthy stepfamily bonding, a realistic new identity, stability (security), and growing pride.

So talk about your merger and compromises together, as you go. ("Wow! This blending is tougher than we realized. How do other step-people get through this?") Your alternatives are to pretend there is no merger or minimize it; admit it but don't discuss it honestly; repress key merger needs, thoughts and feelings; or avoid merger conflicts to "keep the peace," and grow covert frustrations and resentments.

Help each other congratulate family members who find workable compromises, and console your kids and adults suffering broken emotional bonds ("It's really hard having to change all your friends and teachers and go to a strange new school, isn't it? I'm so proud of the way you're being sad and angry about all these tough changes. Doing those good-grief things will help you feel better and enjoy your new friends and school after a while. Keep it up!")

Evolve a Merger Plan Together, Early

Think of the last major plan you made. An effective plan has a clear, attainable goal, specific steps to reach it, and a thoughtful estimate of what resources you need. It will be thoughtful, discussed, shared, and intentional; unconscious, jumbled, unfocused, and conflict-generating; or something in between. Having no plan is the default plan. Some helpful planning options are:

- *Agree together* on who is in charge of managing your merger. One advantage of being in a stepfamily is you have more people who can co-lead—the adults.
- *Encourage each other*, including kids, to name the invisible things you're trying to merge now.
- *Stepfamily adults*, keep your personal, marital, household, and stepfamily priorities clear, vocal, understood, and steady, to guide you in merger conflicts.
- *Develop a merger language* that fits you as unique group members. ("We have a new *standards* clash here, gang ….")
- *Expect merger conflicts*, and learn to name them *without blame*. Who needs what, and what's in the way?

- *Help each other* keep a patient, long-range outlook. Your merger is a multi-year process! Keep reminding each other of your main goal: evolving toward a stable, highly nurturing team years from now.
- *Steadily sharpen your skills* at inner and mutual conflict resolution and win-win compromising.
- *Have periodic "merger meetings"* to discuss and update your plan, inform everyone of it and get their feedback, and negotiate compromises together. Expect such meetings to reveal psychological wounds, unawareness, and the need for harmonizing within individuals.
- *Affirm* your small and large compromise successes as you go. Praise yourselves and each other! This is hard work, which requires every member in your extended stepfamily to change some precious and familiar things. Respect that some changes will be imposed, not chosen. Finally...

As you update and execute your merger plan, keep and enjoy your sense of humor; laughter is a nourishing tonic.

Persecutor-Victim-Rescuer Relationship Triangles

Adults or kids unconsciously play one of three roles, like parts in a play. One person unconsciously chooses the Persecutor role. He or she blames or criticizes the Victim for something, causing the Rescuer to defend the Victim. Each person can switch back and forth between these roles with different situations and different people. Even if people are aware they're doing this, they often can't stop until their self is free to lead their team of sub-selves. Relationship triangles sound like this:

The Persecutor (say a step-dad) scowls and says sarcastically to the Victim (e.g., a step-daughter) *"Boy, you have the brains of a doorknob. How many times do I have to tell you to pick up your toys, so people don't fall over them or step on them and wreck them? You are hopeless!"*

The Victim may whimper and cower, glare and sulk, or talk back defiantly. Either way, the Victim feels guilty, ashamed, and anxious, and may be mad at herself and/or at the Persecutor. She may whine and glance pitifully at...

The Rescuer (say his biological mom), who observes this interaction and feels protective of the poor Victim. So the Rescuer may glower at the Persecutor and say something to the Victim like, *"Honey, I'll help you pick up your toys now. Let me get you a snack."*

The person in the Persecutor role may resent the Rescuer (in this case his partner) siding with the Victim rather than supporting him, the partner.

Unless the adults consciously help each other avoid or defuse these stressful, overlapping triangles in and between their stepfamily dwellings they promote or amplify toxic loyalty conflicts. Unresolved triangles and values conflicts are probably the most common surface reason for our re-divorce epidemic. They can also promote extramarital affairs when seasoned with misdirected sexual energy.

What's Wrong With Triangles?

They promote antagonism, shame, guilt, frustration, hurt, anger, and distrust. These all hinder the bonding and stable new roles co-parents want to grow. Every moment, every child and adult needs to feel comfortable. The three universal comfort factors are feeling respected, safe, and satisfied *now*.

When others' behavior sends us a message that we decode as a criticism or discount, kids and adults alike feel hurt, guilt, angry, defensive, and maybe ashamed. These hardly build highly nurturing relationships.

Triangles always involve an apparent one-upmanship on the part of one or more of the three role-players. "My ideas, values, needs are more important to me than yours right now." In the example above, the Victim receives a hurtful "You're one-down" message from the Persecutor. This upsets the Rescuer, who automatically soothes the poor Victim (which happens especially when the Victim can't or won't assert himself or herself effectively).

To the Persecutor it feels like "Your actions say that you're more concerned with the Victim's needs and feelings right now than mine. That hurts!" And so the Persecutor instantly assumes the Victim role. If someone else is in the room, they may now rescue the new Victim, starting a new wave of triangle communications. So now the Rescuer may feel criticized, misunderstood, disrespected, and hurt; or ignored, cut off, and abandoned.

Although this incident took only about 10 seconds to happen, the feelings from this and similar events may last for hours or days. And though it seems like a simple three-way incident, it isn't. It unintentionally led to all three people feeling upset (hurt, anxious, frustrated, guilty, irritated, and maybe ashamed) and a little less safe in their relationships and home.

If this kind of relationship triangle in various forms continues for months without the adults deciding to change it, what do you suppose will happen to each person's self-esteem, respect, and trust for the others, family bonding and security, and role and relationship stability? Nothing good!

What Can We Do About Our Triangles?

Help each other spot them, avoid them, and encourage other key people to do the same. Here are some options:

Study and discuss the step-dad/stepchild/biological mom example with your stepfamily adult partners. Stress that this is not about blaming anyone, it is about understanding and resolving the problem.

Teach and show your minor and grown kids the three triangle roles. Help younger kids understand the difference between roles and the people in the roles. Neither the roles nor the people are "bad," but the results of a triangle can hurt self-esteem and family safety, trust, bonding, and teamwork.

Triangle spotted: Had the biological mom (Rescuer) been able to spot her own inner Mama-Lion personality part in the above example, she would have been able to say something calmly like, "Whoa! We've got a situation building here, let's back up and look at it, okay?" Step-dad (Persecutor) would trust from experience that his partner wasn't criticizing him, but was alerting all three to their shared risk of a newly hatched triangle. That alerts him to his inner struggle without undue guilt, so he can say something like, *"Mm, yeah, you're right. Sorry. Toby...."* He can then shift intentionally to real problem-solving. That might sound like…

Triangle avoided: If the step-dad becomes aware of feeling frustrated and irritated (and ignored again) when he sees stepdaughter Toby's toys strewn carelessly on the living room floor. He takes a moment to check his impulse to bark sarcastically at Toby. Then he thinks, *"What do I need now?"*

Taking more moments, he decides, *I need to…*

Let Toby know, respectfully and clearly, how her actions affect me, and

Keep working patiently at building her awareness. I also…

Want to model effective listening, assertion, and problem-solving for her. And…

I need Nell's (former Rescuer's) cooperation and help.

There are lots of scenarios that could develop from this beginning. One might sound like this respectful-assertion:

"Toby, when you forget my request to pick up your toys, I feel really frustrated and ticked off. I get worried you or someone else is going to trip and get hurt, or someone'll step on your game and break it. Then you'll feel bad, and we'll all get into an uproar about you earning enough allowance to buy a new game. I don't want those things to happen. How can we solve this problem?"

Loyalty Conflicts

Don't loyalty clashes happen in all families? Sure. And there are at least five reasons why they're more frequent and more stressful in most stepfamilies like yours.

1. There are usually more kids and adults trying to get their complex needs met at the same time. This means that the person in the middle feels pulled in more opposing directions more often than in an average biological family.

2. Most often, the people involved in a stepfamily loyalty competition are usually not all genetically and historically related. Instinct and social training program us to give higher priority to a blood relative than to someone else. Until you've lived with each other for many seasons, new stepparents, stepsiblings, and step-relatives are "someone else."

3. For most of us, blood really is "thicker than water." In a burning stepfamily home, most biological parents' first instinct is to save their genetic children. Biological parents talk about "our son and daughter." Stepfamily adults discuss "your son" and "my daughter," or "my stepson." So despite politeness and pretenses, step-people are more likely to feel second rate with their new housemates and relatives than biological people are, over time. This is especially so in the early years after the wedding.

4. A fourth reason that stepfamily loyalty conflicts feel different from biological versions is that stepfamilies have many new alien roles, like step-mom, stepbrother, half-sister, non-custodial biological father, step-uncle, etc. Relationship *shoulds* and *oughts* are correspondingly unfamiliar, complex, and confusing in and between most step-homes and so far, there's little societal agreement on how step-people are "supposed to" act toward each other, or who is "supposed to" rank first. For instance:

   You love your new spouse, so you *should* love his or her child too, or at least treat them equally with your own, right?

   Your mate *should* always rake your needs higher than their ex's, shouldn't they?

   Who ought to be more important to you: your new spouse or your child? Your "real" brother or your (unreal) stepbrother? Your biological father or your stepfather? Your former daughter-in-law or your new one?

   Can you avoid picking favorites? Whose approval do you need more? Which choice generates less guilt and anxiety?

5. A fifth loyalty conflict is often triggered by major values differences between your three or more merging biological family cultures (e.g., mine, yours, my kid's other parent's, and your child's other parent's).

Forced Priority Choices

Normal stepfamily mergers and daily life generate many forced priority choices for years. Some classic examples, with lots of variations, are:

Titles:	"I feel really good when you call me 'Mom,' but I hear that your biological mother gets hurt and angry when you do (so who should you please?)"
Membership:	"Your ex is *not* part of our new family, even if your son says she is! (You will agree with me, not him, won't you?)"
Rank and authority:	"You tell Stan that he is not your father. *I* am! Just because he lives there, he can't tell you what to do. Your mother and *I* will decide what you need (and I'll feel hurt, disappointed, and resentful of you if you obey your stepfather, no matter what your mother says or does)!"
Household "fairness":	"You let *your* son get away with murder, but micro-manage *my* son. He resents it and complains to me (i.e., wants me to agree and side with him against your unfairness)."
"Fairness" between homes:	"But Mom, Dad and Jean let me watch those videos at *his* house. Why are you so uptight? You're so mean!"

A final uniqueness about stepfamily loyalty conflicts is the probable presence of major guilt, shame, distrust, and insecurities in kids and adults alike. These powerful emotions amplify your stepfamily members' reactivity to feeling rejected and "second best." They flourish because some family members feel they have previously hurt and disappointed other members (e.g., by separating), or they feel betrayed, disrespected, or neglected themselves. New stepfamily relationship wounds can occur before old ones heal.

Most biological parents feel guilty about having forced their children through the trauma of separation and divorce. Some feel guilty and frustrated seeing their kids only on alternate weekends, or not at all. Putting them "second" during visitations or family gatherings seems like further shameful injury.

Dads and moms can feel guilty about child visitation, custody, and financial support hassles, court battles, and/or "inequalities." Custodial biological parents may feel selfish, i.e., bad, about choosing their own happiness over their child's by wanting to share time and activities with their new partner, and making time and setting priorities for their step-kids.

A non-custodial biological parent can feel shame (i.e., "I'm selfish, a bad person") and guilt by choosing an appealing new life in another state and "abandoning" their children. Conversely, custodial parents can feel guilt if they move their kids away from the other biological parent for work or other reasons.

Stepfamily kids may feel "I'm bad" for many reasons, such as…

- Having more fun with a stepparent or step-sibling than with their "real" parent or sibling,

- Resenting or rejecting their friendly stepparent or step-sibling.
- Honestly preferring to live in their non-custodial biological parent's home or with other kin.
- Feeling enraged at their parents for divorcing and one or both remarrying; and
- Having sexual tensions with a step-sibling or a stepparent.

A dual-role stepparent can feel daily self-blame and remorse over nurturing and supporting their mate's custodial kids when their own biological kids are elsewhere, perhaps being co-raised by a stranger.

So stepfamily loyalty conflicts are more frequent and more stressful than those in typical biological families for at least five reasons. Stepfamilies have more members whose needs and values clash; more cultural, genetic, and personal differences; more strange new roles and unclear rules; and more underlying guilt, shame, insecurity, and distrust in kids and adults.

Mastering Loyalty Conflicts Together

Prepare yourselves with a reaffirmation that you adults are all co-managing a normal multi-home nuclear stepfamily together, not separate biological homes. Acknowledge that recurring loyalty conflicts and related "triangles" are usually symptoms that some of your stepfamily adults haven't done enough work on their old psychological wounds. Help each other to assess this and to progress toward the appropriate goals as stepfamily adult *teammates* rather than opponents. If your other stepfamily adults or key relatives aren't cooperative, view them compassionately as wounded people in protective denial. Strive for clarity and focus on the people in your own home. However, you may need to progress on building your stepfamily adults team before you can make progress resolving *inter-home* loyalty conflicts and relationship triangles.

Accept that *inner*-personal and interpersonal conflicts in general, and values conflicts in particular, are normal in any home. They occur because adults and kids try to fill their needs. This means no one among you is bad or wrong when they happen!

Help each other evolve a strategy for spotting and resolving values conflicts in and between each of your stepfamily adults' homes. This usually involves respectfully agreeing to disagree rather than trying to persuade, manipulate, inflame, threaten, or preach. Loyalty clashes are a normal type of values conflict.

Can you finish the following sentence? "When my partner or I see a loyalty conflict among our adults and kids, we've agreed to ...."

It is important that each stepfamily adult accept personal responsibility for resolving your surface loyalty conflicts and the true personal problems beneath them. It's not the kids' or a counselor's job, it's yours! Help each other see that investing time and effort learning how to resolve your values and other conflicts is a high-return choice in the long run, not an annoying, frustrating short-term bother and chore. And finally,

Adopt the belief that when win-win compromises aren't found, putting your holistic health first, your remarriage second, and your kids' short term non-emergency needs third, really puts the kids first, long term. This occurs by protecting them and you from re-divorce anguish and trauma. If any stepfamily adult balks at these priorities or is ambivalent about them, it's probably because their true self is disabled and they don't know it.

Resolving Loyalty Conflicts: Choices

You have many options as you evolve an effective way of resolving your values and loyalty clashes. Notice the theme of these options, as well as the individual choices:

- *Name the conflict* as it occurs rather than ignoring, pretending, repressing, or delaying. Naming can sound like: "Hey, people, we've got another loyalty conflict (or whatever term you like) going!" This can turn into a fun or serious game.
- *Identify clearly who's in the middle and who else is involved* in the current clash, *without blame*. Watch for "invisible" members of the conflict, like non-custodial biological parents, kids at college, the ghost of a dead person, unborn fetuses, or others not physically present, but strongly influencing your conflict's outcome.
- *Strive for an attitude of mutual respect together.* "Each person's needs here are of equal importance to each of us." The implication being that the adults' dignity and needs are (usually) not more important than their kids' needs.
- *Identify as clearly and specifically as you can what each involved person needs* at the time. Distinguish between unconscious needs and surface needs, resource needs versus abstract needs; and immediate needs versus long-term needs. For example: "I need to feel respected, accepted, and co-equal" underneath the surface need of, "I need you to tell your son to clean up the bathroom after he uses it."
- *Stepfamily adults take responsibility* for making enough time and leading win/win compromising (see Chapter Seven). If that doesn't produce an acceptable conflict resolution after your best efforts, then stepfamily adults explore "What option here is best for our relationship long-term?"

A compromise occurs when all people feel they were respectfully heard and genuinely agree to *partially* fill their respective current needs. Popular alternatives are: fighting, arguing, avoiding, submitting, threatening, collapsing, sulking, aggressing, numbing, and manipulating. Many people feel that if win-win problem-solving doesn't work, compromising together is the next best way to resolve conflict.

- *Take the best option*, and honestly acknowledge any hurt, resentment, or anger this choice causes the other people involved. Remind everyone regularly of your long-term goal of building a highly nurturing stepfamily.
- *Praise all the people involved, including yourself,* for your efforts at resolving a tough family dilemma, especially if you found a successful compromise together. Discuss and note what worked well for you about your shared process, and do more of it the next time.

There are no quick fixes here. Values and loyalty conflicts will happen in your stepfamily for years.

Recap

Proactively resolve the many loyalty and other values conflicts that inevitably result form combining your biological families. Three kinds of conflicts are inevitable: disagreements over tangible resources, values and priorities ("lifestyles"), and communication styles. These conflicts are *inner*-personal and interpersonal. Many occur simultaneously among groups of your stepfamily adults and kids for many years.

Co-parents, learn to spot and dissolve Prosecutor-Victim-Rescuer relationship "triangles" in and between your homes. Otherwise, these triangles promote inner- and interpersonal conflicts, hinder your stepfamily bonding and stabilizing, and stress your remarriage.

CHAPTER ELEVEN

HELP EACH OTHER LEARN TO NURTURE EFFECTIVELY AND GROW STEPPARENT-STEPCHILD RESPECT AND TRUST, OVER TIME

Memos From And About Your Stepchild

Set clear limits for me.

I know very well I shouldn't have all that I ask for. I'm only testing you, which is part of my job. I need a parent, not just a pal.

Be firm with me.

I prefer it though I won't say so. It lets me know where I stand.

Lead me rather than force me.

If you force me, I learn that power is what really counts. I'll respond much better to being guided.

Be consistent.

If you're not, it confuses me and makes me try harder to get away with everything I can.

Make promises that you can keep, and keep the promises you make.

That grows my trust in you and my willingness to cooperate.

Know that I'm just being provocative when I say and do things to upset you.

If you fall for my provocations, I'll try for more such excitement and victories.

Say calm when I say "I hate you."

I don't really mean it. I just want you to feel upset and sorry for what I feel you've done to me.

Help me feel big rather than small.

When I feel little, I need to act like a "big shot" or a whiney cripple.

Let me do the things I can do for myself.

Your doing them for me makes me feel like a baby, and I may keep putting you in my service.

Correct me in private.

I can hear you better if you talk quietly with me alone, rather than with other people present.

Talk about my behavior when our conflict has calmed down.

In the heat of battle somehow my listening gets bad and my cooperation is even worse. It's okay for you to take the actions needed, but let's not talk about it until we all calm down.

Talk with me rather than preach at me.

You'd be surprised how well I know what's right and wrong. I need to have my feelings and ideas respected, just like you do—so please listen to them.

Tell me of your anger at my actions without name-calling.

If you call me "stupid" or "jerk" or "clumsy" too often I'll start to believe that. Help me learn how to handle anger without harming.

Help me feel that my mistakes are not sins.

I need to learn from my errors, without feeling that I'm no good.

Talk firmly without nagging.

If you nag over and over, I'll protect myself by growing deaf.

Let my wrong behavior go without demanding big explanations.

Often, I really don't know why I did it.

Accept as much as you can of what I'm able to tell you.

I'm easily scared into lying if my honesty is taxed too much.

When you teach me things, please keep it simple.

If you use big words or get into long confusing explanations, my mind goes somewhere else.

Enjoy me! I have a lot to offer you!

Peter K. Gerlach, M.S.W.

A basic premise in this book is that any family exists to *nurture,* i.e., to steadily fill its adults' and dependents' current and long-term primary needs. Depending on many factors, currently your family may fall somewhere between very low to highly nurturing.

Typically, stepfamily adults can't name most of their kids' (or their own) adjustment needs, or even some of their normal developmental needs covered in previous chapters. As a result, minor kids feel anxious and confused as they try to negotiate alien divorcing-family and stepfamily rules and roles and prepare for independence. That implies that without informed help, as these children become adults, they are in turn at significant risk of unintentionally creating low-nurturing families of their own.

Think of someone you highly respect. Now think of someone you don't. Would you agree that respect refers to admiring a person's attitudes, behaviors, traits, and achievements in general, or some particular role?

A common theme of stepfamily vignettes is a stepparent or a minor or grown stepchild not feeling respected enough by the other person. Significant disrespect fosters uncomfortable relationship triangles in and between your related stepfamily homes and also usually puts the stepparent's partner—the biological parent—in the middle of a stressful loyalty conflict.

Let's explore what causes stepchild-stepparent disrespect, who is responsible, and what can be done to remedy the situation.

Stepfamily Healing and Adjustment Needs

Typical kids of divorce and remarriage need to convert habitual self-doubt, ambivalence, and uncertainty (i.e., inner conflicts) into self-confidence, and grow merited trust in the dependability and good intentions of most caregivers and adult authorities. They need to develop the ability to fully feel and express all emotions within appropriate limits without guilt, shame, or anxiety, as well as the ability to be comfortable enough with others doing the same without anger, sadness, despair, and fear. Failure to develop this ability will seriously inhibit a child's capability to grieve, communicate effectively, and manage interpersonal conflict well, or develop the ability to tolerate change, uncertainty, inner-personal and interpersonal conflict, imperfection, and healthy intimacies.

Typical kids of divorce and remarriage also need to replace toxic ways of self-soothing (e.g., addictions, reality distortions, and avoidance) with holistically healthy habits and healthy sources of comfort and reassurance, and need to strengthen their ability to form real, versus faked, attachments to healthy people, ideas, and goals.

All children need to believe, without ambivalence, that their lives have intrinsic worth, promise, and real meaning, rather than feeling old pessimism, worthlessness, and inner emptiness.

Explore and Reduce the Basic Problems

The nature, mix, and complexity of stepfamily adjustment needs for a given child depend on their:

Age + gender + relations with each biological parent + understanding of the parental divorce + other factors such as the nurturing levels of their pre- and post-divorce homes, school, house of worship, activities, etc.

Because these adjustment needs are usually concurrent with the child's developmental and other family-change needs, use a positive, productive approach to help your stepchildren adjust to their new environment. Help your stepchildren accept less non-custodial biological attention and accessibility. For teens, recognize their growing need to socialize with friends, develop appropriate independence, redefine their personal and family identity, and decide clearly "who is my family now?" Typical step-kids also need to evolve and stabilize several to many un-chosen stepfamily relationships and learn, stabilize, and rank many new family roles (e.g., stepchild, step-sibling, step-grandchild, etc.), as well as learn and adjust to new privacy and sexual conditions in their homes.

They also need to continue grieving old losses and start mourning a complex set of new tangible and invisible losses from the ending of their prior living situation and the merging of several multi-generational biological families over several years. Be aware that a child's "acting out" may be the anger phase of healthy grief and/or appropriate testing of key stepfamily leadership, boundaries, and power.

Your stepchild must now learn to detach from any of their key relatives' or friends' disapproval of their biological parent's remarriage or cohabiting. New stepchildren also need to learn clearly and accept what the rules, boundaries, and consequences are in their two homes and complex stepfamily. Who's really in charge of each of their adults' homes. They need to learn how much power and status they now have in each home, and what roles they are unfortunately expected to play (e.g., peacemaker, entertainer, black sheep, star) and by whom. Further, they need to learn how to handle the differences in the rules, roles, and consequences between their two co-parenting homes. How would you expect a child to react to these webs of values and loyalty conflicts and relationship triangles?

Help your stepchild build trust that *this* home and family are safe to belong to and bond with, because they won't break up like their other one(s) did. Achieving this trust usually requires creative, persistent reality testing over months or years. And, new step-kids also need your help to reduce their feelings of isolation, self-doubt, and "weirdness" because most of their relatives, teachers, and some friends don't really understand what it's like to live in a stepfamily. Minor step-kids need to adjust their identity, roles, loyalties, and "rank" in their home and stepfamily each time their adults have a new child, i.e., a half-sibling, or a biological or step-sibling moves in or out of the home or a key person dies, moves away, remarries, or re-divorces.

The following issues start with common surface problems and progress toward the primary problems that cause them. With which of them do you identify?

1. My stepchild disrespects me despite the concern and consideration I show and the sacrifices I make. S/he is selfish, ungrateful, insensitive, rude, sly, sneak, rebellious, dishonest, lazy…. This is my stepchild's fault—s/he's bad.

2. As a veteran adult and hard-working, well-intentioned stepparent, I deserve respect from my stepchild. I'm the victim here and that's not *my* fault.

3. One or both of my stepchild's biological parents covertly encourage his/her disrespect for me and won't admit or confront it, so it's not *my* fault.

4. I care enough to provide some child discipline that's been missing in their family for too long. My stepchild dislikes that, and me. My stepchild's parents have been too lax, I'm a better parent, and I'm here to rescue this child and create some order in our home. I'm just acting responsibly with good intentions, and I'm going scorned for it.

5. My stepchild is blocked in grieving her/his many losses and doesn't yet have emotional room to grow a relationship with me. *I'm not responsible for the problems we're having.*

6. My stepchild un/consciously hopes that by rejecting me, his/her parents and biological family will reunite. *Solution: We adults are all responsible for helping this child to grieve and release that normal dream.*

7. My stepchild is angry that her/his parents divorced and/or remarried, and s/he is expressing normal anger at me. S/he unfairly feels that their family's breakup is my fault. *Solution: We adults are responsible for validating this child's anger and guiding her/him on how to express (release) it respectfully.*

8. My stepchild is caught helplessly in one or several loyalty conflicts and can't ask for help in getting free or doesn't yet feel consistently safe in forming a relationship with me. Example: My stepchild resents the (disrespectful?) way I treat his/her non-custodial parent, and rejects me by siding with her biological parent "against" me. *Solution: We adults are responsible for resolving our family values and loyalty conflicts and associated relationship triangles.*

9. My stepchild is unconsciously using rejection, rudeness, and "rebellion" to test whether s/he's really safe in this alien new family S/he was powerless to prevent his/her birth family from breaking up, causing agonizing losses. *Solution. S/he has a right to test over and over again to see if s/he's safe from loss and abandonment in this stepfamily.*

   This child may also be doing appropriate testing to clarify who makes the rules in the new home and stepfamily and who enforces them; how the adults rank his or her needs, opinions, and dignity in the family hierarchy; and how much power the adults grant him or her in their lives.

   Unless there are other problems, this testing should subside as your stepchild grows to trust that the adults are dependable, empathic, and wise decision-makers and problem-solvers. The length of this normal "testing phase" will be proportional to how much the child was traumatized before, the number of other significant stressors in and between the stepfamily adults' homes, and the health of your remarriage.

   As stepfamily adults you are responsible for validating the stepchild's need for safety, distinguish that need from "disrespect," and to patiently do what you can to help the child fill her of his developmental and family adjustment needs over time.

10. My stepchild feels disliked and disrespected by me, and is responding with normal hurt, resentment, and hostility. *Solution: I'm responsible for this and can learn to reduce or correct it.*

11. I've avoided acknowledging that we're a stepfamily, and I haven't accepted my responsibility for earning my stepchild's respect as a person and for my stepparent role. I also haven't acknowledged my stepchild's right to express frustration and anger

at being forced into a complex, confusing stepfamily that s/he didn't want or was consulted about. *Solution: We adults are responsible for accepting our stepfamily identity and what is means, validating our kids' feelings as we patiently merge our biological families, and encourage our children, relatives, and supporters to learn stepfamily realities with us.*

12. I've been confusing disrespect with distrust. My stepchild doesn't know how to tell me that s/he doesn't yet trust me to: genuinely like, care about, and enjoy her/him despite irritating traits; consistently respect her/his human rights, boundaries, and values, and not force mine on her/him; and, not cause her/his parent (my mate) to abandon her/him. *One or more of the following solutions may apply:*
    a. *I will be patient and fair with her/him and any siblings.*
    b. *I will not prefer my kids, including "ours" babies to her/him.*
    c. *I will help him/her trust me to be a fun friend as well as a rule-spouting, critical adult.*
    d. *I will be solidly committed to defining and learning my stepparent role because I want to, not just because I have to.*
    e. *I will acknowledge that my stepchild may not yet trust me and will not let her/him manipulate, con, or intimidate me.*
    f. *I will teach, encourage, guide, protect, and empower her/him rather than criticize, demean, order, and use her/him.*
    g. *I will not emotionally or physically abandon her/his parent and her/him.*
    h. *I will co-manage our home and family safely and effectively.*
        Reflect on whether there may be other ways in which your stepchild distrusts, which affect your unique situation.

13. I'm mislabeling my step-teen's normal experimenting with early independence as defiance, disobedience, and personal disrespect. *Solution: I need to change my judgment, affirm my stepchild's healthy goal, and—with my partner—teach this child more acceptable ways of "leaving the nest."*

14. I've not asserted my boundaries and related consequences effectively with this child. *Solution: This is your responsibility to resolve. Read on.*

15. My partner and I are unconsciously using this disrespect conflict to avoid confronting a serious adult-relationship or family problem. My stepchild is confused and anxious about this and may be unconsciously trying to protect us all from greater conflict and anxiety and maybe breaking up. *Solution: Adult partners are responsible for resolving this.*

16. From earlier trauma, my stepchild is often controlled by a fearful, shamed false self. S/he is unconsciously projecting his or her low self-respect (shame) on me. *Solution: Co-parenting adults share the responsibility for helping to empower your stepchild's true self to convert the excessive shame to balanced pride and humility, increase his/*

her security over time, and provide a stable, highly nurturing environment for the entire family.

17. *My personality is ruled by shame-based sub-selves. My own mix of shame, guilt, anxiety, confusion, and self-doubt is distorting my perception of my stepchild and my expectations of myself, my stepchild, and my mate. I need to own all this and investigate personal recovery while learning to prioritize and balance all of our concurrent needs with my partner.*

18. My stepchild senses that I don't respect or trust myself in this alien stepparent role and this promotes her/his disrespect. *Solution: You are responsible for earning your, and other family members', respect in the challenging role you've accepted.*

19. My stepchild and I have "bad chemistry" (many values conflicts) with each other. *Solution: This is no one's fault. Within limits, you can work to affirm the human dignity and potential in your stepchild without disrespectfully pretending to "like" her/him. You can ask, versus. demand, the same from your stepchild. You can also affirm that you and your partner primarily chose each other, not the kids, and sometimes step-relatives just don't like or love each other, without anyone being bad. This doesn't mean that you can't learn to enjoy a highly nurturing stepfamily together! You, your partner and the kids each share responsibility to respect each other's needs, dignity, and integrity, and be honest with each other about these as you evolve your relationships and roles.*

What Does This Apparent Disrespect Mean?

The first thing to notice is that there are many reasons why your stepchild may seem to, or really does, disrespect you in your care-giving role or as a person. Many of them have nothing to do with respect! Your choices are to be boggled and paralyzed with all these reasons, or to realize you have many options within this chapter for improving this situation over time.

The second thing to note is that if you choose to stay at the surface, emotional-reaction level, without going deeper and honestly analyzing each of these possible solutions with your mate, you risk reflexively blaming the child, your partner, or someone else. By criticizing others and avoiding your own responsibility for at least half of the root problems, you'll surely raise others' resentments and anxieties. The most challenging of the scenarios above are those where you are responsible for changing something.

Thirdly, the quality of any relationship is proportional to the thought and time partners *want* to put into it. On a scale of 1 to 10, how much do you really want to *earn* your stepchild's respect? How much do you want to find a new way of respecting his or her spirit and potential, if not the child's values, appearance, and behaviors? If you and your partner aren't talking earnestly about the ideas above, what does that mean about your priorities and awareness?

Another unpleasant implication is that the disrespect you and your stepchild feel may signal a deeper problem you want to avoid, such as: a significant re-marital problem; one or more of you being wounded survivors of major childhood neglect in need of personal recovery; or you and/or your mate having made reactive, unwise relationship and role commitments.

Improve Stepparent – Stepchild Trust

Make it safe to be honest in your home. Distrust is different from a child disliking you. How can you tell if you're trusted? Is your stepchild able to express his or her full range of feelings with you spontaneously, without significant embarrassment (shame), guilt, or anxiety; able to confront you honestly on things he or she doesn't like about you; and spontaneously tell you of daily events that cause him or her major feelings like pride, fear, guilt, shame, excitement, hope, and anger? Please keep an open mind—this is about discovery, not blame.

Another way to gauge your stepchild's trust in you is to reflect on whether he or she voluntarily turns to you for help with school, social, work, and/or family problems. Is there another option? While stressing that you are not on a witch-hunt, ask knowledgeable relatives' and friends' for their opinion.

A final way is to ask your stepchild in age-appropriate language if he or she trusts you to: tell the truth, keep your word, care genuinely (rather than dutifully or falsely), be self-responsible (rather than blaming others), be consistent (predictable), genuinely forgive and be reasonably tolerant, want to listen when you can and to say so when you can't (rather than "faking it"), be on time, say honestly what you mean and need (rather than hinting, lying, or double messages), use "good judgment," provide something tangible (like food) or invisible (like companionship) that they need, and genuinely respect their needs, boundaries, values, opinions, worth, and property.

If you decide your stepchild does trust you enough, enjoy the good feelings that merits and keep doing what you're doing. If not, what might the primary problems be? Your stepchild may be significantly controlled by a fear-based or shame-based self. His or her distrust of you may be generic (all adults, all men or women, all parents, etc.), not personal.

Or perhaps you're not aware of doing something that discourages your stepchild from trusting you. If true, you're challenged to look honestly at your values, habits, and behaviors, and change something familiar. Perhaps you don't really like, respect or care about your stepchild, or you're ambivalent and he or she senses that. A clue is your behavior, such as sending "put down" messages, including not really listening to or avoiding him or her. A deeper problem may be that you made an unwise re-marital decision.

Or, you're taking your stepparent role too seriously, overemphasizing discipline, rules, and (unwanted) advice, rather than genuine listening, play, and friendship-building. A common problem—especially for step-dads—is the feeling that you have to *fix* your stepchild rather than just listening, affirming, encouraging, and getting to know him or her. A deeper problem may be that you're not fully aware of, or accepting, stepfamily realities, or there are sexual tensions between you that no one is taking about.

Or, you covertly disapprove of your partner's and/or their ex-mate's parenting, and resent having to "clean up their mess." Your stepchild senses your criticism, resents or misinterprets it, and may feel covertly protective and combative. This puts you all in a divisive loyalty conflict and probably related relationship triangles.

Are you blurring your stepchild's dislike, disrespect, hostility, overwhelm, blocked grief, or disinterest in you with distrust? Get clear on how each of these differ, separate and assess them, and focus on solving one or two at a time with your mate's help. Be aware that your feelings may actually be the result of doubting your competence as an effective stepparent or that your partner may be projecting uncertainty or ambivalence about your competence. Your stepchild senses this and unconsciously distrusts you as a caregiver, not as a person.

Grow Stepparent – Stepchild Respect

What are your options for resolving the real reasons behind this situation? You can complain, whine, attack, over-analyze, ignore, repress, avoid, endure, catastrophize, or collapse. These choices leave the odds for improvement to chance or "fate."

Or you can make various first-order, i.e., superficial, changes over time, and grow more frustrated, irritated, resigned, cynical, and antagonistic. This and the above choices each inexorably raise your odds of eventual psychological or legal re-divorce.

Or you may choose to assess each of the possible primary problems with your partner honestly, take responsibility for your part, and evolve clear goals and plans together. This option will work best if each of you are guided by your true self, and if you learn and use the communication skills provided in Chapter Seven of this book. Work your plan and monitor what happens over time. Patience and realistic optimism are assets.

Along the way have one or many family meetings, including your stepchild and other key stepfamily members. You adults need to define the agenda, lead the meeting, and stay focused on clarifying, validating, and problem-solving, not blaming, debating, explaining, or punishing! Adopt the view that your "disrespect problem " is a *helpful symptom* of deeper problems and help each other dig down to discern and patiently resolve them a few at a time. If you choose to limit your focus to *forcing* your stepchild to respect you, your problems will surely expand.

Recap

Over the first two decades of their lives, each of your minor kids must fill developmental needs to become independent, self-actualized, productive young adults. Typical kids in stepfamilies, especially from divorced biological families, need informed, patient adult help to fill their adjustment needs to this new family on top of their developmental needs, needs which peers in intact, highly nurturing biological families don't face. Don't confuse your stepchild's repeated testing of new stepfamily relationships for safety with "untrustworthy" behavior and character traits. Every family your stepchild has belonged to has broken up. As least one biological parent has left him or her, love and visitations notwithstanding. These caused agonizing losses, guilt, shame, confusion and fears. Every stepchild instinctively needs to prove that his or her new stepfamily home is a reliable refuge.

In this context, effective stepfamily adults need to nurture their kids and each other patiently. Helping each other to heal your own inner wounds and intentionally providing a highly nurturing family to your step-kids can provide the soil in which your stepfamily can grow and thrive.

It's common for a stepparent or stepchild to feel disrespected by the other—as a person or in their family roles. When that happens, everyone in and between kids' homes feels uncomfortable until the adults act to reduce the significant disrespect that causes divisive relationship triangles and loyalty conflicts. These in turn cause other tensions in and between your stepfamily homes.

What may seem on the surface to be disrespect can really be a mix of several to many unseen personal and relationship problems. To shift stepchild–stepparent disrespect toward acceptance and appreciation, over time, acknowledge that you have significant problem of family "disrespect" rather than one of dislike, distrust, lack of love, or "bad chemistry." Be aware that you want to take responsibility for resolving it, assess for the primary problems, and then brainstorm and try solutions—as teammates, not competitors.

Why? Because stepchild–stepparent tensions, including conflicts over personal rights, boundaries, values, and child discipline, usually put biological parents, siblings, and relatives in the middle of loyalty conflicts and this can turn into a complex re-marital problem.

CHAPTER TWELVE

EFFECTIVE CHILD DISCIPLINE IN STEPFAMILIES

What is *effective* stepfamily co-parenting? How can you reduce the co-parenting barriers between divorced biological parents? What are the key similarities and differences between the complex family roles of stepparent and biological parent? And what are the keys to effective child discipline in and between typical stepfamily homes? What is effective children disciptine and how can it will improve family relationships.

What is "Child Discipline"?

It is both a science and an art unique to each family. An art, because child guidance comes partly from the heart and instincts of the adults. A science in that there are learnable discipline guidelines that family-life experts believe usually yield better short-term and long-term results.

We will define child discipline here as: Sets of behavioral rules and limits, and stated or implied consequences for minor children, which may be enforced or not, by one or more care-giving adults.

For *effective* child discipline in a given home, all of these factors have to work well-enough together. Each factor can contribute to harmony, self-esteem, and mutual respect in a stepfamily's linked homes, or can cause serious relationship problems. To see how, let's look at some ideas about effective child discipline. First, decide...

Why Is Child Discipline Important?

This may sound like a brainless question, but might you agree with these reasons?

1) To *teach* minor children that their actions have consequences for which they are responsible, and which they (usually) can have control over.

2) To *help* maintain order and harmony within the home and family, and so promote feelings of security in everyone.

3) To *nourish* oneself and have mutual love and respect, in and between dependent kids and their stepfamily adults.

4) To *model* a way in which grownups respectfully and lovingly protect, guide, and care for themselves and young people.

5) And, to *show* kids that people have limits to what they will tolerate, and what happens when these limits are not respected.

Together these fall under the general goal "to prepare our kids to one day co-manage their own homes and families effectively."

Would you change this list? How would you rank the order of these (or your) child discipline aims? How would your partner? Each of your parents? Your ex-mate (if any)? His or her new partner? Given their experience to date, would any of your kids be surprised at any of these points? Notice that the words in italics feel positive rather than implying child discipline actions such as punishing, forcing, breaking, or making the child…. The attitude underlying the latter words is about power, not empowering. Such an attitude usually breeds increasing fear, resentment, shame, and defiance in kids over time. Which child-discipline view did your key caregivers and teachers seem to have? By the way, the word *discipline* means "follower" or "pupil." To discipline, then, is to lead, guide, or teach.

What Is Effective Child Discipline?

How do you know if the child discipline in your family is "working" well enough? The answer varies widely with ethnic, local, and birth-family cultures. Your answer depends on your own conscious and unconscious child discipline standards and aims. If you accept all five goals above, then effective child discipline is: "whenever we meet these aims enough." Often, busy, inexperienced, or distracted caregivers do not stop to assess their own child discipline values and goals, especially if their own parents were unclear about theirs.

Many adults often settle for just "we discipline the kids to keep order in our home." While they may achieve this goal, they may lower their kids' self-esteem and damage mutual respect and family harmony in the process. The title of a popular book on career choices applies to the outcome of child discipline, too: *If You Don't Know Where You Want To Go, You'll Probably End Up Somewhere Else.*

Twenty-three Differences of Stepfamily Child Discipline

What makes stepfamily child discipline different from one-home, biological family child discipline? Both "nothing" and A LOT! From one view, setting effective behavior limits in any stepfamily home is no different from any typical biological-family home: i.e., all of the discipline goals above apply to any home. At the same time, because average multi-home stepfamilies are far more complex than one-home biological families, and have many extra tasks to master, effective stepfamily child discipline usually takes much more patience, communication, clarity, and effort by the adults. Here are 23 reasons why:

1) Disciplining minor step-kids involves "your child" or "my child" (or grandchild), rather than "our child." This usually breeds stressful loyalty conflicts, especially in new step-homes.

2) Normally, biological parents discipline their own children without any fear of being lastingly rejected by them—the DNA and ancestral bonds are too strong. Their relationship is not at risk. Many stepparents are sensitive to, and anxious about, rejection by their step-kids, which is always a real possibility, since there is no DNA bond.

3) Remarrying stepfamily adults usually choose each other, rather than each other's kids. Normally, biological kids' wishes about bringing one or two new stepparents into their lives are not given equal weight— "unfairly," from their point of view. A painful reality is that a step-mom or step-dad may not like a stepchild, or vice versa. This makes genuinely respectful child discipline hard!

4) Merging stepfamily adults' households requires an "instant" merger of child-discipline values, priorities, and techniques, as opposed to the gradual shared evolution of those discipline factors in typical biological families. Such sudden mergers can be extra stressful if a new spouse has never parented before (or never parented a teen, a boy, twins, etc.).

5) The remarrying ceremony often instantly causes major changes in adults' and kids' expectations about child discipline. For example: "Yesterday, I was your mom's boyfriend, but today, I'm your stepfather. Now I (suddenly) have both the responsibility and the right to discipline you—but I didn't yesterday." Thus, child discipline may not have been a problem while dating, but may turn into one literally overnight, especially if a stepparent tries to impose many major changes all at once.

6) Where child visitations are involved (which is usual), both kids and adults may experience three conflicting sets of disciplinary standards: (1) Pre-remarriage family rules, and current (2) custodial and (3) non-custodial stepfamily adults' rules. This gets even more complex, considering the added child-discipline values and rules in step- and biological-grandparents' and other step-relatives' homes. From the child's perspective, "there's 'too many' people telling me what I should and shouldn't do. It's too confusing!"

7) If biological dads and moms stay hostile after divorce, the stepfamily adults' child-discipline arguments can fuel their battling. A biological parent's ex-mate can accuse the new stepparent of being too harsh, or favoring their own children, or "interfering with *our* way of child discipline." They may even tell their kids "you don't have to do what (your stepparent) says, they're not your parent!" Or the stepparent may feel "when your kids visit their biological mom(dad), there are no rules at all!" —implying that "they're a bad parent" and "... so *do* something about that or you're a bad parent!"

8) Biological parents may "under-discipline" by the stepparents' (or others') standards because of unresolved guilt over their child's divorce pain. Also, biological parents are often naturally more tolerant of their own kids' behavior than unrelated adults or step-siblings are. Many overloaded single parents had to be more permissive in their homes. A new stepparent's "tightening up" behavior limits and consequences lowers step-kids' freedoms, forces unwelcome changes, and raises their resentment. They did not ask for all this! (Alternatively, a sensitive new stepparent may *promote* new and welcome household order, structure, and clarity!)

   During precious visitations, non-custodial biological dads and moms usually want to have a good time with their kids, not to hassle with rules, limits, and consequences. Stepparents frequently have limited sympathy for this.

9) Where they see the biological parent's discipline as too lax, a stepparent can feel a duty to rescue an "out-of-control" stepchild by becoming the major rule-maker or enforcer. This usually clashes with wanting to be liked and accepted by their step-kid(s), and eventually leads to frustration and resentment at "always being the bad guy." Stepparents can grow to greatly resent "having" to do the custodial or non-custodial biological parents' job(s) —even when they are self-appointed.

10) Stepparents can feel left out, unimportant, and hurt if not invited to participate in stepchild guidance, or if they feel unsupported or unfairly criticized by the biological parent(s) in their discipline efforts. Conversely, kids can resent their biological mom or dad "authorizing" their stepparent to discipline them. If stepfamily adults do not act to improve this situation, frustrated stepparents typically get weary and withdraw, or become autocratic and demanding—which is confusing and stressful to everyone.

11) A biological parent, trying to please both their own children and their new mate, can send confusing, stressful double messages like: "I want you to share in disciplining my kids" and "I don't like what you're doing or how you're doing it (so stop)." Effective verbal communication skills, especially "Process Awareness," can resolve this key cause of stress.

12) New stepparents, especially step-moms, usually work hard to provide "fair and nurturing discipline." Despite the adults' patience and understanding, step-kids often ignore them, and are scornful of, or "ungrateful" for, their stepparent's efforts. Typically, biological parents have less of a need to be thanked by their kids, for obvious reasons.

So, if their mate does not (1) praise and support their child-discipline efforts, and (2) their step-kids ignore them or take them for granted, even the kindest step-dad or step-mom can become resentful and burned out over time. Then motivation for effective stepchild discipline withers and household (and re-marital) conflict rise.

13) Stepchildren over about five or six, especially most teens, are likely to resent discipline by new adults (or older step-siblings) at first, regardless of how fair or justified. This can be especially tough in homes where a new step-mom is caring full-time for her husband's children. It is normal for children in any family to test new behavior rules and limits: "Will they be enforced? By whom? How? How much power do I have here? Will my dad or mom side with me or my stepparent?" If the new adult takes this normal testing (often labeled "defiance" and "rejection") too personally, a stressful relationship will bloom.

14) Because the child-discipline motivations, priorities, and techniques between remarrying adults differ, values conflicts between them are almost certain. These sound like: "You're too strict about Sara's homework!" "No way! You're too soft—look at her grades!" Kids quickly sense this and often try to use such disagreements to their own advantage. Again, stepparents without biological kids may have very idealistic views of child discipline, particularly of stepfamily child discipline.

15) Even if stepfamily adult partners feel okay about the balance of discipline responsibility, kids will often bitterly claim that some stepfamily adult "isn't fair." This is true in any family, but it feels very different in a stepfamily home because it's "your child" or "my kid," not "our child."

16) In some remarriages, older-teen step-kids can be close to the age of a young stepparent, usually a stepmother. This naturally causes awkwardness and role confusion about her step-parental authority, trust, and respect.

17) In a step-home which adds an "ours" child, step-kids or some relatives may see the stepparent as now favoring the new baby. The stepparent, especially if not a parent before, really can favor their own DNA child. That is natural and okay! And, it can really upset hard-won child-discipline harmony, until things rebalance in the home.

18) In new remarriage homes where both adults have prior biological kids (blended stepfamilies), it is normal for each biological parent to emotionally favor their own kid(s) at times. This either clearly shows in "limit-and-consequence" settings or it "leaks" out, despite their real wish to treat biological and step-kids just the same (i.e., to be "fair"). Such adults can be at war *within themselves* ("I shouldn't love my kid more, but I do"), and so send confusing double messages to others in the home. While biological parents often love one biological child more (or differently) than another, such biases feel different in a typical stepfamily, raising self-doubts and loyalty-conflict stress.

19) In new stepfamilies with older teens, the young adults are normally starting to move away from home, just when one or both remarried stepfamily adults want to build stepfamily unity and bonding. This sets up major battles as the teens "defy" new discipline and assert their independence. These conflicts can be especially intense if a teen has not mourned their birth-family's split-up well, or has not accepted their parent's remarriage, their stepparent, or any step-siblings.

20) Even if remarrying adults and their kids reach solid compromises on discipline, grandparents can misunderstand, resent, dislike, or fear the way a new stepfamily adult is "raising" their grandkid(s). These feelings either "leak out" or are obvious, causing another complex stepfamily loyalty conflict. This is extra stressful if grandparents still love their former son- or daughter-in-law, who will "always be their grandkids' dad or mom." Similar loyalty conflicts can bloom with aunts, uncles, and cousins, too.

21) Even after child-discipline harmony develops over time in and between linked stepfamily homes, each time another extended stepfamily adult remarries, many child-discipline values, rules, and consequences must be negotiated and stabilized all over again.

22) If a biological parent is dead, minor and grown kids can torment a stepparent by comparisons: "My real mom (dad) was never so mean/unfair/weird/strict/dumb...(about behavior and household rules)!" The new adult can feel hopeless, being up against a "saint" or "ghost" with whom they can never truly negotiate or "win."

23) Counselors, clergy, and friends who do not know or accept these stepfamily realities may advise new stepfamily adults to have the stepparent(s) discipline their step-kids like biological kids right away. Such well-meant advice usually backfires, adding to personal, marital, multi-home stepfamily stress.

How do you feel now? It is okay to feel pretty overwhelmed. Stepparent adults who think "stepfamilies are pretty much like biological families" normally find these 23 child-discipline differences to be startling, confusing, and stressful at first. A few at a time, they are manageable!

Why Child Discipline Can Be a Big Marital Problem

Basically, biological parents feel unavoidably forced to choose often between their new spouse and their own kids. Typically, the stepparent feels guilty about this; the kids feel anxious, triumphant, or guilty; and each feels resentful if the biological parent chooses the other. If the stepparent accuses the stepchild of "having no manners" or "eating like a cave woman," the biological parent can feel personally attacked ("Oh, so I(we) didn't raise my kid right, eh?"). A natural response is to defend the child or themselves (and even the ex-spouse), polarizing the stepfamily home into biological people versus step-people. This dynamic, especially when cyclical, really stresses the new remarriage!

Another child-discipline dynamic that can strain typical remarriages is inclusion. A stepparent may push for the new family to adopt discipline practices that are different. The proposed changes are not necessarily as important as what they represent: "Agree with my discipline ideas and include them in how our new family functions. If you do, I feel important, valued, and accepted. If you don't, I feel rejected, hurt, and resentful."

Often—especially with insecure stepchildren "resisting" (i.e., testing) —it is easy to focus only on the discipline rule or consequence being debated, rather than on what these stand for. This is why seemingly trivial child-discipline differences between adults can be highly emotional re-marital issues.

So, we have proposed here that (1) stepfamily adults setting child-behavior limits and consequences is both the same and very different from in typical biological-family homes, and that (2) ineffective discipline can really strain stepfamily remarriages.

Guidelines for Effective Stepfamily Child Discipline

These can be grouped into:
- Healthy child-discipline principles for any family, and
- Guidelines unique to typical multi-home stepfamilies.

General Child-Discipline Guidelines

1) Get clear now on your specific parenting and child-discipline goals. Discipline meant mainly to punish (i.e., hurt, get revenge, and grow fear of pain) risks eroding a child's self-esteem and self-confidence, over time, causing shame ("I'm a bad person"), guilt ("I always do bad things"), or anxiety, and either apathy or defiance. Discipline consistently aiming to respectfully teach, guide, and protect fosters self-worth, realistic self-confidence, and feeling secure, over time.

2) Distinguish clearly between the rule or consequence you are communicating about, and how you are communicating about those with your child. When disciplining, your tone of voice and body language immediately tells the child what your present core attitude about them is. These non-verbal "relationship" messages may convey to the girl or boy "I see you right now as a respected person of equal dignity and worth, and I care enough to struggle lovingly with you. I am wiser than you and will consistently guard you against hurting yourself or others. I'm firmly, compassionately in charge here, and *you and your dignity are safe*."

The alternative embedded "relationship" message is "I care more about my immediate needs and wants than yours right now. We are not equals in dignity and worth here. Do what I say or I'll cause you pain."

Which is closest to your current child-discipline style and relationship message?

3) Give yourself guilt-free permission to not always be totally fair or perfect. It is inevitable that you will favor one child a little, that you will sometimes be inconsistent (even with that child), and that your judgment will not always resemble Solomon's. It is also inevitable that your standards will vary by day and by situation from your spouse's (and ex-mate's). Try shooting for...

- Being as consistent as you can.
- Stroking yourself when you are "fair."
- Authorizing yourself to be "imperfect and improving" at achieving child-discipline equality.
- And, listening respectfully to, and acknowledging, your kids' complaints about child-discipline "unfairness"—without guilt!

This last point put into action might sound something like: "Nate, you feel I'm treating Cyndi better than you now. That makes you pretty mad and you really don't like me doing that." Note that "empathic listening" like this does not mean you agree with Nate! It does mean that you *hear* ("with your heart") what he feels now, and why.

4) Try to distinguish between requests you make of your kids and what response ("no," "maybe," or "later" is okay, and demands. It can keep things much clearer if you say something like "this is not negotiable!" (when true).
5) Tell your child clearly, calmly, and specifically what you want, or what rule you are setting and what the related consequence is. Especially on big issues, get specific feedback from your child that they clearly understand what you expect of them, and what will happen if they choose to do otherwise (consequences). For example, specific feedback sounds like "So I hafta be home by 10:30 or get grounded for next weekend, or call if I'm gonna be emergency late," rather than "Okay, okay, I gotta be home on time or else...."

It can be hard on stepfamily adults and kids alike if either limits or consequences are fuzzy or not defined at all. Consequences defined in advance are usually more effective than those created on the spot.
6) Try to fit the consequence to the situation. "You forgot to take out the trash again and I had to do it. You're grounded for the rest of the summer!" may win the battle, but lose the (respect and cooperation) war.
7) When a child breaks a household rule, make the promised consequence happen promptly. Children get scared of their own power and lose respect for a stepfamily

adult if they feel they can often con the adult into backing off a deserved consequence. The well-worn motto here is: "Say what you mean, and mean what you say."

Note the two kinds of consequences: *natural* ("When you leave your bike outside, I worry that it'll be stolen.") and *parental* ("I sure hope that doesn't happen. If it does, I'm not going to buy you another one."). Which kind of consequence do you think is more effective in the long run?

8) Confront discipline problems as soon as you can. Enforcing a consequence two weeks after an incident is far less effective than doing it right away. Among other things, it raises the odds that the situation blurs, letting the child use the "You (or I) never said that!" defense.

9) Especially on major issues, explain calmly and factually how you are affected by a child's ignoring a rule. For example: "If you leave the back door unlocked or standing wide open, *I get scared* someone may come in and take something" is much more "hear-able" and less wounding than "I hate it when you're such a stupid jerk and leave the whole house wide open, so don't, you air-head!"

10) Try to talk about rules and consequences *literally* on the child's (eye) level. You may actually detract from a kid's ability to hear you if you tower over them and have an angry voice and face. Squat, sit, or kneel to reduce the chance they will feel intimidated. If you are feeling extra intense, try to calm down before confronting. Otherwise fright or shame will block the child's hearing and may blast their self-esteem.

11) Reduce the chance that a disobeying child feels shamed by a (parental) consequence by saying something like "I love you *and* (not "but," which negates) I really don't like what you did just now. I'm real angry!" In other words, consistently distinguish between kids' "person-hood" and their actions.

12) Avoid using blaming words ("you're thoughtless/wimpy/yellow/stupid/lazy/ inconsiderate/dumb/weird," etc.) or labels ("you're a nerd/whore/tramp/liar/sorry excuse/ mistake/joke/creep/jackass/jerk/idiot," etc.) when confronting a child. These wreck self-esteem, lower self-confidence, and breed defiance, shame, and guilt. You can protect their self-image and still get your point across forcefully by saying with feeling: "When you (specific behavior), I *really* feel (specific emotion(s)) because (specific effect on your life)!"

13) Expect children who have broken a rule or agreement to be defensive; it does not mean they are being *bad*. It is human nature for all of us, when embarrassed or "wrong," to explain, counterattack, divert, whine, deny, rationalize, and so on. Ridiculing or criticizing children for trying to protect themselves will promote their being sneaky, guilty, and ashamed. Honoring their feelings and human dignity—while firmly sticking to the consequence—will help them feel safe and accepted, and they will be more open to learning the results of their actions.

14) If you feel it is important that a child should learn when and how to apologize, do so yourself. If you never take responsibility for your own mistakes and say (and mean) "I'm sorry," but demand that they do, you may get what you want, but the likely price will be confusion, sullenness, disrespect, and resistance.

15) Encourage cooperation by promptly praising compliance, but only if you really feel like it. False compliments are double messages which breed confusion and distrust. Over-praise, too, dulls the effect. Since some people (especially shamed ones) are embarrassed by praise, it helps to be as specific as possible with why you are praising. This lowers the chance they will discount or minimize your appreciation.

For instance: "Glory, when you cleaned up the dishes, countertop, and trash tonight after your friends left (specific action), I had time to balance the checkbook (specific help to you). You were really thoughtful and considerate—thanks!" is much harder to blow off than "Well, your mess in the kitchen was smaller than usual the other night; maybe there's hope for you after all" (a delayed, negative compliment).

16) Realize that "no limit or rule" (i.e., permissiveness) is a rule. Setting few or no limits—or consequences—is a form of "passive" child discipline. If overdone, a child can decode such actions as "you really don't care that much about me. My actions (or safety) don't seem to matter to you. I must not be very important in this home." Since a child will not ask for limits or consequences, this type of silent shaming will usually go unspoken.

17) Avoid setting limits and consequences when you are very angry, over-tired, or really distracted. Your judgment and focus are impaired, and you may add to household tension rather than reducing it. An option is to say something like: "I'm really upset (worn out, distracted, etc.) right now and I'm not thinking real clearly. When I'm clearer, I'll let you know (about limits and consequences)." If you say a version of this, follow up on it!

18) Get clear on your basic attitude about human "mistakes" and "failures." Mistakes can be seen as *opportunities* for important long-term learning and healthy course corrections. Alternatively, they can be viewed harshly as signs of personal "stupidity," "dumbness," "selfishness," and "badness." Your true attitude about your kids' "failures" and worth will leak out, no matter what you say.

Teaching kids that we all make mistakes, are responsible for them, and can use them to learn better how to get along in the world is *empowering*. Teaching a child how to be a successful "failure" (i.e., how to learn from mistakes and avoid self-shaming) is a priceless gift! Building the habit of calmly describing your own mistakes, even with (non-shaming) humor, and saying briefly what you learned from them, can be powerful positive modeling for your kids. For balance do the same for your successes!

19) Be alert that a strong reaction in you to a child's "mistake" may be more about your senses of parental inadequacy or incompetence than about them. If your personal boundaries are fuzzy, and you see a child's behavior as a clear reflection of your dignity and self-worth, you are requiring your child to carry *your* problem. That may come back to you over time as sullenness, rebellion, furtiveness, avoidance, and/or apathy.

20) Try and stay clear on problem ownership. Encourage kids to take responsibility (within their limitations) for their problems and encourage them to find their own effective solutions. The same applies to you! The wise old adage about the long-range value of teaching a hungry person *how* to fish rather than *giving* them a fish applies here.

21) Many family-life teachers endorse that related stepfamily adults strive for a "united front" in providing limits and consequences for their kid(s). It is confusing and can raise a child's anxiety if one adult says, "You can leave the dinner table when you're done without asking," and the other parenting adult says, "No, you can't!" It's normal for adults to disagree on behavior rules and consequences, but it helps everyone if they can resolve these values conflicts off-line, so they can provide their young people with clear, non-clashing guidelines together.

22) Take the time to identify your own childhood-caregivers' styles and main values about child discipline. Compare those with what your current values, priorities, and styles are (e.g., to shame and punish versus teach respectfully.) Have you thoughtfully designed your own discipline standards or are you unconsciously repeating (or over-avoiding) what you experienced from your caregiver(s)?

23) Be alert for nagging and lecturing, and avoid them. Parents nag when they do not trust their kids (usually from experience), or when they are ambivalent or reluctant to make and enforce consequences because they may promote conflict.

Also, if kids have exceeded a limit, and are scared, guilty, or embarrassed, their ears are emotionally plugged. Kids' attention spans, especially young kids', are limited at best. Droning on and on about why their behavior is/was bad or wrong, and why your rules and consequences are justified and fair, is often a waste of everyone's time. It usually lowers a child's respect for the person who does the droning. Note the major difference between two-way *discussions* about kids' behavior, limits, and consequences, and one-way *lecturing*.

Pause for a moment and thoughtfully compare the guidelines listed above to the guidelines (i.e., "values") that you carry and use. Are there any changes or additions you want to make? How will you do that? What (or who) might get in the way?

Whatever your discipline values and priorities, know clearly what they are. The alternative is disciplining your kids unconsciously and impulsively. Doing so lowers your odds for situational and long-term success.

Guidelines for Stepfamily Child Discipline

Most of the child-discipline guidelines below are especially useful in the first years after remarriage. As a typical stepfamily bonds and grows its own history, traditions, and stability, the need for these special discipline rules decreases.

1) Accept that you all are a normal, unique multi-home stepfamily (rather than "just a family"), with three to six, or more, active stepfamily adults (unless one or more absent biological parents are dead of "uninvolved"). Get clear on which adults, specifically, are responsible for the shared co-parenting of each minor child in your stepfamily.

2) Decide up front if you are all going to try to co-parent your dependent kids as a team of informed, cooperative caregivers, or as independent, competing (or indifferent) adversaries. If you were one of your minor kids, which of these would you want? If divorced biological parents retain hostility and distrust, they are coequally responsible to their minor biological kids for resolving those blocks as best they can, over time.

3) Accept that typical stepfamilies are very different from average one-home biological families, and often need fundamentally different stepfamily rules and standards than typical biological homes. One vital difference, as previously discussed, is that an average minor stepchild may have over 20 unique developmental tasks to master that peers in intact, biological homes don't have. Stepfamily adults in a multi-home stepfamily should learn clearly what these tasks are and base their individual care-giving "job descriptions" on helping each child master their unique mix of these special tasks over time.

4) Identify what all co-parents are trying to do with your stepfamily long-range. Now, based on your specific long-range goals, clearly define how specific responsibilities for each child are to be divided between your three to six, or more, stepfamily adults. Evolve a job description for each adult and keep it current to match new conditions. This is no small task. It really illustrates how complex, challenging, and vital effective stepfamily parenting is.

5) Go slowly on changing pre-remarriage child-discipline rules, and making new rules or consequences. *Kids need to learn to trust in and respect a stepparent before they will award him or her the right to be obeyed.* It often helps if a stepparent acts like an aunt or uncle at first, unless they are the only adult around and must set limits and consequences. In new stepfamily homes, it is often best if the resident biological parent does most of the discipline of their kids for a while, especially enforcing consequences.

6) Expect loyalty (or values) conflicts over child-discipline issues in and between your related homes. A loyalty conflict happens when one family member feels torn between two or more others that he or she loves and wants to please. These clashes are inevitable

and normal. When they happen, no one is doing anything wrong! They happen in any parenting home, but they feel very different in step-homes because they involve "my" or "your" child (or ex-mate), not "our" child.

Do not be surprised if loyalty conflicts erupt soon after the remarriage ceremony, if they did not exist before. Study how to handle these conflicts and discuss them together. Teach your minor and grown kids and key relatives what a loyalty conflict is and how to spot one. When in loyalty-conflict doubt, ask "what's the best option for our marriage here?"

7) Expect dependent step-kids to test and re-test the child-discipline rules in your home. What may look like defiance and rejection can really be a frightened, uncertain child needing to prove that "Yeah, somebody really is steadily in charge here. Maybe this family won't break up like the last ones I was in (birth family and one-parent home); maybe I'm really safe here." How long do you think it takes to build a minor child's trust in this personal safety?

So "rebellion" or "defiance" can really be normal, appropriate testing. It can also be a stepchild acting out part of his or her healthy grief (i.e., anger). Typical step-kids have lost a lot in just a few years. They have much to grieve. "Rebellion" may also be older teens starting to (normally) disengage from the stepfamily. A kid's standard ploy for trying to get a "yes" from one stepfamily adult after the first says "no" (i.e., splitting) applies here, too.

Seeing your step-kids' behavior as testing or part of grieving does not mean you should shrug and avoid setting and enforcing clear behavioral limits and consequences. It does mean you should empathize with and acknowledge their behaviors without blame and stay clear on your own tolerances.

A common way step-kids test is to sarcastically taunt, "I don't have to (obey you), you're not my parent!" An effective way of responding is: (1) First, respectfully acknowledge them; e.g., *"So you feel that because you weren't born to me, I have no right to tell you what to do now."* Then, after they agree, (2) firmly reassert your own position; e.g., *"Yes, you're right, _and_ (not "but")* I am responsible for helping to run our home well and solving problems we all have. That's what I'm doing now."*

As long as the child continues to test, calmly and firmly repeat these two steps until they accept they cannot hook, intimidate, or dissuade you. Ideally, do this with the biological parent present.

8) Try viewing discipline values that clash as *different* rather than good-bad or right-wrong. Imposing one adult's style of child discipline in a step-home can cause resentment and hostility all around. A better way is to experiment with blending different discipline styles over time. Also, open disagreement on discipline styles and values, and on problem-solving, is far better than silent verdicts and resentment, which erode respect and stress remarriages.

9) Help step-kids see and accept that a stepparent is not trying to replace or "become" their biological parent, but is doing parenting things (e.g., guide, teach, comfort, protect) because they care responsibly about their step-kids. Grownup DNA-relatives, or the parents of a child's friend, also do parenting things without trying to replace or "one-up" an absent biological parent. One middle-school stepdaughter spoke for the best case when she said, *"I feel sorry for kids in regular families. They only have two parents—I have four!"*

10) When a stepparent is the only one available to do child discipline, it helps if the biological parent verbally "authorizes" the stepparent in front of the kids to act in his or her place. For instance: *"If* (stepfather*) George asks you to do something, it's just the same as if I asked you, okay?"*

11) If a new stepparent has no parenting experience, it helps everyone if he or she admits that (without guilt or shame) and studies: (a) how kids that are the ages of their stepchildren normally act (especially teens), and (b) effective parenting basics. Help can come informally from veteran friends and relatives, and formally from courses like Parent Effectiveness Training ("P.E.T.") and Systematic Training For Effective Parenting ("S.T.E.P."). Such courses are often offered by local schools, adult education programs, and community mental health centers. If step- and biological parents go to such a course together, their minor kids see both adults taking their jobs and their kids' welfare seriously.

12) Try not to confuse a biological parent's natural tolerance for their own child's behavior with being "too easy." If stepfamily adults' fights on this seem too intense too often, consider counseling to explore if there is a deeper issue here. Typical "deeper issues" are the needs for control, acknowledgment, "order" (i.e., safety), validation (i.e., insecurity), approval, or a fear of "failure." An especially common deeper cause is a biological parent's unresolved guilt from hurting their children with birth-family trauma and breakup and ongoing fights with the other biological parent.

13) Experiment over time with who sets the child-behavior rules, and who enforces them and how. Give all your adults and kids permission to "mess up"; this is alien new ground for all of you! Because multi-home stepfamilies are normally very complex, it usually takes many months (or several years) to find comfortable disciplinary balances among all kids and stepfamily adults. This is a moving target since everyone is evolving together. Aiming for "flexible consistency" is preferable to declaring ironclad right/wrong rules and consequences. *It is okay to take your time and experiment!*

14) Review your parents' styles and values about child discipline to sort out which of their rules work for you and which need revamping for your unique family. If one stepfamily adult comes from a father-run autocratic family and the other from a mother-dominated democratic home, child-discipline power struggles may be natural at first. Note that most birth-family child-discipline habits were not designed to fit a stepfamily. Even if they were, they may not be right for yours.

15) If a stepparent resents a stepchild talking disrespectfully to his or her biological parent, try something like: *"I don't like the way you're talking to my wife (husband). It feels like a put-down and I want you to stop it."* A step-child cannot dispute a stepparent's right to say this, whereas they can dispute *"I don't like the way you're talking to your mother (father),"* by responding, for instance, *" Oh, yeah? It's none of your business how I talk to my own parent, so bug off!"*

16) If step-kids visit their other stepfamily adult(s) regularly, it helps if the adults inform each other of key child-discipline values, rules, and consequences in their respective homes. Where limits and consequences clash, aim for compromises or agreeing to disagree, rather than for converting each other. It is hard for minor kids to abide by two or more different sets of behavior rules. Their natural reactions are frustration, anger, rebellion, depression, anxiety, or extra sensitivity or "energy" after visiting their other home. Ideally, all stepfamily adults will focus on "what's best for our marriages and our kids" rather than trying to prove "we're better parents than you are because...."

17) If other adults or professionals advise on or criticize child discipline in your home, consistently help them understand that you are a multi-home stepfamily, different in over 60 ways from average one-home, two-parent biological families. Be alert for well-meant, but uninformed child-discipline and stepfamily advice. If it is biological family-based, it may well cause more stress rather than less.

How do you feel now? Overwhelmed or intimidated are still okay! If child discipline in stepfamily homes seems complex, it is! These 17 suggestions do not cover every situation. Added to the general child-discipline guidelines, they can help you build stability, consistency, and mutual respect among all your adults and kids as you evolve your stepfamily together.

Co-managing Discipline Values Conflicts

Values conflicts are a common dynamic among members of any home or group. They are normal disagreements about personal or group preferences and opinions, which usually cannot be "proved." For example, "cats are *obviously* 'better' than ferrets as pets!" or "Baptism is *essential*." Values conflicts can include disagreements on priorities too, like "I think honesty is more important than loyalty. You *don't?*"

Values conflicts are different from facts, which can be demonstrated or proved ("If you put your hand on that griddle, you'll get burned").

Average new stepfamily homes are filled with values differences on many subjects. This is because the resident and visiting members usually come from pretty different backgrounds and belief systems. This is especially true for the emotionally loaded subject of effective parenting. Is there a best way of handling the inevitable values and priority clashes between stepfamily members?

Yes. Here are some specific suggestions, based on listening to hundreds of average stepfamily adults describe what works for them:

First, teach everyone who regularly lives in or visits your home clearly what a "values (or preference or opinion) conflict" is as opposed to a "facts" conflict. Encourage all your members, especially kids, to accept that complex stepfamily mergers normally generate lots of these disagreements, so when they happen, no one is wrong or bad!

Second, consider your options for resolving these values conflicts. Here are three:

1) Avoid dealing with them by pretending they do not exist, or minimizing them (e.g., "It's no big deal").
2) Explain, argue, fight, and try assertively (or aggressively) to persuade the disagreeing parties that your opinion is right and theirs is wrong.
3) Or seek, after discussion, to respectfully agree to disagree together and with cooperation; try not to criticize or reject another family member for not agreeing with your value or priority.

Third, in discussing values conflicts cooperatively, grow the habit of explaining in a factual way (rather than judgmental) how the other's opinion affects your life, if at all. If your partner is in a place to listen (rather than vent or defend), this may lead to some practical "problem-solving" that reduces the effect of the values disagreement.

For example, *"Tito, you feel smoking cigarettes in the house is an okay health risk. I don't see it that way* (values conflict). *I respect your right to choose that for yourself* (agreeing to disagree). *When you smoke in our home, the smell makes me feel nauseous and usually distracts me a lot from what I'm doing. When you smoke at a meal, the smell always blocks me from enjoying my food* (specific effects). *If you choose to smoke, would you please either do it outside if I'm at home or wait until I'm gone?"* (Respectful win/win compromising proposal.)

These three ideas apply to any values conflicts about child discipline. For instance: *"You seem to feel it's okay for (your biological daughter) Tammi to swear in front of us. I'm really uncomfortable with that. I feel disrespected when she does* (rather than *'She's so incredibly crude!'*), *and I worry that she'll get in the habit of doing it and accidentally offend some key people in her life, like bosses, co-workers, teammates, or some friends."* (Two specific consequences).

Notice that the latter effect ("I worry...") can stem from a stepparent's belief that he or she shares responsibility for guiding a stepchild to have socially acceptable habits and to "succeed." Is that really *your* job in this family for *that* child? This is why evolving specific job descriptions for stepfamily adults, which spell out clearly what each adult is and is not responsible for, is so vital and helpful.

Recognizing and really resolving normal stepfamily values conflicts, about child discipline and many other areas, are key skills which stepfamily adults can help each other develop over time, in and between their linked homes. Investing time, patience, and energy in doing this cooperatively raises the odds of increasing members' self- and mutual respect, and household and stepfamily teamwork and tranquility. Not doing this inexorably fosters household and marital stress.

How do you all generally handle discipline (and other) family values conflicts? How did your respective parents and former mates? Does your present way "work" well enough for you all? Would each of your kids agree? If you could improve one thing about how you all deal with values conflicts now, what is it and who is responsible for changing it? What is in the way?

This chapter introduced the complex, vital co-parenting art and science of effective child discipline in multi-home stepfamilies. Done well and consistently over time, effective child discipline promotes feelings of teamwork and cooperation in and between linked homes, primarily because every member feels respected and heard enough, over time.

A common key personal issue for step-moms and step-dads is "I lose respect for myself if I'm passive here and don't try to help (my stepchildren) see the trouble they may be causing for themselves." As you see, it can get pretty tricky to stay clear on "how does our values conflict *really* affect *me* and what, specifically, do I need, even if we can respectfully agree to disagree?"

Your rewards for working together toward effective child discipline patiently and cooperatively are tremendous and include:

1. Kids who feel good about themselves and (eventually) their new stepfamily.
2. Adults who feel satisfied and proud they are doing a tough job well.
3. And, a new stepfamily that bonds and grows over five to eight or more years into a nurturing and loving group (usually) enjoyed by all.

Stepfamily adults who consistently put a high priority on learning stepfamily norms and step-kids' special needs can make informed stepfamily mission statements and job descriptions as teammates rather than opponents.

If all two to six, or more, stepfamily adults work over time to develop shared awareness of, and fluency in, the five communication skills you have already read about, they will become more adept at consistently giving clear rules and consequences as unexpected stepfamily challenges unfold. Helping all family members acknowledge and grieve their many losses and proactively heal any post-divorce bitterness and distrust (at least for the kids' sakes) really help, too.

The riskiest approach to stepfamily child discipline is to do it impulsively, by "instinct." Instinct is usually based on biological family realities and traditions. It assumes "what worked in my prior home(s) is good enough for this one!" Unless your prior home was an *informed* stepfamily, that attitude will probably head you all toward inexorably escalating frustration, stress, and conflict.

Guidelines For Effective Child Discipline In Multi-Home Stepfamilies

General Guidelines

- As individual parents and couples, get clear now on your specific long-range parenting and child-discipline goals.
- Distinguish clearly between the rule or consequence you are communicating about, and how you are communicating about those with your child (e.g., respectfully as equals in human dignity to you, or sarcastically putting them down as inferior people).
- Give yourself, and your kids and co-parenting partner(s), guilt-free permission to not always be totally fair or perfect. Be as fair as you can be.
- Distinguish between requests you make of your kids (when "no," "maybe," or "later" are okay responses), and non-negotiable demands.
- Tell your child clearly, calmly, and specifically what you want, or what the limit is that you are setting, and what the related consequence is. On major issues, get clear feedback that they understand these accurately.
- Clear limits and consequences defined in advance give kids clearer choices and let them take responsibility for incurring the consequences.
- Seek consequences that are in proportion to the child's misbehavior.
- If a child breaks a behavior rule, make the promised consequence happen promptly—without humiliation, criticism, sarcasm, triumph, jeering, or smugness. "Say what you mean and mean what you say."
- Decide early which works best to achieve your long-range parenting goals: *natural* consequences, *parental* consequences, or a mix to fit each situation.
- Confront discipline problems as soon as you can.
- Explain calmly and factually how you are (or another is) affected by your child's ignoring a rule or misbehaving.
- Try to talk about rules and consequences literally on the child's eye level, rather than looking down on them. Seek steady, respectful (not intrusive or intimidating) eye contact as you do.
- Consistently distinguish between a child's self and their actions or behavior; e.g., "I love (or respect) you and (*not* 'but') I don't like what you did."
- In reacting to a child's behavior, avoid using blaming words or titles and name-calling. Avoid growing their shame by focusing on the effect of their actions, not on their personal qualities or defects.
- Expect children who have broken a rule or agreement to be defensive; it is normal to be defensive, not weak or bad. Otherwise you teach them "you're bad if you defend yourself or show emotions."
- If you feel it is important that a child learn when and how to apologize, do it yourself.

- Encourage cooperation by promptly praising compliance, if you really feel like it.
- Realize that "no limit or rule" ("permissiveness") *is* a rule.
- Avoid setting important limits and consequences when you are angry, over-tired, or distracted.
- Get clear on your basic attitude about human "mistakes" and "failures." Do you see them as normal, healthy opportunities to learn, or are they symptoms of a child's personal inadequacy and worthlessness?
- Be alert that an extra-strong reaction in you to a child's "mistake" may be more about your sense of parental inadequacy or incompetence than about them.
- Strive to stay clear on behavior-problem *ownership*. Is it the child's problem, yours, someone else's, or a combination? If it is the child's problem, empower them to learn to solve it themselves, rather than always taking responsibility for fixing things for them.
- Stepfamily adults protect kids from confusion and anxiety by striving for a "united front" in presenting limits and related consequences. Resolve your discipline values-differences away from the kids.
- Take the time to identify your own childhood-caregivers' styles, main values, and goals for child discipline and sort out which (if any) work effectively now in your family.
- Get and stay clear on the differences between *explaining* limits and consequences, *nagging*, and *lecturing*.

Special Guidelines for Effective Child Discipline in Typical Stepfamilies

- Accept that you all are a normal, unique multi-home stepfamily (rather than "just a family") with three to six (or more) active stepfamily adults, not just two.
- Decide up front if you are all going to try to co-parent your dependent kids as a team of informed, cooperative caregivers, or as independent, competing (or indifferent) adversaries.
- Accept that typical stepfamilies are very different from average one-home biological families, and often need fundamentally different rules and standards than typical biological homes.
- Early on (ideally before remarriage), draft what you stepfamily adults are all trying to do with your stepfamily, long-range. Evolve a stepfamily mission statement together, as well as related job descriptions for each stepfamily adult.
- Go slowly on changing pre-remarriage child-discipline rules and making new rules and/or consequences. Ideally, biological parents should do much of the discipline with their own minor kids until the kids learn to trust and respect their stepparent(s).

- Expect loyalty (or values) conflicts over child-discipline issues in and between your related homes. Evolve a way to deal with them that works often for your unique stepfamily. When in doubt, put your remarriage first.
- Try viewing discipline values that clash as *different*, not good-bad or right-wrong. Doing so helps avoid destructive, stressful power struggles.
- Expect dependent step-kids to test and retest your home's child-discipline rules. This is (usually) far more about their learning to trust that they are safe in confusing and alien new stepfamily surroundings—or about normal, healthy grieving—than it is about defiance, rebellion, or "badness."
- Help step-kids see and accept that a stepparent is not trying to replace or "become" their biological parent, but is (1) doing parenting things like guiding, teaching, and protecting, and (2) legitimately co-managing his or her own home.
- When a stepparent is the only one available to do child discipline—especially in a new step-home—it helps if the biological parent(s) verbally "authorize" the stepparent in front of the step-kid(s) to act in their place.
- If a new stepparent has no parenting experience, it helps everyone if he or she admits that (without guilt or shame) and studies kids' needs and how to parent effectively.
- Stepparents should try not to confuse a biological parent's natural tolerance for his or her own child's behavior with being "too easy."
- Stepfamily adults should experiment over time with who sets the child-behavior rules, and who enforces them and how. Avoid rigid, black-and-white child-discipline rules.
- A stepparent who resents a stepchild talking disrespectfully to a biological parent should try something like, "I don't like the way you're talking to my wife (husband)" rather than "…to your mom (dad)."
- If step-kids visit their other stepfamily adult(s) regularly, it helps if all stepfamily adults inform each other of key child-discipline values, rules, and consequences in their respective homes, and try for a collective united front where possible.
- And, if other adults or professionals advise on or criticize the child discipline in or between your homes, consistently help them understand that you are a multi-home stepfamily, different in over 60 ways from average one-home, two-parent biological families.

Key Differences in Effective Child Discipline Between Biological Families and Stepfamilies

Setting Clear Limits and Effective Consequences Together Without Wrecking Your Remarriage!

Jack's second wife, Marcia, faces him soberly after dinner one night. *"We have to talk, Jack. Something has to change here. You seem to pick on Rachel* (her custodial daughter) *all the time, but when your daughter visits, she can do no wrong. Rachel's complaining to me and I don't blame her."*

Remarried just over two years, Edward and Joni have grown increasingly concerned about Ed's son Michael's poor school grades. Joni's son, Ethan, also 12, does very well at the same school. *"Mike's smart enough, he just won't buckle down,"* Ed growls. *"I'm gonna pull him off the track team; that'll get his attention!"*

Joni listens, feeling torn. Mike's told her privately he resents his dad's angry punishments and has vowed *"not to let him get to me."* She's not sure what to say. She disagrees with Ed's heavy-handed approach, but when she's suggested a lighter touch, Ed has commented sharply about not having Michael become *"a mama's boy"*—a thinly veiled slam at her and Ethan.

Margaret, nine, complains privately to her grandmother about how strict her stepmother is. *"She has rules for everything. We can't have a corn-flake or a sock out of place, or she goes ballistic! And Daddy just goes along with her. We never had to do all these chores and stuff before **she** came."* Her slender grandmother soothes her, *"Listen, sweetie, I'll talk to your father. Norma shouldn't be making new rules and bossing you around like that. After all, she's **not your mother....**"*

Mark's 10-year-old twins scowl at him and their step-mom, Trish, sullenly, after returning from visiting their biological mother and half-brother, "TJ," over the weekend. The kids want to watch a TV special now, and Mark and Trish have said together, *"Nope. You both know the rule...not until we see that all your homework is done."* Young Alex storms out of the room shouting, *"you guys aren't **fair!** **Mom** never makes us do that! We can watch TV any time, at **her** house!"*

In bed, Georgia rolls up on an elbow and looks at her husband, Frank, beside her. *"I have to tell you, hon, I really can't stand the way you let your kids talk back to you. You're so patient and good with them, and when you ask for some little help around the house, they're sarcastic, rude, whiny, and bitchy. You just let them walk all over you!"*

An ongoing challenge to all members living in or visiting an average stepfamily home is maintaining effective child discipline. Some stepparents have never parented at all before. Others have, but have never raised a boy, a girl, multiple kids, a teen, or a "part-time" child before. Biological parents' and stepparents' discipline values and priorities often differ, sometimes radically. Stepfamily adults in kids' "other" home(s) may cooperate or sabotage. Biological and step-relatives can hassle and criticize. Many step-parents are unsure of their family authority, and so give kids confusing double messages.

Most new step-kids have never experienced a non-related adult "bossing them around," other than teachers at school or house of worship. Many do not like it or do not know how they feel. The main task for average minor step-kids in a new step-home is to test, which unaware (or overwhelmed) stepfamily adults may see as "acting out," "disobeying," or rebelling."

About 90 percent of current U.S. stepfamilies formed following the prior divorce of one or both stepfamily adults. After divorcing, both biological parents may eventually remarry, so their dependent biological kids may come to have three or four stepfamily adults in two homes (and up to eight grandparents) telling them what to do—and when, how, and why.

In all cases, these children have at least one new stepparent who begins to "discipline" them. If the kids and their biological parents feel such discipline is "fair" and does not clash "too much" with what they are used to, then there is little problem. In most multi-home stepfamilies, however, differences over child discipline and parenting values and styles *do* cause at least temporary problems. These can get severe enough to wreck the new marriage.

Keep in mind that the term "discipline" here refers to stepfamily adults' setting behavioral limits and consequences for their live-in and visiting minor kids. You can use the upcoming sections as checklists to note both your family's child-discipline strengths and the things you want to improve. Mark up this chapter as you go: highlight, write notes, underline, amend—let this text work for you!

PART FOUR

SUPPORT YOURSELVES

In conclusion, the following chapter offers ways in which you can organize and grow a blended family and stepfamily support group to support and nurture yourself and others.

CHAPTER THIRTEEN

EVOLVE AND USE A STEPFAMILY AND BLENDED FAMILY SUPPORT NETWORK TOGETHER

How does a group start? What do the people who come to them want? Why do some groups flourish while others fade? Do groups "do any good?" While effective support groups are rare, the answer is "Yes!" and such groups are sorely needed!

This chapter will outline the key steps toward building a support group in which participants feel that their main needs are being met enough in ways that leave each and all members feeling good about themselves and their shared process. This chapter will cover what "support" is, how to get a group started, and how to keep the group going.

What Is Support?

Although support groups in general focus on two categories—*health* problems (cancer, AIDS, limb or organ loss, etc.) and *emotional* health issues (grieving, relationships, career and money problems, aging and retirement, etc.)—all fill the same five sets of human needs.

1. Need to vent
"Venting" is the communication process of talking honestly about current strong emotions and thoughts. *Effective* venting happens when the speaker feels clearly *understood, empathized with* and *accepted* "where they are." When listeners judge or discount the speaker's feelings ("You're *still* grieving your divorce?) or try to fix the situation ("Look, why don't you ...."), venting does not work as the speaker's needs are not filled.

Because typical stepfamilies differ from biological families in many important ways, stepfamily adults often feel painfully little understanding or *real* empathy from their friends and kin. And unless they have had personal experience or special training (which is rare), most clergy and professional counselors also often have trouble *really* empathizing with stepfamily adults (or their kids) who need to vent.

And so, to stepfamily adults who often feel isolated and alone, it's a Godsend to be with a group whose members listen, nod empathically, and say "I *know....*"

2. Need to feel validated

Because many stepfamily members do not know "what's normal" in average stepfamilies, this leaves them unconsciously using *biological*-family standards, expectations, and solutions in coping with *step*family problems. These often don't work well.

Otherwise well-educated, mature women and men struggling with step-kids, ex spouses, and myriad loyalty conflicts can begin to feel literally "crazy." As rosy early remarriage dreams inexorably fade into the stress realities that emerge, partners begin to doubt their own (or each other's) perceptions and abilities to cope. This is especially true for women, who have been trained by our patriarchal society to believe that they are mainly responsible for making their (step)family "happy."

By telling parts of their current stepfamily story, and consistently having other stepfamily adults nod and say, "Yeah, we've had that experience, too," group members can feel almost a tangible relief that they are *normal* after all. They are not imagining or exaggerating their problems, and are not "weird" for having trouble understanding and co-managing them effectively. This second kind of relief is *group validation!*

3. Need to learn

A third need that most support group members seek to fill is to learn about appropriate situational norms, solutions to specific family problems, and resources available. This need for family and parenting information and ideas is often especially acute in average new stepfamily adults—those within two or three years of their remarriage.

Typically, nobody warned them how complex, alien, and confusing their new multi-home, multi-generation family enterprise would feel. The first quest of their learning is usually "What should we be learning?" This is true even for those adults who were raised as step-kids.

Often, stepfamily adults encountering their version of the major tasks covered in this book focus on learning for their kids first (rather than coequally for their remarriage and themselves). A well-organized, effectively run support group can be an excellent source of useful stepfamily information.

4. Need to socialize and help others

Two more reasons why (some) people attend support groups is to help fill their needs for community and belonging, and feeling useful to others. Traditionally adults wired with "female brains" feel the need for relationship and communion more strongly than peers with "male brains." However, if their own, current needs are met, everyone feels good providing meaningful support to others in need.

Effective group leaders periodically poll the members to keep the right current balance between their needs for venting, validating, and learning ("business"), and just *schmoozing* together. A related group benefit some busy remarried mates voice is that their meetings provided a regular "date" night, a scheduled, "legitimate" time alone as adult partners to talk, problem-solve, and just enjoy each other. Also, it is not unusual for some good friendships for adults and their respective kids to evolve from a series of group meetings and multi-family events.

5. Need to grow hope

A last need that effective groups may help to fill applies especially to stepfamily adults in re-marital and stepfamily crisis. Some such adults seek groups frantically because they have finally broken through their denials and have acknowledged they have serious problems. If these frightened people are uneasy with or scared to get professional help, they may hope that going to a group will solve their problems. Usually, that won't work, since support groups and therapy groups are very different in objectives, design, leadership, and process.

If a stepfamily support group's policy is to invite such desperate adults or couples into a meeting, one of the kindest gifts members can bestow is to confront the newcomers with the reality that they need qualified professional help, which the group cannot provide. Ideally, group members would have built a referral list of qualified (i.e., stepfamily-informed) professionals in their area to offer such seekers.

This implies that group members become clear together on what kind of family situations warrant assertive referrals, and which are within the group's own scope. Support groups without a clear policy and guidelines on this important point are at risk of delaying a troubled couple from getting appropriate help for themselves and their kids, or maybe even raising their distress. Even the pain of being "rejected" by a support group (i.e., referred out) can provide validation, information, and direction. These can build some hope for positive family and re-marital change.

More broadly, as average stepfamily adults meet and build awareness of stepfamily realities together, an effective support group can give *everyone* realistic hope that they *can* be among the one-third who "make it," over time.

Here's the bottom line. Adults in typical multi-home stepfamilies often need to vent, feel validated, learn key things, socialize at times, help others, and build and keep realistic hope for themselves as people, couples and stepfamily adults. Because their type of normal family is so complex and different from biological families, step-adults (and their kids!) probably feel these needs more intensely than their peers in typical single-parent, foster-parent, and adoptive-parent families.

Starting a Support Group

The key initial resource needed to establish a successful stepfamily support group is a dedicated person, couple, or core group. You probably would not be reading this unless you are (or might be) such a person. *BRAVO!*

Three general ways to begin are:

1. Group founders set clear criteria and goals in advance, *then* seek participants who agree with these goals.
2. Founders get an initial gathering together, then evolve structure and objectives from their collective unique mosaic of needs; or
3. Combine these: set some loose guidelines first, then refine them to fit whoever shows interest.

The group founders get to decide which of these three modes fits them best. The last option is the one I've seen work most often.

For perspective, let's first look at who might be interested in joining and building a group. Although there is a kaleidoscope of variations, the people who attend stepfamily support groups regularly fall into three general categories:

1. Previously divorced or single people who have a serious new adult relationship growing but are not yet remarried. They may or may not be living together. These people *are aware they're a stepfamily-to-be (*rather than denying that) and want to "get it right" this time for their own and the involved kids' sakes. Such people are probably not in a current stepfamily crisis. Especially if they are previously divorced biological parents, they are self-motivated to learn relevant, accurate how-to information in advance. They are drawn to the chance of hearing either veteran stepfamily adults tell of their experiences (and solutions) or knowledgeable outside speakers describe aspects of stepfamily life.
2. Remarried couples who are feeling confused and somewhat stressed. They have been living together for months or a few years, and are probably finding their family doesn't feel like what they were expecting. One or both may acknowledge they are a stepfamily, but they probably don't really know what that means. These couples are often unbalanced in that one mate (usually a step-mom) is more interested in finding and joining a group than the other.

   These people are likely to be in a custodial (rather than visitation) stepfamily. They often have begun to encounter loyalty conflicts and co-parenting disagreements, and are uneasy about them. They may or may not have biological kids together. One or more of the step-kids may be acting out at home or school, or an ex mate has been causing problems. While open to learning, these people have a higher need for validation than the people in type I described above, because they feel somewhat blamed, misunderstood, guilty, or anxious. The newcomer may feel frustrated his or her spouse is not solidly enthused about coming if attending alone.

3. Adults or couples in major stepfamily (i.e., re-marital) crisis, who are desperate for effective answers to their conflicts. They may or may not be in therapy, and may show interest in the group on their own or because a well-meaning counselor has referred them. These stepfamily adults often challenge group members because they are scared, frustrated, conflicted, and often more interested in blaming and defending than in mutual problem-solving.

These stepfamily adults can use up much group time, repeatedly explaining and justifying their positions and wanting the group to "prove" their mate is "wrong" or "bad." They are probably polarized into his-and-hers camps, are mutually distrustful and cynical, and pose the risk of turning the group into a gripe or attack session. These people often do not know how to do win-win family problem-solving. They may resist learning, out of misplaced pride or unconscious fear.

There is a last *large* group of couples who could really benefit from a stepfamily support group, but they don't know that. They are either dating and committed, or forming a stepfamily. They are living in "benign ignorance" and truly do not know what they do not know about the challenges for which they are headed. If they see an ad for a group, these people think "That doesn't apply to us." Skillful advertising, or the assertive advice of an informed minister, doctor, or friend, may motivate such people to try one meeting. Have some factual handout literature for such folks, to help clarify *why* they should return and learn more.

Planning the First Meeting

If you are considering forming a group, do you have any help so far? It is more fun and less work if you can find at least one other person to team with you in planning and running the first meeting. If you cannot find a partner who will commit to direct participation, can you find an advisor who has started some kind of support group before? Stepfamily couples who work together often seem to harvest important re-marital benefits.

The goal: The basic aim of the first meeting is to meet at least two to five or more other stepfamily adults who are willing and able to join in getting some form of group off the ground.

Set realistic expectations: As an enthused organizer, you probably put a lot of effort into planning and advertising a first group "event." You expect dozens of participants, only to find that three or five people show up. You feel disappointed and frustrated and regard your effort as a failure. Actually, that is a pretty good first turnout.

Here are some apparent realities that could explain why stepfamily adults don't throng to even the best-promoted first meeting:

- Many dating adults about to form a stepfamily often don't identify (yet) as a *step*family. Or if they do, they are apt to believe idealistically "our love will get us though." Either way, they typically see little point in seeking stepfamily support.

- Most middle-class Americans choose jammed lives. They have many activities, responsibilities, and diversions, and feel they have "too little time." Their culture takes family life and parenting for granted, and generally views stepfamilies as "minority" second-class entities. Also, average stepfamilies have more minor kids (say three to six) than their biological family counterparts (one to three.) That means less "free" couple time. (A paradox: Attending a group is one of the best parenting investments of time and energy stepfamily adults can make!)

- Some *veteran* (remarried) stepfamily adults feel "okay enough," so they see little need to get support. Other veterans do acknowledge modest or significant problems, but are uneasy or ashamed to admit it publicly by going to a support group. About 90 percent of current U.S. stepfamily adults have been divorced at least once. To admit that a second (or third) primary relationship feels rocky is pretty scary. It is safer to stay home.

- If the group appears to be linked to a house of worship, hospital, or mental health organization, some stepfamily adults' negative biases get triggered: "Looks like a group for sick divorced people (or "Jesus freaks")—*no thanks!*"

- The least obvious low-attendance factor is that the majority of stepfamily adults seem to come from seriously dysfunctional childhoods. Most grown deprived children learned long ago to be *extremely* independent and not risk asking for or accepting help. This has to do with having been repeatedly let down by key early caregivers. So protecting against repeated disappointments by "not needing" other people becomes a knee-jerk reflex, especially for men. The good news: Grown deprived adults in some form of real personal recovery will gladly use all the help they can get.

- Another reality is that some ethnic groups (e.g., Asians, Hispanics and Latinos, Eastern Europeans, and people of Mediterranean descent) are fiercely private about their family affairs. Relatives can be scathingly critical if a family member "goes public" in a group. Similarly, some religious communities teach that divorce is sinful and remarriage is either invalid or blasphemous. Social pressure can powerfully inhibit such stepfamily adults from trying out a support group.

Are you still enthused about recruiting a group of stepfamily adults? I hope so! Despite these combined factors, I believe there is a select group of stepfamily adults in any community who are motivated to gather together to exchange help.

There are several effective ways to motivate most people to attend an initial gathering. All ways involve some planning and advertising. Here are four options that work and may result in four to eight or more stepfamily adults showing up:

1) ***Advertising an organizing meeting***. This is the least-effort and most direct route. In my experience, it is also the least likely to work. Despite tentative interest, most of us (who may feel over-committed to begin with) are not excited about going to an unknown place to have an "administrative" meeting with some strangers. (Have you ever been to a *"fun"* or *"really* satisfying" organizational meeting?)

Still, it is worth trying. You may harvest even one other person who will team up with you to try another approach. You might also connect with a sponsor. Any advertisement will alert your community that there are stepfamilies "out there," who have needs and issues, too.

2) ***Holding a public information program.*** Given the right advertising "spin," this kind of initial group event can seem very interesting or even fun! Several options include:
- A moderated panel of veteran stepfamily adults or step-teens (or both), describing their stepfamily experiences and recommendations. To raise interest and energy, invite audience questions and supportive comments as part of the process. A panel of about six people provides a lively, interesting meeting.
- A presentation about a key stepfamily topic by a qualified speaker; or

3) ***Making a presentation to a select audience.*** What are "select" (versus "general public") audiences? Excellent prospects are:
- Existing local or national single-parent support groups like *Young Single Parents (YSP)* and *Parents Without Partners (PWP)*.
- Individual or combined (liberal) religious congregations, or their adult-education committees and groups.
- Existing family-related support groups like "Rainbows" and "Tough Love." These groups often have a high percentage of (troubled and *highly* motivated) stepfamily adults.
- Parents who have been notified through a school or district PTO or PTA mailing; and,
- Community college or other local adult education classes focusing on family and parenting topics.

If you connect with such a group, what would you present? Typical topics might be:

- What Are the 20+ Special Needs of Minor Children of Divorce and Remarriage?
- How Do You Know If Your Stepfamily *"Works"*?
- What People Don't Know They Don't Know About Stepfamilies
- What Makes an *Effective* (versus "Good") Stepparent?
- Raising the Odds for Success in Your Remarriage

During the introduction to any of these programs, mention that ideas for, and interest in, an ongoing support group will be invited toward the end of the program. Promoting small and large group discussions during these programs starts a bonding and identity-building process. There is often a surge of enthusiasm as the participants discover mutual stepfamily interests, experiences, and conflicts—and a wish to share more!

At the close of such initial events, ask any people interested in forming a group to meet with you briefly. Allocate time for this. Confirm their initial interest and invite them to a *planning, exploratory,* or *brain-storming* meeting. Get names, phone numbers, referrals to other people or groups who might be interested, and clear commitments for one more meeting. Iron out any scheduling conflicts.

4) **Offering a stepfamily class.** There are several commercial kits available that provide agendas, materials, and leader guides for lay people to lead their own multi-session step-adult class. (See *Sources* at the end of this chapter.)

The "best" class format:

- Comprises 12 to 16 people. Couple attendance is encouraged, but not required.
- Is clearly educational, *not* therapy (i.e., deep emotional venting or serious interpersonal fighting are out of bounds).
- Covers the major interests of the participants over time.
- Mixes presentations with small and large group discussions at each session.
- Focuses on topical problem descriptions and positive *solution options.*
- Includes handouts summarizing key points, and uses worksheets to promote couple and group discussion and value clarifications; and,
- Is informative, supportive, safe, and *fun!*

The distinct benefit to offering a pre-structured class is that real group trust and bonding usually bloom across the class sessions. Often, as such a class ends, the participants don't want to lose the rare feelings of empathy and comradeship that have developed. As a result, they generally welcome the suggestion to continue meeting and perhaps expand the group to include others in the community.

So let's say you have held a first meeting of one of the types suggested above and have harvested several other stepfamily adults solidly interested in forming a group. Now what?

The Second Meeting: Organize

Goals: When this planning meeting (or series) is over, you want to have initial group trust, a feeling of shared purpose and optimism, and a clear-enough-for-now group agreement on issues like those below.

Guidelines: It is helpful to start this planning meeting with a summary of the general purpose and the meeting's agenda. Then ask for some introductions: preferred names; a little background on each person's stepfamily structure, status, and experience to date; and what they want to both get from and give to the group (e.g., "Tell us why you're interested.") Ask if anyone has had experience in organizing or participating in a support group before.

Within your own comfort level, learn if anyone present has any special concerns for *this* meeting about (1) smoking, (2) confidentiality (e.g., any stepfamily information shared here stays among us, unless it's okay with the speaker to tell others), and (3) ending times. Set the tone by stating that you are gathered to brainstorm and that *any* ideas or thoughts are welcome, no matter how "nutty" or far-fetched.

ALERT! Time after time, as such a planning meeting unfolds, one extra-needy person or couple will vent at great length and take the meeting over. One way of avoiding that is to remind everyone before they come AND as you start that this is primarily a planning meeting, and that your future meetings will provide the chance for stepfamily sharing and exchange. You (the facilitator) may have to be assertive on this point during the meeting to help people feel it was productive at the end. Stay focused on *planning* as your process unfolds!

The key questions to resolve at this organizing meeting include:

Useful Organizing Topics

What are our key *group* goals?
Who is our group for and *not* for?
How will we recruit new members?
Who do we want to make referrals to us? How shall we invite that?
What kind of image do we want to present to our community, if any?
Should we limit our size? How big?
Where will we meet?
What should our meeting format be?
How often should we meet? For how long (per meeting)?
What group-process rules and guidelines will help us meet our goals?
Will we need to raise funds? For what? When? How?
Do we want a sponsor or local affiliate organization? If so, who? Costs and benefits?
Should we try to compile a resource library? Of what? How?
Should we have a newsletter? For just group members or others, too? Containing what?
Do we need professional (clinical) back-up and/or other resource people? Why? Who? Should we offer child care?
Should we have a group name? A logo?
Who's in charge of what for now?

Add any questions that pertain to your unique situation. The resulting list forms a working agenda for your organizational meeting(s). As you see, there is much to decide. If this looks daunting, one option is to draft rough answers to some or most of these questions and evolve firmer policies as you gain members and group experience. You don't have to decide all these at once.

Review all these questions together. Decide those you can, then ask for volunteers to work on options for some or all of the remaining questions. Have them bring back their ideas and recommendations to the next planning meeting. Investing patient, focused effort in group design (rather than jumping right in) *really* pays off over time!

After personal experience with a number of groups, I have learned that there is no one best group design. The mosaic of personal, couple, and stepfamily situations that your participants bring will form a unique blend of combined needs. To succeed, your group members should value—and *risk*—getting honest and clear on their needs, and then working cooperatively together to help fill them.

Perspectives

Your group's evolved list of answers collectively forms your *policy statement*. For clarity and consistency, summarize and write down your policies for advertising the group and accepting new people. Here are some thoughts on each of the questions above.

Q: What are your group goals?

Job-counseling author David P. Campbell has titled his book, *"If You Don't Know Where You're Going You'll Probably End Up Somewhere Else (Finding a Career and Getting a Life)."* In the same vein, a group without clear goals is like the proverbial boat without a rudder. I suggest evolving a concise (i.e., one or two paragraphs), clear mission statement early in the process, and reading it at the start of each meeting. This is especially helpful when new people are present.

Basically, you are coming together to fill members' special needs to (1) vent, (2) feel validated and accepted, (3) get effective solutions to stepfamily problems, (4) learn of relevant resources, (5) reduce stepfamily adult isolation, (6) socialize and enjoy each other's company, (7) raise the quality of co-parenting your respective biological and step-kids, and (8) offer a vital resource for each other and the people of your community. Discussion and your increasing group experience may generate other key goals for you all.

It's a good idea (I think) to have a clear policy asking people who are drunk or high on chemicals to stay home or leave.

Q: *Who is our group for and not for?*

A stepfamily support group may be for: any remarried adults, adults considering remarriage, or both; stepparents only, or step *and* biological parents ("stepfamily adults"); or couples only, or any interested individuals or whole stepfamilies.

Some groups are open to the public, while others are limited to members of a sponsoring religious congregation or community.

In my experience, the best option is to invite *all* interested prospective and veteran stepfamily adults, up to your group size-limit (if any). Couple attendance is strongly encouraged, but individuals are welcome. All-stepfamily gatherings or events may happen several times a year (e.g., a holiday meeting), with group consensus.

Having separate meetings for the members' kids is wonderful and a *lot* of work. If you have several adults who are experienced and willing to commit to organizing and supervising periodic meetings for your older preteens or teens, great.

An important membership consideration has to do with the depth of people's needs. Unless you have a qualified therapist attending and facilitating regularly, be clear that your group is *not* meant as a substitute for professional counseling. State that in any verbal and media advertising, and include it in your mission statement.

Some signs indicating that professional help is warranted include: (even joking) comments about suicide or murder; extreme depression, anxiety, paranoia, or reality distortion; descriptions of family physical or verbal abuse or neglect; obvious addiction to chemicals, activities, or people; couples arguing violently in the group; inappropriate sexual conduct at home or in the group; and the like.

Q: *How shall we recruit new members?*

Q: *Who do we want to make referrals to us? How shall we invite that?*

Once you are clear on what you are all trying to do, and for whom, you are in a place to advertise. From my experience, here are some *Do's* and *Don'ts* about effectively publicizing your group for either an initial meeting or an established group.

Terminology can be key. Some people may either be turned off by, or not understand, the terms "stepfamily" or "stepparent" (associations: "wicked," second-best," etc.). Alternative publicity adjectives are *"blended"* or *"reconstituted"* (also confusing) family, "remarriage" or "second-marriage" family. Fortunately, the negative bias against "step-" seems to be mellowing with time as people get used to this "new" type of normal family (estimated to be about one out of five or six U.S. households, in many places).

Advertising a *"stepparents'"* group potentially leaves out the many biological parents who are married to a stepparent, but have no step-kids. *They need just as much support!* Better alternatives are to say clearly you are a group for "stepfamily adults" or "stepparents and their partners"—if you are.

The most effective support-group recruiting publicity seems to be periodic human interest stories in your community paper, with a photo or two. Focusing on an actual couple or family will get people's attention, and lead them into reading about and considering your group. Notices in the community meeting section of local papers, as well as radio and cable and network TV public-service announcements (usually free) work well. These often need to be submitted in writing to the newspaper or broadcast station two to three weeks in advance of the event. Other places to advertise include:

➢ Bulletins and newsletters from a house of worship.

➢ Middle- and high-school district PTO/PTA newsletters.

➢ Local government and organization flyers; e.g., park district, junior college, hospital, or public mental health center adult education programs.

➢ Private counseling agencies, including hospital outpatient departments, and mental health, family-medicine, and family-law private practitioners, are usually glad to know of support groups to which they can make selective referrals.

➢ Have your members tell their doctors, pediatricians, and dentists of your support group when they visit. Perhaps 20 percent of their patients may be in stepfamilies. Divorce-mediation and family-law lawyers can be helpful, too (if they clearly understand you do not need emotionally chaotic or warring people).

➢ Colorful posters can attract wide attention in high-traffic places like libraries, grocery and drug stores, fast-food outlets, copying centers, video rental stores, entrances to public transportation, etc.

➢ Local banks or realty offices may allow reputably sponsored organizations to include group flyers in their mailings.

➢ Local single-parent support groups may have newsletters which will advertise your group. Even if they do, visit their meetings periodically and describe your group. About 70 percent of U.S. single parents remarry within five to seven years.

➢ See if local organizations are sponsoring any "Rainbows" (grief support) groups. Often the kids in them are in stepfamilies. Also, a majority of the adults in "Tough Love" support groups are (pretty troubled) stepfamily adults of teens.

➢ Some (liberal) clergy may agree to make referrals and/or post notices. Clergy who remarry couples are potentially the best people to alert new stepfamily adults to the challenges ahead. Clergy (and other counselors) are often handicapped by lack of *informed* training and direct experience.

➢ One way of advertising is to invite stepparents to sit in on a meeting or two (especially if they are remarried). Often, human-service professionals have no comprehensive idea of the scope and kind of problems with which stepfamily adults and their kids are routinely faced. When they hear some typical stories from your members, they may gain empathy and motivation to refer to your group.

Build a mailing list of potential referral sources from your phone book and send a descriptive flyer quarterly or so. The more planned and thought-out your group design, and the more established you are, the more likely it is that you will attract referrals from such organizations and people (particularly those who are *in* a stepfamily).

Q: What kind of image do we want to present to our community?

Several suggestions about key themes you want the public to "get" about your group from your advertising are that:

- We are here for *all* (adult ?) members of potential or actual stepfamilies with live-in or visiting, minor or grown step-kids.
- We are (not) affiliated with any local religious or mental health organization, or any 12-step movement.
- Our primary purposes are *education* and re-marital and stepfamily *support* (versus therapy), because about two-thirds of U.S. stepfamilies ultimately re-divorce.
- We are an open, drop-in (or call-first) group with clear confidentiality policies (if you are).
- We strive to be realistic, informed stepfamily and remarriage optimists committed to helping our members find effective solutions to their problems. We are not a gripe or ain't-it-awful group (if true).

Q: Should we have a group size limit? How big is too big?

Between eight and 16 people per meeting is optimal. Less than seven or eight people seems to under the "critical mass" that will attract and hold group loyalty. That is partly because there are so many stepfamily variations that a small group lowers the chance attendees will meet "someone a lot like me/us." More people means more potential experience, wisdom, and creativity to draw on for solutions.

More than around 16 participants risks too many who need to vent at a meeting, and some winding up feeling "cut-off" or frustrated. Large-group decision-making gets lengthy and cumbersome, too. Often, a major factor in deciding group size are the capacity and facilities of the meeting site. Either can determine the other.

Q: What should our meeting format be?

Your stepfamily support group can be on a continuum from totally structured to completely unstructured. Moderately structured often works best. That means have a loose, standard format like an opening followed by a "working" segment, a short refreshment break, some socializing/ administrative time, and a closing.

The opening is an important ritual that builds group identity and "gets everyone in the mood." Some options are: welcoming and introducing any new or resource people present; someone reading the group's brief mission (and maybe policy) statement; sharing a prayer if appropriate; reviewing the meeting's agenda; or asking "who needs air time?"

"Working time" is where you all attend to your main needs to vent, be validated, learn, problem-solve, and belong. Again, you have several options:

- Invite each member to "check in" (or "pass") by introducing themselves if new people are present; describing briefly how they are doing; and telling the group about any important stepfamily or re-marital events, problems, and successes. This may be the place to learn if they need air time.
- Have a guest speaker focus on some topic relevant to most (or ideally all) people present, followed by discussion.
- Have "air time," where a few members speak at length about their current stepfamily situation and get feedback if desired.
- Do focused problem-solving for a member who asks for it, and if you are doing a self-led stepfamily class together, go through one of the session modules.

Take a break, get refreshed, and regroup. Then either attend to any administrative business (funding, advertising, recruiting, planning, etc.), just relax and socialize, or complete any unfinished matters from the "working time."

Finally, have a closing that fits you. This could be a (physical) friendship circle, a prayer, a summary of what you have just done together (especially positive options and solutions that emerged), and/or an expression of thanks and encouragement to troubled members and to all. This final segment, though brief, is a powerful way of forging group identity, loyalty, community, and continuity. Some 12-step and other groups close with "keep coming back—it (our group) *works!*"

The "looseness" of such a meeting format comes from your ability to mold each segment to fit your collective circumstances at the time. Sometimes you will have a speaker, other times not. Sometimes you will have many administration tasks, other times little or none. Sometimes many people will need air time, other times everyone will be in a pretty good space and will just enjoy socializing.

The one constant at every meeting is your participants' set of common needs: to vent/validate/learn/problem-solve/belong to/socialize, and build *hope*.

My experience is that groups whose meeting agendas are consistently free-form (no structure) don't last long. Similarly, groups that are run with an over-rigid schedule and format are a turn-off for all but people with high structure needs. Look for a dynamic balance of these that usually *works* for most of you.

An important periodic administrative task is for the leader(s) to poll all members on their comfort level with the average meeting format, and to adjust the format if enough people want to. You will evolve your own best-fit routine over time.

Q: *Where will we meet?*

The major options are (1) members' homes or (2) somewhere else. The basic needs are a nearby bathroom, moveable chairs (ideally), enough elbow room and quiet, a sink and counter space, an accessible public phone, perhaps a refrigerator, and a place for stowing any heavy-weather clothes.

Many stepfamily support groups rotate the hosting responsibilities among the members, partly because they could not find a suitable outside site. The advantages of this approach are economy (free), simplicity (no outside people to negotiate with), and all sharing the site-prep and refreshment responsibilities. The disadvantages are that group size may be limited to fit the smallest homes, and often, phones, kids, and pets can be distracting.

Possible non-home sites can include: meeting rooms at a local church, school, civic building (library, park district, city hall, etc.), hospital, business, or a public or private mental health agency. One Chicago group found a comfortable (free) home in a local realty office's conference room. Again, where choice exists, you may lower the chances of limiting group attendance by avoiding church and mental health sites, and people's (unfortunate) related biases. Conversely, some people would be attracted *because* you were in a church.

Q: *Meet when, how often, and how long?*

These choices will evolve from your group's unique personality. The norm I have seen is to meet once or twice a month, on a week night or Sunday evening, for two to two-and-a-half hours. For eight or more people, meeting for less than that often doesn't allow enough air and administrative time, which breeds frustration and drop-outs.

Q: *What kind of group-process rules or guidelines would help us meet our goals?*

From my experience, there are several aspects of how a group functions that greatly influence how successful it is. I recommend you evolve early—and enforce respectfully—group policies on the following points.

Punctuality. Most members will feel better about the group if they can count on knowing when each meeting will start and end. People arriving after the meeting has started—or leaving before the end—disrupts focus, mood, and momentum, which takes everyone's time to rebuild. If meetings consistently run longer than advertised or agreed upon, members (especially those with baby sitters) can feel stressed and resentful, and lean toward dropping out. You may find it useful to ask that if people are unavoidably detained, they be responsible for calling and letting the host/leader know that. Every group will have a unique blend of members' needs about timeliness. If in doubt what your group's blend is, *ask* everyone what they need!

Smoking and other drug usage. An increasing number of people consider second-hand tobacco smoke as both unpleasant and unhealthy. Further, even one person who attends a group meeting "under the influence" will probably be a major distraction to most others and a turn-off for new people. If your group tolerates members being high or drunk, you are, in effect, enabling them (promoting an unhealthy habit). That is opposite to your (presumed) shared goal of fostering personal and family health. At the very least, poll all members on this point when you organize and agree on (and enforce) a clear policy. Note that if your policy says "we ask that people who have just used mind-altering drugs not attend," that implies if someone comes in high, your host/leader will have to assertively ask them to leave.

Confidentiality. Effective groups feel safe in that they allow members to reveal personal or even intimate details of their lives without fear of ridicule or leaking sensitive things to the outside world. It can help to build group trust and intimacy if you remind everyone at the start of each meeting that *"what's said here stays here,"* or some such theme. An ongoing option is for people who are sharing sensitive information to ask everyone to keep it within the group. Obviously, if someone discloses probable criminal behavior, or child abuse or neglect, you have a moral (and *legal*) obligation to report those immediately to the appropriate authorities.

"Air time" and interruptions. A standard group task at each meeting is to balance the time available with members' needs to vent, discuss, and get feedback. One way of doing that is for the leader to ask people to state during their initial check-in if they want group air time. Then try to manage the group process so that those who need time get enough. A fairly structured way of doing this is to divide the "business" time available by the number of people who want time, and allocate the resulting number of minutes to each person.

Have the group stay alert to how interruptions feel to them as they speak and listen. Some interruptions can feel very supportive while others can distract from where the speaker is "going" or derail him or her completely. Talk together about how you all want to handle the latter. One option is to give responsibility to the speakers for their own tolerance for interruptions and for inviting respectful assertions.

Confrontations. A challenging aspect of any support group is how to handle members' inevitable disagreements on stepfamily decisions. People's values on stepfamily parenting, marriage, and "family health" vary widely. Your group will evolve a policy, spoken or unspoken, on what you all do when one member describes something that some others strongly disagree with.

Average stepfamilies are riddled with emotional, controversial topics: child discipline, visitation, and custody; money management; relations with ex mates; grieving; stepparent rejection; privacy; etc. I recommend that when values disagreements occur in your group (and they will), the people who disagree provide their reaction in the form of a respectful *"I message,"* rather than a blaming or accusatory statement. *"I messages"* avoid name-calling or using adjectives like "stupid," "idiotic," and "ridiculous." They sound like: *"Jack, when you describe using a belt to reprimand your stepson, I get really uncomfortable. I'm afraid that kind of action will generate fear, resentment and shame in Georgie. Are you open to feedback on other possible ways of enforcing your discipline?"*

The focus here is on the reaction of the person who disagrees, rather than blaming or accusing the original speaker. The group-divisive alternative is to come out with something like, *"Jack, that's outright child abuse. How can you do that? Millie, how can you let him do that to your son—are you crazy!?"*

Also, build a professional referral list that you can use for people to take positive action when conflicted. Stay focused that you are a support group, not the Grand Inquisition. If someone is doing some parenting (or marital) thing that seems harmful, then respectful, constructive confrontation is a gift. Not confronting the issue is potentially hurtful and erodes self-respect. Also, stay aware that you are not there to win the Stepfamily Adult Olympics. Hopefully, members come to encourage and learn, not compete with others.

Griping and conflict versus problem-solving. Probably the biggest group-killer is that group meetings turn into predictable "bitch sessions." Those can make people walk out feeling like stepfamily life is gloomy, awful, and chaotic, with no way out or reason to hope.

A fundamental decision that all founding members need to make is whether they are meeting to find effective solutions to their confusing stepfamily dilemmas or not. It's easy to complain, whine, and play "ain't it awful." It is harder, and far more rewarding, to use the group's empathy, wisdom, and creativity to seek clear, effective resolutions.

The next step here is for the leader or another member to confront the gripers. Say something like, *"I feel we're over-focusing on your problem. Are you ready to shift now to getting clearer on what you want and options for getting that?"* Another way of confronting *respectfully* is for any member to ask the speaker, "What do you want (or *need*) from us right now?"

Couples arguing. A normal group-process issue is learning how to handle stepfamily parenting partners' arguing or fighting excessively in the group. Suggestions include:

Hear and validate them: "You two are really having trouble finding a win-win compromise here. You're in a standard loyalty (or values) conflict, and your high frustration and anger seem to be blocking you each from hearing each other."

Refocus them: "Are you willing to have us help you problem-solve now?" (What if they say "No"?)

Limit them: Major re-marital and adult firefights in one couple can consume an entire meeting. Honor them and other members by calling time on a warring couple, after hearing them, and asking what they need. That will be easier if everyone has a clear idea on what the group's air-time policy is.

Refer them: Unless you have a trained clinician present and are a therapy rather than support group, assertively suggest to a couple having the same problems meeting after meeting that they seek professional counsel. Ideally, evolve a list of stepfamily-knowledgeable local professionals to whom you can refer. Lastly,

Learn from them: Conflicted couples are the main reason groups exist. If a couple is at an impasse in your group, observe them empathically and see why they get stuck. It is often far easier to see the causes in another couple than in your own primary relationship!

Giving feedback. Verbal communication exists to fill people's needs at the moment. Key basic needs are to (1) feel respected, (2) cause action, (3) vent, i.e., feel understood and *non-judgmentally*

accepted, (4) get or give new ideas or information, (5) regulate the emotional distance between the speaker and listener(s), or (6) break uncomfortable silence.

Unless members specifically ask for help or suggestions on a situation, avoid a barrage of advice-giving. If a group member says, "Well, what you should do is...," it can feel like a shaming discount. It implies that the "fixer" is wiser and one-up and knows how the listener should live "right."

One helpful alternative to "fixing" is to focus constructively on *how the person or couple is trying to solve their problem,* i.e., focus on their *process.* Often, that's the *real* problem. Another alternative is to join with the speakers (when they're ready) and cooperatively group-brainstorm alternatives they can pick from.

Group leadership. This factor alone can make or break the eventual success of your group. Like functional families, functional support groups need one or two motivated leaders. A key reason most groups end (or never get going) is because the leader(s) are either burned out or ineffective. What does this key role entail? Some typical responsibilities include:

- Provide the initial group vision, spirit, and dedication. Organize and conduct the initial meeting(s).
- Hold planning meetings to determine the support group's aims, policies, and logistics.
- Arrange for volunteers to share the group's administrative tasks. Delegate to and co-ordinate them, resolve conflicts in and among them, and recognize and appreciate them regularly for their efforts.
- Conduct each support meeting effectively, or delegate that to another effective co-leader. Set each meeting's tone (e.g., optimism, not gloom) and agenda—and follow it, unless unexpected crises arise. Balance each meeting's content dynamically between stepfamily business and group administration tasks. An effective meeting is one in which most of those attending get their major needs met in a way everyone feels good enough about.
- Act as community spokesperson for the group, or delegate that job and monitor it.
- Stay aware of general and special group needs, and coordinate the talents and resources of group members and the community to meet them.
- Balance personal stepfamily needs with all group members' needs. Avoid overusing the group as a personal resource.
- Make clear, timely administrative decisions about group process. Confront problems promptly and assertively. Facilitate group problem-solving supportively when members conflict.
- Negotiate with guest speakers (if any) and co-ordinate their time, focus, and participation.
- Monitor what group members come for, and whether they are getting enough of their needs met. If not, take responsibility for problem-solving that.

- Take (or delegate) overall responsibility for recruiting appropriate new members and do so.
- Groom another effective leader and hand over the baton when feeling burned out or personally "done." Then, let go. And,
- Enjoy doing all this, over time!

Q: Do we need to raise funds? For what? When? How?

How will you pay for postage, advertising, printing, space, refreshments, speakers, educational kits, and supplies? Many groups use a combination of passing the hat at each meeting, fundraisers, and soliciting community or participant donations (of supplies, copying service, or space, rather than money).

Fundraisers can take many forms: car washes, bake and garage sales, wine tasting or meet-the-cast parties, artist benefit performances, mail solicitations, raffles, etc. These can be fun group-building events as well as work, and they provide good advertising, too.

Experience suggests that unless your group gets "big," the idea of fixed dues and membership is generally a turnoff. Dues take time to account for, can imply exclusivity or formality, and will tie up periodic group time in discussion and haggling. Their advantage, of course, is that they provide regular and (fairly) predictable income, enabling more or "wider" activities.

Who in your group will handle the money management responsibilities?

Q: Do we want a sponsor or local affiliate organization? If so, who? Costs and benefits?

A well-known community organization's endorsement of your group can lend it instant credibility. Mental health agencies, hospitals, clinics, or churches, however, carry a mix of associations for prospective attendees. If any such sponsor already has a good community reputation for unbiased and positive family-life education programs, fine. Otherwise, if you advertise such sponsorship prominently you may get credibility while limiting the scope of the people who will try out the group because of biases against such organizations.

One possible endorsement deserves special note—that of the non-profit Stepfamily Association of America (SAA). SAA promotes the formation of non-profit chapters around the country. To quality for sponsorship (become a "chapter"), a group has to pay SAA membership dues and follow its bylaws and organizational requirements. SAA benefits include: high group credibility; some help in group setup, marketing, and maintenance; rebates of a percentage of the members' required annual SAA dues (I think); networking with other SAA chapters; discounts on SAA's stepfamily materials (including group kits) and attendance fees to the annual national conference; and, occasional advance notice of local or national news relating to stepfamilies (laws, media events, resources, etc.). Call SAA for more information at 1-800-735-0329.

Q: Should we try to compile a resource library? Of what? How?

One of the five main reasons stepfamily couples re-divorce is benign ignorance. Stepfamily adults often do not know what they do not know about stepfamily norms, tasks, and effective solutions. One solution to this is to interest them in—and provide—informed stepfamily education. That implies collecting realistic information, making it available to stepfamily adults, and motivating them to read and *use* it. Your group is a perfect place to do this! Refer to the resource list at the end of this chapter to see some available materials and where to get them.

Q: Should we have a newsletter? For just group members or others, too? Containing what?

Although hard work, a group newsletter is an effective way of welcoming new members; advertising your group's presence, agendas, events, and any donors' or sponsors' services; distributing useful stepfamily facts or articles; and promoting a feeling of togetherness and continuity. Contact SAA or the Self Help Center listed at the end of this chapter for self-help group newsletter samples.

Q: Do we need professional (clinical) backup and/or other resource people. Why? Who?

Besides your participants, there are three kinds of resource people that can add much to the quality and effectiveness of your support group: knowledgeable speakers, qualified clinicians, and support-group consultants.

"Knowledgeable speakers" are any local people who have stepfamily-relevant knowledge, and the time and heart to share it. At the head of the list of experts are *your* older step-kids! Close behind are your co-grandparents and other stepfamily relatives. Other options include family-law lawyers or judges, professional (post-divorce) mediators, specialized teachers and therapists (including clergy), and consultants on child development, relationships, parenting, verbal communications, and family finances.

"Qualified clinicians" can be psychiatrists, clinical (rather than research) psychologists, clinical and psychiatric social workers, or marriage-and-family counselors. Qualified here means they have, in addition to therapy fundamentals and experience, some special interest, training, and experience with any of the following: divorce dynamics and mediation; stepfamily norms and stressors; stepfamily adult dynamics and issues; filling step-kids' special needs; remarriage dynamics and issues; promoting healthy grieving; diagnosing and managing addictions; verbal communication skills; and, facilitating personal adult recovery from childhood abuse and neglect.

Experience has shown that, sadly, most (say 75 percent) of remarried adults come from moderately to highly dysfunctional childhoods. Further, most of these people mysteriously pick each other for partners, *time after time*. This inexorably generates compound personal, marital, and parental "mental-health" stressors, which usually justify some qualified help along the way.

Because of this, it is a great asset to any group to build and use a referral list of qualified local therapists and support organizations for step-people in crisis. Such resource people *may* also make excellent speakers for selected stepfamily meeting topics. A quick test to ascertain a clinician's qualification is to ask them to:

> Highlight any special training in stepfamily dynamics they have had.
> Spontaneously list at least 10 structural and family-dynamics' differences between average biological families and stepfamilies.
> Summarize the 10 key unique issues that most remarried stepfamily adults normally encounter; and,
> Name at least 10 of the almost two dozen special stressors that average minor step-kids must usually master.

If a clinician fumbles with these, or resents your asking, look elsewhere—without guilt.

Do not hesitate to ask qualified clinicians to help your group. Most mental health professionals are highly interested in the opportunity to help, and possibly be introduced to rich sources of client or patient referrals. A number of such professionals are stepfamily adults, too!

The third type of helpful resources are consultants who have special experience or training in establishing and maintaining a flourishing non-therapy support group. Such people may be lay or professional, and local or distant. The volunteer leaders of National Stepfamily Resource Center many chapters around America (see: Resources) are a pool of seasoned (non-professional) group consultants. They are usually glad to trade ideas by phone.

Often, both mental health agencies and larger religious organizations sponsor several support groups. They may have a group liaison or coordinator who would advise for free or point you to other resource people.

Q: Should we have a group name? A logo?

Like various athletic teams, some members feel more group pride and loyalty if they have cooperatively forged a name and logo, or even have picked a symbolic or real mascot. Whether these would help *you* depends totally on who you all are as a unique group. The adjective "step" offers possibilities for fun, nutty, or inspiring titles. Enjoy kicking this around at a meeting from time to time. Your step- and *inner*-kids are rich sources of ideas and energy here!

Keeping Your Group Thriving

After the first session, what will keep stepfamily adults coming back? What will attract new people? Both questions hinge on "what do typical stepfamily adults need?"

Again, typical key stepfamily adult needs include: To vent and feel empathically heard about their stepfamily frustrations, confusions, and successes; to get consistent respect, acceptance, validation, and encouragement from knowledgeable peers; to learn realistic step norms, and effective parenting and re-marital solutions, via caring feedback and suggestions; to commune and belong with similar-enough women and men; to be compassionately confronted (rather than enabled) when appropriate; to get away together for a while and enjoy time as a couple; to share your thoughts helpful to peers and kids; and to build and keep realistic (rather than idealistic) stepfamily and re-marital optimism, faith, and hope.

What most busy stepfamily adults don't need includes: Wasting their time, energy, and money; listening to pessimistic others complain, whine, blame, fight, and drone on endlessly; being ignored, interrupted, criticized, lectured to, competed with, or discounted; feeling overwhelmed by the depth and complexity of some other member's situation and needs; and being overburdened with group administration trivia.

As your group evolves, if its leaders keep these two sets of typical needs in clear sight and motivate everyone to strive to fill them together in a balanced way, you will thrive! There will always be stepfamily adults in your area who need your group!

We strongly encourage you to evolve and *use* a concise, flexible group mission statement, and a policy statement to keep everyone focused on what you are trying to do together and how.

Screening New People

The quality and long-range effectiveness of your group depends largely on whether the needs of the members match the capabilities of the group. One way of trying to optimize this balance is to screen people before they come to the group or after they have come once. The main thing to ascertain in your screening is whether they need support or professional therapy. With any verbal or media advertising of your group, it is a good idea to have prospective participants call a designated group member and describe something of their stepfamily situation, what they are looking for, and why.

Some indicators that therapy is probably more appropriate are when the inquiring person describes recent or current: Suicidal or homicidal thoughts or family events; chemical addictions to alcohol, food, or prescription or street drugs; probable or certain physical, verbal, spiritual, or emotional (including sexual) abuse in the home or family; serious adult talk of re-marital separation or re-divorce; hospitalizations for emotional conditions (e.g., major depression) or a family member taking medications for such conditions; repeated "excessive" interference in the stepfamily's life by a relative; reported extra-marital affairs, or law-breaking behaviors or events by stepfamily members; kids running away, being kidnapped by biological relatives, or custodial biological parents refusing child visitation; prolonged court battles between ex mates over child custody, support, visitation, or other issues; or an ex mate stalking, making phone threats, harassing or engaging in other excessively hostile acts.

This isn't a complete list, but you can see the theme. Grow the group attitude that the best way of supporting stepfamily adults involved in such situations is to compassionately and assertively point them at qualified professional help, and then give them full responsibility for their own choices.

Kindly and firmly telling a group applicant that you feel, after listening to them, that they would really be better off getting professional help (and giving them referral names, if you have them) helps both them and your existing group members. If in doubt, call your group's qualified mental health consultant or find one.

Again, if anyone in your group ever describes what you feel is probable or certain current child or spousal abuse (or illegal activity), you have a moral (and very probably a legal) obligation to call the police immediately to report that.

Meeting Content Suggestions

There is a rich array of options to choose from:

- Build your own course. If you choose to have a series of educational stepfamily topics as one part of your meeting (rather than just talking), what are some topics? There are over a dozen that are of general interest to most stepfamily adults. One option is to use this book as a blueprint to make your group curriculum. This book contains self-discovery topics, which generate rich couple and group discussions.
A related option is to use the titles of these chapters as a guide for picking topics for guest speakers to address.
- Have a panel of older step-kids. Although sometimes tricky to organize, this can be enormously rewarding. If you are blessed with four to six teen or preteen step-kids who would agree to "instruct" your stepfamily adult group on what they experience and need, ask them!
At a pre-panel group meeting, ask your members to develop questions like those below. Consider writing them out and giving them to the panelists in advance, so they can think about them:

  ➢ What do you *like* about being in your stepfamily?
  ➢ What's hardest for you these days about being a step-kid?
  ➢ Who do you include as real members of your "family" now?
  ➢ What would you change in your (multi-home) stepfamily if you could?
  ➢ What's it like having a step(sibling)?
  ➢ What's it like being split between two homes?
  ➢ How do you feel about the way visitations (with non-custodial biological parents) are going for you all now?
  ➢ What worries you the most about your (multi-family) stepfamily now?

> ➤ If you could teach stepparents one thing, what would it be?

Have an *unrelated* adult act as "talk show host" and invite the kids to honestly react to such open-ended questions one at a time. ***Guidelines***: *no blaming, judging, interrupting, or arguing!* One option for avoiding the awkwardness of kids speaking in front of their own stepfamily adults: hold the panel without the adults and videotape it for replay and group discussion.

- Consider having a couple of all-family events during the year as part of your program. Picnics, bowling, Halloween costume parties, or camp-outs are some (of many) options. Such gatherings help everyone turn abstract names into real people, and raise the level of exchanged interest and caring among members. They are apt to be fun, too! Because at first most of the kids and adults haven't met, it can help to start with a safe "ice-breaking" exercise or game to help everyone relax and join in. Ask your kids for ideas.

Group "Problem Solving"

When people leave a group meeting with some practical new ideas on how to manage a difficult situation at home, *everyone* feels good! Some suggestions on how to promote that include:

1) After someone has vented for a while, ask something like: "Do you need to be heard more now, or do you want us to help problem-solve?" If they choose the former, honor that. If the speaker(s) want to problem-solve, ask them to honestly answer three questions:
   Specifically, what do you (each) want in this situation?
   What, specifically, have you tried, and what did you get?
   What's in the way (of you each getting most of what you want)?
2) Be careful not to judge or discount the speakers, or tell them what they want—they are the experts on their own needs, feelings, and limits. Be alert for the speakers unconsciously using biological family expectations rather than appropriate stepfamily realities in forming their goals.
3) Paraphrase back to the speaker(s) concisely and specifically what you hear their wants are (including any guesstimated step-kids' wants), until you get agreement. This nonjudgmental feedback process usually generates more clarity on what people *really* want. It can sound like: "So you want your stepson to acknowledge you more when you sit across from him at dinner, and you want your mate to support you in this."
4) Usually, stepfamily conflicts and dilemmas come in layered clusters rather than neatly packaged one at a time. Help the speaker distill down and separate their layers and

clusters. Pick one specific problem at a time to work on. Be alert for generalities. For example, "I want us to feel more like a regular family" is too big and too general. Refine such generalities down to small targets. "I want to get clear on how much money to contribute to my stepdaughter's college fund" is specific and manageable.

5) Commonly, after loyalty conflicts the next most "popular" group of stepfamily stresses usually involves unfinished (or new) conflicts with ex mates. Note your inevitable decision about whether such ex mate stepfamily adults are legitimate members of each of your stepfamilies or not. Your kids certainly include them!

   If you exclude them, and do not try to consider their needs coequally with your kids' and your own, I believe your chance of effective problem-solving is slender or nonexistent. You also guarantee putting your kids painfully "in the middle"— which promotes their shame, frustration, insecurity, acting out, and rejecting their stepparent(s).

6) Consider asking a member of your group to volunteer to role-play each of the speaker(s)' missing stepfamily members who are involved in this problem-solving situation, including ex mates and absent stepparents. Ask them to "speak for" the missing adult or child in as realistic a way as possible, and say honestly what they feel and want.

7) Once agreed on who wants what, brainstorm as a group on options that may get *everyone's* needs met, not just the speaker(s)'. Don't shoot down ideas as they emerge—just collect possibilities. Be free to be as nutty and creative as possible. Focus steadily on what might work rather than on what won't. Avoid turning this into a contest over "who can think of the best idea." This is a team effort in which everybody can win, for the process usually generates helpful ideas for all members on their own family issues.

8) Stay focused on stepfamily members' needs, not their personalities or actions. Also, stay focused on your shared problem-solving process, and don't get sidetracked by other members' issues or stories. Stay with this process until either the speakers say "thanks, that's enough," or you run out of time.

9) Stay clear on who "owns" the stated problem—the speaker does, not your group or another group member. Each of you retains responsibility for attending to your own needs.

10) If a member who requested group brainstorming does not offer feedback on the outcome over time, ask them respectfully "what happened?" You are *all* students here, and everyone can learn from each other's co-parenting and re-marital experiments and actions.

Leader(s), stay focused on your group's "problems-solving" process. If at any time it turns into a competition, a lecture, or a blaming festival, rather than a team effort, stop and refocus the group on its own process. Ask how the current process feels and whether it feels productive ("Is this why you came here?").

Stay aware that some people need to vent more than to problem-solve at times, but that can be done to excess. Incidentally, you can use this same problem-solving format on group-process projects and problems, just like stepfamily conflict.

You can see that this multi-step "problem-solving" process takes time, dedication, and concentration to harvest its full benefits. If you use a group session for "problem-solving," allocate at least 30 or more minutes for one problem. If you have too much other business, including too many people who need to vent, postpone this process, or encourage the problem owner(s) to do it at home and share the outcome.

Notice that this group democratic problem-solving process invites your group to operate like a functional, healthy family. What would happen if each member took this process home and practiced it consistently in and between their stepfamily homes?

Using a "Phone Tree"

As a way of extending your group's support, ask members to participate (voluntarily) in setting up a phone or calling tree—a continually updated list of names and phone numbers, and okay times to call. That way, group members who fall into a stepfamily crisis will have some other people to contact immediately rather than waiting a week or more for the next meeting.

Option: The receiver of such a call for support can use thegroup's established set of needs to guide his or her response. Does the caller need to vent, be validated, or learn ideas, resources, and solution options? When in doubt of the caller's need, ask—then listen! If the caller wants to do more than just vent, consider using some version of the problem-solving steps above.

Also, a phone tree can help effectively broadcast group news (e.g., "meeting canceled, rescheduled, or moved because...."). This helps protect the group's leader(s) from telephone burnout.

Summary

Average American stepfamilies are far more complex and stressful than typical biological families. Stepfamilies are at high risk of eventual re-divorce. Typical remarried stepfamily adults and their kids need *a lot* of education, patience, and knowledgeable support for years after their nuptials. A well-designed and effectively run stepfamily adult support group can be a Godsend. Few communities have them now.

Stepfamily support groups are hard work to set up and get going, yet they can be enormously satisfying and gratifying. The real beneficiaries of such group efforts are all the stepfamily adults' minor step-kids.

This chapter has suggested the human needs such groups can fill, and some ways to fill them effectively as a team of empathic stepfamily adult peers. Each group is unique with its own mosaic of personal needs, backgrounds, resources, and personalities. And, paradoxically, all groups are the same, in aiming to help empower their members to be the best stepfamily adults they can be.

SELECTED RESOURCES

Worksheets
By Peter K.Gerlach, M.S.W.
"Break The Cycle!"
http://sfhelp.org/site/worksheets.htm
Three Way to Prevent Family Stress and Divorce
An Overview of the Toxic (Wounds + Unawareness) Cycle
High-nurturance Family Traits
Common False-self vs. True-Self Behaviors
An Inventory of Personal Intangible and Tangible Losses
Identify and Compare Your Grieving Values
A Grief Assessment Worksheet
Learn Your Values About Losses and Grieving
Am I Remarrying he Right People (Adults and Kids)?
Am I Remarrying for the Right Reasons?
Am I Remarrying at the Right Time?
Common Stepfamily Expectations
Why and How to Draw Your Stepfamily Map ("Genogram")
Sample Structural Maps of High and Low-nurturance Biofamilies and Stepfamilies
A Stepfamily Identity Questionnaire
Clarify Which of Your Stepfamily Adults Are Responsible For What
Common Communication Blocks
A Conflict-resolution Inventory
25 Tips For Effective Communication
Our Co-parents Strengths as Committed Couples
Typical Primary Partnership Needs
Relationship Strength and Stressors Inventory
How High Does Our Primary Relationship *Really* Rank Now
How We Handle Values Conflicts Now
How We Handle Loyalty Conflicts Now
How We Handle Relationship Triangles
Discover Your Child Discipline Values
Resources for Stepfamilies

ORGANIZATIONS

National Stepfamily Resource Center

The Center's primary objective is to serve as a clearinghouse of information, resources, and support for stepfamily members and the professionals who work with them. Current and planned activities include: resources for stepfamilies, Facts and FAQs about stepfamilies, posted research summaries and annotated bibliographies of stepfamily research, training institutes for family life and marriage educators, training institutes for therapists and counselors, media consulting on stepfamily issues, expert consulting on special projects, programs, and products targeting stepfamilies; and development of educational materials for use with stepfamilies. Web site: http://www.stepfamilies.info; E-mail: Stepfamily@auburn.edu

The Stepfamily Foundation, Inc.

333 West End Avenue, New York, NY 10023
(212) 877-3244; FAX: (212) 362-7030
24 hour information line (212) 799-STEP
Web site: http://www.stepfamily.org; E-mail: Stepfamily@aol.com

The Stepfamily Foundation, Inc., headquartered in New York City is a not for profit founded in 1975. Their mission is to assist you in making your family, as it is now, function well. "We have created a successful management system for the stepfamily – who unfortunately, is the unacknowledged majority. We address the issues of; organization, partnership, couple strength, conflict of loyalties, roles, discipline, the ex spouse and much, much more. We also serve faith based organizations and individuals."

The Stepfamily Foundation, Inc., offers a program "Start Your Own Stepfamily Support Group" for professionals, clergy and people living in stepfamilies who want to form educational groups and/or earn extra income. Order from Stepfamily Foundation, Inc. the Leader's Manual (120 pages), as well as one copy of the Participant's Manual. The Leader's manual offers information and skill building homework assignments.

Group Leaders and Participants Manual. "We will lead you through the vital and often hidden issues that cause the high break up rate (two out of three) among these new partners with children of prior relationships. You will be directed in informing participants of the special dynamics of The 21st Century Family and the solutions."

National Council on Family Relations (NCFR)

3989 Central Avenue, N.E., Suite 550, Minneapolis, MN 55421, (617) 781-9331

NCFR has a Focus Group on re-marriage and stepfamilies, which maintains an extensive bibliography of lay and professional resources (available on paper and computer media). Web site: http://www.ncfr.org; E-mail: info@ncfr.org

The Illinois Self-Help Coalition

3050 W Touhy Ave.., Chicago, IL IL 60645, (773) 857-5901

A non-profit effort founded in May of l995, to help area Self help groups via group-leadership training, advocacy, and referrals. Web site:

http://www.wecaretoo.com/Organizations/IL/selfhelp-illinois.html ; E-mail: dipeace@aol.com

Rainbows

2100 Golf Road, Suite 370, Rolling Meadows, IL 60008, (847) 952-1770.

Materials, leader training, and consultation for organizations sponsoring divorce, death, and re-marriage grief-support groups for children, teens, and adults. "Rainbows educates and builds awareness about the growing number of children suffering significant loss issues in their lives and produces high quality programs offered at no cost to children and youth," believing that, "grieving youth deserve supporting, loving listeners as they struggle with their feelings and is available to participants of all races and religions, serving as an advocate for youth who face life-altering crises."

Web site: http://www.rainbows.org; E-mail: info@rainbows.org

Hotlines

National Runaway Switchboard

This 24-hour hotline service for US parents and youth offers crisis intervention , message service, educational information, referrals, and runaway searches.

1-800-RUNAWAY; 1-800-786-2929

Web site: http://www.1800runaway.org

Alateen and Al-Anon Family Group Headquarters

Al-Anon Family Group Headquarters, Inc.

1600 Corporate Landing Parkway, Virginia Beach, VA 23454-5617

(800) 344-2666

For over 55 years, Al-Anon (which includes Alateen for younger members) has been offering strength and hope for friends and families of problem drinkers. It is estimated that each alcoholic affects the lives of at least four other people... alcoholism is truly a family disease. No matter what relationship you have with an alcoholic, whether they are still drinking or not, all who have been affected by someone else's drinking can find solutions that lead to serenity in the Al-Anon/Alateen fellowship.

Web site: http://www.al-anon.alateen.org; E-mail: wso@al-anon.org

National Alcohol Substance Abuse Information Center
800-784-6776

The National Alcoholism and Drug Addiction Treatment Information Center is primarily a provider of drug alcoholism addiction treatment facts and detailed information. It was established and designed specifically to help provide fast, accurate information about every aspect of alcoholism and drug addiction treatment. It was created because we understand all too well that finding current, accurate, relevant facts about drug and alcoholism addiction treatment can be difficult.
Web site: http://www.addictioncareoptions.com

School Program

BANANA SPLITS RESOURCE CENTER: a school/parent support program for children of divorce. Entering voluntarily and with parental permission, "Splits" kids, grouped by age and grade level, meet every two or three weeks to air the frustrations and successes of their altered family lives. A volunteer teacher or counselor guides the discussions and offers individual attention for a serious problem or crisis. A big part of the program is when other kids help a group member move through a particularly tough situation such as a child-custody hearing or learning to get along with a stepparent.

This program offers more than group counseling, however. Its "curriculum" includes special art Steps that help younger children express their concerns through drawing; in other activities, they air their anxieties by playing with stuffed animals and toys. Older children and youths do several activities: develop a more sophisticated graffiti wall as a springboard for discussion of common problems; acts as peer counselors as well as set up activities for younger "latch-key" children; construct collages; write and act out skits; do paintings; and plan social activities for the whole group (e.g., an end-of-year "Banana Splits Picnic"). Finally, the program contains directions for setting up parent groups to meet in the evenings.

Banana Splits is organized and presented in a three-ring notebook with eight tab sections and 116 pages. At no cost to participants, the notebook cost is $40. For more information contact:
Web site: http://www.bananasplitsresourcecenter.org;
E-mail: info@bananasplitsresourcecenter.org

INTERACT, Box 997-BS93, Lakeside, California 92040, (619) 448-1474 or toll-free 1-800-359-0961

Home Program Available:

Videotape series *Portrait of a Family.* Each half-hour videotape is $29.95; shipping and tape cost included. These videotapes are for private home viewing only with text material sold separately.

Portrait of a Family, produced by the Southern California Consortium, takes a close look at marriage and family with the focus on stepfamilies. Module IV: *The Family in Transition* offers material on: Stepparenting, A Big Challenge in Re-marriage; Being a Stepmother; and, Stepparenting: Some Tips.

Family Board Games

LifeStories

FNDI Limited Partnership, 701 Decatur Ave. North, #104, Golden Valley, MN 55427.

A win-win board game providing "entertaining conversation between family, friends, and people you have just met; 2 to 8 players, ages 6 to 106." FutureStories is a similar game for sharing hopes and dreams.

The Stamp Game: A Game of Feelings by Claudia Black, Ph.D.

The purpose of the Stamp Game is to help players to better identify, clarify, and discuss feelings. Players will be able to relate more honestly to others as they learn to express feelings. As a result, players become more effective problem-solvers and the identification and expression of feelings brings clarity to players' needs, which in turn leads to enhanced self-esteem. The game is a wonderful tool to equalize those who use words as a defense but have difficulty being emotionally honest, and for those who have great difficulty being articulate on any level. Playing The Stamp Game is a novel, fun and meaningful way for players to learn about themselves and each other. Available at Amazon.com, etc.

The Ungame

Non-competitive fun board game to help people learn safely about each other - ideal for stepfamilies. Optional materials for couples, families, children (5 and up), and teens. Available at Amazon.com, etc.

Web Sites

Family Surfboard: http://familysurf.com

Family World: http://www.family.com

The Mommy Times: http://www.mommytimes.com

Parent Soup: http://parenting.ivillage.com

Parents Helping Parents: http://www.php.com

Parents Place: http://www.parentsplaceonline.org

Positive Parenting Online: http://www.positiveparenting.com

"Break The Cycle!" by Peter K. Gerlach, M.S.W.:http://sfhelp.org

The Stepfamily Foundation:http://www.stepfamily.org

Internet World Wide Web::http://www.yahoo.com (or other Web "search engine"), and search on "stepfamily," "blended family," or "step-parent" for the latest resources.

On-Line Chat Groups:America on Line (AOL), Prodigy, compuServe (CIS), and the Microsoft Network (MSN) all have Stepfamily co-parents chat groups. They make take some digging to find.

AFCC (Association of Family Conciliation Courts) - AFCC is an organization of lawyers, judges and mental health people who promote, and learn together about, best practices for kids and families in the courts. www.afccnet.org

American Family Therapy Academy - AFTA is a non-profit organization of leading family therapy teachers, clinicians, program developers, researchers and social scientists, dedicated to advancing systemic thinking and practices for families in their ecological context. www.afta.org

The Association for Couples in Marriage Enrichment - Building Better Marriages. The mission of ACME is to promote marriages by providing enrichment opportunities that strengthen couple relationships and enhance personal growth, mutual fulfillment, and family wellness. www.bettermarriages.org

Bonus Families - A non-profit organization dedicated to peaceful coexistence between separated or divorced parents and their new families. www.bonusfamilies.com

"Break The Cycle!" - This nonprofit, research-based, educational site by Peter K. Gerlach, M.S.W., is for prospective and current stepfamily members and their supporters. It suggests 12 ongoing projects that stepfamily adults can work at together to overcome five re-divorce hazards, and build a highly nurturing stepfamily. Browse over 450 Web pages on understanding and resolving typical stepfamily problems. http://sfhelp.org/site/intro.htm

Children's Rights Council - A national nonprofit organization based in Washington, DC that works to assure children have meaningful and continuing contact with both their parents and extended family regardless of the parent's marital status. http://www.crckids.org

CoMamas Association – CoMama's goal is to teach step-wives and their families how to develop cooperative and respectful relationships so they can end their war and get along for the sake of the children. http://www.comamas.com

Designing Dynamics Stepfamilies - Bringing the pieces to peace. www.designingdynamicstepfamilies.com

Family, friendly, fun - Offers a wide variety of family fun, family life and family health topics including adoption, baby care, celebration and parties, children and teens, disabilities, and special needs for babies to grandparents. www.family-friendly-fun.com

Family Medallion - Celebrating and strengthening family ties. Help children feel included in the wedding plans and a tangible symbol of being embraced by the new family. http://www.familymedallion.com

Forever Families - Practical, scholarly, and faith-based information for strengthening and enriching families of all denominations. www.foreverfamilies.net

Getting Remarried - Information for planning a second marriage or renewing your wedding vows. www.idotaketwo.com

InStep Ministries - Practical resources for stepfamilies. www.instepministries.com

The Institute for Equality in Marriage - A resource where people can get action oriented information and support in all stages of their relationship. www.equalityinmarriage.org

It's My Life - Kids and teens. It's My Life deals with life and the stuff that we deal with every day. Whatever problem you're dealing with, believe it or not, other kids and teens have gone through the same thing. Read informative articles, share your stories, play games, share feelings and experiences, get advice. http://pbskids.org/itsmylife

Life in a Blender - A forum with the main ingredients of respect, compassion and positive interaction. www.lifeinablender.org

Parenting With Dignity- A resource where parents learn new, essential parenting skills and gives them the tools necessary to create an encouraging, and loving home for their children. www.ParentingWithDignity.com

Selfgrowth.com - Provides a central resource for information on Self Improvement, Self Help and Personal Growth on the Internet. www.selfgrowth.com

ShareKids.com - A Stepfamily co-parenting system designed to assist individuals in managing child sharing between homes. www.sharekids.com

Smart Marriages - A resource-rich national clearing house for premier educational and support programs for couples. www.SmartMarriages.com

Step and Blended Family Institute - An organization that exists to support stepfamilies and the individuals in them, to succeed at the enormous task of building and nurturing their new families. www.stepinstitute.ca

StepCarefully for Stepparents - An organization created by stepparents, for stepparents We offer on-line support, as well as a to-the-point series of resources for step-parenting needs, and a newsletter designed to help stepfamilies not only survive, but succeed. www.stepcarefully.com

Stepfamilies (United Kingdom) - Advice, Contacts & Support. www.stepfamilies.co.uk

Stepfamilies in Seattle - Helping stepfamilies in Seattle create healthy relationships. www.stepfamilyseattle.com

Stepfamily Association of Victoria, Inc. - A self-help, non-profit organization offering support, education, and resources to stepfamilies in Australia. www.stepfamily.org.au

The Stepfamily Life - A column from life in a blender. www.thestepfamilylife.com/index.html

Stepfamily Living - Stepfamily information and resources from veteran stepfamily educator and therapist Elizabeth Einstein. www.stepfamilyliving.com

The Stepfamily Network - A nonprofit organization dedicated to helping stepfamily members achieve harmony and mutual respect in their family lives. www.stepfamily.net
Stepfamily Solutions -Offers individual, couple, family and group counseling for stepfamilies. Workshops and classes provide training to mental health professionals and organizations. www.stepfamilysolutions.net

The Stepfamilyzone - The Stepfamily Association of South Australia Inc. and Stepfamily Australia - Our aim is to actively promote the positive aspects of Stepfamily Life. Stepfamilies can work and be successful! We believe that providing information is the first step towards successful stepfamily life. www.stepfamily.asn.au

Stepping Stones Counseling Center - Created with the goal of improving and enriching the quality of stepfamily life. "We not only work with stepfamily issues, we face them every day in our personal lives." www.stepfamilies.com
TheStepStop.com - Offering resources, information, and support for all stepfamily members. www.thestepstop.com

Successful Stepfamilies - Christian resources for Church and Home. This site offers articles, resources, and conferences for stepfamilies and ministry leaders. It also offers couples an opportunity take the online Couple Checkup to understand and enhance their relationship. www.SuccessfulStepfamilies.com

Winning Stepfamilies - Offers immediate help to get you through rough spots, and the long term support you need to successfully blend your family. www.winningstepfamilies.com

Stepmother/Second Wives Links

Bride Again Magazine - A magazine designed for the encore bride. Quarterlies cover issues, both psychological and material, that meet the unique needs of the thousands of women planning to walk down the aisle again. www.brideagain.com

reMarriage **Magazine** – "Before, during & happily ever after", this online magazine is designed for people in second marriages by offering support, information, and a blog for answering questions. www.remarriagemag.com

The Second Wives Club - A comprehensive, interactive site touted as "the online haven" for second wives and step-moms! www.secondwivesclub.com

StepTogether - Provides "virtual" support and educational material resources for all women and persons who are, or have been stepmothers, stepfathers, or in a stepfamily as a stepchild or otherwise related to a stepfamily environment. www.steptogether.org

Stepmom's Retreat - Comfort and support for stepmothers, and wives of blended families. www.geocities.com/heartland/plains/6663

StepMom Magazine - an on-line publication that features monthly articles about: step-life, marriage, divorce, parenting, exes, in-laws, custody, finance and legal matters. By subscribing, you'll join a group of women from all over the US and Canada and become a member of the magazine's support group forum - a private place where StepMoms can post questions, get advice, discuss common concerns and share successes. www.stepmommag.com

WIFE - The non-profit Women's Institute for Financial Education provides financial education and net-working opportunities to women of all ages. A dynamic on-line magazine updated several times each month. www.wife.org

"Younger Women, Older Men" - Practical information for managing the complexities surrounding May-December relationships when you are younger than your partner - and maybe even younger (or just slightly older) than his children! Connect with the author. www.beliza.com

Stepfather / Biological father Links

National Fatherhood Initiative - A non-profit, non-partisan, non-sectarian national civic organization founded in 1994 to stimulate a society-wide movement to confront the growing problem of father absence, and is dedicated to improving the well-being of children by increasing the number of children growing up with involved, responsible, and committed fathers. www. fatherhood.org

Father 4 Kids - Information about, and referrals to, attorneys and other professionals who understand fathers' issues, and effectively represent the interests of fathers and children in family court in all jurisdictions. www.fathers4kids.org

American Coalition for Fathers and Children - We dedicate ourselves and our efforts to the creation of a family law system, legislative system, and public awareness, which promotes equal rights for ALL parties affected by divorce and the breakup of a family, or establishment of paternity. www.acfc.org

United Fathers of America - The goal of United Fathers is to provide an interactive medium for people experiencing the effects of dissolution, parenting arrangements and other family law issues. Our secondary purpose is to provide information and resources in the aid of Internet Legal Research. www.ufa.org

National Center for Fathering - Inspires and equips men to be better fathers. They conduct research on fathers and fathering and develop practical resources to prepare dads for nearly every fathering situation. www.fathers.com
Divorce Support and Legal Issues Links

American Responsible Divorce Network - Options for making divorce gentler on families; offers a monthly newsletter. http://proactivechange.com/divorce/responsible
Divorce Central - Has developed this service to offer help, support, and information, and to give you the opportunity to communicate with others who are in various stages of decision-making. www.divorcecentral.com

Divorce Help for Parents - A site devoted to helping divorced parents navigate the complex waters of parenting after divorce. www.divorcehelpforparents.com

Divorce Info - Designed to help you get through divorce, and move on with your life. www. divorceinfo.com

Divorce Net - State by State resource center, and interactive bulletin boards (forums) dealing with various divorced family and stepfamily issues. www.divorcenet.com

Divorce Online - An electronic resource for people involved in, or facing the prospect of, divorce. www.divorceonline.com

DivorceSource.Com - Offers State-specific divorce information and stepfamily issues. www.divorcesource.com

Divorce Support - Offers support with divorce, child custody and family law. www.divorcesupport.com

Dad's Divorce Rights - experienced attorneys help fathers with litigation and negotiation strategies while always focusing on what is best for the child(ren). www.dadsrights.com

DivorceInteractive.com - A comprehensive divorce resource with survival tools, information and helpful resources for divorce. www.divorceinteractive.com

Divorce Step - Providing consultation and direct service in the area of divorce and stepfamily relationships. www.divorcestep.com

Equality In Marriage - Educating women and men about the importance of equality in marriage and divorce. www.equalityinmarriage.org

Kids' Turn - A non-profit organization to help kids and parents through divorce. www.kidsturn.org

Legal Help USA - Professional legal aid available from a nationwide team of expert lawyers that provide help and assistance with all legal related issues. www.legal-help-usa.org

MillennumDivorce.com - A divorce site devoted to providing information and help. Developed and written by divorce lawyers and family law attorneys to answer your questions. www.millenniumdivorce.com

Support Groups At The Time Of This Printing
National Stepfamily Resource Center

Local chapters of the former Stepfamily Association of America provide essential support and education to co-parents. Active support groups do this via regular meetings where stepfamily members discuss problems and successes, and find that they're not alone!

Support groups usually offer organized discussion groups, speakers, an 8-step program for successful stepfamily living, and other education and support opportunities.

ARKANSAS

Step-Carefully
Bobby Collins
Fort Smith, AR 72917
479-522-7490
www.stepcarefully.com
step@stepcarefully.com

ARIZONA

Valley Steps
Matthew Lissy
Scottsdale, AZ 85260
480-614-6614
valleysteps@cox.net

Southwestern Stepfamilies
Michael Harmon
Scottsdale, AZ 85259
480-551-2115

CALIFORNIA

Placer County
Laudon Rowen
Rocklin, CA 95677
916-251-1050

Sacramento County
Steve & Barbara Straub
745 Oak Ave. Parkway
Folsom, CA 95630
(800) 946-8112
steve.straub@winningstepfamilies.com

MISSOURI

Kansas City SAA
Brad Nowlin
Kansas City, MO 64114
913-579-8526
bnow45@kc.rr.com

Step Forward
Joanne Gramann
Platte City, MO 64079
816-858-4241
hazelcj7@aol.com

NEVADA

Life in a Blender, LLC
Lisa Doyle
Reno, NV 89512
775-329-4025
lmzaro@netscape.com
lisa@lifeinablender.org

NEBRASKA

Lincoln Stepfamilies
CJ Johnson
Lincoln, NE 68505
402-441-4349

NEW MEXICO

Albuquerque Chapter
Kerin Groves
Albuquerque, MN 87184
505-884-9411

Los Angeles Area

Los Angeles
Yaffia Balsam
P.O. Box 2481
Los Alamitos, CA 90720
714-527-8111
www.yourheartfeltsolutions.com

Orange County
Vincent Redmond
Santa Ana. CA 92670
714-358-9831

Bay Area

Oakland/East Bay
Anthony Carpentieri
Berkeley, CA 94609
510-653-6344 or 510-849-1626

Silicon Valley
Susan English
Los Gatos, CA 95030
408-395-7448

Santa Cruz
Kit Siemer
Scotts Valley, CA 95062
831-335-2601
kit@siemerclan.com

San Diego North
Pam Laidlaw
San Diego, CA 92130
858-759-2263

COLORADO

Tri-Lakes
Kari Ann Kimbrel
Monument, CO 80132
719-487-2942/719-205-1358
kariannkimbrel@aol.com

FLORIDA

Central Florida Stepfamilies
Jesse Davis
Orlando, CL 32804
407-293-2199
cflsaa@yahoo.com

NEW YORK

Buffalo
Christopher Pino
Buffalo, NY 14214
716-832-1434
docpi9no@aol.com
geocities.com/drcjpino

Rochester
Estalyn Walcoff
Rochester, NY 14618
585-442-3440
estalyn@sprintmail.com

OHIO

Stepfamilies of Stark Co.
Francine Crist
Canton, OH 44718
330-453-2827
cristfk@aol.com

OKLAHOMA

The Stepping Stones
Traci Walden
Oklahoma City, OK 73159
405-703-0560
twcoolgirl@os.com

PENNSYLVANIA

Stepping Forward NEPA
Jennifer Mason
Tunkhannock, PA 18657
570-833-5715
daisies07@yahoo.com

Hispanic Support Group
"Tuyos, Míos y Nuestros"
Dora Capelluto
Weston, FL 33327
954-881-6099
www.familiesnewmillennium.org

Stepfamilies of North Central Florida
Heather Remer
Gainesville, FL 32608
352-281-0412
heather.remer@cox.net

GEORGIA

INSTEP
T. Raymond McCranie
Dalton Church of God
1007 Underwood Street
Dalton, GA 30721
706-271-0293
harborhouse@alltel.net

IDAHO

Southwest Idaho
Marion Summers
Boise, ID 83704
208-376-3720

ILLINOIS

Illinois Chapter
Brenda Nemeth
Arlington Heights, IL 60004
847-255-6736 or 815-455-6736
icsaa1@ameritech.net

Insightful Steps
Dave Freckleton
Peoria, IL 61615
309-689-5774 or
cell 309-696-3113
insightfulsteps@email.com

Harrisburg/Hershey Stepfamilies
Carolyn Wolf
Harrisburg, PA 17111
717-545-2571

North Hills of Pittsburgh Group
Anna and Tom Gay
www.stepfamilyconnection.org

Pittsburgh South Hills
Heather & Robert Trivus
Pittsburgh, PA 15228
412-343-1009 or 412-531-2520
http://home.attbi.com/~pittsburghsaa/
pittsburghsaa@attbi.com

NWPA Support Group
Kimberly Fabrizio
North East, PA 16428
814-725-2025
kfabrizio@wgln.org

Stepfamily Connection
Dr. Anna McManus-Gay
62 Seldom Seen Road
Bradfordwoods, PA 15015
724-799-2123
stepfamilyconnection@zoominternet.net

SOUTH CAROLINA

Stepping Into Grace
Tara Keathley
Charleston, SC 29422
843-406-2770
tkeathley@steppingn2grace.org
www.steppingN2grace.com

Stepfamily Support Group of Decatur
Theresa Miller
Decatur, IL 62521
217-425-2998
otiefam@aol.com

INDIANA

Step Together
Carolyn Hittle
Rushville, IN 46173
765-938-2502
carolyn_hittle@yahoo.com

KANSAS

Kansas City SAA
Brad Nowlin
Kansas City, KS
913-579-8526
bnow45@kc.rr.com

KENTUCKY

Louisville
Sally Connolly, LCSW, LMFT
St. Matthews Baptist Church
Meetings take place the third Sunday of each
month
502-473-0766

LOUISIANA

Monroe Area Group
Christine Murphy
8478 Old Monroe Road
Bastrop, LA 71220
318-283-2747 (Home)
318-348-7126 (Cell)
chmurphy@sudden.net

TENNESSEE

Blended Family Educational
Group
Douglas and Creel Pittman
Harpeth Hills Church of Christ
1949 Old Hickory Blvd
Brentwood, TN 37027
615-370-8177
PittmanLLC@cs.com

Greater Nashville
Brian Foti
Spring Hill, TN 37174
615-573-9161
brianfoti@yahoo.com

TEXAS

Stepfamilies of Houston and Texas
Jayna Haney
3139 W. Holcombe Blvd. #705
Houston, Texas 77025
713-.664-7888
info@stepfamiliesoftexas.com
www.stepfamiliesoftexas.com

VIRGINIA

Arlington County
Miriam Gennari
Arlington, VA 22202
703-549-1422
pmgennari@comcast.net

WASHINGTON

Puget Sound
Laureen Miki
Kirkland, WA 98033
425-985-3890
www.expage.com/localstepfamily

MARYLAND

Baltimore
Neil & Debbie Zimmerman
Baltimore, MD 21236
410-529-7176 or 410-965-8294
.http://neil_and_debbie.tripod.com

Montgomery
Amy Scott
Bethesda, MD 20814
301-656-3225 or
202-244-8855 x2
afscottmsw@verizon.net

Howard County
Barbara Fowler
Columbia, MD 21045
410-381-2402

MASSACHUSETTS

StepFamily Association of Bedford
Jon Land
Bedford, MA 01730
781-929-1253
micheleandjon.land@comcast.net

MICHIGAN

Stepfamilies of Kalamazoo
Brita Boer
Portage, MI 49002
269-377-9585
jbboer@aol.com

Step by Step
Pam Willemstein
Jenison, MI 49428
616-457-4033
pam@mistepbystep.org
mistepbystep.org

WISCONSIN

Metro Milwaukee
Grant Anderson
Brookfield, WI 53005
414-541-5580 or 262-821-1893

CANADA - British Columbia

Abbotsford
Katheryn J. Doell
Northview Community Church
32040 Downes Rd.
Abbotsford, BC V4X 1X5
(604) 853-2931 / fax (604) 853-9921

CANADA - Ontario

London
Al Gayed
London, ON N6K3B2
519-472-3544 or 519-472-2442

Toronto
Terri OBrien
Toronto, ON M4N 1Y7
416-485-8386
terri_obrien@sympatico.ca

VIRTUAL (on line)
StepTogether
Toril Oien Eller
757-329-8315
www.steptogether.org

One Step At a Time
Jennifer Wezensky
Battle Creek, MI 49015
269-565-3379
wezensky0650@attbi.com

MINNESOTA

Big Lake
Lynn Corcoran Roberts
Big Lake, MN 55309
763-458-9255
solidsteps@charter.net
http://webpages.charter.net/solidstepsmn

Related Publications

Selected readings

Bolton, Robert, Ph.D.: <u>People Skills</u>; 1979. Prentiss Hall, Inc. Spectrum Books; Englewood Cliffs, NJ. A 300 pp. Paperback, selected by the American Management Association.

Brandon, Dr. Nathaniel: <u>If You Could Hear What I Cannot Say - Learning to Communicate With The Ones You Love</u>; 1983. Bantam Books, New York, NY. A 293 pp. Paperback text and workbook.

Einstein, Elizabeth; Albert, Linda: <u>Strengthening Your Stepfamily</u>; 2005. Impact Publishers, 272 pp.

Farber, Adele and Mazlish. Elaine: <u>How To Talk So Kids Will Listen & Listen So That Kids Will Talk</u>, 1980. Avon Books, New York, NY. A clear, helpful 241 pp. Paperback.

Ginott, Dr. Haim G.: <u>Between Parent and Teenager</u>; 1971. Avon Books, New York, NY. A classic 255 PP paperback, including bib.

Gordon, Dr. Thomas: <u>P.E.T. in Action</u>; 1976. Plume Books, New American Library, Inc., New York, NY. A 334 PP paperback on *Parent Effectiveness Training*; applies to all relationships.

Lerner, Harriet G., Ph.D.: <u>The Dance of Anger</u>, 1985. Harper and Rowe, Publishers, Inc., New York, NY. A 239 PP paperback. Though slanted toward women, this is an excellent book for anyone wishing to express and use anger constructively.

Miller, S., Nunnally, E., and Wackman, D.: <u>Couple Communication 1 - Talking Together</u>, 1979. Interpersonal Communications, Inc., Minneapolis, MN; 174 PP softbound. Also available: a 1982 4-session workshop guide with 2 audiotapes, based on the book.

Satir, Virginia: <u>The NEW Peoplemaking</u>, 1988. Science and Behavior Books, Inc., Palo Alto, CA. A 400 PP paperback update of the classic on healthy personal and family relations.

Stone, Hal, Ph.D. and Winkelman, Sidra, Ph.D.: <u>Embracing Our Selves - The Voice Dialog Manual</u>, 1989. New World Library, San Rafael, CA. An interesting 257 PP paperback that introduces the many selves that clamor and compete within us.

Tannen, Deborah, Ph.D.: <u>You Just Don't Understand - Women and Men in Conversation</u>, 1990. Ballentine Books, New York, NY. A highly readable, practical 300 PP paperback on the differing communication styles of men and women, by a linguistics professor.

Adler, Allen, and Archambault, Christine. *Divorce Recovery.* New York, Bantam, 1992

Baker, Nancy. *New Lives for Former Wives.* New York: Anchor Press/Doubleday, 1980

Bayard, Robert, and Bayard, Jean. *How to Deal with Your Acting-Up-Teenager - Practical Self-Help for Desperate Parents.* San Jose, CA: The Accord Press, 1981

Beer, William R. *Relative Strangers: Studies of Stepfamily Processes.* New York: Rowman and Littlefield, 1988. *American Stepfamilies.* New Brunswick, N.J.: Transaction Publishers, 1992.

Berman, Claire. *Making It as a Stepparent: New Roles, New Rules.* New York: Harper & Row, 1986. *What Am I Doing In a Stepfamily?* New York: Carol Publishing Co., 1992. *A Hole In My Heart - Adult Children of Divorce Speak Out.* New York: A Fireside Book, Simon and Schuster, 1991.

Bernard, Jessie. *Remarried: A Study of Marriage.* New York: Russell and Russell, first edition, 1956, second edition, 1971.

Bernstein, Anne. *Yours, Mine, and Ours: How Families Change When Remarrieds Have a Child Together.* New York: Mac Millan, 1989

Bloomfield, Harold H., with Kory, Robert B. *Making peace in Your Family: Surviving and Thriving as Parents and Stepparents.* New York: Hyperion, 1993

Bloomfield, Harold H., with Felder, Leonard. *Making Peace With Your Parents.* New York: Ballantine Books, 1985

Bradshaw, John. *The Family.* Pompano Beach, FL: Health Communications, Inc., 1988.

Burger, Stuart. *Divorce Without Victims.* Boston: Houghton Mifflin, 1983

Burns, Cherie. *Stepmotherhood: How To Survive Without Feeling Frustrated, Left Out, or Wicked.* New York: Harper & Row, 1986

Burt, Mala. *Stepfamilies Stepping Ahead.*

Coale, Helen. *All About Families the Second Time Around.* Atlanta: Peachtree Publishing, 1980

Cohen, Miriam. *Long Distance Parenting: A Guide for Divorced Parents.* New York: New American Library, 1989

Covey, Stephen. *The 7 Habits of Highly Effective People.* New York: Simon and Schuster, 1989.

Dodson, Dr. Fitzhugh. *How To Father.* New York, A Signet Book, New American Library, 1975.

Duberman, Lucille. *The Reconstituted Family: A Study of Remarried Couples and Their Children.* Chicago: Nelson-Hall, 1975.

Ecker, James. *Step-by-Stepparenting.* Crozet, VA: Betterway Publications, 1988

Engel, Marjorie. *Weddings for Complicated Families*

Einstein, Elizabeth. *The Stepfamily: Living, Loving and Learning.* New York: MacMillan, 1982

Ephron, Delia. *Funny Face: Us, the Ex, the Ex's New Mate, the New Mate's Ex, and the Kids. New York: Viking, 1986.*

Espinoza, Renata, and Navaman, Yvonne. *Stepparenting.* DHEW Publications no. ADM 89-579, U.S. Government Printing Office. Washington, D.C., 1979

Faber, Adele and Mazllish, Elaine. *How To Talk so Kids Will Listen and Listen So Kids Will Talk.* New York: Avon Books division of Hearst Corp., 1980.

Frydenger, Tom, and Frydenger, Adrianne. *The Blended Family.* Grand Rapits, MI: Chosen Books, 1984

Furstenberg, Frank F., Jr., and Spanier, Graham B. *Recycling the Family: Re-marriage After Divorce.* Beverly Hills, CA.: Sage Publications, 1984.

Gordon, Dr. Thomas with Judith Gordon Sands. *P.E.T. In Actions.* Wyden Books, 1976.

Hirschfield, Mary, Jd., Ph.D. *The Adult Children of Divorce Workbook.* Los Angeles, CA.: Jeremy Tarcher, 1992

Ihinger-Tallman, Marilyn, and Paley, Kay. *Re-marriage.* Newbury Park, CA.: Sage Publications, 1987.

Keshet, Jamie. *Love and Power in the Stepfamily: A Practical Guide.* New York: McGraw-Hill, 1986

Krementz, Jill. *How It Feels when Parents Divorce.* New York: Knopf, 1984.

Kuzma, Kay. *Part-Time Parent.* New York, Wade Publishing, 1980.

Lamanna, Mary Ann, and Riedmann, Agnes. *Marriages and Families.* Bemont, CA: Wadsworth Publishing Co., 5th Edition, 1993

Lewis, Helen. *All About Families, The Second Time Around.* Atlanta: Peachtree Publishing, 1980.

Lintermans, Gloria. *The Newly Divorced Book Of Protocol: How To Be Civil When You Hate Their Guts.* New York, Barricade Books, (1-800-59 BOOKS), 1995

Lintermans, Gloria. *The Healing Power of Grief: The Journey Through Loss to Life and Laughter,* (Sourcebooks, Inc.), 2006

Lintermans, Gloria *The Healing Power of Love: Transcending The Loss of a Spouse to New Love*, (Sourcebooks, Inc.), 2006

Maddox, Brenda. *The Half Parent.* New York: Evans, 1975

Maglin, Nan Bauer, and Schneidewind,Nancy. *Women and Stepfamilies: Voices of Anger and Love.* Phadiladelphia: Temple University Press, 1989.

Mala, Burt. *Stepfamilies Stepping Ahead: An Eight-Step Program for Successful Family Living.* Lincoln, NE: Stepfamily Association of America, 1989.

Mastrich, Dr. Jim with Bill Birnes. *The ACOA's Guide To Raising Healthy Children.* New York: Collier Books, Macmillan Publishing Co., 1989.

Messinger, Lillian. *Re-marriage: A Family Affair.* New York: Plenum Press, 1984.

Noble, June, and Noble, William. *How to Live with Other People's Children.* New York: Hawthorne Books, 1977.

O'Gorman, Patricia and Oliver-Diaz, Philip. *Breaking The Cycle of Addiction - A Parents Guide to Raising Healthy Kids.* Pompano Beach, FL: Health Communications, Inc., 1987.

Pasley, Kay, and Ihinger-Tallman, Marilyn. *Re-marriage and Stepparenting: Current Research and Theory.* New York: Guilford Press, 1987.

Prilik, Pearl. *Stepmothering-Another Kind of Love.* New York: Berkeley, 1990.

Robinson, Bryan E., and Robert L. Barret. *The Developing Father.* New York: Guilford, 1986.

Roosevelt, Ruth, and Lofas, Jeanette. *Living In Step: A Re-marriage Manual for Parents and Children.* New York: Stein & Day, 1976

Rosenberg, Maxine B. *Talking About Stepfamilies.* New York: Bradbury Press, 1990.

Rosin, Mark Bruce. *Stepfathering: Stepfathers' Advice on Creating a New Stepfamily.* New York: Simon and Schuster, 1987.

Satir, Virginia. *The New Peoplemaking.* Mountain View, CA: Science and Behavior Books, 1988.

Savage, Karen, and Adams, Patricia. *The Good Stepmother: A Practical Guide.* New York: Crown, 1988.

Smith, Donna. *Stepmothering.* New York, St. Martin's Press, 1990.

Stuart, Richard B., and Jacobson, Barbara. *Second Marriage: Make it Happy! Make it Last!* New York: W. W. Norton & Company, 1985.

Tatelbaum, Judy. *The Courage To Grieve.* New York: Perennial Library, Harper & Rowe, 1980.

The Family Resource Coalition. *Starting and Operating Support Groups: A Guide for Parents.* Chicago, IL 60604, (312) 341-0900, Fax (312) 314-9361

Visher, Emily, and Visher, John. *How to Win as a Stepfamily.* New York: Brunner & Mazel, 1991.

Visher, Emily, and Visher, John. *Stepfamilies Stepping Ahead.* Lincoln, NE: Step-Families Press, 1989.

Visher, Emily, and Visher, John. *Stepfamilies.* New York: MacMillan, 1990.

Wallerstein, Judith and Blakeslee, Sandra. *Second Chances.* New York: Ticknor & Fields, 1989.

Woititz, Janet Ed.D. *Healthy Parenting - An Empowering Guide for Adult Children.* New York: Fireside Book, Simon and Schuster, 1992.

Helpful Books for Stepchildren Ages 3 - 9

Boyd, Lizi. *The Not-So-Wicked Stepmother.* New York: Viking Kestrel, 1987.

Bradley, Buff. *Where Do I Belong? A Kids Guide to Stepfamiles.* Reading, MA: Addison-Wesley, 1982

Brown, Laurence Krasney, and Brown, Marc. *Dinosaurs Divorce.* New York: Little, Brown & Co., 1988.

Burt, Maria Schuster, and Burt, Roger B. *What's Special About Our Stepfamily: A Participation Books for Chidlren.* New York: Doubleday, 1983.

Byars, Betsy. *The Animal, the Vegetable and John D. Jones.* New York: Delacorte, 1982.

Evans, Marla. *This is Me and My Two Families.* New York: Magination Press, 1988.

Gardner, Richard. *The Boys and Girls Books About Divorce.* New York, Bantam, 1971.

Goff, Beth. *Where Is Daddy: The Story of Divorce.* Boston: Beacon Press, 1978.

Green, Phyllis. *A New Mother for Martha.* New York: Human Science Press, 1978.

Helmering, Doris W. *I Have Two Families.* Nashville: Abingdon, 1981.

Hunter, Evan. *Me and Mr. Stenner.* New York: J.B. Lippincott, 1976.

Jasinek, Doris, and Ryan, Pamela Bell. *A Family is a Circle of People Who Love You.* Minneapolis: CompCare, 1988.

Kremetz, Jill. *How It Feels When a Parent Dies.* New York: Knopf, 1981.

LeShan, Eda. *What's Going to Happen to Me?.* New York: Avon Books, 1976.

Lewis, Helen. *All About Families: The Second Time Around.* Atlanta: Peachtree Publishing, 1980.

Shyer, Marlene, Fanta. *Stepdog.* New York: Charles Schibner's Sons, 1983

Sobol, Harriet. *My Other Mother, My Other Father.* New York: Macmillan, 1979.

Stenson, Janet. *Now I Have a Stepparent and It's Kind of Confusing.* New York: Avon Press, 1979.

Vigna,Judith. *Daddy's New Baby.* Morton Grove, IL: Whitman, Albert & Co., 1982

Vigna, Judith. *Grandma Without Me.* Morton Grove, IL: Whitman, Albert, & Co., 1984.

Vigna, Judith. *She's Not My Real Mother.* Morton Grove, IL: Whitman, Albert & Co., 1980.

Helpful Books for Step-Teens ages 10 - 18

Berger, Terry. *A Friend Can Help.* Milwaukee: Raintree Editions, 1975

Berman, Claire. *What Am I doing in a Stepfamily?* New Jersey: Lyle Stuart, 1992.

Craven, Claire. *Stepfamilies: New Patterns in Harmony.* New York: Julian Messner, 1982.

Eichoness, Monte. *Why Can't Anyone Hear Me?* Ventura, CA: Monroe Press, 1989.

Getzoff, Ann, and McClenahan, Carolyn. *Step-kids: A Survival Guide for Teenagers in Stepfamilies.* New York: Walker, 1984.

Hawley, Richard. *The Big Issues in the Adolescent Journey.* New York: Walker, 1988.

Wesson, Carolyn McLenahan. *Teen Troubles: How to keep Them From Becoming Tragedies.* New York: Wlaker, 1988.

*** **Please note** that this list does not include every book, organization, private program, videocassette, audiocassette, Web Site or literature that deals with the various aspects of step-parenting. Inclusion on this list does not constitute endorsement by the authors or publisher of this book.

INDEX

About the Author

Gloria Lintermans has 25 years of professional journalistic experience. She is the author of *The Healing Power of Grief: The Journey Through Loss to Life and Laughter, The Healing Power of Love: Transcending the Loss of a Spouse to New Love, The Newly Divorced Book of Protocol: How to Be Civil When You Hate Their Guts,* and *Retro Chic: A Guide to Fabulous Vintage and Designer Resale Shopping in North America & Online.* She has written dozens of articles for local and national magazines, and is a retired newspaper columnist whose column has been syndicated in English and Spanish language newspapers worldwide. Lintermans is a step- and biological mother and grandmother.

LaVergne, TN USA
10 March 2011

219578LV00002B/77/P